Lecture Notes in Computer Science 15345

The series Lecture Notes in Computer Science (LNCS), including its subseries Lecture Notes in Artificial Intelligence (LNAI) and Lecture Notes in Bioinformatics (LNBI), has established itself as a medium for the publication of new developments in computer science and information technology research, teaching, and education.

LNCS enjoys close cooperation with the computer science R & D community, the series counts many renowned academics among its volume editors and paper authors, and collaborates with prestigious societies. Its mission is to serve this international community by providing an invaluable service, mainly focused on the publication of conference and workshop proceedings and postproceedings. LNCS commenced publication in 1973.

Albert Meroño Peñuela · Oscar Corcho ·
Paul Groth · Elena Simperl · Valentina Tamma ·
Andrea Giovanni Nuzzolese ·
Maria Poveda-Villalón · Marta Sabou ·
Valentina Presutti · Irene Celino ·
Artem Revenko · Joe Raad · Bruno Sartini ·
Pasquale Lisena
Editors

The Semantic Web: ESWC 2024 Satellite Events

Hersonissos, Crete, Greece, May 26–30, 2024 Proceedings, Part II

Springer

Editors
Albert Meroño Peñuela
King's College London
London, UK

Oscar Corcho
Universidad Politécnica de Madrid
Madrid, Spain

Paul Groth
University of Amsterdam
Amsterdam, Noord-Holland, The Netherlands

Elena Simperl
King's College London
London, UK

Valentina Tamma
University of Liverpool
Liverpool, UK

Andrea Giovanni Nuzzolese
National Research Council
Bologna, Italy

Maria Poveda-Villalón
Universidad Politécnica de Madrid
Madrid, Spain

Marta Sabou
Vienna University of Economics and Business
Vienna, Austria

Valentina Presutti
University of Bologna
Bologna, Italy

Irene Celino
Cefriel - Politecnico Di Milano
Milan, Italy

Artem Revenko
Semantic Web Company
Vienna, Austria

Joe Raad
University of Paris-Saclay
Gif-sur-Yvette, France

Bruno Sartini
Ludwig-Maximilians-Universität München
Munich, Germany

Pasquale Lisena
EURECOM
Biot, France

ISSN 0302-9743 ISSN 1611-3349 (electronic)
Lecture Notes in Computer Science
ISBN 978-3-031-78954-0 ISBN 978-3-031-78955-7 (eBook)
https://doi.org/10.1007/978-3-031-78955-7

This Springer imprint is published by the registered company Springer Nature Switzerland AG
The registered company address is: Gewerbestrasse 11, 6330 Cham, Switzerland

Preface

This volume contains the satellite proceedings of the 21st edition of the European Semantic Web Conference (ESWC 2024). ESWC is a major venue for discussing the latest in scientific results and innovations related to the semantic web, knowledge graphs, and web data. This year we aimed at acknowledging recent developments in AI with a special tagline, "Fabrics of Knowledge: Knowledge Graphs and Generative AI". The satellite events are an important aspect of facilitating the main conference discussion as well as fundamental questions about how we acquire, represent, use, and interact with knowledge in the advent of Generative AI and large language models.

To reflect this year's special topic, the satellite events of ESWC 2024 featured a Special Track on Large Language Models for Knowledge Engineering, in addition to the poster and demo session, the PhD symposium, the industry track, project networking, and workshops and tutorials. Due to scheduling, the papers from these events are published as post-proceedings.

The Special Track on Large Language Models for Knowledge Engineering provided a venue for scientific discussion and community building for early work on this exciting new area of research. The track had 52 submissions, demonstrating the importance of research in this direction, of which 10 were accepted. In addition to the accepted papers, the track had a community discussion session that synthesised and mapped directions forward in this area.

The poster and demo track received 51 submissions of which 17 posters and 20 demos were accepted. All submissions received 2 to 3 reviews. Posters and demos highlight new research trajectories and ideas within the community and allow for discussions of the latest results. Here, we see topics such as ontologies, knowledge graph, multi-modality, domain application, methods for dealing with data sources, and advances in semantic technologies and machine learning.

The PhD symposium is an important venue for doctoral students to present and receive feedback on their research. In total, 18 submissions were received, of which 14 papers were accepted. Both the review and guidance processes were intensive and tailored to helping the students to improve their research plans. This included 3 reviews for each paper as well as peer review by the students themselves. Additionally, all papers were guided by mentors who are senior members of the community. Importantly, senior members of the community attended each presentation to give in-depth feedback. The symposium also featured a social event for students only aimed at facilitating networking among new community members.

The industry track featured papers that discuss the adoption and usage of semantic technologies within organisations. Importantly, papers must have a co-author with a non-academic affiliation. We received 10 submissions of which 7 were accepted. All papers received between 3 and 6 reviews. The industry track featured papers from a wide variety of organisations including Siemens, DATEV, Munich Airport, Dun & Bradstreet,

Beamery, AddQual, and PANTOPIX. Topics included scalability of semantic technologies in real-world cases, the application of knowledge graphs to product management systems and value chains, FAIR and dataset management, and combining knowledge graphs with large language models for ontology modelling, knowledge extraction, and rule optimisation. The accepted papers cover concrete scenarios from a broad range of industries and markets, including manufacturing, industrial IoT, transportation, product data, sales and supply chain, smart building, and human resources.

ESWC 2024 featured a record-breaking selection of 16 workshops and 2 tutorials covering topics ranging from knowledge graph construction to deep learning with knowledge graphs. Workshops and tutorial highlights were summarised in a main conference presentation, describing their outcomes to the entire community, and highlighting the impact of generative AI and large language models in their contributions. Later in this volume you will find a selection of the best papers from the workshops, which have been extended and fast-tracked to be hosted in the ESWC satellite proceedings.

While not formally part of the proceedings, ESWC has a history of providing network opportunities for projects and in particular EU projects. We would like to thank Cassia Trojahn and Sabrina Kirrane for organising this part of the program for this year.

April 2024

Albert Meroño Peñuela
Oscar Corcho
Paul Groth
Elena Simperl
Valentina Tamma
Andrea Giovanni Nuzzolese
Maria Poveda-Villalón
Marta Sabou
Valentina Presutti
Irene Celino
Artem Revenko
Joe Raad
Bruno Sartini
Pasquale Lisena

Organization

General Chair

Albert Meroño Peñuela	King's College London, UK

Research Track Program Chairs

Anastasia Dimou	KU Leuven, Belgium
Raphaël Troncy	EURECOM, France

Resource Track Program Chairs

Mehwish Alam	Télécom Paris, Institut Polytechnique de Paris, France
Heiko Paulheim	University of Mannheim, Germany

In-Use Track Program Chairs

Olaf Hartig	Linköpings Universitet, Sweden
Maribel Acosta	Ruhr University Bochum, Germany

Special Track on Large Language Models for Knowledge Engineering

Oscar Corcho	Universidad Politécnica de Madrid, Spain
Paul Groth	University of Amsterdam, Netherlands
Elena Simperl	King's College London, UK
Valentina Tamma	University of Liverpool, UK

Workshops and Tutorials Chairs

Joe Raad	Paris-Saclay University, France
Bruno Sartini	Ludwig-Maximilians University of Munich, Germany

Poster and Demo Chairs

Andrea Nuzzolese	ISTC-CNR, Italy
María Poveda-Villalón	Universidad Politécnica de Madrid, Spain

PhD Symposium Chairs

Marta Sabou	Vienna University of Economics and Business, Austria
Valentina Presutti	University of Bologna, Italy

Industry Track Program Chairs

Irene Celino	Cefriel, Italy
Artem Revenko	Semantic Web Company GmbH, Austria

Sponsorship

Nitisha Jain	King's College London, UK
Jan-Christoph Kalo	University of Amsterdam, Netherlands

Project Networking

Cassia Trojahn	IRIT, France
Sabrina Kirrane	WU Vienna, Austria

Web and Publicity

Stefano De Giorgis	University of Bologna, Italy
Tabea Tietz	FIZ Karlsruhe, Germany

Proceedings and Conference Metadata

Pasquale Lisena	EURECOM, France

Program Committee

Nora Abdelmageed	Friedrich-Schiller-Universität Jena, Germany
Ghadeer Abuoda	Aalborg University, Denmark
Maribel Acosta	TU Munich, Germany
Shqiponja Ahmetaj	TU Wien, Austria
Aljbin Ahmeti	Semantic Web Company GmbH and TU Wien, Austria
Mehwish Alam	Télécom Paris, France
Céline Alec	Université de Caen-Normandie, France
Vladimir Alexiev	Ontotext Corp., Bulgaria
Panos Alexopoulos	Textkernel B.V., Netherlands
Alsayed Algergawy	University of Jena, Germany
Reham Alharbi	University of Liverpool, UK
Bradley Allen	University of Amsterdam, Netherlands
Doerthe Arndt	TU Dresden, Germany
Natanael Arndt	eccenca GmbH, Germany
Luigi Asprino	University of Bologna, Italy
Ghislain Auguste Atemezing	ERA, France
Maurizio Atzori	University of Cagliari, Italy
Sören Auer	TIB Leibniz Information Center for Science and Technology, Germany and University of Hannover, Germany
Carlos Badenes-Olmedo	Universidad Politécnica de Madrid, Spain
Booma Sowkarthiga Balasubramani	University of Illinois at Chicago, USA
Konstantina Bereta	National and Kapodistrian University of Athens, Greece
Abraham Bernstein	University of Zurich, Switzerland
Russa Biswas	Hasso Plattner Institute, Germany
Christian Bizer	University of Mannheim, Germany

Peter Bloem	Vrije Universiteit Amsterdam, Netherlands
Martin Blum	University of Trier, Germany
Carlos Bobed	University of Zaragoza, Spain
Fernando Bobillo	University of Zaragoza, Spain
Pieter Bonte	Ghent University, Belgium
Andreas Both	DATEV eG, Germany
Alexandros Bousdekis	Institute of Communication and Computer Systems-National Technical University of Athens, Greece
Loris Bozzato	Fondazione Bruno Kessler, Italy
Janez Brank	Jožef Stefan Institute, Slovenia
Adrian M. P. Brasoveanu	MODUL Technology GmbH, Austria
Olivier Bruneau	University of Lorraine, France
Carlos Buil Aranda	Universidad Técnica Federico Santa María, Chile
Maxime Buron	Inria, France
Davide Buscaldi	Université Sorbonne Paris Nord, France
Jean-Paul Calbimonte	University of Applied Sciences and Arts Western Switzerland, Switzerland
Pablo Calleja	Universidad Politécnica de Madrid, Spain
Antonella Carbonaro	University of Bologna, Italy
Valentina Anita Carriero	Cefriel, Italy
Sylvie Cazalens	LIRIS - INSA de Lyon, France
Irene Celino	Cefriel, Italy
Renato Cerqueira	IBM Research - Brazil, Brazil
Yoan Chabot	Orange Labs, France
Javad Chamanara	Technische Informationsbibliothek, Germany
Pierre-Antoine Champin	LIRIS, Université Claude Bernard Lyon1, France
David Chaves-Fraga	Universidade de Santiago de Compostela, Spain
Lihu Chen	Inria Saclay, France
Gong Cheng	Nanjing University, China
Philipp Cimiano	Bielefeld University, Germany
Andrea Cimmino Arriaga	Universidad Politécnica de Madrid, Spain
Michael Cochez	Vrije Universiteit Amsterdam, Netherlands
Diego Collarana	Fraunhofer IAIS, Germany
Pieter Colpaert	Ghent University, Belgium
Oscar Corcho	Universidad Politécnica de Madrid, Spain
Francesco Corcoglioniti	Free University of Bozen-Bolzano, Italy
Julien Corman	Free University of Bozen-Bolzano, Italy
Marco Cremaschi	University of Milano-Bicocca, Italy
Claudia d'Amato	University of Bari, Italy
Mathieu D'Aquin	LORIA, University of Lorraine, France

Jennifer D'Souza	TIB Leibniz Information Centre for Science and Technology University Library, Germany
Enrico Daga	Open University, UK
Jérôme David	Inria, France
Jacopo de Berardinis	King's College London, UK
Victor de Boer	Vrije Universiteit Amsterdam, Netherlands
Stefano De Giorgis	Alma Mater University of Bologna, Italy
Ben De Meester	Ghent University, Belgium
Daniele Dell'Aglio	Aalborg University, Denmark
Gianluca Demartini	University of Queensland, Australia
Elena Demidova	University of Bonn, Germany
Kathrin Dentler	Triply, Netherlands
Danilo Dessì	GESIS – Leibniz Institute for the Social Sciences, Germany
Gayo Diallo	University of Bordeaux, France
Stefan Dietze	GESIS – Leibniz Institute for the Social Sciences, Germany
Dimitar Dimitrov	GESIS – Leibniz Institute for the Social Sciences, Germany
Anastasia Dimou	KU Leuven, Belgium
Christian Dirschl	Wolters Kluwer Germany, Germany
Daniil Dobriy	Vienna University of Economics and Business, Austria
Milan Dojchinovski	Czech Technical University in Prague, Czech Republic
Ivan Donadello	Free University of Bozen-Bolzano, Italy
Mauro Dragoni	Fondazione Bruno Kessler, Italy
Kai Eckert	Mannheim University of Applied Sciences, Germany
Vasilis Efthymiou	Harokopio University of Athens, Greece
Shusaku Egami	National Institute of Advanced Industrial Science and Technology, Japan
Fajar J. Ekaputra	Vienna University of Economics and Business (WU), Austria
Vadim Ermolayev	Ukrainian Catholic University, Ukraine
Paola Espinoza Arias	Universidad Politécnica de Madrid, Spain
Lorena Etcheverry	Universidad de la República, Uruguay
Pavlos Fafalios	Technical University of Crete and FORTH-ICS, Greece
Alessandro Faraotti	IBM, Italy
Catherine Faron	Université Côte d'Azur, France
Anna Fensel	Wageningen University and Research, Netherlands

Javier D. Fernández	F. Hoffmann-La Roche AG, Switzerland
Mariano Fernández López	Universidad San Pablo CEU, Spain
Jesualdo Tomás Fernández-Breis	Universidad de Murcia, Spain
Sebastián Ferrada	Universidad de Chile, Chile
Agata Filipowska	Poznań University of Economics, Poland
Erwin Filtz	Siemens AG Österreich, Austria
Giorgos Flouris	FORTH-ICS, Greece
Flavius Frasincar	Erasmus University Rotterdam, Netherlands
Naoki Fukuta	Shizuoka University, Japan
Michael Färber	Karlsruhe Institute of Technology, Germany
Mohamed H. Gad-Elrab	Bosch Center for Artificial Intelligence, Germany
Alban Gaignard	CNRS, France
Luis Galárraga	Inria, France
Fabien Gandon	Inria, France
Aldo Gangemi	Università di Bologna and ISTC-CNR, Italy
Raúl García-Castro	Universidad Politécnica de Madrid, Spain
Andrés García-Silva	Expert.ai, Spain
Daniel Garijo	Universidad Politécnica de Madrid, Spain
Manas Gaur	Wright State University, USA
Yuxia Geng	Zhejiang University, China
Genet Asefa Gesese	FIZ Karlsruhe – Leibniz-Institut für Informationsinfrastruktur, Germany
Pouya Ghiasnezhad Omran	Australian National University, Australia
Martin Giese	University of Oslo, Norway
Jose M. Gimenez-Garcia	Universidad de Valladolid, Spain
Francois Goasdoue	University of Rennes, France
Jose Manuel Gomez-Perez	Expert.ai, Spain
Simon Gottschalk	Leibniz Universität Hannover, Germany
Floriana Grasso	University of Liverpool, UK
Damien Graux	Huawei Research Ltd., UK
Paul Groth	University of Amsterdam, Netherlands
Claudio Gutierrez	Universidad de Chile, Chile
Peter Haase	metaphacts GmbH, Germany
Mohad-Saïd Hacid	Université Claude Bernard Lyon 1, France
Torsten Hahmann	University of Maine, USA
George Hannah	University of Liverpool, UK
Andreas Harth	Friedrich-Alexander-Universität Erlangen-Nürnberg and Fraunhofer IIS, Germany
Olaf Hartig	Linköping University, Sweden
Oktie Hassanzadeh	IBM, USA
Ivan Heibi	University of Bologna, Italy

Veronika Heimsbakk	Capgemini, Norway
Nicolas Heist	University of Mannheim, Germany
Lars Heling	Stardog Union, Germany
Nathalie Hernandez	IRIT, France
Daniel Herzig	metaphacts GmbH, Germany
Ryohei Hisano	ETH Zurich, Switzerland
Pascal Hitzler	Kansas State University, USA
Rinke Hoekstra	Elsevier, Netherlands
Aidan Hogan	Universidad de Chile, Chile
Andreas Hotho	University of Würzburg, Germany
Wei Hu	Nanjing University, China
Thomas Hubauer	Siemens AG Corporate Technology, Germany
Andreea Iana	University of Mannheim, Germany
Luis Ibanez-Gonzalez	University of Southampton, UK
Ana Iglesias-Molina	Universidad Politécnica de Madrid, Spain
Filip Ilievski	Vrije Universiteit Amsterdam, Netherlands
Antoine Isaac	Europeana & Vrije Universiteit Amsterdam, Netherlands
Hajira Jabeen	GESIS – Leibniz Institute for the Social Sciences, Germany
Nitisha Jain	King's College London, UK
Mustafa Jarrar	Birzeit University, Palestine
Ernesto Jimenez-Ruiz	City, University of London, UK
Milos Jovanovik	Ss. Cyril and Methodius University in Skopje, N. Macedonia
Simon Jupp	Elsevier, Netherlands
Jan-Christoph Kalo	University of Amsterdam, Netherlands
Eduard Kamburjan	University of Oslo, Norway
Maulik R. Kamdar	Optum Health, USA
Katariina Kari	Inter IKEA Systems B.V., Finland
Tomi Kauppinen	Aalto University, Finland
Mayank Kejriwal	University of Southern California, USA
Natthawut Kertkeidkachorn	Japan Advanced Institute of Science and Technology, Japan
Ali Khalili	Deloitte, Netherlands
Sabrina Kirrane	Vienna University of Economics and Business, Austria
Tomas Kliegr	Prague University of Economics and Business, Czech Republic
Matthias Klusch	DFKI, Germany
Haridimos Kondylakis	Institute of Computer Science, FORTH, Greece
George Konstantinidis	University of Southampton, UK

Stasinos Konstantopoulos	NCSR Demokritos, Greece
Roman Kontchakov	Birkbeck, University of London, UK
Manolis Koubarakis	National and Kapodistrian University of Athens, Greece
Kozaki Kouji	Osaka Electro-Communication University, Japan
Maria Koutraki	Leibniz Universität Hannover, Germany
Anelia Kurteva	TU Delft, Netherlands
Tobias Käfer	Karlsruhe Institute of Technology, Germany
Birgitta König-Ries	Friedrich Schiller University of Jena, Germany
Jose Emilio Labra Gayo	Universidad de Oviedo, Spain
Frederique Laforest	INSA Lyon, France
Sarasi Lalithsena	IBM Watson, USA
Andre Lamurias	NOVA School of Science and Technology, Portugal
Davide Lanti	Free University of Bozen-Bolzano, Italy
Danh Le Phuoc	TU Berlin, Germany
Maxime Lefrançois	École des Mines de Saint-Étienne, France
Huanyu Li	Linköping University, Sweden
Sven Lieber	Royal Library of Belgium (KBR), Belgium
Stephan Linzbach	GESIS – Leibniz Institute for the Social Sciences, Germany
Anna-Sofia Lippolis	University of Bologna and ISTC-CNR, Italy
Pasquale Lisena	EURECOM, France
Wenqiang Liu	Xi'an Jiaotong University, China
Giorgia Lodi	Istituto di Scienze e Tecnologie della Cognizione (CNR), Italy
Vanessa Lopez	IBM, Ireland
Pierre Maillot	Inria, France
Maria Maleshkova	Helmut-Schmidt-Universität/Universität der Bundeswehr Hamburg, Germany
Maria Vanina Martinez	IIIA-CSIC, Spain
Miguel A. Martinez-Prieto	University of Valladolid, Spain
Jose L. Martinez-Rodriguez	Autonomous University of Tamaulipas, Mexico
Patricia Martín-Chozas	Universidad Politécnica de Madrid, Spain
Edgard Marx	Leipzig University of Applied Sciences (HTWK), Germany
Philipp Mayr	GESIS – Leibniz Institute for the Social Sciences, Germany
Jamie McCusker	Rensselaer Polytechnic Institute, USA
Lionel Medini	CNRS, France
Albert Meroño-Peñuela	King's College London, UK
Franck Michel	Université Côte d'Azur, CNRS, I3S, France
Nandana Mihindukulasooriya	IBM Research AI, USA

Nada Mimouni	CEDRIC lab - CNAM Conservatoire National des Arts et Métiers, France
Daniel Miranker	University of Texas at Austin, USA
Victor Mireles	Semantic Web Company, Austria
Pascal Molli	University of Nantes, France
Pierre Monnin	Université Côte d'Azur, Inria, CNRS, I3S, France
Boris Motik	University of Oxford, UK
Enrico Motta	Open University, UK
Diego Moussallem	Paderborn University, Germany
Paul Mulholland	Open University, UK
Varish Mulwad	GE Research, India
Raghava Mutharaju	IIIT-Delhi, India
María Navas-Loro	Universidad Politécnica de Madrid, Spain
Fabian Neuhaus	University of Magdeburg, Germany
Vinh Nguyen	National Library of Medicine, NIH, USA
Andriy Nikolov	AstraZeneca, UK
Nikolay Nikolov	SINTEF, Norway
Andrea Nuzzolese	ISTC-CNR, Italy
Cliff O'Reilly	City, University of London, UK
Femke Ongenae	Ghent University, Belgium
Francesco Osborne	Open University, UK
Ankur Padia	UBMC, USA
George Papadakis	National Technical University of Athens, Greece
Pierre-Henri Paris	Télécom Paris, France
Heiko Paulheim	University of Mannheim, Germany
Terry Payne	University of Liverpool, UK
Tassilo Pellegrini	St. Pölten University of Applied Sciences, Austria
Maria Angela Pellegrino	Università degli Studi di Salerno, Italy
Bernardo Pereira Nunes	Australian National University, Australia
Romana Pernisch	Vrije Universiteit Amsterdam, Netherlands
Catia Pesquita	Universidade de Lisboa, Portugal
Rafael Peñaloza	University of Milano-Bicocca, Italy
Guangyuan Piao	University of Galway, Ireland
Francesco Piccialli	University of Naples Federico II, Italy
Lydia Pintscher	Wikimedia Deutschland, Germany
Dimitris Plexousakis	Institute of Computer Science, FORTH, Greece
Axel Polleres	Vienna University of Economics and Business, Austria
Livio Pompianu	University of Cagliari, Italy
María Poveda-Villalón	Universidad Politécnica de Madrid, Spain
Nicoleta Preda	University of Versailles Saint-Quentin-en-Yvelines, France

Valentina Presutti	University of Bologna, Italy
Joe Raad	Paris-Saclay University, France
Alexandre Rademaker	IBM Research and EMAp/FGV, Brazil
Helen Mair Rawsthorne	École des Mines de Saint-Étienne, France
Simon Razniewski	Bosch Center for Artificial Intelligence, Germany
Diego Reforgiato	Università degli studi di Cagliari, Italy
Artem Revenko	Semantic Web Company GmbH, Austria
Mariano Rico	Universidad Politécnica de Madrid, Spain
Célian Ringwald	Université Côte d'Azur, Inria, CNRS, I3S, France
Giuseppe Rizzo	LINKS Foundation, Italy
Mariano Rodríguez Muro	Google, USA
Sergio José Rodríguez Méndez	Australian National University, Australia
Edelweis Rohrer	Universidad de la República, Uruguay
Julian Rojas	Ghent University, Belgium
Maria Del Mar Roldan-Garcia	Universidad de Málaga, Spain
Oscar Romero	Universitat Politècnica de Catalunya, Spain
Miguel Romero Orth	Universidad Adolfo Ibáñez, Chile
Henry Rosales-Méndez	University of Chile, Chile
Catherine Roussey	INRAE, France
Sebastian Rudolph	TU Dresden, Germany
Anisa Rula	University of Brescia, Italy
Alessandro Russo	STLab, ISTC-CNR, Italy
Marta Sabou	Vienna University of Economics and Business, Austria
Harald Sack	FIZ Karlsruhe, Leibniz Institute for Information Infrastructure & KIT Karlsruhe, Germany
Afshin Sadeghi	Fraunhofer IAIS, Germany
Angelo Antonio Salatino	Open University, UK
Muhammad Saleem	University of Leipzig, Germany
Bruno Sartini	Ludwig-Maximilians University of Munich, Germany
Felix Sasaki	Cornelsen Verlag GmbH & TH Brandenburg, Germany
Fatiha Saïs	Paris-Saclay University, France
Ralf Schenkel	Trier University, Germany
Stefan Schlobach	Vrije Universiteit Amsterdam, Netherlands
Daniel Schwabe	PUC-Rio, Brazil
Mario Scrocca	Cefriel, Italy
Juan F. Sequeda	data.world, USA
Umutcan Serles	University of Innsbruck, Austria
Bariş Sertkaya	Frankfurt University of Applied Sciences, Germany

Marieke van Erp	KNAW Humanities Cluster, Netherlands
Frank Van Harmelen	Vrije Universiteit Amsterdam, Netherlands
Miel Vander Sande	Meemoo, Belgium
Guillermo Vega-Gorgojo	Universidad de Valladolid, Spain
Ruben Verborgh	Ghent University, Belgium
Maria-Esther Vidal	TIB, Germany
Serena Villata	CNRS, France
Fabio Vitali	University of Bologna, Italy
Domagoj Vrgoc	Pontificia Universidad Católica de Chile, Chile
Kewen Wang	Griffith University, Australia
Ruijie Wang	University of Zurich, Switzerland
Xander Wilcke	Vrije Universiteit Amsterdam, Netherlands
Honghan Wu	King's College London, UK
Zhe Wu	eBay, USA
Josiane Xavier Parreira	Siemens AG Österreich, Austria
Guohui Xiao	University of Bergen, Norway
Nadia Yacoubi Ayadi	Université Claude Bernard Lyon1, France
Fouad Zablith	American University of Beirut, Lebanon
Hamada Zahera	Paderborn University, Germany
Ondřej Zamazal	Prague University of Economics and Business, Czech Republic
Xiaowang Zhang	Tianjin University, China
Ziqi Zhang	Accessible Intelligence, UK
Yihang Zhao	King's College London, UK
Antoine Zimmermann	École des Mines de Saint-Étienne, France
Sara Zuppiroli	ISTC-CNR, Italy
Hanna Ćwiek-Kupczyńska	University of Luxembourg, Luxembourg
Kārlis Čerās	University of Latvia, Latvia

Additional Reviewers

Akaichi, Ines
Antakli, Andre
Babaei Giglou, Hamed
Bruns, Oleksandra
Cardellino, Cristian
Cintra, Paul
D'Adda, Fabio
Djeddi, Warith Eddine
Efthymiou, Vasilis
Fanourakis, Nikolaos
Fischer, Elisabeth
Gaur, Manas
Gautam, Nikita
Gui, Zhou
Inizan, Olivier
Kommineni, Vamsi Krishna
Lippolis, Anna Sofia
Mahdavinejad, Mohammad Saeid
Martín Chozas, Patricia
Montiel-Ponsoda, Elena
Morales Tirado, Alba Catalina
Nayyeri, Mojtaba

Olivier, Inizan
Omeliyanenko, Janna
Ondraszek, Sarah Rebecca
Patkos, Theodore
Peng, Yiwen
Pons, Gerard
Qu, Yuanwei
Ragazzi, Luca
Raoufi, Ensiyeh
Ratta, Marco
Ringwald, Célian
Saki Norouzi, Sanaz
Samuel, Sheeba
Schlör, Daniel
Schraudner, Daniel
Shao, Chen
Soulard, Thibaut
van der Weijden, Daniel
Viviurka Do Carmo, Paulo Ricardo
Xiong, Bo
Yumusak, Semih
Zuppiroli, Sara

Sponsors

Platinum Sponsors

videolectures.net
exchange ideas & share knowledge

VideoLectures.NET is an award-winning free and open access educational video lectures repository. The lectures are given by distinguished scholars and scientists at the most important and prominent events like conferences, summer schools, workshops and science promotional events from many fields of Science. The portal is aimed at promoting science, exchanging ideas and fostering knowledge sharing by providing high quality didactic contents not only to the scientific community but also to the general public. All lectures, accompanying documents, information and links are systematically selected and classified through the editorial process taking into account also users' comments.

Gold Sponsors

ontotext

Ontotext is a global leader in enterprise knowledge graph technology and semantic database engines. Ontotext employs big knowledge graphs to enable unified data access and cognitive analytics via text mining and integration of data across multiple sources. Ontotext™ engine and Ontotext Platform power business critical systems in the biggest banks, media, market intelligence agencies, car and aerospace manufacturers. Ontotext technology and solutions are spread wide across the value chain of the most knowledge intensive enterprises in financial services, publishing, healthcare, pharma, manufacturing and public sectors. Leveraging AI and cognitive technologies, Ontotext helps enterprises get competitive advantage, by connecting the dots of their proprietary knowledge and putting in the context of global intelligence.

Silver Sponsors

Springer is part of Springer Nature, a leading global research, educational and professional publisher, home to an array of respected and trusted brands providing quality content through a range of innovative products and services. Springer Nature is the world's largest academic book publisher, publisher of the world's most influential journals and a pioneer in the field of open research. The company numbers almost 13,000 staff in over 50 countries and has a turnover of approximately €1.5 billion. Springer Nature was formed in 2015 through the merger of Nature Publishing Group, Palgrave Macmillan, Macmillan Education and Springer Science+Business Media.

Founded over 350 years ago, the **University of Innsbruck** today is the most important research and educational institution in western Austria, offering a wide range of programmes across all disciplines. Located in the heart of the Alps, it offers 28,000 students and 5,500 employees the best conditions.

Bronze Sponsors

metaphacts is a German software company that empowers customers to drive knowledge democratization and decision intelligence using knowledge graphs. Built entirely on open standards and technologies, our product metaphactory delivers a low-code, FAIR

Data platform that supports collaborative knowledge modeling and knowledge generation and enables on-demand citizen access to consumable, contextual and actionable knowledge. metaphacts serves customers in areas such as life sciences and pharma, engineering and manufacturing, finance and insurance, retail, cultural heritage, and more. For more information about metaphacts and its products and solutions please visit www.metaphacts.com.

eccenca Corporate Memory is cutting-edge Knowledge Graph technology. It digitally captures the expertise of knowledge workers so that it can be accessed and processed by machines. The fusion of human knowledge with large amounts of data, coupled with the computing power of machines, results in powerful artificial intelligence that enables companies to execute existing processes as well as innovation projects of all kinds at high speed and low cost. And it creates an impressive competitive advantage.

Through eccenca.my you can register and create a eccenca Corporate Memory Community Edition Sandbox for evaluation. Join pioneers like BOSCH, SIEMENS, Astra Zeneca and many other global market leaders – our world-class team of Linked Data Experts is ready when you are.

Contents – Part II

Contents – Part I

Special Track on Large Language Models for Knowledge Engineering

Industry

Posters and Demos

PhD Symposium

Optimisation of Reasoning over Ontologies on Embedded Hardware for Avionics-Context Semantic-Aware to Generate Minimisation of Computation Time and Memory Footprint

Youssef Amari[1,2](✉)

[1] Thales,Toulouse, France
yamari@laas.fr
[2] LAAS-CNRS,Toulouse, France

Abstract. Current advances in Artificial Intelligence (AI) technologies pave the way to consider new services that assist aircrew, possibly in embedded systems. Semantic reasoning using ontologies provide both opportunities and challenges for these services. Recent studies showcase that those reasoning approaches suffer from long and unpredictable execution times, and high memory consumption. Such limitations currently refrain the use of this approach in embedded systems. The objective of this work is to explore ways to deploy such reasoning in embedded architectures focusing on optimisations of time/memory envelope and benchmarking. We first explore the related work on existing optimisations of some implementations to get a clear view on reasoning techniques, then we investigate the variability sources to get a clear view on what is going inside a reasoner. The results are (i) a better overview of reasoner methodologies, (ii) a notable categorisation of optimisation families and (iii) a clearer view of impacts concerning reasoning time determinism.

Keywords: Semantic Reasoning · Symbolic AI · Avionics · Embedded System · Ontology · Description Logic · OWL · Reasoner · Optimisation

1 Introduction/Motivation

Semantic reasoning dealing with ontologies was mostly initiated by the Semantic Web started in 2001 by the World-Wide Web Consortium (W3C). The goal of its founder, Tim Berners-Lee, was to ease the navigation on the Internet using semantic [13]. This has prompted an interest of a sheer number of researchers to extract prominent inventions using the potential of semantics, ontologies and reasoning over many domains of interest such as life science [6], mobiles [12] or avionics. In aeronautics, one of the envisioned applications can be the assistance to the aircrew in order to circumvent human workload limitations.

Y. Amari—Early Stage Ph.D.

A. Meroño Peñuela et al. (Eds.): ESWC 2024, LNCS 15345, pp. 3–12, 2025.
https://doi.org/10.1007/978-3-031-78955-7_1

1.1 Use Case: a Virtual Assistant

Thales is developing a virtual assistant exploiting symbolic AI technologies in order to solve tasks related to the assistance of the aircrew. This assistant will be deployed in embedded operational environment with limited computational power and time response constraints. We study the feasibility of implementing an ontology coupled to a reasoner in an embedded system.

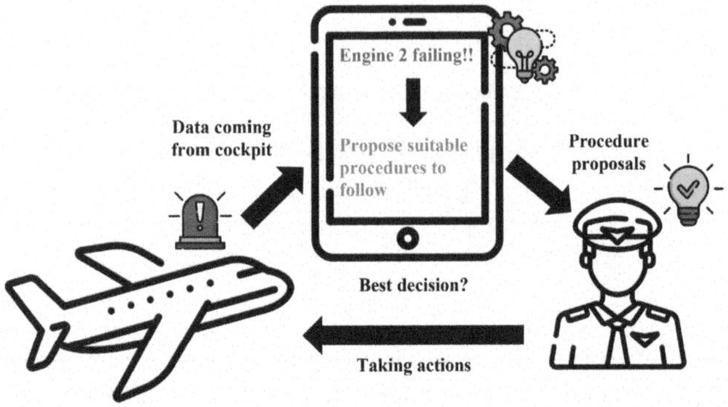

Fig. 1: Schema of a possible situation in our use case (icons from Flaticon.com)

Imagine in a cockpit a warning light shows up so then the pilot has to assess, as quickly as possible, the seriousness of the alarm in order to evaluate the criticality of the situation (see Fig. 1). Due to stringent real-time constraints, monitoring is consequently one of the most complex and critical features in the aviation domain. If perception and prediction steps can be performed by data-based approaches, the comprehension step of this situation must use aeronautic domain knowledge to give a structured meaning of the alarm using explainability feature of reasoning [10]. Notwithstanding, for such case, even if we detain constraints on time and memory space we bound to have a minimal and deterministic reasoning time to help the pilot to understand the situation in time. [8] relates our work and gives a concrete view of time constraint: in the test campaign, 1 s is the maximum time response and some runs exceeds this limit and also show non-determinism of reasoning time for consistency or explanation service. This in not acceptable in the real-time context of avionics!

1.2 Ontologies and Reasoners

We are dealing with knowledge bases in ontology format and these ontologies are formalised using the Web Ontology Language (OWL) based on Description Logics (DL). Typically an aircraft ontology can consist of the two regular boxes:

- a TBox which is the skeleton of the domain of aircraft, describing it using concepts and relations such as an aircraft detains two wings and wheels,
- an ABox which is the base of individuals related to our domain such as an Airbus A380 or Boeing 737 aircraft.

According to [4], a semantic reasoner is a *a piece of software able to infer logical consequences from a set of asserted facts or axioms.* [...] *The inference rules are commonly specified by means of an ontology language, and often a description logic language.*

1.3 Constraints in On-Board Systems

Embedding ontologies and reasoner(s) is a challenge because these technologies were not initially thought for embedded devices. On the one hand, according to [7,12], the world of embedded systems such as mobiles or constrained devices imply many constraints concerning the deployment of a reasoner. In fact, numerous state of the art reasoners are too resource-intensive to be implemented on a such system. On that kind of systems the memory space, power, or running time are hugely limited. On the other hand, some studies show up that those technologies are known to suffer from long and unpredictable execution times, usually saturating memory capacities of usual computers such as in [8].

Additionally in our case, another fully-fledged constraint is added: Time-constraints associated to Real-Time usage. In other words, we coerce time response but even more we need to bound it to meet the time directives.

2 State of the Art

In this section, we showcase the *sine qua non* of fundamentals to serenely tackle our problematic, the existing work that seems well to tackle our research question and the different efforts made to perform embedded reasoning with a coarse grained focus on all embedded devices targeted in the literature.

2.1 Reasoning

Background: Description Logics, Web Ontology Language, and Misc. Description Logics (DL) are a decidable fragment of first-order logic (FOL). It is characterised by a syntax ("symbols") and a semantics ("formal meaning"). The Web Ontology Language (OWL) is an ontology standard language for the semantic Web and RDF is a protocol for web data. OWL has two versions, OWL 1 and 2, both consisting of fragments with a specific expressivity. A case in point, OWL 2 contains the profiles [3] OWL 2 EL, QL, and RL.

State of the Art Reasoners. The first step of our work was to gather well-known reasoners in the literature in order to have clues on which one(s) could guide us towards a concrete direction for our problematic. To this extent, we deeply studied 38 reasoners coming from [2] and *LiRoT* [7]. These reasoners have been considered due to their popularity and last update date (at least 2012). Moreover, only official reasoners have been considered because of their recognition and the associated solid community, hence ignoring prototypes implementations.

Importantly, a preliminary phase was to break down the inside of a reasoner by firstly dealing with the structure of its backbone which is the reasoning methodology. We have identified 5 main reasoning approaches among the considered list: *Tableau*, *Hypertableau*, *Consequence-based*, *Datalog rewriting*, or *RETE*. Furthermore, we have extracted the existing standard reasoning tasks such as satisfiability, classification, or consistency that are used to accompany reasoning process.

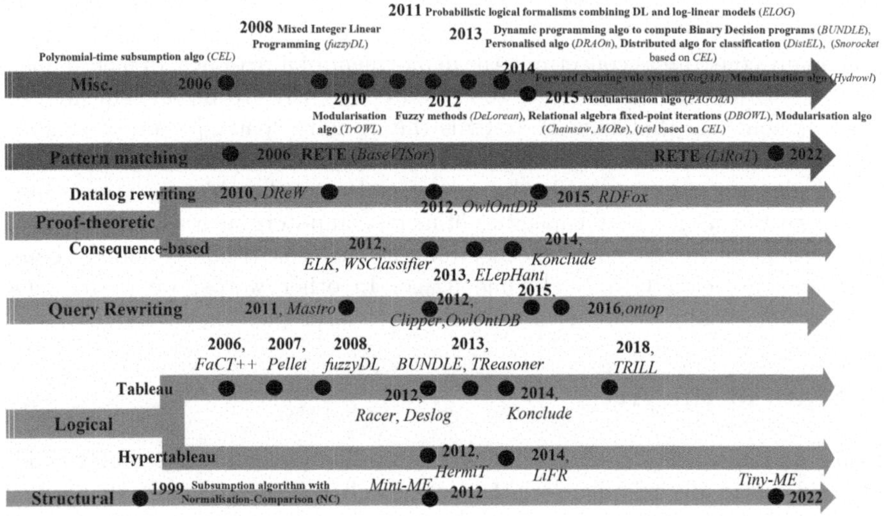

Fig. 2: Timeline regarding reasoning approaches appearance with their associated reasoners from 1999 to 2022

We have categorised the reasoners relatively to their methodology over time, as shown in Fig. 2. The purpose was to determine the active and inactive methodologies in order to stay update. In this figure, we observe that (*hyper*) *Tableau* algorithms were regularly used over time, this is the same observation for miscellaneous approaches whereas pattern matching approach, particularly RETE, was less implemented but the trend is apparently changing with the 2022 contribution. The same is for structural family. Moreover, to tackle performance issues concerning memory and time usage, we have thoroughly studied the existing and notable optimisations (see Sect. 6) of the considered reasoners in order to evaluate how these improvements are suitable with our approach.

2.2 Is Embedding Reasoning Conceivable?

Furthermore, we have extended our research to the reasoners dedicated to embedded systems to examine ups and downs in this area. There are few papers with the development of various approaches such as for Internet of Things (IoT).

Some fairly well-known reasoners are straightforwardly aimed at embedded architectures such as: *Pocket KRHyper* [12,20], *μOR* [5], *MiRE4OWL* [11], *ELepHant* [18], *COROR* [24], *Mini-ME* [16] and *Tiny-ME* [15], or *LiRoT* [7] used in IoT context called Semantic Web of Things (SWoT).

[23] depicts a mobile reasoner which implements an extension of Tableau algorithm. In fact, they trade inference result exactness for gain in efficiency, if the latter is needed. The authors describe their solution such as an improvement of *Pellet* [21] reasoner. [17] presents an OWL reasoner for embedded devices by constructing a global architecture using OWL 2 RL and CLIPS [1] rule engine. In [9], the authors describe a reasoner dedicated for Programmable Logic Controllers (PLC) which implements per se a consequence-base approach in order to classify ontology from the OWL 2 EL fragment. This profile was chosen because of its convenience with diagnostic models. The consequence-driven classification algorithm used is the same inside the *CEL* [6] reasoner. [14] proposes an interesting approach that resembles our work direction. They developed the Delta-reasoner based on OWL 2 RL and SWRL[1] concerning context-aware applications. Also, some efforts have been made on optimising algorithms towards the embedding reasoning such as: m-Tableaux [22] which role is to give the possibility to use Tableaux algorithm on mobile architectures, or RETE_{pool} [25] that is dedicated to resource-constrained devices. It gathers RETE memory mechanisms in order to get a better memory footprint.

This is an interesting related work because it shows a plethora of implementations for a specific use case towards embedded or constraints hardware. But, the problem of implementing a reasoner on embedded hardware still exist with a continuous interest to the community. Plus, this encourages us even more to find a solution to our problematic.

3 Problem Statement and Contributions

Accordingly, the objective of our thesis is to propose an efficient reasoning over ontologies to be embedded in avionics-context by introducing optimisation to generate minimisation of reasoning time and memory consumption by tackling the next questions:

- How efficient are current reasoners to handle our problematic?
- Can we combine existing optimisations[2] from standard reasoners to achieve our goal?
- Can current reasoners for embedded systems provide more clues on optimisation techniques and hardware technologies choices?
- How to experiment the limits of reasoning runtime and guarantee a Worst-case Execution Time for embedding applications?

[1] Language for the Semantic Web used to symbolise rules and logic.

[2] Means the features principally geared towards better running time and/or memory footprint.

4 Research Methodology and Approach

We aim to explore optimisation methods for ontology reasoning with this approach:

1. Establish a state of the art on reasoners and those dedicated to embedded architectures to classify optimisations to see what exist and could help us towards an efficient solution;
2. Test Bench: generate an ontology corpus, using e.g. [19], and use a list of reasoners to test. The goal is find out the different ontology metrics and different processing steps that could impact the reasoners performances and their existing optimisations;
3. Based on the outcomes of the test bench step, we will propose new optimisation methods of reasoners to enhance performances thereof and then tackle embedding constraints.
4. Develop efficient mapping on (new) architectures such as a Graphics Processing Unit (GPU);
5. Implement the solution on the real case of virtual assistant for validation and assess how understandable are the outputs for different users such as the consumer or the builder.

Our current work is focused on whether we can optimise reasoning approaches and how, and importantly understand the sources of reasoning runtime variability (non-determinism). In parallel, we are separating the wheat from the chaff in order to undertake the deemed necessary levers concerning our use case such as which reasoning tasks do we need or what is the targeted expressiveness? We are not reinventing the wheel, we mean that this is not a classical research question, as it arises in embedded systems. The real challenge would be whether the reasoning execution is mastered, verifiable, and importantly bounded in memory space and reasoning runtime.

5 Evaluation Plan

During our evaluation process, we envisioned to mainly scrutinise the different causes of a low reasoning runtime and an high memory space usage. To do so, we will address the following tasks:

- Make tests with existing benchmarks, such as [19], to explore various features of ontologies such as expressiveness or size of ABox against a set of reasoners and therefore get a global view of relations between ontology metrics, memory space and reasoning runtime. To avoid generic results, we will tailor them towards avionic-context;
- Conduct reasoning experiments on different hardware architectures and compare each in turn. More specifically, we will deeply study the given reasoner over ontologies through a scalability process regarding notable metrics such as its TBox size or expressiveness. We will use a profiler to highlight for instance

the number of processes used during the reasoning, or the appearing hotspots means the functions highly demanding in runtime. Also, a huge concern will be on the operations used at the low-level, their dependency, data location in memory, or the algorithmic structure used by the reasoning approach.

We will also shed light on the following questions to help us get a grip on our problem: Which reasoning tasks (e.g. classification) are relevant for our use case? Which level of expressiveness is needed? What is the size of the ontology? Which reasoning methodologies the reasoner is using and which one could be pertinent? How to accelerate reasoning? By constraining the expressiveness, optimising algorithms, or both? When the ontology cannot be restricted, can we find efficient reasoners to deal with (very) highly expressive ontologies? Also, we need to analyse which hardware architecture could suit our needs.

6 Preliminary Results

Two preliminary results w.r.t our work are: on the one hand, we have built a categorisation in Fig. 3 corresponding to the different optimisation families from studied existing reasoners, organised in a logical order from those concerning low-level to software ones.

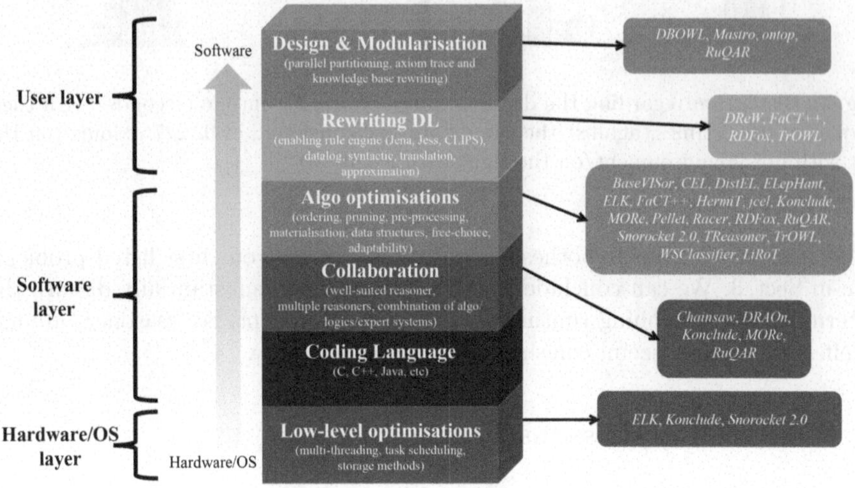

Fig. 3: Categorisation of different optimisation families from studied existing reasoners

This figure shows different families, each one concerning particular techniques of related optimisations. This optimisations tiling gives us more clues on which techniques could be useful for our use case.

On the other hand, we have conducted a first experiment by running 1,000 times *HermiT* against the same ontology (9,227 axioms) on a classical laptop with a noisy environment[3]. We used Owlready2 package from Python language[4]. In Fig. 4, on the left, we observed that runtime is non-immutable. Hence, we need to master this variability in order to obtain determinism concerning runtime. This finding spurred us to deepen the explanations of that and our first and logical hypothesis could be interferences caused by background services. Hence, we need to restrain interferences by measuring runtime of the reasoning process in an isolated work environment as it could be in a classical embedded device. Consequently, on another computer we isolated our reasoning from pollution of services/processes. We conducted the same experiment, and obtained the results in Fig. 4, on the right. In this last experiment, the distribution of running time is hugely more concentrated between 19 and 20 s whereas in the former one the data are more widely dispersed showing a high variability.

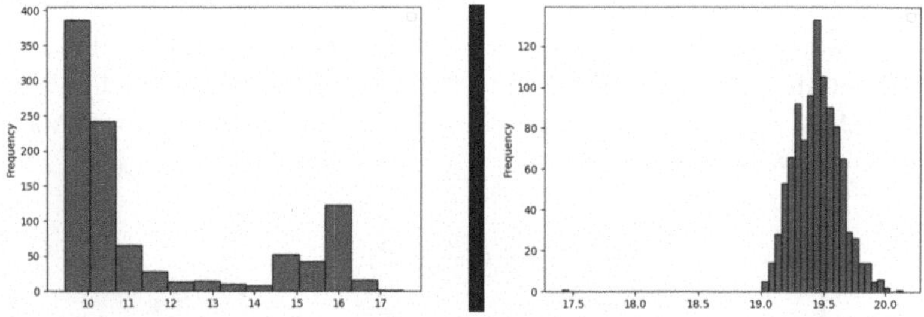

Fig. 4: Histogram regarding the distribution of *HermiT* runtime (seconds) with their frequency, 1000 times, against the same ontology consisting of 9, 227 axioms (on the left with noisy environment/on the right with isolation)

It is clear that our hypothesis is answered but also our first listed problematic in Sect. 3. We can conclude that the interferences substantially disturb the determinism of reasoning runtime in a work environment. So, reasoners are not as effective as they seem, concerning time predictability.

7 Conclusions/Lessons Learned

Our literature review has shown that all reasoners have various features and restrictions, related to their optimisations, for mastering their time and space footprint. We presented the first steps towards providing a clear evaluation phase in an embedded system context. At this step of our work, one question could be: can one dreams of an efficient reasoning in embedded systems? To the best of our knowledge, the answer should be positive.

[3] Signifies services/process running in background.

[4] Reminder: Hermit is based on Java and hence a Java Virtual Machine is used.

Our future work include investigating how embedded architectures and hardware acceleration techniques can go in pair with optimisation of algorithms. Our ultimate goal is to implement a solution in the real case of virtual assistant.

Acknowledgments. I would like to express my gratitude to my supervisors M. Roy (LAAS-CNRS), F. De Grancey (Thales), and H. Waeselynck (LAAS-CNRS).

References

1. CLIPS: a tool for building expert systems. https://www.clipsrules.net/
2. List of reasoners. http://owl.cs.manchester.ac.uk/tools/list-of-reasoners/
3. OWL 2 Web Ontology Language Profiles (Second Edition). https://www.w3.org/TR/owl2-profiles/
4. Semantic reasoner (2024). https://en.wikipedia.org/w/index.php?title=Semantic_reasoner&oldid=1193724481
5. Ali, S., Kiefer, S.: A micro OWL DL reasoner for ambient intelligent devices. In: Advances in Grid and Pervasive Computing. Springer, Heidelberg (2009). https://doi.org/10.1007/978-3-642-01671-4_28
6. Baader, F., Lutz, C., Suntisrivaraporn, B.: CEL a polynomial-time reasoner for life science ontologies. In: Automated Reasoning. Springer, Heidelberg (2006). https://doi.org/10.1007/11814771_25
7. Bento, A., Médini, L., Singh, K., Laforest, F.: Do arduinos dream of a efficient reasoners? In: The Semantic Web. Springer, Cham (2022). https://doi.org/10.1007/978-3-031-06981-9_17
8. De-Grancey, F., Audouy, A.: Towards the deployment of knowledge based systems in safety-critical systems. In: The Semantic Web: ESWC 2023 Satellite Events. Cham (2023). https://doi.org/10.1007/978-3-031-43458-7_35
9. Grimm, S., Watzke, M., Hubauer, T., Cescolini, F.: Embedded EL+ reasoning on programmable logic controllers. In: The Semantic Web ISWC 2012. Springer, Heidelberg (2012). https://doi.org/10.1007/978-3-642-35173-0_5
10. Ilkou, E., Koutraki, M.: Symbolic Vs Sub-symbolic AI methods: friends or enemies? (2020). https://www.semanticscholar.org/paper/Symbolic-Vs-Sub-symbolic-AI-Methods%3A-Friends-or-Ilkou-Koutraki/9d80b0382d4576676610f502abb954e10b4e6037
11. Kim, T., Park, I., Hyun, S.J., Lee, D.: MiRE4OWL: mobile rule engine for OWL. In: 2010 IEEE 34th Annual Computer Software and Applications Conference Workshops (2010). https://doi.org/10.1109/COMPSACW.2010.62
12. Kleemann, T.: Towards mobile reasoning (2006)
13. Matthews, B.: Semantic Web Technologies. E-learning **6** (Jan 2005)
14. Motik, B., Horrocks, I., Kim, S.M.: Delta-reasoner: a semantic web reasoner for an intelligent mobile platform. In: Proceedings of the 21st International Conference on World Wide Web. New York, NY, USA (2012). https://doi.org/10.1145/2187980.2187988
15. Ruta, M., et al.: A multiplatform reasoning engine for the semantic web of everything. J. Web Semant. (2022). https://doi.org/10.1016/j.websem.2022.100709
16. Scioscia, F., et al.: Mini-ME matchmaker and reasoner for the semantic web of things (2018)
17. Seitz, C., Schönfelder, R.: Rule-Based OWL Reasoning for Specific Embedded Devices. In: Aroyo, L., et al. (eds.) ISWC 2011. LNCS, vol. 7032, pp. 237–252. Springer, Heidelberg (2011). https://doi.org/10.1007/978-3-642-25093-4_16

18. Sertkaya, B.: The ELepHant reasoner system description (2013)
19. Singh, G., Bhatia, S., Mutharaju, R.: OWL2Bench: a benchmark for OWL 2 Reasoners. In: The Semantic Web ISWC 2020 (2020). https://doi.org/10.1007/978-3-030-62466-8_6
20. Sinner, A., Kleemann, T.: KRHyper in your pocket. In: Automated Deduction CADE-20. Lecture Notes in Computer Science, Springer, Heidelberg (2005). https://doi.org/10.1007/11532231_33
21. Sirin, E., Parsia, B., Grau, B.C., Kalyanpur, A., Katz, Y.: Pellet: a practical OWL-DL reasoner. J. Web Semant. (2007). https://doi.org/10.1016/j.websem.2007.03.004
22. Steller, L., Krishnaswamy, S.: Efficient mobile reasoning for pervasive discovery. **10**(1145/1529282), 1529562 (2009)
23. Steller, L.A., Krishnaswamy, S., Gaber, M.M.: A weighted approach to partial matching for mobile reasoning. In: Bernstein, A., Karger, D.R., Heath, T., Feigenbaum, L., Maynard, D., Motta, E., Thirunarayan, K. (eds.) ISWC 2009. LNCS, vol. 5823, pp. 618–633. Springer, Heidelberg (2009). https://doi.org/10.1007/978-3-642-04930-9_39
24. Tai, W., Keeney, J., OSullivan, D.: Resource-constrained reasoning using a reasoner composition approach. Semantic Web (2015). https://doi.org/10.3233/SW-140142
25. Van Woensel, W., Abidi, S.S.R.: Optimizing semantic reasoning on memory-constrained platforms using the RETE algorithm. In: The Semantic Web. Cham (2018). https://doi.org/10.1007/978-3-319-93417-4_44

Computational Approaches for Addressing Problematic Terminology in Museum Catalogues: A Knowledge Graph of Museum Critical Cataloguing Guidelines

Erin Canning(✉)

University of Oxford, Oxford OX1 2JD, UK
erin.canning@eng.ox.ac.uk

Abstract. Many museums are interested in addressing the presence of problematic terminology in their catalogue data but are uncertain of what they should look for and what do to when a problematic term is encountered. There is an opportunity to address the lack of guidance and scarcity of resources available for museums looking to engage with this work through the use of linked open data in order to create a knowledge graph that links together machine-readable versions of terminology guidance from multiple sources and then further connects them to additional lexicographical resources. The resulting knowledge graph can then be leveraged to support critical cataloguing tasks—namely confirming a term as problematic in a given context and making a decision of how to proceed—by providing cataloguers with the information they need to perform their work. This approach seeks to meet the needs of museum professionals to have access to domain best practice while allowing for localization of recommendations. This research seeks to understand what kinds of language museums are concerned with, how museums are thinking about what makes a term problematic, what possible reparative actions museums feel are appropriate given different contexts, and what kinds of information museum professionals look for to make a decision about which action to take. This work is taking place as part of a Collaborative Doctoral Partnership studentship co-supervised by the University of Oxford and the Victoria and Albert Museum, and as such the Victoria and Albert Museum serves as the case study for the exploration of this research area.

Keywords: ontology · knowledge graph · linked open data · cultural heritage · problematic terminology

1 Introduction and Motivation

The Victoria and Albert Museum (V&A) first opened its doors to the public as the South Kensington Museum in 1857 and today contains an extraordinarily diverse collection of close to 1.7 million works of art and design objects. Just as diverse as the objects are the catalogue records that accompany them: this catalogue data contains evidence of the colonial history of the museum and of the relationship between Britain and the areas of the

A. Meroño Peñuela et al. (Eds.): ESWC 2024, LNCS 15345, pp. 13–22, 2025.
https://doi.org/10.1007/978-3-031-78955-7_2

world in which Britain had colonial or proto-colonial interests, as objects from these parts of the world make up a significant portion of the museum's collection. This evidence can appear in various forms, including the presence of "problematic terminology": harmful and offensive language, colonial naming practices, euphemisms, clichés, and more. This issue is not unique to the V&A, and the museum field as a whole is wrestling with how to best address the problematics in their data.

One of the challenges for museums in addressing problematic terminology in catalogue data, also called critical cataloguing, is in determining where to begin: many museums may be interested in addressing issues in their data but are uncertain of what they should look for and what do to when a problematic term is encountered. The lack of guidance and scarcity of resources available for museums looking to engage with this work is well known [1–3]. There is an opportunity to address this through the use of linked open data (LOD): museum professionals can benefit from having a structured resource that makes clear how different terms are understood by different institutions, and how different museums are approaching critical cataloguing work. The use of LOD will enable the creation of a knowledge graph that can link together machine-readable versions of terminology guidance from multiple sources and then further connects them to additional lexicographical resources. The development of this resource will contribute to the understanding of how museums are thinking about what makes a term problematic and what reparative actions are possible given different contexts, as well as supporting museum workers engaged in this work by addressing the need to develop sector-wide guidance and support cross-institutional knowledge exchange.

2 Related Work

2.1 Addressing Problematic Terminology in Museum Catalogue Data

The Museums Association Decolonization Working Group produced a decolonization support guide in 2021, two pages of which are dedicated to collections cataloguing [3]. Resources aimed at the museum community have also been developed by individual people and institutions; for example, [4] includes a glossary of problematic terminology and suggestions for what other museums could do when encountering the terms in their own catalogue data. In the UK, [5] published a set of recommendations for conducting critical cataloguing work and [6] produced a guide for critical cataloguing in archives building on those recommendations. There is also now [7], a collaborative resource intended to "promote cross-institutional collaboration on inclusive description issues" [1]. Although these resources started locally, they respond to a field-wide need and seek to contribute to a collective effort.

Individual institutions are working to put these guidelines into action, and museums are forming internal terminology and cataloguing review groups to audit and remediate their catalogue data. Auditing involves reviewing catalogue data for instances of harmful language, such as specific words, or for colonial, dehumanizing, or otherwise problematic framings. Once problematic terminology has been identified it can be addressed in a number of ways; there is no single rule that would be appropriate in all cases and it is essential to take the context and purpose of the work into consideration [2, 8]. When documented locally, these lists of problematic terms and suggested reparative actions become terminology guidance documents for the use of cataloguers within a museum.

2.2 Ontologies for Addressing Problematic Terminology in Cultural Heritage

While numerous lists of offensive, sensitive, and problematic terminology exist, the most relevant related work is in ontologies for the representation of terminology and cultural heritage data. This is because the focus of this project is not producing a list of problematic language, but on enabling both an understanding of what "problematic terminology' means in the context of cultural heritage data, and facilitating cross-institutional sharing of information on terms and suggested reparative actions. Therefore, the focus of this work is not on the terms themselves, but instead on how they are framed and considered by cultural heritage institutions, as evidenced by the structure and contents of terminology guidance documents. The most relevant existing ontologies are:

- CIDOC Conceptual Reference Model (CIDOC CRM): an ontology for the representation of cultural heritage data [9]. It is a stable standard widely used in the cultural heritage community and has been an ISO standard since 2006 (and updated in 2023).
- Ontology Lexicon (OntoLex): an ontology for the representation of linguistic data, namely lexica and dictionaries. It is a stable standard, and the most widely used model for publishing these linguistic resources as linked open data [10].
- Simple Knowledge Organization Schema (SKOS): an ontology for the representation of thesauri and terminology lists. It is a stable standard and is widely used for publishing controlled vocabularies as linked open data. It has been used to create LOD critical cataloguing vocabulary resources such as Homosaurus [11].
- Cultural Contexts Concept Scheme for Contentious Terminology (CULCO): an ontology developed in 2022 as part of the "Culturally Aware AI" project to describe [6]'s glossary section [12].

These ontologies do not exist in isolation: points of connection link them together into a base that can then be further developed (see Sect. 6 below). CULCO, OntoLex and CIDOC CRM all assert relationships to SKOS, making it key for bringing them together. While these connections are usually encoded as inheritance relationships, others are more informally proposed in scope notes or wider documentation. Alignment between OntoLex and CIDOC CRM has also been previously proposed [13].

3 Problem Statement and Contributions

3.1 Research Questions

This project seeks to examine the high-level question of if and how computational approaches can support the goals of, and work involved in, critical cataloguing. In pursuit of knowledge towards this goal, this research aims to answer the following questions:

RQ 1. How can domain knowledge about the identification and remediation of problematic terminology in museum catalogues be structured as a data schema that is actionable for use in a technical system?

This research question addresses the hypotheses that textual terminology guidance documents produced by museums can serve as knowledge sources for building an ontology and actionable knowledge graph of the informational needs of reparative critical cataloguing practitioners, that a linked open data solution that makes use of an ontology for the representation of terminology guidance documents will promote inter-institutional collaboration and knowledge sharing in this area in a way that also allows for each location to retain their local specificity, and that combining the terms listed in terminology guidance documents with additional information from linked open data resources will enable us to understand what kinds of language museums consider to be potentially problematic.

RQ 2. How can museum records containing potential indicators of the presence of biased language be identified using existing computational methods?

This research question addresses the hypothesis that providing access to information about the historical and contemporary meanings of terms, along with information about the different reparative methods suggested by the museum field, will enable critical cataloguing practitioners to review records and take remediative actions with greater confidence and efficiency.

RQ 3. Can computational approaches enable critical engagement with catalogue data, and if so, how can they be developed? What might a methodology for the development and application of computational methods informed by the theoretical foundations and concerns of critical cataloguing look like?

This research question addresses the hypotheses that computational approaches can enable critical engagement with catalogue data when they are developed not to address only specific existing work practices but to meet the goals of critical cataloguing work as a movement in the museum field, and that the theoretical foundations and concerns of critical cataloguing can inform the methodology for developing computational tools and methods for working critically with catalogue data.

3.2 Outputs and Contributions

This project will produce three distinct yet connected technical outputs: an ontology for representing problematic terminology and suggested actions, a populated and linked knowledge graph that incorporates multiple terminology guidance documents and additional linked open data vocabularies, and a computational environment that supports target knowledge graph usage by enabling the exploration of museum catalogue data through the components of the knowledge graph: the presence of identified terminology alongside the display of information about the term and suggested remediative actions.

The contributions to knowledge that this project seeks to make include:

- Understanding what kinds of problematics museums are concerned with, evidenced by what kinds of information make up terminology guidance documents.
- Comparing between institutions what is being looked for, how it is being identified, and what is being recommended when instances are encountered.
- Demonstrating how computational approaches can aid in identifying catalogue records that have the potential to contain bias.

– Demonstrating how concepts from critical theory can inform methodology for data engineering projects situated in this domain.

4 Research Methodology and Approach

The initial modeling work for the design of an ontology for the representation of problematic terminology guidelines (described below in Sect. 6) was undertaken using the Victoria and Albert Museum Terminology Guidance Document as the source document for analysis. Knowledge was elicited from the structure and content of this document, and was used to enumerate the requirements of the schema. These requirements were then compared to the affordances of existing ontologies, a gap was identified, and a modelling solution was proposed. The design approach taken for this intends to minimize the creation of new classes and instead focus on ways to further bring together existing LOD resources and the communities involved in their development, therefore bringing this project into conversation with the data communities most relevant to the work being undertaken on this project and contributing towards the reuse of existing resources in the linked open data domain. The design approach builds off of two ontology engineering approaches: the approach to designing and adopting ontologies for use in domain of cultural data from a feminist methodological perspective discussed in [14], and the method of lean ontology development [15]. Feminist theory is one of the fields of critical theory that directly informs critical cataloguing [16], and therefore this methodological approach is highly relevant for this project. The lean ontology development method discussed in [15] has also been trialed in the setting of a feminist linked open data project which validates the suitability of this approach for this project. These approaches will be used as the foundations for exploring an ontology engineering methodology informed by the theoretical foundations and concerns of critical cataloguing.

This model will be validated through review with museum staff, as well as through the integration of two additional terminology guideline documents relevant to the field: the glossary section of [4] and the contents of [7]. These are frequently cited resources: [4] is regularly looked to as a guiding document in this field, and [7] is crowd-sourced and expansive. Integrating these sources will validate the proposed schema as applicable beyond the single context, and comparisons of terms and suggestions between different sources could be analyzed as a form of inter-researcher or inter-institutional agreement. Linking this knowledge graph to other LOD resources will involve looking for term matches in the Getty Art & Architecture Thesaurus (a commonly used controlled vocabulary) and the Homosaurus vocabulary (a community-developed LOD vocabulary that is already working in the space of critical cataloguing) to assert relationships to terms published by those sources. This will work to expose how problematic terminology may be introduced into catalogue data through the use of externally-sourced vocabularies and highlight community-developed vocbularies as alternatives.

This project also seeks to incorporate the perspectives of museum professionals engaged in critical cataloguing by means of an ongoing set of interviews which have been taking place since December 2023. Findings from these interviews about the requirements, pain points, and goals of critical cataloguers inform project developments.

5 Evaluation Plan

Evaluation will be done in three ways: through review with V&A staff, through the integration of additional guidelines, and through the use of competency questions over the final knowledge graph. The initial validation involved reviewing the conceptual model with key stakeholders from the V&A staff. These are staff who are responsible for creating and maintaining the museum's Terminology Guidance Document (TGD), and therefore are best positioned to evaluate whether the conceptual model matches their understanding of the document and domain. A second validation review was then carried out with the same staff to confirm that the suggestions had been accurately translated into the model. This was an important area for confirmation as the "suggestion" section is the core purpose of the TGD, and accuracy is therefore critical for the validity of the knowledge graph. Integrating [4] and [7] will confirm the interoperability of the structure of the ontology. This validation test will determine whether the kinds of information found in the TGD are the same kinds of information as found in other terminology guidelines, or if there are additional kinds of knowledge and relationships that will need to be accommodate, thus requiring revision of the ontology. This validation is being performed after the reviews with V&A staff to ensure that the base model being compared is a stable foundation for this stage of the work. Validation through competency questions will be performed once the additional terminology guidelines have been integrated and links to the additional vocabularies sources have been made. These questions will be developed in collaboration with the V&A stakeholders involved in the earlier validation work, and will be formulated to answer questions that they had when creating the original document and when engaging in catalogue review.

Evaluation of the computational environment will return to review with V&A staff. This evaluation will be intended to consider whether the use of the information contained in the knowledge graph is indeed useful for the practical or conceptual work involved in critical cataloguing: namely, if it enables cataloguers to review records and take remediative actions with greater confidence and efficiency, and if working with catalogue records through this lens supports a critical engagement with catalogue data. This evaluation step is closely related to the competency question validation step, but will move beyond it to include the experiences of stakeholders who would potentially use the outputs of this project in their own work.

6 Results

6.1 Conceptual Model of the V&A Terminology Guidance Document

The V&A holds regular cross-departmental meetings to discuss terminology questions and concerns, with the goal of coming to recommendations about how to address general and specific cases. Decisions are documented and inform the V&A Terminology Guidance Document (TGD): a living document, developed in collaboration with the Interpretation Department and additional staff-led internal advisory groups, that is intended to support staff in making decisions of how to proceed when they encounter problematic terminology in catalogue records. The TGD contains three main sections:

1. Potentially problematic terms: in addition to a central term, the document lists common variants and forms that a cataloguer might encounter in object records.
2. Term description: a number of different ways that the term has been used or understood across different times and places, reminiscent of a diachronic dictionary.
3. Suggestions: a list of suggestions that could be considered based on specifics of the term encounter, such as who or what is being described, the original intended use of the term in the record, and the field in the record where the term is found.

The conceptual modelling stage of work separates each of these elements into separate entities and defines the relationships between them. There is also information about the TGD itself: as a living document, both the guideline and individual entries are written, edited, and informed by the expertise of various people over time. Therefore, the document itself as an information object is a necessary element of the model.

6.2 Gap Analysis of Existing Ontologies

The next stage of this work was to review existing linked open data ontologies in order to evaluate whether or not a new ontology is required to represent this information. CIDOC CRM, OntoLex, SKOS, and CULCO covered many of the periphery elements found in the TGD conceptual model, but lacked in core coverage as well as actions involved in the work of the domain. However, due to their existing formal and informal relationships, this set of ontologies provide a robust foundation to build from.

CULCO represents the glossary of [4]: this resource lists terms along with descriptions of their history, use, and possible sensitivities, as well as suggestions of actions for cataloguers to take when they encounter in the term in a museum record. The CULCO model is comprised of three classes and six properties. Individual terms are classed as *ContentiousIssues*, which have labels (*skosXL:Label*)—the way that they are written—and *Suggestions*. This *Suggestion* class is the closest existing class for a suggestion as it is understood in the context of the TGD, but it is too lightweight to be used for an accurate translation of the conceptual model of the TGD as it does not expand on the concept of labels, to which it is directly connected, beyond using SKOS-XL directly. This is similar to how Homosaurus uses *skos:altLabel* for their "use for" concept [11]. As such, it was found to be a strong foundation but not sufficient on its own.

OntoLex, conversely, introduces a level of complexity in modelling lexical information beyond what is required for the representation of the TGD: using OntoLex to model term forms and descriptions would require the use of classes such as *LexicalConcept* that, for the purposes of this context, would be purely intermediary and beyond the requirements. Similarly, CIDOC CRM introduces a level of complexity in modelling information about cultural heritage objects that exceeds the requirements of the TGD. Even with these added levels of complexity, the core elements elicited during the conceptual modelling stage are not sufficiently covered by existing ontologies.

6.3 Proposed Ontology

The ontology proposed at this stage addresses this gap by declaring six new classes and ten new properties—labelled with the prefix "caapt" for "Computational Approaches for Addressing Problematic Terminology"—as subclasses and subproperties of elements from one or more of these four ontologies. The new classes represent core concepts for the ontology: the types of authority documents being detailed in this space (*caapt:Guide* and subclasses *caapt:TerminologyGuide* and *caapt:StyleGuide*), the terms described in terminology guidance documents (*caapt:TermRoot*), the contexts of term uses (*caapt:UseContext*), and the suggestion instructions (*caapt:Suggestion*).

The ten proposed properties can be grouped by their constraints and superproperties:

- Properties which describe the details of use contexts: *caapt:used_where*, *caapt:used_when*, *caapt:used_why*, *caapt:about_who*. These take *caapt:UseContext* as domain, different classes as ranges, and are subproperties of *ontolex:usage*.
- Properties which describe relationships between different suggestions: *caapt:use_along_with*, *caapt:preferred*, *caapt:if_not_possible_use*. These take *caapt:Suggestion* as domain and range, and are subproperties of *crm:P69_has_association_with*.
- Properties which describe relationships between terms and suggestions: *caapt_suggests_replacement*, *caapt_suggests_amendment*. These take *caapt:Suggestion* as domain, *caapt:TermRoot* as range, and have no declared superproperty.
- A property which describes the relationship between a suggestion and the type of catalogue record field that the suggestion takes as part of its context: *caapt_encountered*. This takes *caapt:Suggestion* as its domain, *skos:Collection* as its range, and has no declared superproperty. Initial label values for instances of this class are "historical context" and "contemporary context" as this is the language used in the TGD.

6.4 Knowledge Graph Population

The knowledge graph has been structured according to the proposed ontology and populated with the contents of the V&A TGD using a combination of manual and automated methods. The TGD was transformed by hand from its original text document form into a set of CSVs, which were then used as the input for conversion scripts.

6.5 Validation with Domain Experts

Validation has been carried out with V&A staff to review the conceptual model and the populated contents of the "suggestions" section of the knowledge graph. The first review was conducted using diagrams of the model and its components as the stakeholders largely hold non-technical roles and therefore an illustrative diagram was a better artifact for communication than data files or code for this audience. In addition to the model itself, an example from the TGD was shown in this structure in order to illustrate how the ontology would be used to represent a real-life example familiar to the V&A staff. An OWL file of the ontology and TTL file of the example record were also made available so that interested parties would be able to review these materials, but the review discussions were driven by the diagrams. This review was successful, with only one change being required: in the TGD, entries often have a note saying "consult with" followed by the name of an organization external to the V&A. While that had initially been interpreted as meaning "if a question comes up regarding this term that we cannot resolve internally, this is an identified expert to consult with", the review revealed that the meaning was in fact an internal note between the document authors and not intended as a permanent component of the TGD. As such, this relationship was removed from the modelling. As the second review was focused on contents as opposed to structure, a spreadsheet was used as the primary artifact for consideration. In order to create this spreadsheet, SPARQL was used to query the knowledge graph and return *Suggestion* labels and comments, along with relationships to other suggestions (*preferred*, *if_not_possible_use*, *use_along_with*), grouped by *TermRoot*. The results of this review were also successful: the primary change that resulted from this review meeting was the addition of the *use_along_with* property between a greater number of *Suggestions*.

7 Conclusion

The ontology and knowledge graph have been validated by V&A staff, and the original design appears to be fit for purpose. The next step in this work will be to validate it against additional terminology guidance resources before linking it to wider LOD resources. The steps taken so far have built a solid foundation for the development of interoperable, machine-readable terminology guidelines for museums to learn from, use, or adapt to their local contexts. This project is well positioned to make a number of contributions to knowledge through the approach that is taken as well as outputs that are produced. The work that has been completed to date is already evidence of this: the gap analysis of existing LOD schemas and resulting model that makes use of existing structures where possible to enable conversations across currently loosely connected domains, along with the identification of currently unmet data representation needs, will become the first contribution to knowledge made by this project. The resulting knowledge graph has the potential to address a significant pain point for museum staff seeking to engage in critical cataloguing in both the V&A and the wider museum field.

Acknowledgments. This research is taking place as part of the AHRC-funded Collaborative Doctoral Partnership scheme grant AH/X004775/1.

Disclosure of Interests. The author has no competing interests to declare that are relevant to the content of this article.

References

1. Chew, C.: Decolonising description: addressing discriminatory language in Scottish public heritage and beyond. J. Irish Scottish Stud. **11**, 3 (2023). https://doi.org/10.57132/jiss.213
2. Dalal-Clayton, A., Rutherford, A.: Against a new orthodoxy: decolonised "objectivity" in the cataloguing and description of artworks (2020). https://photoarchive.paul-mellon-centre.ac.uk/groups/against-a-new-orthodoxy
3. Museums Association: Supporting decolonisation in museums (2021). https://www.museumsassociation.org/campaigns/decolonising-museums/supporting-decolonisation-in-museums/
4. Tropenmuseum: Words matter: an unfinished guide to word choices in the cultural sector (2018). https://www.materialculture.nl/en/publications/words-matter

5. Chilcott, A.: Towards protocols for describing racially offensive language in UK public archives. Arch. Sci. **19**, 359–376 (2019). https://doi.org/10.1007/s10502-019-09314-y
6. Kennedy, L.: Finding the words: addressing language in archive collections as archivists, heritage professionals and volunteers (2022). https://bathandcolonialism.org/wp-content/uploads/2022/04/Finding-the-Words-booklet.pdf
7. Chew, C.: Welcome to CHTNUK. https://culturalheritageterminology.co.uk/. Accessed 28 Apr 2023
8. Frick, R., Proffitt, M.: Reimagine descriptive workflows: a community-informed agenda for reparative and inclusive descriptive practice. OCLC Research (2022)
9. Bekiari, C., et al.: CIDOC conceptual reference model, Version 7.1.2 (2022). https://cidoc-crm.org/Version/version-7.1.2
10. Khan, F., et al.: When linguistics meets web technologies. recent advances in modelling linguistic linked open data. Semantic Web. **0**, 1–62 (2021)
11. Hardesty, J., Nolan, A.: Mitigating bias in metadata: a use case using homosaurus linked data. Inf. Technol. Libr. **40** (2021). https://doi.org/10.6017/ital.v40i3.13053
12. Nesterov, A., Hollink, L., van Erp, M., van Ossenbruggen, J.: A knowledge graph of contentious terminology for inclusive representation of cultural heritage. In: Pesquita, C., et al. (eds.) The Semantic Web, pp. 502–519. Springer Nature Switzerland, Cham (2023). https://doi.org/10.1007/978-3-031-33455-9_30
13. Khan, F., Salgado, A.: Modelling lexicographic resources using CIDOC-CRM, FRBRoo and ontolex-lemon. In: Presented at the SWODCH: Semantic Web and Ontology Design for Cultural Heritage (2021)
14. Canning, E., Brown, S., Roger, S., Martin, K.: The power to structure : making meaning from metadata through ontologies. KULA Knowl. Creation Dissemination Preserv. Stud. **6**, 1–15 (2022). https://doi.org/10.18357/kula.169
15. Cummings, J., Stacey, D.: Lean ontology development. In: Proceedings of the 10th International Joint Conference on Knowledge Discovery, Knowledge Engineering and Knowledge Management, pp. 367–374 (2018). https://doi.org/10.5220/0006963003670374
16. Watson, B.M.: Critiquing the machine: the critical cataloging database. TCB Tech. Serv. Relig. Theol.. **31**, 1–17 (2023). https://doi.org/10.31046/tcb.v31i1.3216

PErsoNal Genome QUery IN Healthcare and Clinical Practice (PENGQUIN)

Elias Crum[1,2(✉)]

[1] IDLab, Department of Electronics and Information Systems, Ghent University - imec, Ghent, Belgium
elias.crum@ugent.be
[2] Flemish institute for Technological Research (VITO), Mol, Belgium

Abstract. Medical care is in the process of becoming increasingly personalized through the use of patient genetic information. At present, data useful for clinical care, including genetic data, is commonly diffuse, organized arbitrarily, and stored in data silos. Thus, unstructured organization, high costs for data storage and generation, and tight privacy restrictions pose serious challenges to scaling personalized clinical strategies. I propose an early stage Ph.D. that aims to improve the connectedness and shareability of genomic data storage(s), while preserving data privacy, to decrease the costs of using patient genome data in clinical practice. In this pursuit, I will integrate various domains of semantic web research into a novel, holistic framework designed for use in clinical practice. Specifically, I will (a) store patient data using Solid pods, (b) represent personal genome sequence data in RDF as Linked Data, (c) attach policies to stored data, and (d) query data through link traversal queries.

Keywords: Solid · Linked Data · Querying · Genomic Data Sharing

1 Introduction/Motivation

As our understanding of genomics deepens, the role of Personal Genome Sequencing (PGS) in healthcare is expanding. At the time of writing, there are multiple domains of clinical practice where patient PGS data is now used to inform medical decision making, including drug development [13], cancer diagnosis and treatment [17], and rare genetic disease identification and treatment [15]. How this integration is deployed varies by clinical domain, but improved outcomes have generally been observed [16]. Despite great promise, barriers to adoption remain [22]. One major challenge is presented by the digital representation, storage, and access to the PGS data that underlies clinical usage. With my Ph.D., I aim to address the challenges presented by PGS data usage in clinical practice by leveraging decentralized storage, data representation, and querying technologies.

PGS Data Storage and Sharing. PGS data are expensive to both generate and store. The average human genome is slightly over 3 billion base pairs in length (3 Gbp). During a whole genome sequencing workflow, various sequence

A. Meroño Peñuela et al. (Eds.): ESWC 2024, LNCS 15345, pp. 23–32, 2025.
https://doi.org/10.1007/978-3-031-78955-7_3

formats that offer different sets of information are produced [6]. Of these, Variant Call Format (VCF) files [10] serve as the state-of-the-art for most clinical genomic applications. VCF files are typically between 100–1000 s MBs within computer memory and represent around 3 million nucleotide positions of an individual' s PGS. For these genomic data, there are also significant privacy considerations. Unfortunately, the relationship between privacy and cost is largely antagonistic within the current technological framework. Increases in privacy protections often lead to increases in data siloing and increased costs for both patient and provider. For instance, if a patient moves hospitals, it is common for PGS data and genomic tests to be regenerated and indefinitely stored in that new location because of the lack of data sharing between institutions. One strategy for reducing costs is through increased data sharing and data discoverability between hospital systems. Another increase in efficiency could be achieved by greater connectivity of a single patient' s data, such as previous test results, PGS data, medical history, etc. Increasing patient data connectedness and accessibility for authorized users is not a trivial problem while also maintaining privacy. It is at this crossroads that the current state-of-the-art in clinical data storage technology is largely incapable of achieving both goals.

A Solid Solution. A possible solution to the challenges faced is through reorganization of how data is stored and discovered. The citizen-centric model places the patient at the center and is not an entirely novel concept [8]. Within the current system, a citizen-centric model is difficult to implement due to technological challenges presented by centralized databases. The Solid protocol [9], a decentralized data storage approach, is composed of specifications more conducive to construction of a citizen-centric data storage strategy for clinical data. Specifically, Solid offers the ability to granularize data privacy, allow authorized data access over the web, and represent stored data as Linked Data, all features that can work to remove some of the antagonism between cost reduction and privacy preservation.

Project Motivation. Despite there being no real solutions to the current antagonism between privacy and cost reduction for PGS data usage in healthcare, there is also a conspicuous gap in the current scientific discourse around the development and implementation of a proposed solution. This gap underscores the necessity of my Ph.D. I aim to improve the connectedness and shareability of genomic data storage(s) while preserving data privacy, through the integration of various domains of semantic web research into a novel, holistic framework designed for use in clinical practice. My Ph.D. will also aim to demonstrate the limitations of current state-of-the-art semantic web technologies in this novel application domain with the intention of driving innovation and discovering future research pursuits.

2 State of the Art

Current Clinical Data Storage. Most clinically relevant health data, including PGS data, is stored using an institution-centric approach characterized by the hospital or hospital system isolating its stored data into one or more centralized or cloud-based databases that are governed and maintained solely by the owner institution or a contracted organization [19]. The predominant organization of these databases is a relational structure, although alternative non-relational methods like NoSQL or RDF have become slightly more popular in recent years [14]. Due to technological limitations imposed by relational database structure, maintaining stored data privacy results in strict data accessibility policies that severely restrict data sharing potential. With the enlarged threat of hacking, phishing, and login credential compromisation that is only increasing [4], health care institutions have taken steps to enact tighter restrictions on data access and increase cyber security budgets. Collectively, these state-of-the-art approaches to PGS data storage inhibit the scalability of PGS data usage in clinical practice due to data siloing and resulting high costs.

PGS Data Sharing in Academic Research. In academic research, the development of infrastructure that allows for sharing of genome data between institutions, creating federated centralized databases, can be observed in initiatives such as GA4GH Beacons [20]. Despite this step towards increased sharing and cost reduction, advancements in state-of-the-art infrastructure and standards are not directly translatable to clinical practice.

Solid, RDF, and Linked Data in Clinical Practice. The Solid specifications have been shown to provide competent infrastructure for preserving the privacy of sensitive stored data [11]. Further, it has been shown that additional safeguards can be imposed using privacy policies represented in RDF triples, allowing more granular discoverability controls [7].

In recent years, there have been initiatives for representing biological data as RDF [21], specifically extending into clinical biology recently [24]. Past experiments have shown that general linked data integration into clinical practice results in improved outcomes [12]. There is also precedent for investigation into the representation of genomic information as RDF [18,24]. Solid pods could provide the infrastructure for such data storage strategies, while also preserving possibilities for non-linked data stored in the pod, such as test result files, to be linked to genomic data, improving data connectivity.

Link Traversal Query Processing (LTQP). To make sense of linked genomic and clinical data approaches to parsing and querying that data must also be investigated, especially to encourage greater data discoverability and usage in clinical practice. Recent work has established that the querying of Linked Data in decentralized environments is possible [23], but these results were obtained with assumptions different than those presented by patient genome pods. Here, querying will be performed over a potentially large number of data pods containing large amounts of linked data, a situation not extensively investigated.

3 Problem Statement and Contributions

My Ph.D. is situated to provide a proof-of-concept PGS data storage and querying framework for use in clinical practice. In this pursuit, my core research question is: *Can combining the Solid specifications for data storage with other compatable cutting-edge innovations in data policy, linking, and querying be instantiated and deployed as a framework that provides advantages over the existing PGS data storage protocols in health care?*

To address this central question, I will investigate the more specific questions: A) Can the decentralized storage protocol Solid [9] offer suitable infrastructure for PGS data? B) Do the specifications provided by Solid provide for adequate control of PGS data privacy while also allowing for increased authorized sharability? C) Can querying over these sources be achieved through the use of modified LTQP algorithms? D) Can these features be combined into a cohesive web application and deployed together?

My hypothesis is that such a framework can be developed and would offer unique advantages over the existing state-of-the-art institution-centric PGS data storage solutions.

The following five objectives will be undertaken to test my hypotheses: (1) Solid Pod PGS Data Storage, (2) Genomic data as Linked Data, (3) Data policies, (4) Data querying, (5) Framework deployment.

Together, these objectives will serve as the components of an operational framework. The framework, once produced, will be compared to existing strategies for storing and sharing PGS data to assess the efficacy of transitioning toward product production and specific clinical use case adaptation. The proposed scientific approach also aims to test the application of numerous fields of semantic web research to a clinical knowledge domain. Explicitly, an approach to how decentralized storage specifications can be applied to sensitive medical data storage, how genomic and medical data can be represented and queried as Linked Data, how existing Linked Data querying algorithms perform over genomic and health data, how granularized data policies impact querying and linking data in a medical context, and how the combination of these semantic technologies could provide an improvement over existing state-of-the-art clinical PGS data storage and usage strategies, are specific questions my Ph.D. aims to answer.

4 Research Methodology and Approach

My Ph.D. will be split into four component work packages (WPs) with a fifth work package where the components will be unified into a cohesive framework with an accompanying web application. This workflow is reflected in Fig. 1.

4.1 Work Package 1: Storing and Publishing Personal Genomic Data in a Decentralized Environment

I will test the viability of Solid data pods as storage infrastructure for patient PGS data, thus, testing my hypothesis that Solid can support PGS data storage.

A test dataset will be constructed using publicly available Illumina platinum genome files [3]. These files will be used as representative "patient" PGS data for experimentation.

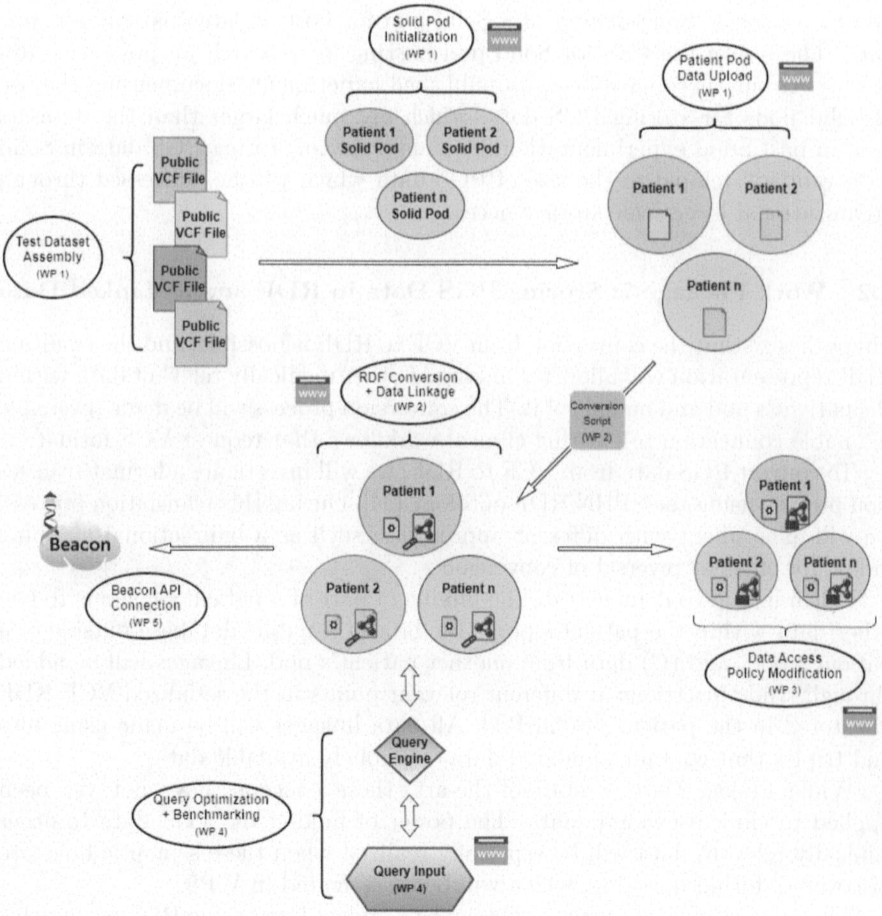

Fig. 1. PENGQUIN Ph.D. workflow. White circles represent milestones to be achieved in respective work packages (WP) that are denoted in parentheses. The small blue "WWW" box seen next to some objectives represents integration of that item into the framework' s web application. WP 1 will achieve the assembly of a VCF file test dataset, the initialization of simulation Patient Solid Pods, and the upload of simulation patient VCF files into that patient's Solid pod. WP 2 will convert VCF file data into a serialized RDF representation and link parts of that VCF data to other simulated medical data. WP 3 will establish data access policies for patient Solid pods and specific data stored within them. WP 4 will experiment with querying approaches for discovering and accessing data stored in patient Solid pods through the use of user provided queries and the use of a query engine. WP 5 will establish the connection of the patient's Solid pod to the Beacon network.

I will also create server-hosted Solid pods using the Community Solid Server (CSS) implementation of Solid [1]. Each pod will be a storage container for a single individual' s PGS data. I will upload a single VCF file, into one "patient's" pod to test basic functionality of a Solid pod for hosting large patient genomic data. The use of the CSS for Solid pod hosting for research purposes is state-of-the-art, but there have been no published experiments documenting the use of Solid pods for storing PGS data, which are much larger than the datasets used in past Solid experimentation. The main risk of storing PGS data in Solid data vaults is related to the size of PGS data which will be addressed through organizational large-scale storage access.

4.2 Work Package 2: Storing PGS Data in RDF and as Linked Data

I hypothesize that the conversion from VCF to RDF is possible, and the resulting RDF representation will allow for linking of other medically relevant data within the patient's pod and outside of it. The conversion process will be made reversible to enable connection to existing clinical workflows that request VCF format.

To convert PGS data from VCF to RDF, we will investigate a format translation process using the SPHN RDF ontology [24]. During this translation process, we will experiment with different approaches, such as a bidirectional mapping index, for efficient reversal of conversion.

I then intend to demonstrate the linking of part of a patient's genome to (A) other data within the patient's pod, (B) data in a public database outside of a patient's pod, and (C) data from another patient's pod. Linkages will be added through triple insertions at different relevant points in the serialized VCF RDF file stored in the patient's Solid Pod. All data linkages will be made using files and triples that contain simulated data or publicly available data.

While Linked Data is state-of-the-art, these concepts have not yet been applied to clinical genomic data. The power of linking the VCF data to other clinically relevant data will be especially realized when these semantic links are discovered during querying, which will be investigated in WP5.

The main risk of converting PGS data to Linked Data using RDF is that this conversion requires an ontology. The conversion process will utilize the publicly available SPHN RDF ontology [24] and if this ontology is insufficient, I will work with members of the IDLab at UGhent with experience in ontology definition to make changes or additions where necessary.

4.3 Work Package 3: PGS Data Privacy Policies

In this work package, I will experiment with the design and implementation of multiple levels of authorization as well as methods that allow for dynamic control over data discoverability, read/write access, and data access consent requests within a patient's Solid pod. I hypothesize that various levels of authorization can be implemented and provide protections for maintaining the privacy of PGS data stored in Solid pods.

I will develop and test three functionalities for privacy modifications. (1) registration of a pod to an individual patient, (2) submission of a request to access stored data from a data requester, the notification of the patient, and the consent or denial by the patient, and (3) permission revoking capabilities as well as an opt-in option to share their data with researchers. All of these methods will be integrated into the framework's web application. To utilize these methods, various levels of access to pod read and write privileges will be created and filled to represent a real clinical PGS workflow.

Assigning the above permissions within Solid is an open area of research and there are currently state-of-the-art protocols implemented in the CSS that allow their implementation. The described access schema has not been attempted in the presented level of detail for clinical genomic data. If the above proposed schema for privacy policies cannot be achieved, a simpler and more generalized schema will be devised and implemented. Privacy is a nuanced subject, especially in terms of governance and here, I aim to show the possibilities presented by Solid in this framework, not dictate suggestions for its deployable implementations.

4.4 Work Package 4: Querying over PGS Data in One and Many Pods

This work package will establish a querying mechanism for patient pod data that incorporates user permissions and data linkages. I hypothesize that a querying functionality that utilizes a query engine computational strategy will be able to query over patient Solid pods and return query results.

I will execute queries across PGS data contained in patient pod(s) through the use of the query language SPARQL [5]. Query execution requires a source for computation which is not currently provided by the Solid pods themselves. I will investigate the use of a query engine, such as that offered by Comunica [2], to perform the queries apart from the data stores.

For PGS data querying, I will benchmark and build upon the link traversal query processing (LTQP) paradigm [23], which has been shown to be an effective method for querying Linked Data between Solid Pods. A significant challenge is presented by the storage landscape of a large number of large data sources. I will look to innovate established LTQP algorithmic approaches by integrating strategies that leverage the unique structure of PGS data such as the use of pre-computed indexes, like the one generated for RDF-VCF conversion, as a guide for faster query processing.

I aim to adapt this querying approach to the specific domain of genomic and health data which has not been attempted before. There is a risk that I cannot devise solutions to incorporating indexes in LTQP algorithms and/or these algorithm modifications do not improve performance enough to be usable. If these challenges are encountered, I will first investigate imposing limits on query complexity and reducing the number of data vaults that are included in the possible query space, then, if still unsuccessful, look to investigate the implementation of algorithms utilized by centralized SPARQL endpoints that are known to be able to query large sets of data.

4.5 Work Package 5: Component Consolidation and Framework Deployment

To improve data flows for research purposes, I intend to connect the proposed framework to the international Beacon initiative [20]. In this aim, I will investigate the establishment of patient Solid pods, containing PGS data, as beacon endpoints that can be discoverable and queried via the Beacon API. The connection of a decentralized, citizen-centric storage framework to the Beacon network is novel in nature as all other existing endpoints are institution-centric relational databases maintained by hospitals or research institutions. Any issues within this aim will be addressed through collaboration with creators of the Beacon initiative.

All other functionalities will also be packaged into a web application with supporting documentation for final deployment and exhibition of how such a framework could function in clinical practice. This framework would be the first of its kind.

5 Evaluation Plan

WP1. All tasks within WP1, including test dataset assembly, Solid pod creation and hosting using the CSS, and test data uploading to Solid pods will be evaluated only for functionality.

WP2. Direct conversion between VCF and RDF will be evaluated in terms of computational overhead, conversion time, and memory usage, both in the Solid pod and during conversion. The same evaluations will also be performed on the process when an intermediate mapping index file is used. Comparisons will be documented in a formal benchmarking study. Functionality of data linkage aims will be assessed by data querying in WP4.

WP3. Attaching differing levels of authorization to data will be assessed by creating various profiles that reflect clinical roles and access levels and attempting to access data via user-mediated, application requesting, and querying approaches.

WP4. Query engine functionality will be evaluated using query execution time and computational load metrics as well as query results assessment. Query results will establish the functionality of data linkages from WP2. Benchmarking will be done for existing LTQP algorithms and altered query algorithms that utilize genomic index files and results will be compared. Ideally, success will be determined by queries that return correct results in under 10 min for users and potentially longer for applications. In a clinical setting, time constraints are not as important as accuracy and reliability of results, although excessive query times decrease the usefulness of such a tool for physicians in clinical practice.

WP5. Beacon API connection will be evaluated on functionality and integrate all previous work package components. Similarly, evaluation of the web application from which a user can interact with the framework will also be based on functionality.

6 Preliminary Results

During the first months of my Ph.D., I have been composing a scoping review paper on the current landscape of clinical genomic data sharing. I plan to submit the review paper for publication in a peer-reviewed journal in the coming months. Within WP1, I have successfully assembled the test dataset and set up CSS pod instances. I have also successfully uploaded VCF files into these pods signalling completion of WP1.

7 Conclusions/Lessons Learned

With the emergence of patient genomic data as a tool for clinicians, establishing the infrastructure for patient genomic data sharing that maintains patient data privacy is an economic niche that is largely unfilled. My Ph.D. framework is poised to provide the outline of necessary technological implementation considerations while hopefully contributing to future product development. More generally, my Ph.D. is designed to assess the potential in applying cutting-edge semantic web research to modern clinical challenges with the hope of gaining insight into the efficacy of these applied implementations while identifying future research directions.

Acknowledgments. I acknowledge my Ph.D. promoters Ruben Taelman[1], Bart Buelens[2], Gokhan Ertaylan[2], and Ruben Verborgh[1] for their help and guidence.Funding provided from VITO NV (`UG_PhD_2303_contract`).

References

1. CommunitySolidServer/CommunitySolidServer: An open and modular implementation of the solid specifications. https://github.com/CommunitySolidServer/CommunitySolidServer
2. Comunica - a knowledge graph querying framework. https://comunica.dev/
3. Platinum genomes. https://emea.illumina.com/platinumgenomes.html
4. Ransomware attacks on hospitals have changed | cybersecurity | center | AHA. https://www.aha.org/center/cybersecurity-and-risk-advisory-services/ransomware-attacks-hospitals-have-changed
5. SPARQL 1.1 query language. https://www.w3.org/TR/sparql11-query/
6. Bagger, F.O., Borgwardt, L., Jespersen, A.S., Hansen, A.R., Bertelsen, B., Kodama, M., Nielsen, F.C.: Whole genome sequencing in clinical practice **17**(1), 39. https://doi.org/10.1186/s12920-024-01795-w
7. Benaribi, F.I., Malki, M., Faraoun, K.M., Ouchani, S.: A SPARQL-based framework to preserve privacy of sensitive data on the semantic web **17**(3), 183–199. https://doi.org/10.1007/s11761-023-00368-6
8. Brands, M.R., Gouw, S.C., Beestrum, M., Cronin, R.M., Fijnvandraat, K., Badawy, S.M.: Patient-centered digital health records and their effects on health outcomes: systematic review **24**(12), e43086. https://doi.org/10.2196/43086
9. Capadisli, S., Berners-Lee, T., Verborgh, R., Kjernsmo, K.: Solid protocol. https://solidproject.org/TR/protocol

10. Danecek, P., et al.: 1000 genomes project analysis group: the variant call format and VCFtools **27**(15), 2156–215. https://doi.org/10.1093/bioinformatics/btr330
11. Esposito, C., Hartig, O., Horne, R., Sun, C.: Assessing the solid protocol in relation to security & privacy obligations. http://arxiv.org/abs/2210.08270
12. Farinelli, F., Barcellos de Almeida, M., Linhares de Souza, Y.: Linked health data: how linked data can help provide better health decisions. **216**, 1122 (2015)
13. Ko, Y.K., Gim, J.A.: New drug development and clinical trial design by applying genomic information management. **14**(8), 1539. https://doi.org/10.3390/pharmaceutics14081539
14. Kotsilieris, T.: An efficient agent based data management method of NoSQL environments for health care applications. **9**(3), 322. https://doi.org/10.3390/healthcare9030322
15. Marwaha, S., Knowles, J.W., Ashley, E.A.: A guide for the diagnosis of rare and undiagnosed disease: beyond the exome. **14**(1), 23. https://doi.org/10.1186/s13073-022-01026-w
16. Mathur, S., Sutton, J.: Personalized medicine could transform healthcare. **7**(1), 3–5. https://doi.org/10.3892/br.2017.922
17. McLeod, H.L.: Cancer pharmacogenomics: Early promise, but concerted effort needed. **339**(6127), 1563–156. https://doi.org/10.1126/science.1234139
18. Prasanna, S., Rao, D., Simoes, E., Rao, P.: Scalable knowledge graph construction and inference on human genome variants. https://doi.org/10.48550/arXiv.2312.04423
19. Quantin, C., Jaquet-Chiffelle, D.O., Coatrieux, G., Benzenine, E., Auverlot, B., Allaert, F.A.: Medical record: systematic centralization versus secure on demand aggregation **11**, 18. https://doi.org/10.1186/1472-6947-11-18
20. Rambla, J., et al.: Beacon V2 and beacon networks: a "lingua franca" for federated data discovery in biomedical genomics, and beyond. **43**(6), 791–799. https://doi.org/10.1002/humu.24369
21. SIB swiss institute of bioinformatics RDF group members: the SIB swiss institute of bioinformatics semantic web of data **52**, D44–D51. https://doi.org/10.1093/nar/gkad902
22. Stefanicka-Wojtas, D., Kurpas, D.: Barriers and facilitators to the implementation of personalised medicine across Europe **13**(2), 203. https://doi.org/10.3390/jpm13020203
23. Taelman, R., Verborgh, R.: Evaluation of link traversal query execution over decentralized environments with structural assumptions. https://doi.org/10.48550/ARXIV.2302.06933
24. Van Der Horst, E., et al.: Bridging clinical and genomic knowledge: an extension of the SPHN RDF schema for seamless integration and FAIRification of omics data. https://doi.org/10.20944/preprints202312.0373.v1

Enhancing Hypoglycemia Prediction in Type 1 Diabetes Through Semantic Knowledge Integration and Machine Learning Optimization

Jennifer I. Daniel Onwuchekwa[1(✉)], Christian Weber[1], and Maria Maleshkova[2]

[1] Digital Health Sciences and Biomedicine, University of Siegen, Siegen, Germany
Jennifer.DOnwuchekwa@uni-siegen.de

[2] Data Engineering, Helmut Schmidt University, Hamburg, Germany

Abstract. Managing type 1 diabetes (T1D) is challenging due to unpredictable hypoglycemia episodes that can lead to serious health risks. To address this issue, this research aims to develop and evaluate a novel hybrid artificial intelligence (AI) model that integrates deep semantic knowledge and optimizes machine learning (ML) model frameworks to improve the prediction of hypoglycemia in patients with T1D. The proposed model incorporates comprehensive knowledge graphs (KGs) derived from patient-specific contextual data and evidence-based information, leveraging ML approaches to provide accurate and personalized predictions. The research methodology involves data collection, ontology development, KG construction, and utilization of knowledge graph embeddings (KGEs) to convert entities within the constructed graph into numerical vectors to enhance ML predictions. Preliminary findings indicate that integrating semantic knowledge with ML techniques can reveal complex patterns and patient-specific factors and hence, demonstrate promising performance in improving the predictive accuracy of hypoglycemia and enabling more personalized, effective management strategies. Future work will focus on developing the hybrid AI model to improve early detection and proactive management of hypoglycemia, implementing real-world validation for personalized hypoglycemia prediction, as well as evaluating its scalability and generalizability across diverse populations and clinical settings.

Keywords: Semantic Integration · Machine Learning · Hypoglycemia · Type 1 Diabetes · Predictive Models

1 Introduction/Motivation

Hypoglycemia is a serious medical condition characterized by an abnormal drop in blood glucose levels, usually equal to or less than 70 mg/dL or 3.9 mmol/L [6]. It can have life-threatening consequences, including seizures, loss of consciousness,

Supported by DRK Hospital, Kirchen, Germany.

A. Meroño Peñuela et al. (Eds.): ESWC 2024, LNCS 15345, pp. 33–44, 2025.
https://doi.org/10.1007/978-3-031-78955-7_4

and even death [9]. Patients receiving insulin treatment for diabetes, especially those with type 1 diabetes (T1D) are at a higher risk with hypoglycemic episodes occurring three times more frequently than in patients with type 2 diabetes (T2D) [17]. The occurrence and onset of hypoglycemia can differ from patient to patient, occur at different times of the day (daytime, postprandial, nocturnal), and at different glycemic thresholds [1,3]. In some cases, symptoms like tremors, sweating, headaches, anxiety, and hunger, that serve as warning signals can be subtle or completely absent, making it harder to anticipate or prevent its occurrence [17]. These variations in frequencies and occurrence of hypoglycemic episodes among patients emphasize the critical need for personalized detection and predictive strategies for T1D management [6,34]. Given these complexities, various traditional machine learning (ML) techniques including Random Forest [27], Support Vector Regressors [10], and Multi-Layer Perceptron Neural Networks [27] have been explored using different input parameters and training algorithms for hypoglycemia detection and prediction [24,25]. However, these models often lack personalization and struggle with feature selection, model portability, interpretability, and handling complex healthcare data [10,27,31].

Furthermore, in addition to known factors such as age, type of diabetes, long-term diabetes, recurrent hypoglycemia, and poor glycemic control [21], there are other potential predictors not routinely measured in clinical settings. For instance, possibilities like physical activities, food intake, and medication use influence when hypoglycemic events may occur or be most impactful [17]. The pervasive use of wearable and mobile sensing devices, automated insulin delivery systems, and continuous glucose monitors have accumulated extensive data for monitoring hypoglycemic events in real-world contexts for individual patients susceptible to hypoglycemia [13,15]. Studies have shown non-invasive detection of hypoglycemia by analyzing continuous sensor data including electrocardiogram, heart rate, respiratory rate, and lifestyle activity data from wearable devices [20]. However, a comprehensive method to analyze these multifaceted variables, inter- and intra-patient variability, time lag between sensor monitoring data and actual blood glucose values, and the combined effects of manually entered and largely unquantified variables like stress, carbohydrate intake, physical activity, and infections on hypoglycemia is still lacking. To address these challenges, customized data collection and semantically enhanced ML models are necessary.

In this context, ontologies and knowledge graphs (KGs) play a vital role in enabling the integration of data from various sources, including clinical records, psychosocial databases, and wearable/mobile technologies. By leveraging ontologies and KGs, researchers can extract, manage, interpret, and use semantically nuanced information associated with complex health conditions like diabetes [33]. This integration of data semantics allows for the generation of more relevant features, handling noisy and ambiguous data, and optimizing ML models to interpret the context, patterns, relationships, and data meaning more efficiently [33]. Moreover, medical repositories offer valuable information for understanding patients' conditions and developing personalized treatment plans [16]. Hence, the utilization of ontologies and KGs provides a comprehensive view of a patient's health status, ultimately improving the complexity, performance, and accuracy of prediction models [12,30].

Moreover, the state of the art in semantic analysis and KG-based ML for diabetes management and prediction is still evolving, with limited works specifically addressing the technical aspects of the use case [16]. Therefore, this research focuses on developing advanced predictive models for hypoglycemia events in T1D patients by harnessing the synergistic potential of advanced semantic technologies and ML optimizations. Ontologies enrich KGs by providing structured data representation [4], while knowledge graph embeddings (KGEs) preserve the semantic relationships within these graphs, converting complex graph data into vector representations for ML algorithms [32]. These embeddings integrate KGs with ML frameworks, broadening the predictive scope and fostering tailored hypoglycemia prediction and management. Techniques such as TransE and Graph Convolutional Networks (GCNs) generate these embeddings, facilitating feature selection and enhancing the accuracy of ML predictive algorithms [5,32]. Therefore, the objective of this research is to uncover latent connections crucial to revolutionizing personalized health management by leveraging semantically enhanced ML models to parse T1D data and identify patterns beyond human expertise [5,12,30]. By enhancing ML applications in predicting health outcomes, this approach promises to improve interoperability, advance personalized diabetes management, and have transformative prospects beyond diabetes, extending to fields in e-health, personalized medicine, and health delivery systems. This paper presents the problem statement, contributions, research methodology, approach, and evaluation plan for the developed hybrid AI model.

2 State of the Art

Despite advances in prediction model optimization, the integration of ML models with semantic knowledge from diverse sources remains underexplored. This section reviews the extraction and representation of semantic knowledge within medical AI, focusing on technologies like KGs and ontologies. These studies bridge biological knowledge with medical histories and health outcomes of individual patients [28] [18]. Research has aimed to enhance disease information management, improve disease assessments, and support decision-making, potentially reducing errors in disease treatment and patient care by analyzing semantic knowledge from medical literature [25]. For example, Wang *et al.* (2022) [28] investigated personalized disease-specific KGs in cardiology and cardiovascular medicine, highlighting how KGs encapsulate critical patient information, including clinical symptoms, activities, diagnostic results, medical history, medications, and potential surgeries. This review also elucidates how KGs identify common risk factors among patients, thereby facilitating the discovery, sharing, and application of new knowledge by health professionals in diagnosis, treatment, and disease management [28].

Furthermore, a study explored the link between Kawasaki disease - a cardiac condition of unknown etiology primarily affecting children under five years of age - and two frequently mentioned viruses using semantically enabled searches and medical KGs. Another contribution reviewed the link between dietary factors and cardiovascular outcomes such as acute myocardial infarction and fatal coronary heart disease, using data from the Nurses' Health Study to build KGs. The KGs served as decision support tools in clinical settings [28].

Although limited research on KGs and their implications in diabetes management and treatment has been done, one study [29] successfully combined expert-reviewed clinical evidence to construct a KG encompassing diabetes complications such as retinopathy, diabetic nephropathy, foot issues, and depression. The data used for constructing the graph included T2D information such as lifestyle risk factors, clinical test results, medications, and their associated complications. The strength of relationships between these entities was determined through systematic evaluations and meta-analyses, providing insights into odds ratios, correlations, and relative risks.

3 Problem Statement and Contributions

This research contributes to semantic web research, ML, and the medical domain by developing a personalized, predictive solution for hypoglycemia in individuals with T1D that captures the effects of lifestyle factors like diet, physical activity, stress, and infections on blood glucose levels. The contributions of this work are manifold and innovative, including:

1. Construction of comprehensive knowledge graphs from patient-specific and evidence-based medical data, leveraging varied data sizes, types, velocities, and sources such as publications, databases, repositories, and evolving knowledge bases, captures patient-specific data inferring glucose variability and hypoglycemia in T1D individuals [2]. This research employs knowledge discovery techniques to mine bio-text corpora, uncover concepts and attributes, and establish correlations between data concepts organized within an interpretable and structured knowledge graph. These graphs serve as the backbone for ML algorithms, providing structured and semantically rich data to enhance predictive performance.
2. Developing a hybrid AI model that integrates deep semantic knowledge of hypoglycemia and T1D into a custom ML framework. While feature engineering and deep learning enable the extraction of predictive features and pattern identification within datasets, they often overlook semantic meanings, and the contextual information is incomplete, ambiguous, and messy [18]. This work incorporates a personalized approach to identify, characterize, and integrate high-quality, multidimensional data, leading to the identification of patterns and correlations across vital parameters derived from multiple sensors, paving the way for more accurate hypoglycemia prediction models. This research promises a more individualized and context-aware prediction capability by acknowledging each patient's intricacies.
3. Application of graph embeddings and advanced analytics to improve early detection and proactive management strategies for hypoglycemia. Knowledge graphs are gaining popularity for information storage and retrieval as the field shifts toward systems biology [14]. This work can be used as a reference

for developing hypotheses and responding to inquiries about hypoglycemia, elevating the clinical utility of the predictive models.

4. Enhanced Predictive Performance through a substantial reduction in prediction error rates and increased accuracy, sensitivity, and specificity of hypoglycemia predictions. These improvements are critical for real-world clinical applications due to the potential costs of inaccuracies.
5. Integration of this work into clinical settings offers the opportunity to enhance day-to-day clinical practices by developing more accurate preventive measures and personalized treatment options for improved patient outcomes. Additionally, it creates a dynamic model that benefits from continuous improvement through real-world application [2]. The hybrid AI model and knowledge graphs in clinical scenarios contribute to an evolving knowledge base. Feedback from healthcare professionals and patient outcomes refines the AI algorithms and knowledge graph accuracies, ensuring sensitivity to the changing patient health data, reducing prediction errors, and increasing reliability [18] [14]. Implementing machine learning models in the clinical environment, along with ongoing assessment and adaptation, strengthens the bridge between computational innovation and medical praxis, signifying a progressive step towards an adaptive, learning healthcare system.

These contributions address a critical need in diabetic care and represent a significant step in adopting AI and semantic analysis in precision medicine.

3.1 Aim and Research Questions

This research aims **to develop and evaluate a hybrid AI model that integrates semantic knowledge and optimizes ML models to improve the prediction of hypoglycemia in patients with T1D**. The goal is to address the limitations of current prediction models by integrating a comprehensive KG and advanced embedding techniques for personalized predictions, leading to proactive hypoglycemia management. To achieve this aim, several sub-research questions will be addressed:

- RQ1 **Insights from the Knowledge Graph**: What novel insights can KGs uncover regarding the factors contributing to hypoglycemia in patients with T1D? To what extent do these findings improve our understanding beyond traditional databases towards a more interconnected representation of patient data and biomedical knowledge?
- RQ2 **Role of Knowledge Graph Embeddings**: What role do KGEs play in improving the semantic representation and usability of patient data for predicting hypoglycemia in patients with T1D?
- RQ3 **Comparison with State-of-the-Art Approaches**: How does the semantic-based ML model compare with existing state-of-the-art approaches, particularly in terms of model performance-accuracy, sensitivity, specificity, and interpretability?
- RQ4 **Personalization and Subgroup Analysis**: How can KGs facilitate identifying and analyzing patient subgroups within T1D to personalize hypoglycemia prediction models?

4 Research Methodology and Approach

This section elaborates on the research plan depicted in Fig. 1 and the systematic approach to leveraging KGs for hypoglycemia prediction in patients with T1D, as shown in Fig. 2.

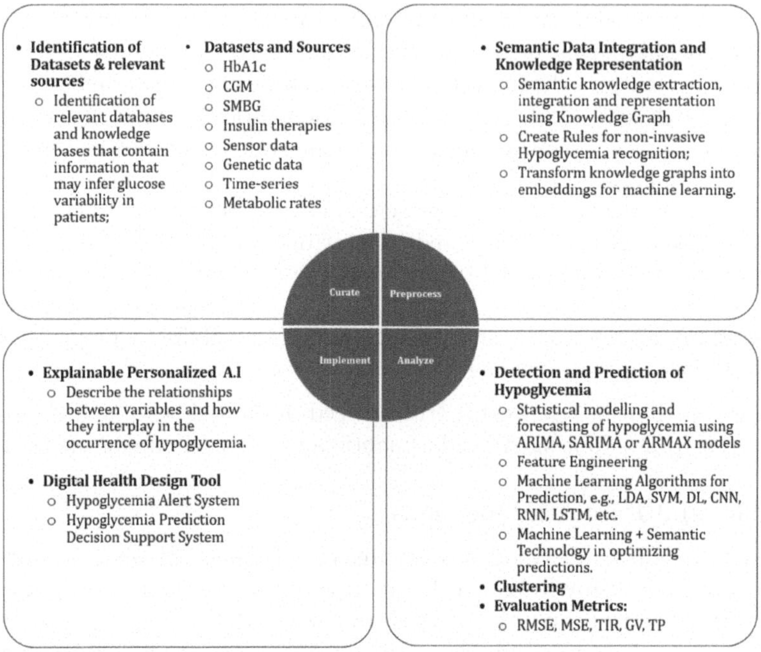

Fig. 1. Research Plan and Activities

4.1 Data Collection and Preparation

Structured and Unstructured Patient Data: To enrich our understanding of hypoglycemia in T1D, electronic health records (EHRs), patient databases, such as MIMIC-III database [11,22], the OhioT1DM Dataset, and the D1NAMO Dataset [8] are accessed. These sources provide a wealth of structured clinical records alongside unstructured data captured from doctor's consultation notes and discharge summaries using natural language processing (NLP) techniques.

Systematic Reviews and Medical Guidelines: It is pertinent to ensure that the ontology's definitions align with the latest scientific findings. Hence, evidence-based recommendations gathered from medical journals, healthcare organizations, and clinical trial repositories across various articles including

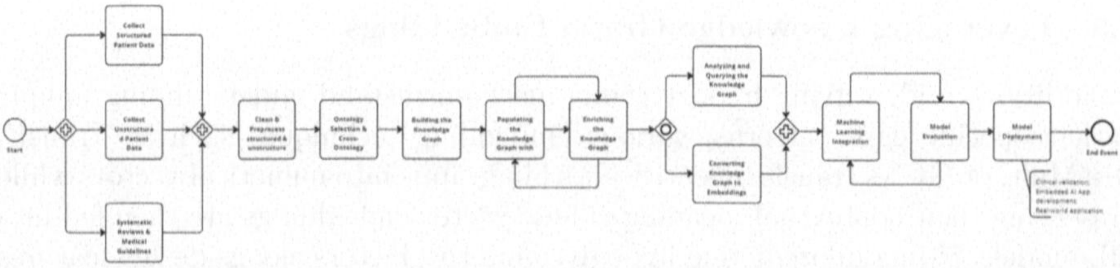

Fig. 2. A Process Map for Semantic Knowledge Integration and Machine Learning Optimization

systematic reviews [7,19,26] - are essential for providing valuable insights into understanding the disease mechanisms and treatment outcomes and guiding clinical decisions.

4.2 Ontology Development and Knowledge Graph Construction

Ontology Selection: A variety of related ontologies, such as the Diabetes Mellitus Ontology (DMO), Symptom Ontology (SYMP), Human Phenotype Ontology (HPO), SNOMED-CT, LOINC, RxNorm, and the Semantic Sensor Network Ontology (SSN), are meticulously curated to construct an extensive KG. The integration of these ontologies captures diabetes-related data, clinical symptoms and phenotypes, detailed classifications of symptoms and treatments, standardized laboratory test results and measurements, medication information, wearables, and sensor data integration, respectively. Additionally, the TimeML ontology is utilized to capture temporal dynamics related to T1D events.

Building the Knowledge Graph: The selected ontologies are harmonized into a unified framework that serves as the schema for standardizing and mapping data from diverse sources onto the KG. This ensures semantic consistency through consistent representation of concepts and relationships while synthesizing overlapping ontology elements to maintain integrity within the semantic model.

Populating and Enriching the Knowledge Graph: Structured patient records are imported to populate the KG, and each element is aligned with defined entities and relationships from the ontology. Moreover, additional details from unstructured data, such as patient-specific clinical notes and medical literature, help fill in missing connections between entities. This process allows for integrating global medical knowledge along with personalized insights derived from patient records.

4.3 Leveraging Knowledge Graph Embeddings

In addition to identifying hypoglycemia mechanisms and understanding unique patient-specific care patterns, various embedding techniques such as TransE, DistMult, or GCNs transform entities within graphs into numerical vectors while preserving their contextual meaning. These vector embeddings are then fed into ML models, aiding in predicting hypoglycemia risk factors alongside key features and patterns associated with hypoglycemia events.

4.4 Model Evaluation, Refinement, and Deployment

The KG and models are continuously assessed and enhanced, utilizing specified evaluation metrics, feedback from healthcare professionals, and new data to fine-tune the predictions and insights. This iterative process of model evaluation and refinement involves ongoing feedback loops aimed at boosting accuracy and reliability. Ultimately, validated models are implemented in clinical settings where they are monitored and adjusted based on real-world performance, as well as evolving healthcare developments.

5 Research Evaluation/Evaluation Plan

The effectiveness and quality of the proposed hybrid hypoglycemia prediction model are evaluated comprehensively. This involves delving into various aspects of the research questions to ensure thorough analysis and high-quality results.

RQ1 Insights from the Knowledge Graph Evaluation Plan: To evaluate this research question, various feature importance techniques, such as decision tree-based algorithms or Pearson's correlation coefficient, will be employed. These methods will rank the importance of each feature and determine the statistical relationship between numerical features and blood glucose levels. Additionally, the utilization of SHapley Additive exPlanations (SHAP) values will enhance interpretability and derive insights from individual features on predictions.

RQ2 Role of Knowledge Graph Embeddings Evaluation Plan: To assess the role of knowledge graph embeddings in improving the semantic representation and usability of patient data for hypoglycemia prediction, several metrics will be considered. The evaluation will include measures such as the accuracy, completeness, disambiguation, semantic validity, and consistency of the knowledge graph embeddings. Visualization techniques like t-Distributed Stochastic Neighbor Embedding (t-SNE) and Principal Component Analysis (PCA) will also be employed to qualitatively assess the meaningful representation of patient data and biomedical knowledge within the embeddings.

RQ3 Comparison with State-of-the-Art Approaches Evaluation Plan: The proposed semantic-based ML model will be rigorously compared with existing state-of-the-art approaches, including traditional ML models and baseline models such as the Auto-Regressive Integrated Moving Average (ARIMA) model [23]. The evaluation will involve statistical tests and measures like accuracy, mean squared error (MSE), and root-mean-square error (RMSE). These evaluations will aid in selecting the optimal algorithm for hypoglycemia prediction and provide insights into the performance, accuracy, and interpretability of the semantic-based ML model.

RQ4 Personalization and Subgroup Analysis Evaluation Plan: To evaluate personalized hypoglycemia prediction and subgroup analysis, advanced clustering algorithms optimized for high-dimensional and temporal data, such as dynamic time warping (DTW), will be applied. These algorithms will help identify patient profiles, glucose variability patterns, clustering distance metrics, and visualize patterns or inspect anomalies. The evaluation will focus on efficient customization possibilities within patient subgroups, facilitating personalized hypoglycemia prediction models.

6 Results

Preliminary findings from analyzing structured data in the MIMIC-III dataset are presented. The research utilized a combination of the ARIMA model and selected ML algorithms to predict blood glucose levels in T1D patients. Table 1 presents a detailed comparison of the performance of the models compared to the lagged model which predicts glucose values from previous ones, showing promising results.

Table 1. Blood Glucose Prediction Model Performance Evaluation Metrics of a MIMIC-III patient with participant ID-96232

Metric	Naive (Lagged) Model	ARIMA	XGBOOST	LSTM
MSE	5.1763	4.3032	0.0030	0.0006
RMSE	2.2751	0.0066	0.0547	0.0238

Furthermore, this research provides a comprehensive semantic representation of hypoglycemic events from the integration of various relevant data sources including blood glucose levels, insulin regimens, patient-specific wearable and sensor data, as well as multiple variables like time of day (e.g., during sleep), physical activity, and diet. A summary of concepts and attributes extracted from the MIMIC-III dataset can be found in Table 2.

Table 2. Sample Semantic Concepts identified in the MIMIC-III Curated Dataset

Semantic Concept	Details/Examples
Enumerate Terms	subject_ID, hospital_admission_ID, ICU_stay_ID, LOS_ICU_days, first_ICU_stay, timer, start_time, GLC_timer, end_time, input, input_hours, GLC_level, GLC_source, insulin_type, event, infusion_stop
Define Classes	Patient, Hospital, Intensive Care Unit, Glucose, Insulin
Define Properties	Time, ID, GLC_Source, Insulin_Type, Insulin_Regimen
Create Constraints	Boolean, String, Integer
Create Instances	Fingerstick/Blood Glucose Test, Short-Acting/Long-Acting Insulin, Bolus Injection/Infusion/Bolus Push Insulin Regimen

7 Conclusions/Lessons Learned

This research is still in its early stages and focuses on developing a personalized, predictive solution for hypoglycemia in T1D patients through the integration of semantic knowledge and optimization of ML models. The research methodology implies the extension of state-of-the-art ML algorithms, including constructing and refining KGs by integrating, representing, and storing diverse information that can infer hypoglycemia, incorporating graph embeddings, and evaluating the models. The results of this research have the potential to improve the prediction accuracy and personalized management strategies for hypoglycemia in T1D patients. This research also indicates the need for semantic domain knowledge to improve the performance of ML models for hypoglycemia detection and prediction in T1D. Although hypoglycemia is a complex condition influenced by several factors, the ability to predict its occurrence can help prevent dangerous and potentially life-threatening situations and ultimately improve the quality of life of patients with T1D.

References

1. Alhaddad, A.Y., et al.: Sense and learn: recent advances in wearable sensing and machine learning for blood glucose monitoring and trend-detection. Front. Bioeng. Biotechnol., 699 (2022)
2. Chandak, P., Huang, K., Zitnik, M.: Building a knowledge graph to enable precision medicine. Sci. Data **10**(1), 67 (2023)
3. Chehregosha, H., Khamseh, M.E., Malek, M., Hosseinpanah, F., Ismail-Beigi, F.: A view beyond HBA1C: role of continuous glucose monitoring. Diab. Therapy **10**, 853–863 (2019). https://doi.org/10.1007/S13300-019-0619-1

4. Chen, J., Hu, P., Jimenez-Ruiz, E., Holter, O.M., Antonyrajah, D., Horrocks, I.: OWL2VEC*: embedding of owl ontologies. Mach. Learn. **110**(7), 1813–1845 (2021)
5. Chen, J., Chen, H.: Edge-featured graph attention network. arXiv preprint arXiv:2101.07671 (2021)
6. Cryer, P.E.: Hypoglycemia in type 1 diabetes mellitus. Endocrinol. Metab. Clin. **39**(3), 641–654 (2010)
7. Diouri, O., Cigler, M., Vettoretti, M., Mader, J.K., Choudhary, P., Renard, E., Consortium, H.R.: Hypoglycaemia detection and prediction techniques: a systematic review on the latest developments. Diabetes Metab. Res. Rev. **37**(7), e3449 (2021)
8. Dubosson, F., Ranvier, J.E., Bromuri, S., Calbimonte, J.P., Ruiz, J., Schumacher, M.: The open d1namo dataset: a multi-modal dataset for research on non-invasive type 1 diabetes management. Inf. Med. Unlocked **13**, 92–100 (2018). https://doi.org/10.1016/J.IMU.2018.09.003
9. Eljil, K.S., Qadah, G., Pasquier, M.: Predicting hypoglycemia in diabetic patients using time-sensitive artificial neural networks. Int. J. Healthc. Inf. Syst. Inf. (IJHISI) **11**(4), 70–88 (2016)
10. Jensen, M.H., Dethlefsen, C., Vestergaard, P., Hejlesen, O.: Prediction of nocturnal hypoglycemia from continuous glucose monitoring data in people with type 1 diabetes: a proof-of-concept study. J. Diabetes Sci. Technol. **14**(2), 250–256 (2020)
11. Johnson, A.E., et al.: Mimic-iii, a freely accessible critical care database. Sci. Data **3**, 1–9 (2016). https://doi.org/10.1038/sdata.2016.35, https://www.nature.com/articles/sdata201635
12. Kipf, T.N., Welling, M.: Semi-supervised classification with graph convolutional networks. arXiv preprint arXiv:1609.02907 (2016)
13. Laha, S., Rajput, A., Laha, S.S., Jadhav, R.: A concise and systematic review on non-invasive glucose monitoring for potential diabetes management. Biosensors **12**(11), 965 (2022)
14. MacLean, F.: Knowledge graphs and their applications in drug discovery. Expert Opin. Drug Discov. **16**(9), 1057–1069 (2021)
15. Makroum, M.A., Adda, M., Bouzouane, A., Ibrahim, H.: Machine learning and smart devices for diabetes management: systematic review. Sensors **22**(5), 1843 (2022)
16. Moonian, O., et al.: Recent advances in computational tools and resources for the self-management of type 2 diabetes. Inform. Health Soc. Care **45**(1), 77–95 (2020)
17. Mujahid, O., Contreras, I., Vehi, J.: Machine learning techniques for hypoglycemia prediction: trends and challenges. Sensors (Basel, Switzerland) **21**, 1–21 (2021). https://doi.org/10.3390/S21020546, https://www.ncbi.nlm.nih.gov/pmc/articles/PMC7828835/
18. Ping, P., Watson, K., Han, J., Bui, A.: Individualized knowledge graph: a viable informatics path to precision medicine. Circ. Res. **120**(7), 1078–1080 (2017)
19. Pratiwi, C., Mokoagow, M.I., Kshanti, I.A.M., Soewondo, P.: The risk factors of inpatient hypoglycemia: a systematic review. Heliyon **6**(5), e03913 (2020)
20. Ranvier, J.E., Dubosson, F., Calbimonte, J.P., Aberer, K.: Detection of hypoglycemic events through wearable sensors. In: CEUR Workshop Proceedings, vol. 1588, pp. 21–26 (2016)
21. Rewers, A., et al.: Predictors of acute complications in children with type 1 diabetes. JAMA **287**(19), 2511–2518 (2002)
22. Robles Arévalo, A., et al.: Data-driven curation process for describing the blood glucose management in the intensive care unit. Sci. Data **8**(1), 80 (2021)

23. Shumway, R.H., Stoffer, D.S., Shumway, R.H., Stoffer, D.S.: Arima models. Time series analysis and its applications: with R examples, pp. 75–163 (2017)
24. Site, A., Nurmi, J., Lohan, E.S.: Systematic review on machine-learning algorithms used in wearable-based ehealth data analysis. IEEE Access **9**, 112221–112235 (2021)
25. Tao, X., et al.: Mining health knowledge graph for health risk prediction. World Wide Web **23**(4), 2341–2362 (2020). https://doi.org/10.1007/s11280-020-00810-1
26. Tsichlaki, S., Koumakis, L., Tsiknakis, M., et al.: Type 1 diabetes hypoglycemia prediction algorithms: systematic review. JMIR Diab. **7**(3), e34699 (2022)
27. Vahedi, M.R., et al.: Predicting glucose levels in patients with type1 diabetes based on physiological and activity data. In: Proceedings of the 8th ACM MobiHoc 2018 Workshop on Pervasive Wireless Healthcare Workshop, pp. 1–5 (2018)
28. Wang, H., et al.: Application of medical knowledge graphs in cardiology and cardiovascular medicine: a brief literature review. Adv. Ther. **39**(9), 4052–4060 (2022)
29. Wang, L., et al.: Construction of a knowledge graph for diabetes complications from expert-reviewed clinical evidences. Comput. Assist. Surg. **25**(1), 29–35 (2020)
30. Weston, J., Bordes, A., Yakhnenko, O., Usunier, N.: Connecting language and knowledge bases with embedding models for relation extraction. arXiv preprint arXiv:1307.7973 (2013)
31. Woldaregay, A.Z., et al.: Data-driven modeling and prediction of blood glucose dynamics: machine learning applications in type 1 diabetes. Artif. Intell. Med. **98**, 109–134 (2019)
32. Yang, B., Yih, W.t., He, X., Gao, J., Deng, L.: Embedding entities and relations for learning and inference in knowledge bases. arXiv preprint arXiv:1412.6575 (2014)
33. Zemmouchi-Ghomari, L.: Ontology and machine learning: a two-way street to improved knowledge representation and algorithm accuracy. In: International Conference on Paradigms of Communication, Computing and Data Analytics, pp. 181–189. Springer (2023). https://doi.org/10.1007/978-981-99-4626-6_15
34. Zhang, L., Yang, L., Zhou, Z.: Data-based modeling for hypoglycemia prediction: importance, trends, and implications for clinical practice. Front. Public Health **11**, 1044059 (2023)

Knowledge Graph Repair

Robert David(✉)

Institute for Data, Process and Knowledge Management, Vienna University of Economics and Business, Vienna, Austria

robert.david@semantic-web.com

Abstract. The Semantic Web provides standards for knowledge graphs (KGs), which have become popular for solving data heterogeneity problems in enterprises, since they allow for flexible data modelling and integration via linking of graphs. This flexibility requires standards to ensure data quality and consistent state, such as the Shapes Constraint Language SHACL. However, SHACL does not provide the means to explain why constraint violations occur and how the KG can be repaired to conform to the constraints. Also, repairs for a KG can come with a high number of different alternative choices to pick from, where we need a way to determine preferences in practice. Finally, knowledge in the KG itself can be exploited for repairs to determine fresh values and preferred choices and to identify incorrect data from a real-world perspective. For these challenges, we aim to develop a system that combines logic-based repairs and data-driven analysis for a repair approach that concludes KGs towards a quality fix point. The approach will not only be defined at the formal level, but we also will provide prototypical implementations for practical experiments, thereby positioning it at the intersection of theoretical and applied research. Use cases shall be provided from companies, projects and open data to better understand how repairs can be applied effectively in practice. With this work we contribute to improving the quality of KGs by providing intelligent knowledge graph repair.

Keywords: Knowledge Graphs · Shapes Constraint Language · SHACL · Data Repair · Data Quality · Logic Programming · Data-Driven Anaylsis · Hybrid AI

1 Motivation

Knowledge graphs (KGs) [13] are often used in enterprises for consolidation of heterogeneous data sources. The flexible approach of modelling graphs using the Resource Description Framework (RDF) makes it possible to link together various data sources and thereby integrate them into an enterprise knowledge graph (EKG) [11]. However, problems like inconsistencies and incomplete data can be introduced. These problems generally represent quality issues that need appropriate mechanisms to detect and manage them in practice. This generally applies to KGs, but it is especially important in an enterprise scenario, where business decisions depend on the consolidated information.

A. Meroño Peñuela et al. (Eds.): ESWC 2024, LNCS 15345, pp. 45–54, 2025.
https://doi.org/10.1007/978-3-031-78955-7_5

The Semantic Web traditionally uses open world reasoning based on RDFS and OWL [3], which has very limited use regarding the detection of inconsistencies. While OWL can express restrictions, an OWL reasoner uses them for classification and not as constraints on the data. The later introduced Shapes Constraint Language SHACL [15] can detect data inconsistencies based on constraints and return a report about violations. However, these reports do not explain why a violation has happened and they do not provide sufficient information on how to correct the data. In a data consolidation scenario, we mostly consider changing the KG itself without changing the underlying schema. Knowledge graph refinement, as discussed in [18], focuses on adding missing knowledge to the graph and identifying wrong information in the graph, and thereby increasing the quality of the graph regarding the schema. As the quality of graph data is of high importance in practice, having a system which can determine such refinements so that constraint violations can be repaired would be of high value.

In the following, we present the state of the art for graph standards, ontology and database repairs and data-driven analysis. Then we continue with formulating research questions and contributions our work will provide. In the research methodology and approach section, we show how we plan to incrementally address the questions, followed by the evaluation plan. We then provide a report on the intermediary results up to now. Finally, we present conclusions and next steps.

2 State of the Art

The state of the art related to this thesis covers knowledge graph technologies, which are the foundation of our work. We also look into approaches to repair data for ontologies and relational databases and the complexity of the repair problem. Finally, we need to understand the broad field of data-driven analysis methods, which can be used to determine repair choices.

2.1 Knowledge Graphs and the Semantic Web

The Semantic Web [16] is a set of standards for knowledge representation for the world wide web. It includes languages to describe the semantics of (graph) data, RDF Schema RDFS and the Web Ontology Language OWL [3]. These languages allow for reasoning about the data in the form of logical conclusions. Because links to graphs can be created by anyone on the web, these conclusions use the open world assumption for monotonic reasoning, but thereby accepting problems introduced by contradicting data.

Enterprise Knowledge Graphs. Originally created for open data publishing, the Semantic Web standards were discovered to be sufficiently flexible and expressive to be used in enterprise contexts to solve data integration problems under the term Enterprise Knowledge Graphs (EKG) [11]. On the organisational side,

EKGs differ from public knowledge graphs usually by being limited to the enterprise's data sources and the need for high quality to avoid false information which might become problematic from a business point of view. Therefore, the quality of graph datasets needs to be defined in a principled manner in order to be able to detect conflicts and possibly repair them [7].

Graph Constraint Languages. There are currently two constraint languages for knowledge graphs. The shapes constraint language SHACL [15] is the W3C recommendation for constraint validation in the Semantic Web. The shape expressions language ShEx [19] is developed in a W3C community group and publicly available. SHACL and ShEx are both based on the idea of shapes that group together constraints to be evaluated on nodes in the knowledge graph. They differ in syntax, and in some details regarding constraint validation and reporting, and they define different semantics for recursion. Semantics for shape validation are discussed in general in the scientific community regarding what makes sense for data quality. Generally, the provided information should assist in fixing the data to achieve conformance with the constraints and thereby improve the quality of the graph data.

2.2 Repair Approaches

Relational Database Repairs. Inconsistent data, as a consequence of violating integrity constraints, is well-researched for relational databases. Two strategies for coping with inconsistent relational data are presented in [5]. First, consistent query answering (CQA) does not resolve the inconsistencies but provides answers to queries based on a consistent subset of the data. Second, data cleaning repairs the inconsistencies while trying to preserve as much information as possible by making minimal changes. This strategy can result in different choices on how to change the data. One way of specifying and implementing repairs is to represent them as logic programs, e.g. using disjunctive Datalog with stable model semantics, which is described in [5]. These programs modify a database to achieve conformance with a set of integrity constraints.

Ontology Repairs. Related to our work are also reasoning tasks for explanations and repairs for ontologies, often in the context of Description Logics. Debugging and repair of OWL ontologies [14] addresses logical contradictions in OWL-DL ontologies and proposes a framework to repair such defects. Examples of work on explanations for negative query answers can be found in [8,9]. A recent work on Description Logic ontologies is [4], which addresses optimal repairs in the scenario where the schema (TBox) is assumed to be correct, while the data (ABox) needs to be repaired. Optimal repairs in this context are repairs which preserve as much as possible from the logical consequences of the ontology. Similar, an approach to repair EL ontologies is presented in [17] using a combination (or trade-off) of weakening and completing to mitigate the negative effects of removing wrong axioms. Finally, the relation between Description Logics and

SHACL is discussed in [6]. The idea is to bridge the two communities and provide work about Description Logic as a formal foundation for future SHACL developments.

Rule-based Repairs. Rule-driven inconsistency resolution is described in [12], which assumes rule-generated descriptions of entities in KGs by using ontologies. In this scenario, quality problems can be introduced when ontology terms are used without alignment with the rules, thereby leading to violations of restrictions defined by the ontologies. A rule-driven methodology is introduced which determines refinements which should be applied to the rules and the ontology. Experts still need to decide manually if the rules or the ontology should be changed.

2.3 Data-Driven Analysis

Some aspects of repairs cannot always be covered by formal constraints alone. A source of repair information is the data graph itself, which can be analysed to decide on fresh values, pick repair choices and identify false data from a real-world perspective beyond formal constraints. The field of concluding new knowledge from sample data is very broad and there are many different approaches to do so, with the most prominent being machine learning methods like Graph Neural Networks [20]. The field of Knowledge Graph Completion [10] focuses on predicting graph structures and values based on statistical analyses of existing graph data. It contains many different approaches, which range from probabilistic methods to modern machine learning techniques, like deep learning and large language models. Such data-driven analyses, when combined with crisp semantic descriptions from the data set, can be a source of practically viable repair options.

3 Problem Statement and Contributions

In the course of the thesis, we plan to address the following research questions and develop solutions for knowledge graph repair. On the theoretical side we provide novel formalisms to analyse graphs regarding repairs based on constraints. On the practical side, we apply prototypes to practical scenarios to gain further insights for practically viable repairs. With this work we aim to contribute to the advance of the academic discourse on knowledge graph quality. In the following, we identify 3 main research questions.

3.1 Explaining and Repairing Constraint Violations

The first main research question is about how to define and implement repairs for graph data based on constraints. This is an open question in the research community that was not yet addressed. To limit the scope, our work focuses on SHACL as a constraint language. In the following, we provide a motivating example for the repair problem.

Example 1. Assume a shapes graph with a shape StudentShape (left) and a data graph (right), written in Turtle syntax:

```
:StudentShape a sh:NodeShape;          :Ben :studentID "2119110",
    sh:targetNode :Ben;                                 "1716110".
    sh:property [
        sh:path :studentID;
        sh:maxCount 1;
    ].
```

The StudentShape defines that a student must not have more than one student ID. In this example, we can see that *Ben* has two student IDs. *Ben* is a target node for StudentShape and violates the *sh:maxCount* constraint.

SHACL is designed to identify quality problems by specifying constraints grouped into shapes and then checking if the graph data satisfies them. The process of validation returns reports for constraint violations. However, reports do not provide an explanation for why a constraint is violated and how this can be solved. In example 1, we could delete either one of the student IDs to make *Ben* validate StudentShape, so there are two (minimal) repair choices. Providing automatic solutions for violations in more complex scenarios is not trivial. Explanations are non-deterministic and have to be determined globally for a data graph. Currently, it is open how to compute such repairs for knowledge graphs.

To develop a solution for repairs, we first need a formal definition for explanations to represent why these non-validations of SHACL constraints happen. These explanations are a preliminary step and the basis to determine how to change the data graph to achieve conformance with the constraints. We also discuss which kinds of explanations we would like to have from a practical point of view. For example, we can argue for minimality of changes, because we want to preserve as much of the original data graph as possible. Second, we investigate how to transfer existing repair approaches for relational databases to knowledge graphs and how to combine them with SHACL.

RQ1: How can we compute repairs that correct graph data to conform to SHACL constraints and how can this be implemented?

- *RQ1.1: What is our understanding of an explanation for SHACL constraint violations?*
- *RQ1.2: How can we compute SHACL repairs based on explanations and provide an implementation?*
- *RQ1.3: How well does the repair approach scale for practical purposes?*

3.2 Repair Strategies

The second main research question continues from the first main research question and asks about ways to represent user preferences for the repairs on top of what SHACL repairs can express. The motivation for this question comes from two open issues which are not addressed by the first question.

- First, users might decide for certain elements of the data graph that they should not be added or deleted by the repairs, which basically means that they are read-only. In a less restrictive situation the user might still allow these elements to be added or deleted, but it would not be a preferred situation to pick them if there are alternative choices to repair the data graph.
- Second, in the situation where there is a high number of possible and equally optimal repair choices, users can decide on preferences to reduce the number of choices and thereby make it easier to pick one choice.

Technically, preferences can be addressed by weighing different repair choices and determining the optimally weighted repair. We will apply this approach to extend the basic SHACL repair implementation.

RQ2: Based on our definition of repairs, how can we provide formalized repair strategies so that users can define optimal repair choices for specific use cases.

3.3 Data-Driven Repairs Choices

The third main research question again continues from the previous main research questions and brings in data-driven methods to SHACL repairs for determining repair preferences. The idea is to create a hybrid system of formal and data-driven approaches.

This question is motivated at first by the question of how to come up with fresh values if a SHACL repair needs the addition of data. Such values usually cannot be determined by looking at the constraints and need to come from a different source. An approach is to take into account information from the (existing) data graph that can provide insights into how to choose values. Also, we can determine which choices to preferably pick for repairs. Finally, we can determine outliers which might be incorrect data. As described, data-driven analysis to determine such values is a broad and well-researched field. In our work, we focus on the integration of such methods for repair strategies and will not research new data-driven methods.

RQ3: How can we formally integrate data-driven methods into repair strategies to conclude missing values, detect outliers and pick from multiple choices?

3.4 Future Questions

Finally, we would like to point out other interesting research questions, which were identified, but will not be addressed in this work because of scope reasons.

- Are there alternative notions of explanations and repairs?
- How do repairs interact with ontological reasoning with RDFS and OWL?
- How can we address recursive dependencies of shape targets and repairs?
- Given the high complexity of the repair problem, how can we improve the scalability in practice?

- How far does the integration of data-driven methods for repair strategies improve the quality of a KG from a practical point of view?

These questions are future work outside of the scope limits of this thesis.

4 Research Methodology and Approach

The research methodology for this thesis addresses the combination of theoretical and applied research. We develop our work incrementally by starting with the formal basis on the theoretical part and then going towards implementation and experiments to apply our approach to practical use cases.

4.1 Methodology

The initial question of this thesis is how we can identify and repair quality problems in enterprise knowledge graphs. We started with a gap analysis regarding this question and identified open issues that we will address. We then determined the main research questions based on a high level understanding of this problem. The research questions are stated to clearly define and narrow down the scope in the broad field of knowledge graph quality. The main research questions of this thesis will be addressed incrementally, with each answer to a question providing the context for the next question. At the beginning we will address *RQ-1* and provide a formal basis and a prototypical implementation. Then we follow with *RQ-2* and *RQ-3*, which have a focus on applied research in the context of specific use cases, where we will verify the applicability of our approach and incorporate the insights into our work.

- For *RQ-1*, we will investigate how to calculate repairs for SHACL constraint violations, while considering practical aspects, like minimal changes done by repairs to preserve as much as possible of the existing data. We will also discuss the computational complexity of repairs and choose an appropriate technology for implementation.
- For *RQ-2*, we will consider the scenario where users want to provide preferences for different repair choices. *RQ-2* will be answered in the context of use cases, where we will specifically answer the question of what users would accept as a high quality repair in such a scenario.
- For *RQ-3*, we will look into integration of data-driven methods for inferring values in knowledge graphs as an extension of the outcomes of *RQ-2*. Answering *RQ-3* will allow us to integrate formal repairs with data-driven analysis methods into a hybrid approach and we will provide a prototypical implementation. *RQ-3* will also be answered in the context of use cases.

The proposed methodology aims to develop a system for knowledge graph repair built on a strong formal basis and developed in practical scenarios. To the best of our knowledge, our approach is novel in the way how we address data quality for knowledge graphs and our implementation is an innovation where no similar solutions currently exist.

5 Evaluation

The evaluation of our work has 3 aspects. First, we will verify the correctness of the repairs against the SHACL validation. After computing a repair, the repaired data graph must always validate against the constraints. If it is not possible to repair all the violations, the repairs provide a maximal consistent data graph and report the targets which were not repaired. This evaluation can be done by using a SHACL processor for validation and can be tested automatically. We will provide unit test cases and also test against the published SHACL test suite[1]. Second, the program needs to return repairs with only minimal changes to the original data graph from all the repairs it can compute. We aim to solve this formally on the technical level by using (existing) optimization implementations which always identify the optimal repairs. Third, the approach developed is intended to be applied in practice. We will select real-world use cases and evaluate how well our approach can be used to solve them from a qualitative point of view. An important question is to understand what users would accept as repairs for these use cases in the sense that it improves the quality of the data graph from a real-world perspective. We will then evaluate if such repairs can be formally represented using repair strategies. Currently, we plan to look into two use cases for repair strategies.

- Automatic processing of contract data, which needs data consistency to satisfy legal requirements originating in the GDPR [2]. We will use real-world contract data and introduce inconsistencies to simulate system defects.
- Modifying existing OWL ontologies to make them compliant with a given use case-specific OWL fragment, while preserving as much as possible of the original ontology in a syntactic and semantic sense. We will select existing and publicly available ontologies as data for this use case.

Finally, for evaluating the integration of data-driven methods we will select another use case, which contains an appropriate data graph to explore missing values, pick preferred choices and identify outliers. We will evaluate how we can integrate these analyses as part of the repair strategies.

6 Results

The research questions are intended to incrementally build up a knowledge graph repair system. We will publish intermediary results and provide implementations for proof of concept and practical experiments that complement the theoretical work and build up a unified analysis and repair system. Currently, we have published two intermediary results as conference papers.

- In *Reasoning about Explanations for Non-validation in SHACL* [1] we explain non-validation using the notion of a repair as a collection of additions and

[1] https://w3c.github.io/data-shapes/data-shapes-test-suite/.
[2] https://gdpr.eu/what-is-gdpr/.

deletions whose application on a data graph results in a repaired graph that satisfies a set of SHACL constraints. This publication answers research question *RQ1.1* and provides the foundation for the next steps.
- In *Repairing SHACL Constraint Violations using Answer Set Programming* [2] we propose an algorithm to compute repairs by encoding the repair problem into an answer set program. We introduce several optimisations to the program that aim to maximise the benefit for practical scenarios. This publication answers research question *RQ1.2*, builds on the previous outcomes and is the first step towards practical experiments.

With these two contributions, we already gained insights into the topic of this thesis and shared them with the research community.

7 Conclusions and Next Steps

Our work aims to contribute to research by providing a formal foundation and a prototypical implementation to compute repairs for knowledge graphs based on SHACL constraints. The next steps will cover user preferences and the integration of data-driven methods.

- For user preferences, we intend to publish the results with one publication for each use case described in Sect. 5, where we share insights into what kind of repairs users would accept as high-quality repairs.
- For integrating data-driven methods, we still need to identify an appropriate use case and then see how we can integrate with data-driven methods. Here we will publish the results in one publication.

With our work, we contribute to improving the quality of large data graphs, especially in an enterprise knowledge graph scenario, by providing intelligent knowledge graph repair.

Acknowledgments. This Ph.D. is done under the supervision of Axel Polleres (Ph.D. advisor, Vienna University of Economics and Business) and Shqiponja Ahmeta (Vienna University of Technology).

References

1. Ahmetaj, S., David, R., Ortiz, M., Polleres, A., Shehu, B., Simkus, M.: Reasoning about explanations for non-validation in SHACL. In: Bienvenu, M., Lakemeyer, G., Erdem, E. (eds.) Proceedings of the 18th International Conference on Principles of Knowledge Representation and Reasoning, KR 2021, Online event, 3-12 November 2021, pp. 12–21 (2021). https://doi.org/10.24963/kr.2021/2
2. Ahmetaj, S., David, R., Polleres, A., Šimkus, M.: Repairing SHACL constraint violations using answer set programming. In: The Semantic Web - ISWC 2022: 21st International Semantic Web Conference, Virtual Event, October 23-27, 2022, Proceedings, pp. 375–391. Springer-Verlag, Heidelberg (2022). https://doi.org/10.1007/978-3-031-19433-7_22

3. Allemang, D., Hendler, J.: Semantic Web for the Working Ontologist: Effective Modeling in RDFS and OWL, 2nd edn. Morgan Kaufmann Publishers Inc., San Francisco, CA, USA (2011)
4. Baader, F., Koopmann, P., Kriegel, F., Nuradiansyah, A.: Optimal ABox repair w.r.t. static EL TBoxes: from quantified ABoxes back to ABoxes. In: The Semantic Web: 19th International Conference, ESWC 2022, Hersonissos, Crete, Greece, May 29 - June 2, 2022, Proceedings, pp. 130–146. Springer-Verlag, Heidelberg (2022). https://doi.org/10.1007/978-3-031-06981-9_8
5. Bertossi, L.: Database repairing and consistent query answering. Synth. Lect. Data Manag. **3**(5), 1–121 (2011)
6. Bogaerts, B., Jakubowski, M., Van den Bussche, J.: SHACL: a description logic in disguise. In: International Conference on Logic Programming and Nonmonotonic Reasoning, pp. 75–88. Springer (2022). https://doi.org/10.1007/978-3-031-15707-3_7
7. Bonifati, A., Fletcher, G., Voigt, H., Yakovets, N., Jagadish, H.V.: Querying Graphs. Morgan & Claypool Publishers (2018)
8. Calvanese, D., Ortiz, M., Simkus, M., Stefanoni, G.: Reasoning about explanations for negative query answers in DL-Lite. J. Artif. Intell. Res. **48**, 635–669 (2013). https://doi.org/10.1613/jair.3870
9. Ceylan, İ.İ., Lukasiewicz, T., Malizia, E., Molinaro, C., Vaicenavicius, A.: Explanations for negative query answers under existential rules. In: Proceedings of KR 2020, pp. 223–232 (2020). https://doi.org/10.24963/kr.2020/23
10. Chen, Z., Wang, Y., Zhao, B., Cheng, J., Zhao, X., Duan, Z.: Knowledge graph completion: a review. IEEE Access **8**, 192435–192456 (2020)
11. Galkin, M., Auer, S., Vidal, M.E., Scerri, S.: Enterprise Knowledge Graphs: A Semantic Approach for Knowledge Management in the Next Generation of Enterprise Information Systems. In: ICEIS (2). pp. 88–98 (2017)
12. Heyvaert, P., De Meester, B., Dimou, A., Verborgh, R.: Rule-driven inconsistency resolution for knowledge graph generation rules. Semant. Web **10**(6), 1071–1086 (2019)
13. Hogan, A., et al.: Knowledge graphs. Synthesis Lectures on Data, Semantics, and Knowledge, Morgan & Claypool Publishers (2021). https://doi.org/10.2200/S01125ED1V01Y202109DSK022
14. Kalyanpur, A.: Debugging and repair of OWL ontologies. University of Maryland, College Park (2006)
15. Knublauch, H., Kontokostas, D.: Shapes constraint language (SHACL). Tech. rep., W3C (2017). https://www.w3.org/TR/shacl/
16. Lassila, O., Hendler, J., Berners-Lee, T.: The Semantic Web. Sci. Am. **284**(5), 34–43 (2001)
17. Li, Y., Lambrix, P.: Repairing EL ontologies using weakening and completing. In: European Semantic Web Conference, pp. 298–315. Springer (2023). https://doi.org/10.1007/978-3-031-43458-7
18. Paulheim, H.: Knowledge graph refinement: a survey of approaches and evaluation methods. Semant. web **8**(3), 489–508 (2017)
19. Prud'hommeaux, E., Labra Gayo, J., Solbrig, H.: Shape expressions: an RDF validation and transformation language. In: ACM International Conference Proceeding Series **2014** (2014). https://doi.org/10.1145/2660517.2660523
20. Scarselli, F., Gori, M., Tsoi, A.C., Hagenbuchner, M., Monfardini, G.: The graph neural network model. IEEETNN **20**(1), 61–80 (2009). https://doi.org/10.1109/TNN.2008.2005605

Towards an Ontology of Data Sovereignty and Ownership in Cyberspace

Giacomo De Colle[1,2](✉)

[1] University at Buffalo, Buffalo, NY 14260, USA
gdecolle@buffalo.edu
[2] National Center for Ontological Research, Buffalo, NY, USA

Abstract. To improve data analysis in cybersecurity, I present a plan to build a formal ontological representation of data ownership and sovereignty in cyberspace, alongside with the cyberattacks that threaten them. I argue that modelling these phenomena by making use of ontologies allows for coherent integration of data coming from diverse sources, automated reasoning over such data, as well as their analysis and reuse. Existing ontological tools in cybersecurity can be ameliorated by connecting them to neighboring domains such as law, regulations, governmental institutions, and documents. Moreover, they will benefit from the introduction of clear competency questions and of the technical terminology to answer them. In the course of the paper, I propose metrics to evaluate currently existing ontological tools to create formal representations in this domain, and I provide a plan to develop such representations and to extend current ontological tools when they are lacking.

Keywords: Ontologies · Cybersecurity · Cyberspace · Data Sovereignty · Data Ownership · Basic Formal Ontology

1 Introduction and Motivation

Cyberspace, provisionally understood as the aggregate of computing artifacts, the information they process and the connections between such artifacts, is the source of an immense and variegated body of data. Analyzing this data is at the heart of multiple computer science disciplines, including those that are broadly located in, or related to, the field of cybersecurity, such as digital forensics, network analysis, attack response, intelligence analysis, and identification of cybercrime. Coherent integration of cyberspace data with data from neighboring fields is nevertheless impossible without a shared semantical framework such as the one that can be specified by a commonly adopted ontology. An ontology able to represent cyberspace and the operations that take place in cyberspace would allow for data sharing between different organizations, thus enabling the breaking of data silos and supporting querying, reasoning, and analysis of large bodies of data coming from different sources.

Take as an example the following case, illustrated in a simplified way in Fig. 1. An unknown device is starting a TCP handshake process, thus asking to access a certain

A. Meroño Peñuela et al. (Eds.): ESWC 2024, LNCS 15345, pp. 55–63, 2025.
https://doi.org/10.1007/978-3-031-78955-7_6

(part of) a website containing healthcare data. This process is recorded in logs which contain information about data packets shared between different devices, and that convey information about, for example, the IP address of the device starting the TCP request. Can we automatically detect whether the request was warranted, or rather a potential attack coming from a malicious actor? In order to do so, we have to identify the type of information that the device was trying to access, as well as whether the device itself has features that are suspicious. This is possible only if we connect information from at least three different sources: the cyber operation itself (the TCP request), the type of data accessed and what it refers to (the patient and their health history), and security and criminal data, for example whether the device owner is listed in a watchlist.

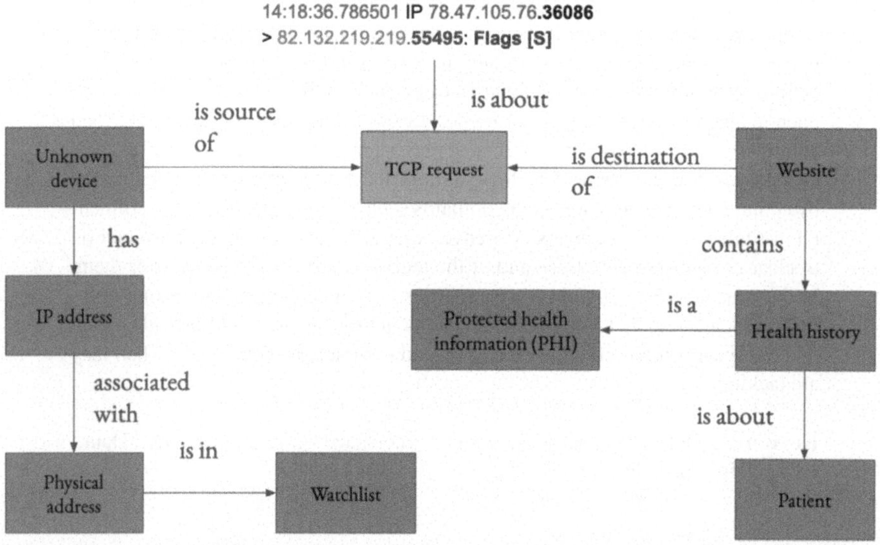

Fig. 1. Simplified representation of a use case for an ontology of cybersecurity. Green represents BFO: occurents, blue represents BFO: continuants. Data packet information refers to different entities involved in the TCP request. (Color figure online)

Connecting the three data sources is of course possible through direct manual intervention, but such an approach is not scalable given that it requires an exponential growth of mappings the more data sources are added (see [1] for a discussion of a similar issue in the representation of occupation data). On the other hand, an ontology structuring the data coming from these different sources would allow for its coherent integration and execution of federated queries, for example in the shape of SPARQL queries, to single-handedly identify whether the request represented in Fig. 1 is a potential cyberattack. Using semantic web technologies such as ontologies, SPARQL queries and reasoners is especially crucial when the type of information we are trying to extract from this body of data is interdisciplinary, as in the case of cyberspace information being connected with the legal domain for identification of privacy violation and other types of cybercrime.

In the rest of this paper, I will present a plan to use ontological resources for the modelling and formal representation of cyberspace, with a focus on the representation of digital sovereignty and data ownership. When these ontological resources are missing, I will discuss venues to develop them. Data ownership and sovereignty can be provisionally understood as the rights that state or private actors have over data regarding them. For example, the case in Fig. 1 can potentially lead to a case of breaching of one's rights over their data. But that can only be detected in an automated way if we are able to create an ontological representation of what data ownership is. In the case represented above, the fact that the device was trying to access health record data about one's own health history makes it plausible that it is a case of data ownership breach, but this cannot be inferred and classified as such unless one has axioms connecting health data to data ownership itself.

I will begin by presenting already existing ontological efforts in the field of cyber security, and I will motivate the adoption of the Basic Formal Ontology (BFO) and the Common Core Ontologies (CCO), respectively as a top-and mid-level architecture [2, 3]. I will then present more in detail the main research question and its sub questions, alongside with associated steps in representation, formalization and ontological implementation. I will conclude with a brief presentation of the first obtained results, which currently consist in the identification of a research question, a first literature review and the creation of simple ontology design patterns for the representation of information in BFO and CCO.

2 State of the Art

The necessity for a formal representation of the knowledge surrounding cybersecurity has been discussed by different authors [4–6]. The extensive literature review presented in [7] shows that almost 40 efforts exist in the field of ontological representations of domains related to cybersecurity, and good ontology engineering practice requires for existing resources to be reused when possible. Recall the use case presented above in Fig. 1: in order to ontologically represent such a scenario, there is need for an ontology which is able to bridge data from cyberspace with data in neighboring do- mains, especially those of documents, agents, intelligence operations, and social entities. This means that the desiderata that such an ontology or ontologies need to satisfy are the following: being non-parochial, which means that they are able to be employed for different use cases of cyberspace representation; as a cognate notion, being able to be used as a hub for extensions; adopting a top-level ontology, which allows for the coherent integration of data already tagged with other ontologies, in order to avoid the creation of an ontology data silos; and the presence of technical terminology, in the ontology, which is directly tied to the domain of interest, and that doesn't suffer from being too generic. These desiderata compose metrics, which will also be used as part of the evaluation for the ontology resources I will myself develop, as discussed later on in this paper.

As shown in Table 1, many of the existing projects in the field are not tied to a top-level ontology or are developed for narrow uses such as malware recognition or risk analysis. The ontologies in question are then not able to be adopted for the type of use case presented in Fig. 1, which requires an ontology that can be used for tying together disparate data sources. The Unified Cyber Ontology (UCO), which is now part of a Linux Foundation project, was recently mapped into top-level ontologies such as BFO, but this mapping is only partial [5]. CRATELO, which adopts DOLCE as a top-level architecture [6], and the Cyber ontology, currently developed as part of an IEEE initiative, which adopts BFO and CCO as top- and mid-level architectures [8, 9], are the two projects which better satisfy the presented desiderata.

Many of the use cases for ontologies representing cyberspace will interact, directly or indirectly, with neighboring areas such as intelligence analysis, directives and legal documents, defense, and counterterrorism. CCO and BFO have been recently adopted as baseline standard ontologies by the intelligence and defense communities [10] and are thus required to be used in U.S. initiatives in these fields. Moreover, CCO and other projects in the BFO community already provide a baseline for representing many of the entities related with cyberspace. Of particular interest for the purpose of this presentation are information artifacts [11], software [12], military operations [13], intelligence analysis [14], counterterrorism [15], and agents [3]. As such, BFO and CCO appear to be the privileged starting points for developing such ontological representations.

Notable efforts neighboring the ontology field are ATT&CK and D3FEND, vocabularies developed by MITRE that respectively document cyberattack and cyberdefense techniques and which are extremely valuable as data and terminology sources for the cybersecurity community. The terms included in the two vocabularies will provide a guideline for which technical terms need to be introduced in an ontology aiming to represent cyberspace.

Table 1. Existing ontologies of cyberspace and cybersecurity, evaluated alongside different metrics on a scale from 0 to 2, where 0 represents an ontology which doesn't satisfy the criterion, 1 represents an ontology which partially satisfies the criterion, and 2 represents an ontology which fully satisfies the criterion.

Ontology	Non-parochial	Uses top-level	Technical	Hub
CRATELO	2	2	1	2
Cyber Ontology	2	2	1	2
UCO	2	1	1	2
COoVR, MALOnt, etc.	1	0–1	1	0

3 Problem Statement and Contributions

The literature review presented in the section above identified the Cyber ontology, based on CCO and BFO, as a starting point for developing an ontological representation of cyberspace. The Cyber ontology itself, as an active development project, will eventually include more precise technical terms. The main research question that the project presented here addresses is whether ontologies can be used to enhance data sharing and analysis practices aimed at identifying breaches of data ownership and sovereignty, by answering competencies questions that are not yet answerable due to the disparity and variety of the data in question. Moreover, whether such ontological representations can be built in a way which is not fragmented and which connects data from the cybersecurity domain with neighboring domains. The metrics presented in the previous section are a first attempt at measuring success conditions for this kind of application. This main research question breaks naturally down in two sub-questions. The first, regarding the ontological representation, formalization and implementation, is whether it is possible to ontologically represent cyberspace and the state and private actors that inhabit it, alongside with the laws and regulations that permeate it. Such a representation would be able to get high scores in all the metrics introduced in Sect. 2, as well as to be able to be expanded into neighboring domains and reusable for related practices. The second, which regards the operationalization of ontologies, is whether this ontological representation can be used to identify breaches of data ownership and sovereignty perpetuated by state and private actors.

The two main sub questions can furthermore be scaffolded into multiple and more narrow objectives. A first set of questions breaks down the first question on building an ontological representation and correspond to the first steps taken in top-down ontology engineering [16]. For what purely regards representing cyberspace and cyber operations, these questions include, for example, "what is an act of information processing?", "what is an act of information sharing over a network?", "what is a malicious actor, and what is a cyberattack?". For what regards the interplay of data ownership and sovereignty with the cyberspace, these questions include, for example "what is digital sovereignty?", "what is data ownership?", "what is an act of cyber warfare?", "what is an act of legal compliance in cyberspace?". Answering these questions from an ontological perspective will give birth to definitions, axioms and design patterns used in ontology development.

The second set of questions breaks down the operational part of the ontology engineering practice, thus corresponding to the data-driven approach taken in bottom-up ontology development [17]. These questions will identify the applications that the ontology engineering steps undertaken or identified in other parts of the project can have. Some of these questions include, for example, "what are the formats and types that cyberspace data takes?", "what are the formats and types that digital legal documents on data ownership and sovereignty take?", "how can privacy infringement and data sovereignty be represented in knowledge graph format, so that data coming from different sources can be queried for identification of these phenomena?", "what are the types of digital forensics and data analysis tasks that need to be automated and integrated with data regarding regulations?". Answering the second set of questions will provide the project with a more precise understanding of the type of data to be structured, and of the competency questions that such data can be used to answer.

4 Research Methodology and Approach

The first step of the project will involve identifying with more precision the specific type of legal phenomena surrounding data sovereignty and data ownership [18, 19]. For example, data sovereignty for citizens of the E.U. is largely concretized in regulations such as the GDPR. Once these regulations and related phenomena are identified, it will be possible to narrow down what type of cybersecurity terms need to be used in order to identify actions that in compliance or breaking of such regulations. For example, what kind of cyberattack constitutes an act of violation of the data ownership of a certain individual under a certain regulation? What kind of act in cyberspace constitutes a violation of the digital sovereignty of a certain country?

Answering these types of questions within concrete existing regulations and cyber security terminologies will allow for the creation of a first set of competency questions, that will be subsequently made more precise the more ontological terminology is identified to specify them. These competency questions will eventually take the form of SPARQL queries and will be one of the evaluation tools used to assess the success or failure of the project. This first step allows for the creation of a list of *desiderata* that ontologies need to be able to satisfy, as well as a list of core terms coming from the field of law, political science and cybersecurity that are required for the success of an ontological project.

The next step involves the review of already existing ontology projects and frameworks, as well as the study of already existing neighboring non-ontological projects such as vocabularies and taxonomies. For example, MITRE's taxonomies DEF3ND and ATT&CK are the main resources that are used to represent knowledge of cybersecurity experts and that are already employed as terminological standards in the field. Other similar projects to be properly investigated are the Structured Threat Information eXpression (STIX), developed by MITRE for the DHS. On the side of notions of digital sovereignty, warfare and ownership and related documentation, similar studies of foundational texts and of existing ontologies will be undertaken in order to identify existing resources and evaluate them [20]. The resources thus identified, alongside with the ontologies described in Sect. 2, will then be evaluated for their capability of representing the competency questions and terms identified in the previous step. Moreover, this step will involve identifying the shape taken by data in these fields, so that the ontology can be properly structured in such a way that it mirrors it.

Once these competency questions are identified, proper development of ontology resources can begin. As previously discussed in this paper, the Cyber ontology acts as a starting resource, as well as cognate ontologies in CCO and the BFO community such as the Information Artifact Ontology (IAO), the Agent ontology, the Information Entity Ontology (IEO), and the Geospatial ontology. The method adopted in the process of ontology engineering will follow the two types of questions introduced in Sect. 3 of this paper, thus effectively merging bottom-up and top-down ontology development in an exercise of the so-called middle-in ontology development strategy [21]. In this way, the ontological resources created can extend from the top-and mid-level layers of BFO and CCO, while also being developed with an eye to the structure of data that needs to be integrated by ontologies and to the competency questions that domain experts need to answer, as identified during previous steps of this process.

5 Evaluation Plan

The different steps described in the previous section can be evaluated in the course of the project in different ways. Recall that step 1 involves the identification of the notions in legal and political science which are needed in order to identify violations of state and private actors' rights over their data. This can be tested by creating definitions that are built and confronted not only with other ontologists in the community, but also with domain experts in both fields of cybersecurity and legal and political science. Success in step 1 is represented by the identification of core terms and notions in the respective fields and by the creation of first tentative definitions for them. Step 2 involves the formalization of competency questions that use terms and notions identified in the previous step. These competency questions will act as primary benchmark and use case for the ontological representations created in next steps. Step 2 will also involve the identification of the type of data that the ontologies will be created for – for example, data packet logs, server logs, access logs, and legal regulation data. Success of step 2 is marked by the creation of a satisfying set of competency questions, that are checked with the domain experts and ontologists contacted in step 1.

Step 3 will include the identification of missing terms in existing ontologies, that need to be added in order for them to represent and answer the competency questions created in previous steps. This step involves the creation of terms and definitions to be added to the ontologies mentioned above and will be evaluated by the acceptance of the terms by the ontology communities to which they are proposed to. The final step of the project will involve the ingestion of instance level data, for example taken by MITRE's database, and the testing of the ontology by means of the competency questions identified in previous steps. If the queries can be successfully applied to the knowledge base thus constructed, reasoning and implicit knowledge extraction will successfully prove the quality of the ontology and its applicability. This final part of the project will include evaluation by making use of the metrics introduced in Sect. 2. A successful step 4 will mark a final positive result for the ontology resources created, identifying previously unidentified instances of breaking of data sovereignty or ownership. The various steps of the project can each furthermore be tested by presenting results to existing ontology conferences in the field of ontologies and law, as well as ontology and cybersecurity, such as FOIS and JURIX.

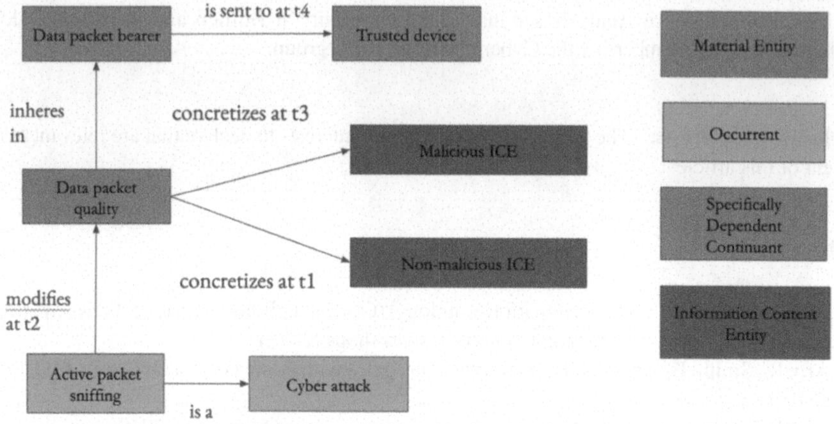

Fig. 2. Simple design pattern for the representation of information sharing in CCO and BFO. The scenario depicted represents an active packet sniffing attack, where the content of an intercepted data packet is injected with malicious code.

6 Results

The stage of the research is at the moment at its beginnings. Preliminary results include an extensive literature review and evaluation of the existing semantic web projects in cybersecurity, presented in Sect. 2 of this paper. As part of these preliminary studies, I have also started identifying data sources and already adopted terminological standards in the field, such as MITRE's ATT&CK and D3FEND, NIST recommendations, ISO standards such as ISO 27005, and STIMS. A study of foundational notions of cybersecurity has also begun, as well as contacting cybersecurity experts. One of the first objectives in the development of the project is to identify basic design patterns in CCO and BFO that can be used to represent information processing and sharing in the domain of interest of cybersecurity. Figure 2 is an example of such first results.

7 Conclusions

The preliminary studies undergone so far show the need for a framework to relate efforts in ontology of cyberspace and cybersecurity with neighboring domains. To remedy this issue, I have proposed the evaluation and further development of ontological resources in cybersecurity and their interaction with ontological representations in the domain of data ownership and data sovereignty. Such a project will achieve interoperability between heterogeneous data sources from the cybersecurity domain and the domain of data sovereignty and ownership. Given the difficulties proper of cybersecurity and intelligence analysis in data integration, this is an issue of primary concern in an era where analyzing big data for informatic vulnerabilities, sovereignty and rights infractions will exponentially develop as a focal problem.

Acknowledgments. The author wishes to acknowledge the help gained from comments and insightful discussions with Barry Smith, John Beverley, the members of the 2024 Ontology Engineering and Intelligence Analysis seminar at the University at Buffalo and in particular Max Farrington, and the members of the Cyber Ontology IEEE group.

Disclosure of Interests. The author has no competing interests to declare that are relevant to the content of this article.

References

1. Beverley, J., et al.: The occupation ontology (OccO): building a bridge between global occupational standards. In: Joint Ontology Workshops (2023)
2. Arp, R., Smith, B., Spear, A.D.: Building Ontologies with Basic Formal Ontology, MIT Press (2015)
3. CUBRC: White Paper. An Overview of the Common Core Ontologies (2019)
4. Maathuis, C., Pieters, W., van den Berg, J.: Developing a cyber operations computational ontology. J. Inf. Warfare **17**(3), 32–49 (2018)

5. Casey, E., Barnum, S., Griffith, R., Snyder, J., Beek, H.V., Nelson, A.: The evolution of expressing and exchanging cyber-investigation information in a standardized form. In: Biasiotti, M., Mifsud Bonnici, J., Cannataci, J., Turchi, F. (eds) Handling and Exchanging Electronic Evidence Across Europe. Law, Governance and Technology Series, vol. 39. Springer, Cham (2018)
6. Oltramari, A., Cranor, L.F., Walls, R.J., Mcdaniel, P.: Building an ontology of cyber security. Semant. Technol. Intell. Defense Secur. **2014**, 54-61 (2014)
7. Martins, B.F., et al.: A framework for conceptual characterization of ontologies and its application in the cybersecurity domain. Softw. Syst. Model. **21**(4), 1437–1464 (2022). https://doi.org/10.1007/s10270-022-01013-0
8. Donohue, B., Jensen, M., Cox, A.P., Rudnicki, R.: A common core-based cyber ontology in support of cross-domain situational awareness. Defense Secur. (2018)
9. IEEE Cyber Ontology Working Group: Cyber Ontology Releases. IEEE Open Source. https://opensource.ieee.org/cyber-ontology-working-group/cyber-ontology-releases. Accessed 25 Feb 2024
10. Wade, L., Martell, C.: Baseline Standards for Formal Ontology within the Department of Defense and the Intelligence Community. Chief digital and artificial intelligence officer council members intelligence community chief data officer council members (2024)
11. Ceusters W. An information artifact ontology perspective on data collections and associated representational artifacts. *Stud Health Technol Inform*, pp. 68–72. PMID: 22874154. (2012)
12. Malone, J., et al.: The software ontology (SWO): a resource for reproducibility in biomedical data analysis, curation and digital preservation. J. Biomed. Semant. **5**, 25 (2014)
13. Morosoff, P., Rudnicki, R., Bryant, J., Farrell, R., Smith, B.: Joint doctrine ontology: a benchmark for military information systems interoperability. Semant. Technol. Intell. Defense Secur. (2015)
14. Mandrick, B., Smith, B.: Philosophical foundations of intelligence collection and analysis: a defense of ontological realism. Intell. Nat. Secur. **37**, 809–819 (2022)
15. Mandrick, B.: An ontological framework for understanding the terror-crime nexus. SOF Role Comb. Transnational Organized Crime 147–162 (2016)
16. Keet, C.M.: An Introduction to Ontology Engineering, ch. 6 (2018)
17. Keet, C.M.: An Introduction to Ontology Engineering, ch. 7 (2018)
18. Floridi, L.: The fight for digital sovereignty: what it is, and why it matters, especially for the EU. Philos. Technol. **33**, 369–378 (2020)
19. Floridi, L., Mariarosaraia, T.: The Ethics of Information Warfare. Springer (2014)
20. Scherenberg, F.V., Hellmeier, M., Otto, B.: Data sovereignty in information systems. Electron. Mark. **34**, 15 (2024)
21. De Colle, G., Hasanzadeh, A., Beverley, J.: Ontology development strategies and the infectious disease ontology ecosystem. In: International Conference on Biomedical Ontology (2023)

Personalized Query Engine Optimization for Link Traversal-Based Query Processing over Structured Decentralized Environments

Ruben Eschauzier(✉)

Ghent University - Imec, Ghent, Belgium
ruben.eschauzier@ugent.be

Abstract. The scale of decentralization envisioned for the presently centralized web requires querying approaches that can query numerous small data sources instead of a few large ones. Link Traversal-based Query Processing (LTQP) is a promising candidate for querying highly decentralized environments that executes queries with zero knowledge of the queried data and discovers data sources on the fly. However, as the engine does not know in advance what data will be queried, creating an optimized query plan before executing the query is challenging. Presently, LTQP is employed for client-side querying, where one engine instance services a single client. Despite this, current engines do not utilize client-specific engine query usage patterns to implement personalized query optimization algorithms. This paper will describe the proposed research approach for implementing personalized query optimization techniques, such as caching or learned query optimizers, for LTQP. The objective is to improve query optimization algorithms through the analysis of historical query engine usage, instead of depending on additional prior information. Personalized optimization will be based on existing work in SPARQL optimization literature and fundamental database theory, adapted to LTQP, and aimed at repeating their success in reducing query execution time. As a result, query engines will gain the capability to query large decentralized environments, enabling applications to function within this emerging decentralized web landscape.

1 Introduction

Currently, web user data is stored in centralized silos controlled by massive companies like Facebook, Google, and Amazon. These companies control the data generated by web users, restricting innovation [1]. Rather than adopting a 'vertical' approach where all user data from a single service is stored in one central location, various decentralization efforts [2, 3], advocate for a 'horizontal' approach. This approach disperses data, resulting in many smaller data entities. For instance, all data pertaining to an individual would be stored in a singular location. As a result, data becomes highly decentralized, spread over possibly millions of sources. Decentralized querying approaches must support cross-source queries, as, for example, social media applications frequently aggregate content from various users to construct a homepage. Initiatives like Solid use the Resource Description Framework (RDF) to store data in a machine-readable format. Traditional

A. Meroño Peñuela et al. (Eds.): ESWC 2024, LNCS 15345, pp. 64–73, 2025.
https://doi.org/10.1007/978-3-031-78955-7_7

SPARQL query algorithms are designed to query a singular RDF store, which is known beforehand. This approach is insufficient for decentralized environments, as there are multiple sources, and the number of sources is not known beforehand.

Federated SPARQL query algorithms [4, 5] are built to query a few large sources [6, 7] known ahead of time and do not support fine-grained access control. This is insufficient for decentralized environments comprising numerous, small, and highly personal data requiring access control. Instead, querying over these decentralized environments can be done by Link Traversal-based Query Processing (LTQP) [8]. LTQP is an integrated querying approach where the query engine dynamically discovers sources by following hyperlinks discovered in documents of previously dereferenced URIs. This approach allows for fine-grained access control, as an LTQP engine can ignore any document it cannot dereference and continue traversing to new documents. Furthermore, LTQP requires no prior knowledge of the location of data sources, as this is discovered on the fly.

Despite these advantages, LTQP still suffers from significant limitations [9], as discerning relevant from irrelevant data sources during query execution is difficult [10], and query planning without pre-computed statistics often produces suboptimal query plans. Current literature on LTQP considers each query as a separate event without considering the usage of shared engine state between query executions. However, LTQP is a client-side query approach where an engine instance exclusively services a single client. As seen in, for example, browser usage [11], clients exhibit patterns when using applications or browsing the internet. These patterns translate to observable patterns in the queries issued to the query engine. For example, users might primarily use a singular application, which only requires a subset of all data available in the decentralized ecosystem. Additionally, users form sub-communities [12] within applications, which can potentially induce sub-graphs of data that are more frequently accessed by members of the sub-community. Query engines should quantify these patterns and leverage them for significantly improved query optimization. When an engine has already seen a large portion of the data in previous queries, it can use previously computed answers, statistics, and indexes to improve query performance. To address this gap in research, *I will reformulate the query optimization problem from singular queries to a sequence of (possibly) correlated queries.* As such, query engines can apply personalized client-specific query optimizations based on the statistical properties of these patterns to improve average query sequence execution time.

2 State of the Art

First, existing approaches for LTQP optimization must be considered. Then, the following sections will discuss existing SPARQL optimization approaches that can be adapted for personalized LTQP optimization.

2.1 Optimizing LTQP

The literature on LTQP optimization aims to improve the execution plan of queries and the prioritization of query-relevant documents. Identifying query-relevant documents is relies on link prioritization algorithms, which aim to identify query-relevant documents and access them first. On the other hand, LTQP query planning relies on heuristics [13]. These heuristics, which use no prior knowledge, employ four rules to establish the evaluation order of operators. Firstly, they prioritize triple patterns with a designated seed document, except when the seed document represents vocabulary terms. Moreover, they favor query plans featuring filtering triple patterns in proximity to the seed triple pattern. Finally, they create an order where preceding triple patterns contain at least one query variable of the subsequent pattern.

While multiple algorithms [10] for link prioritization exist for the Open Linked Data Web, none show a definitive advantage over others. However, in structured decentralized environments like Solid, previous work [9], demonstrates improved query execution speed when leveraging structural information inherent to such environments.

These studies usually assume limited prior data knowledge. However, if our engine frequently queries the same dataset, the hypothesis is that leveraging prior knowledge obtained from previous query executions can boost query performance.

2.2 SPARQL Caching Strategies

In SPARQL, server-side caching optimizes query performance by storing and reusing computations [14, 15]. While caching entire query results is possible, most strategies focus on frequently encountered basic graph patterns (BGPs) [15]. These BGPs can substitute joins in query plans and influence join optimization [14]. Canonical labeling algorithms assign distinct labels to isomorphic BGPs, ensuring that all isomorphic BGPs receive equivalent labels [14]. Other server-side caching approaches [15] utilize data summaries to compute join reductions and cache these reductions rather than caching query results. Client-side caching aims to minimize requests to SPARQL endpoints by caching complete query results [16] and implementing proactive query fetching [17]. The efficacy of such strategies heavily depends on the cache hit rate. To decide which queries to prefetch, machine learning techniques predict probable subsequent queries based on the current query [16]. When the cache reaches capacity, cache eviction algorithms, such as Least Recently Used (LRU), remove the least recently requested entry.

2.3 Auxillary Data Structures

In this section, we'll briefly examine data structures used by query engines to optimize query plans. While these are typically precomputed offline, making them impractical for LTQP, caching and dynamically discovering them during LTQP query execution could allow the LTQP engine to use traditional SPARQL optimization strategies. Potential structures include:

- **Dataset summaries**, such as the Vocabulary of Interlinked Datasets (VoID) [18], describe statistical information of the underlying dataset. This information can include the number of triples, distinct subjects or predicates, and the occurrences of predicates.
- **Characteristic sets** [19], **which** define entities sharing the same predicate set present in the data. Characteristic sets are instrumental in estimating the cardinality of star-shaped joins, thereby enhancing join planning. These sets can be estimated using sampling techniques [20], reducing the cost of computing them.

- **Approximate Membership Functions (AMFs)**, which determine whether a dataset can potentially contain answers to a query. Examples of AMFs are Prefix-Partitioned Bloom Filters (PPBFs) [21] and the extended Semantically Partitioned Bloom Filters (SPBFs) [22].
- **Indexes**, which are utilized to accelerate the lookup of matching triples to triple patterns. Engines calculate different combinations of SPO indexes depending on their implementation.

2.4 Learned Optimizers

Recent literature on learned query optimizers in relational databases [23, 24] is gaining traction, utilizing reinforcement learning to train the optimizer. Queries are transformed into numeric vectors containing information crucial for query planning, with various featurization methods, such as one-hot encoding join predicates [25] or utilizing advanced graph neural networks on the query graph [23]. The next step involves greedily constructing a join plan to minimize predicted execution cost or latency. To predict latency, ReJOIN [25] employs a feed-forward neural network, while newer approaches use tree-based neural networks to handle the tree structure of join plans [23, 24]. The model is trained to minimize the difference between predicted and actual query latency or cost. While most approaches train optimizers from scratch, Bao [24] augments traditional optimizers by learning to select optimal query hints from a predefined set, reducing training costs significantly while improving over traditional optimizers. In the SPARQL query optimization literature, several cardinality estimation techniques [26] using machine learning are highly successful. Learned optimizers operate under the assumption that there is prior knowledge of the data to be queried, allowing models to be trained offline. However, in the case of an LTQP engine, the data queried is not known beforehand and dependent on the queries issued, rendering offline model training impractical. Thus, the model must learn optimization strategies dynamically as users actively issue queries.

3 Problem Statement and Contributions

Building upon the existing work in Sect. 2, this thesis will use personalized query optimization to overcome the performance issues outlined in Sect. 1. Personalized query optimization adapts the optimization procedure to the client-specific query usage patterns of the engine. As such, the engine will keep a state that stores optimization-relevant information. The hypothesis underlying this work is:

- **Hypothesis 1:** Personalized query engines can significantly improve query execution times compared to non-personalized query engines by leveraging client-specific query patterns to improve query optimization.

Before any work on personalized query optimization can proceed, real-world client query usage patterns must be identified. These patterns can include but are not limited to, application data requirements, query requirements for different applications, and data update frequency. After the identification of query patterns, they should be translated to an extensive benchmark that can validate the performance of personalized query optimization algorithms in real-world applications. As such, we define research question I.

- **RQ I:** How do client-specific query patterns manifest in real-world usage scenarios, and how can we accurately capture and represent them within a benchmark?

This thesis will explore two approaches to personalized optimization. The use of caching auxiliary data structures or (intermediate) results, and learned query optimizers. Two natural candidates for cached content are intermediate results sets for queries or auxiliary data structures that improve query planning. However, LTQP uses the *cMatch* criterion [27] *to* extract links to dereference, changing the queried data depending on what predicates are used in the query. Consequently, queries with overlapping sub-BGPs, but different sets of predicates will dereference different documents during query execution. As reusing the result set for the overlapping sub-BGPs of one query on another can generate wrong results, it is vital to evaluate the effectiveness of caching strategies under these conditions. These conditions lead to research questions I & III.

- **RQ II:** Can (intermediate) result caching be effectively utilized during Link Traversal-based Query Processing to enhance query execution performance when the queried subweb of data changes between queries?
- **RQ III:** How does caching auxiliary data structures during Link Traversal-based Query Processing impact the performance of query execution?

Our caching approaches will build upon and extend methods introduced in Sect. 2. The primary challenge to overcome in LTQP is the dynamic nature of the queried data, as it can differ between queries, influencing cache validity.

Finally, learned optimizers are a promising candidate for extracting query usage patterns from sequences of queries. Formulating the client query usage patterns as a data-generating process (DGP) and the queries as samples from this process, we can use learning methods to approximate this DGP. However, learning methods can be data and compute expensive and require exploring sub-optimal query plans to learn the entire optimization space. As learned optimizers will be trained in an online scenario where the client actively uses the engine, we must design any solutions with data and compute efficiency in mind. This gives us research questions IV & V:

- **RQ IV** Can training a query optimizer lead to improved query performance in Link Traversal-based Query Processing?
- **RQ V:** Does the query performance benefit of training a query optimizer during query execution outweigh the model training cost?

To answer these research questions, the proposed methods will build upon existing literature for learned cardinality and join plan estimation. From this foundation, data and compute efficiency approaches will be included to facilitate the usage of learned estimation for LTQP.

4 Research Methodology and Approach

The work in this thesis is divided into three packages. The first aims to answer **RQ I**, the second provides an answer to **RQ II & III**, and finally the third will investigate **RQ IV & V**.

4.1 Identification and Simulation of Client-Specific Query Usage Patterns

Evaluating the effectiveness of personalized query optimization algorithms requires a benchmark simulating real-world query patterns. To identify these patterns, the first step is a literature review on sub-communities in social media networks and the use of linked data in existing applications. This literature review will be used in the creation of a theoretical framework outlining various client query usage patterns in social media and linked data.

An existing benchmark, SolidBench [9], simulates a social network application's data that is fragmented to represent Solid data vaults. Extending SolidBench using the theoretical framework of client query usage patterns allows for simulated client-specific query sequences, representing real-world sub-communities and access patterns. The degree of fragmentation and separation between communities and the probability of within-community queries will be an adjustable parameter to enable the analysis of how varying degrees of client-specific query patterns influence personalized query optimization performance.

4.2 Caching in the Context of Link Traversal-Based Query Processing

While caching entire query results is straightforward, caching intermediate results in LTQP is complicated as the queried data changes depending on the query predicates. Intermediate result caches must be aware of the underlying documents that produced these results to allow the engine to identify over what data these intermediate results are valid and what data is not included in the cached results. To answer **RQ II**, an adaptive query planner that can adaptively change its execution plan to include intermediate results that are valid for the currently dereferenced documents is needed. Using cached intermediate results, we can reuse computation, quickly check document cache validity through ETags, and produce first results faster. This query planner will need to consider three cases. The first case is where the intermediate results contain results produced using undiscovered data. In this case, careful pruning of cache elements is required. Second, the cache can contain less data than discovered during query execution. In this case, the query planner should first use all valid intermediate results to quickly produce answers before including the additional data in the query execution to ensure result completeness. Finally, these two cases can occur simultaneously, which will require a combination of the solutions of the previous cases. The proposed query planner must be adaptive, as the validity of the cache can change as more documents are discovered.

For **RQ III**, an investigation into the effect of the data structures described in Subsect. 2.3 is required. Data structures like approximate membership functions, dataset summaries, and characteristic sets can be used to determine whether a document can produce answers to a given query. Documents that will never return results to the query can be pruned, reducing the queried data size and improving query execution times. Additionally, dataset summaries and characteristic sets can be used to improve cardinality estimation as they are discovered. This allows the engine to improve its query plan resulting in reduced computational complexity of the query. Finally, the possible upside of indexes is clear. Currently, these indexes are computed as the engine dereferences a document, which is computationally intensive. If the engine can reuse indexes from previous queries, we bypass the need to re-compute them.

The fundamental risks of all caching approaches are the overhead of maintaining the cache and the possibility of cache invalidation. If searching the cache for relevant entries is too computationally intensive and the cache hit rate is low, the engine will spend more time searching the cache than it saves using cache entries. To account for this risk, this thesis will first investigate caching approaches requiring the least complex cache keys, like document-based caching, or query result caching. After successfully applying the straightforward caching approaches complex tasks will be considered. For cache invalidation, we must account for the possibly rapidly changing data landscape in social media applications. However, even when many *new* posts are added, cached information for old and unchanged content remains valid and can improve query execution performance. Furthermore, even if the query is primarily over the subset of data that rapidly changes, caching the static content in social-media applications can inform the engine of their (ir)relevancy, reducing the queried data size and improving performance. To determine whether a cached entity is valid, we can use the ETag header or introduce data vault server-side data structures that indicate the last change to a resource.

4.3 Learned Query Optimization in Link Traversal-Based Query Processing

To answer **RQ IV**, personalized query engines need learned query optimization algorithms that work in an online setting since LTQP engines do not know what data they will query in advance. As such, any offline training algorithm that requires millions of training examples is infeasible. My previous work in SPARQL join order optimization [28] shows that while reinforcement learning-based join order optimization is promising, it is computationally expensive to train an optimizer from scratch. Instead, learned query optimization hint approaches [24, 29] train models that give hints to existing optimizers, like what join operator to use. These approaches require significantly less training time and are thus more suitable for online learning. To answer **RQ IV & V**, relational learned query optimization hints will be adapted for use in LTQP.

5 Evaluation Plan

The evaluation of this work will be done by implementing prototype algorithms on their own, or in combination with other prototypes.

- The prototypes will be built into a modular open-source LTQP query engine [5]. By implementing our approach as modules, other researchers can easily replicate and extend these approaches.
- The primary evaluation method is the benchmark introduced in Subsect. 4.1. The benchmark will simulate varying intensities of observed query patterns to determine the impact this has on performance. Further evaluation on different benchmarks will be included if valuable and compatible with LTQP.

The evaluation of query optimization performance will follow evaluation approaches of previous work on LTQP. In practice, the following metrics are often used as gauges of performance:

- **Query execution time**, indicating overall query execution efficiency.
- **First *k* result arrival times**, as LTQP is a streaming querying approach, producing first results quickly improves the client experience.
- **Diefficiency** [30], **measures** the efficiency of result arrival times during query execution. Engines that quickly produce many results are considered better.
- **Result completeness**, as any caching or document pruning strategy could introduce mistakes, result completeness will be verified and ensured during evaluation.

These metrics will be used to compare the state-of-the-art approaches for non-personalized LTQP optimization to our intended personalized optimization algorithms.

For further analysis of the caching approaches in Subsect. 4.2, cache hit rate and overhead will be investigated. The preceding metrics will provide a clear picture of the effectiveness of personalized query optimization for LTQP.

6 Preliminary Results

Initial work was primarily focused on the exploration of the literature around relational database optimization, SPARQL query optimization, caching theory, learned optimization, and more. Following an extensive literature review, the next step was an exploration of the problem space. To facilitate an understanding of LTQP, I produced an early-stage visualization tool of how LTQP engines explore the decentralized environments and an in-depth analysis of the document links discovered during query execution [31]. Moreover, I established a software framework to facilitate the subsequent implementation of LTQP optimization algorithms. This was achieved by enabling the engine to associate metadata with each triple processed during query execution.

7 Conclusion

In this thesis, the query optimization problem is reformulated as an optimization problem over a sequence of correlated queries. These correlations are hypothesized to occur due to client-specific query usage patterns during the usage of LTQP query engines. In this context, personalized query optimization can identify patterns in sequences of queries and use them to adapt the query optimization approach. This thesis aims to use caching and learned query optimizers to identify and leverage patterns in query sequences. As a result, LTQP engines will become more efficient without relying on pre-computed statistics and optimizations. The enhanced efficiency of LTQP engines will subsequently improve the responsiveness and practicality of decentralized applications, thus bringing a decentralized web one step closer.

Acknowledgements. The research for this work has been supported by SolidLab Vlaanderen (Flemish Government, EWI and RRF project VV023/10).

References

1. Verborgh, R.: A data ecosystem fosters sustainable innovation (2020)
2. Kuhn, T., Taelman, R., Emonet, V., Antonatos, H., Soiland-Reyes, S., Dumontier, M.: Semantic micro-contributions with decentralized nanopublication services. PeerJ Comput. Sci. **7**, e387 (2021)
3. Mansour, E., et al.: A demonstration of the solid platform for social web applications. In: WWW (2016)
4. Saleem, M., Potocki, A., Soru, T., Hartig, O., Ngomo, A.-C.N.: CostFed: cost-based query optimization for SPARQL endpoint federation. Procedia Comput. Sci. **137**, 163–174 (2018)
5. Taelman, R., Van Herwegen, J., Vander Sande, M., Verborgh, R.: Comunica: a modular SPARQL query engine for the web. In: ISWC. Springer (2018)
6. Dang, M.-H., Aimonier-Davat, J., Molli, P., Hartig, O., Skaf-Molli, H., Le Crom, Y.: FedShop: a benchmark for testing the scalability of SPARQL federation engines. In: ISWC. Springer (2023)
7. Qudus, U., Saleem, M., Ngonga Ngomo, A.-C., Lee, Y.-K.: An empirical evaluation of cost-based federated SPARQL query processing engines. Semantic Web. **12**, 843–868 (2021)
8. Hartig, O., Bizer, C., Freytag, J.-C.: Executing SPARQL queries over the web of linked data. In: ISWC (2009)
9. Taelman, R., Verborgh, R.: Link traversal query processing over decentralized environments with structural assumptions. In: ISWC (2023)
10. Hartig, O., Özsu, M.T.: Walking without a map: Ranking-based traversal for querying linked data. In: ISWC (2016)
11. Adar, E., Teevan, J., Dumais, S.T.: Large scale analysis of web revisitation patterns. In: SIGCHI conference on Human Factors in Computing Systems (2008)
12. Ferrara, E.: A large-scale community structure analysis in Facebook. EPJ Data Sci. **1**, 1–30 (2012)
13. Hartig, O.: Zero-knowledge query planning for an iterator implementation of link traversal based query execution. In: ESWC. Springer (2011)
14. Papailiou, N., Tsoumakos, D., Karras, P., Koziris, N.: Graph-aware, workload-adaptive SPARQL query caching. In: SIGMOD (2015)
15. Madkour, A., Aly, A.M., Aref, W.G.: Worq: workload-driven RDF query processing. In: ISWC (2018)
16. Zhang, W.E., Sheng, Q.Z., Yao, L., Taylor, K., Shemshadi, A., Qin, Y.: A learning-based framework for improving querying on web interfaces of curated knowledge bases. ACM Trans. Internet Technol. **18** (2018)
17. Zhang, W.E., Sheng, Q.Z., Qin, Y., Yao, L., Shemshadi, A., Taylor, K.: SECF: improving SPARQL querying performance with proactive fetching and caching. In: Annual ACM Symposium on Applied Computing (2016)
18. Alexander, K., Cyganiak, R., Hausenblas, M., Zhao, J.: Describing linked datasets with the VoID vocabulary (2011)
19. Neumann, T., Moerkotte, G.: Characteristic sets: accurate cardinality estimation for RDF queries with multiple joins. In: ICDE (2011)
20. Heling, L., Acosta, M.: Estimating characteristic sets for RDF dataset profiles based on sampling. In: ESWC (2020)
21. Aebeloe, C., Montoya, G., Hose, K.: Decentralized indexing over a network of RDF peers. In: ISWC (2019)
22. Aebeloe, C., Montoya, G., Hose, K.: The lothbrok approach for SPARQL query optimization over decentralized knowledge graphs. Semantic Web **14**, 1121–1165 (2022)

23. Yu, X., Li, G., Chai, C., Tang, N.: Reinforcement learning with tree-LSTM for join order selection. In: ICDE (2020)
24. Marcus, R., Negi, P., Mao, H., Tatbul, N., Alizadeh, M., Kraska, T.: Bao: making learned query optimization practical. In: SIGMOD (2021)
25. Marcus, R., Papaemmanouil, O.: Deep reinforcement learning for join order enumeration. In: Proceedings of the First International Workshop on Exploiting Artificial Intelligence Techniques for Data Management (2018)
26. Schwabe, T., Acosta, M.: Cardinality estimation over knowledge graphs with embeddings and graph neural networks. Proc. ACM Manag. Data **1**, 1–26 (2023)
27. Hartig, O., Freytag, J.-C.: Foundations of traversal based query execution over linked data. In: ACM Hypertext Conferenceand Social Media, pp. 43–52 (2012)
28. Eschauzier, R., Taelman, R., Morren, M., Verborgh, R.: Reinforcement learning-based SPARQL join ordering optimizer. In: ESWC (2023)
29. Woltmann, L., Thiessat, J., Hartmann, C., Habich, D., Lehner, W.: FASTgres: making learned query optimizer hinting effective. Proc. VLDB Endow **16**, 3310 (2023)
30. Acosta, M., Vidal, M.-E., Sure-Vetter, Y.: Diefficiency metrics: measuring the continuous efficiency of query processing approaches. In: ISWC (2017)
31. Eschauzier, R., Taelman, R., Verborgh, R.: How does the link queue evolve during traversal-based query processing? In: QuWeDa/MEPDaW@ ISWC, pp. 26–33 (2023)

GraphWiseLearn: Personalized Learning Through Semantified TEL, Leveraging QA-Enhanced LLM-Generated Content

Wolfgang Fahl[1,2](✉)

[1] RWTH Aachen University, Computer Science i5, Aachen, Germany
wf@bitplan.com
[2] BITPlan GmbH, Willich, Germany

Abstract. In today's educational landscape, from traditional schools to MOOC platforms, the prevalent model is a one-size-fits-all approach to learning content, often overlooking the unique needs and learning paces of individual students. This gap between the ideal personalized instruction by a team of personal trainers and the practicalities of standardization presents significant challenges, including diminished engagement and understanding. My PhD research proposes a Knowledge Graph-based application of core Technology Enhanced Learning (TEL) components, aiming to bridge this divide with a cost-effective method targeted to individual learning objectives and paths.

The core elements of the approach are structured around five key components: Knowledge Graphs (KGs), Large Language Models (LLMs), Flashcards, Visualization of Dynamic Competence Maps (DCMs), and a Quality Assurance (QA) review and feedback workflow.

The approach will collect empirical data on students needs and misconceptions which allow to apply learning analytics for continuous improvement of the learning material.

We hypothesize that this approach will provide a viable method for digitization and entering into a quality improvement cycle based on the rating results, offering a concrete solution for the transition from traditional learning materials.

Keywords: Technology Enhanced Learning · Knowledge Graphs · Large Language Models · Dynamic Competence Map

1 Introduction

The landscape of education and learning methodologies is undergoing a transformative shift with the integration of technological solutions. Traditional educational models often implement a standardized approach to learning, delivering the same material in a uniform manner to all students. This generalized strategy, while logistically straightforward, fails to accommodate the diverse and nuanced needs of individual learners. It overlooks the unique learning styles, pace, and backgrounds of students, resulting in a learning experience that may not fully

A. Meroño Peñuela et al. (Eds.): ESWC 2024, LNCS 15345, pp. 74–83, 2025.
https://doi.org/10.1007/978-3-031-78955-7_8

harness each student's potential. Shemshack's comprehensive analysis of personalized learning components [15] shows the general potential of such approaches as they may be found in current scientific literature.

In response to these challenges, our research introduces a novel combination of KG and TEL approaches designed to provide a personalized learning experience by tailoring educational content to individual needs.

Five key components are applied: Knowledge Graphs (KGs), Large Language Models (LLMs), Flashcards, Visualization of Dynamic Competence Maps (DCMs), and a Quality Assurance (QA) review and feedback workflow.

At the heart of this framework is a knowledge graph capturing the learning content. A semi-automatic semantification of learning content from various sources-such as PowerPoint slides, PDFs, and plain texts-is employed to populate the knowledge graph, emphasizing alignment with specific learning goals. The complexity of this KG, with a hierarchical representation of a Competence Tree as the leading structure, is mitigated by visualizing the learning progress using Dynamic Competence Maps (DCMs). Individual learning paths aligned with the learning goals are provided by using Language Model-generated (LLM) flashcards and assessments. The assessments enable decisions about the most effective learning content to be offered next. This combination not only enables a personalized learning journey but also ensures that the content is dynamically aligned with each learner's progress and understanding. Since LLM-generated content may still be of poor quality at the current state of the art, a quality assurance workflow is applied, involving cost-effective human interaction through a star-rating approach.

The subsequent sections of this paper will outline the architecture of our proposed framework, the methodology employed to curate and structure educational content into a knowledge graph, and the interactive learning platform that leverages Large Language Models (LLMs) for content generation and assessment-feedback cycles. We will explore the effectiveness of this approach through empirical research, aiming to validate our hypothesis that such a personalized, technology-enhanced learning model provides a viable path from traditional learning approaches to a continuous improvement, TEL-based approach while maintaining or improving outcomes, motivation, satisfaction, and overall learning experience.

2 State of the Art

Technology Enhanced Learning: Justin Reich argues in *Failure to Disrupt* [13] that despite the potential of Technology Enhanced Learning tools[1] such as Massive Online Courses (MOOCs) [14], Learning Management Systems (LMS), Adaptive Learning Technologies, Flipped Classrooms, Educational Games and Gamification, Personalized Learning, Online Peer Tutoring, Collaboration Platforms, Automated Scoring and Feedback Tools these technologies alone cannot significantly improve learning outcomes without addressing deeper systemic

[1] https://cr.bitplan.com/index.php/TEL_approaches.

issues in education. Continuous Improvement (CI) principles, specifically the DMAIC (Define, Measure, Analyze, Improve, Control) methodology, are presented by Carnovale et al. [3] as a necessary approach for the pedagogical assessment of online learning programs, potentially addressing the limitations highlighted by Reich.

Learning Taxonomies and Ontologies: Defining clear learning goals is foundational to all learning activities. Learning taxonomies proposed by Miller, Bloom, and Anderson and Krathwohl [1,2,11] provide a structured approach to this. Heist et al. [7] introduce a competency ontology aimed at competency management in rapidly evolving fields such as AI, utilizing knowledge graphs for better integration and scalability.

Flashcard Learning and Zettelkasten: Heinrich Schliemann's method evolved into the flashcard technique, further refined by Sebastian Leitner [9] to employ spaced repetition for efficient memorization. Research by Malashenko et al. [10] validates the effectiveness of digital flashcard systems in improving learning effectiveness.

Personalized Learning Paths: The work of Durand, Belacel, and LaPlante [4] on using graph theory to recommend personalized learning paths addresses the sequential and dependent nature of learning materials. Learning styles based on Experience Learning Theory (ELT) are explored by Bo Heffler [6], highlighting the importance of aligning educational approaches to individual learning preferences.

Personal Knowledge Graph. E. Ilkou discusses the development and evaluation of Personal Knowledge Graphs (PKGs) in e-learning platforms [8], demonstrating their potential to enhance learning by linking user activities to broader knowledge graphs for personalized content delivery. It outlines future research directions, including privacy enhancements and integration with semantic technologies to provide personalized educational recommendations and more interactive learning experiences.

Yang's PKG (Personal Knowledge Graph) [17] approach for recommendations is not considered state-of-the-art anymore with the rise of large language models (LLMs) because it requires extensive collection and manual structuring of entities and relationships specific to individual users, a process that is resource-intensive and less scalable. In contrast, LLMs can dynamically generate personalized recommendations by understanding and processing vast amounts of data across contexts, providing more flexibility and efficiency without the need for pre-constructed user-specific graphs.

Dynamic Competence Maps: The term "Kompetenzbilanz" (Skills/Competency balance) has been introduced in 2003 by Erler [5]. Triebel wrote his PhD thesis on "Kompetenzbilanzierung" [16]. According to Preißer and Völzke [12] competency assessment in adult education inconsistently applies definitions, Methods, varying from descriptions and observations to measurements, may occur in real-time ("in actu") or retrospectively, and range from standardized to qualitative, often based on self or external evaluations, prioritizing usability, practicability and cost over precise validity. Dynamic Competence Maps capture individual competency balance results over time and allow to visualize these as a skills wheels or radar charts.

LLM Generated Learning Material: Yue Yin's thesis [18] demonstrates the capability of LLMs like ChatGPT4 to create individualized learning content, despite limitations in semantic richness and accuracy, marking a step forward in the application of AI in education.

3 Problem Statement and Contributions

Our research is centered on addressing the lack of personalization and adaptability in traditional learning environments. The one-size-fits-all approach, prevalent in most educational systems, fails to consider individual differences in learning styles, pace, and background knowledge, leading to suboptimal educational outcomes.

Technology Enhanced Learning (TEL) approaches are not living up to their promises yet. A viable approach for the transition from traditional learning approaches to digitization, continuous improvement and personalized learning is needed.

3.1 Research Hypothesis

We hypothesize that the integration of five core elements will enhance the learning process in a cost/benefit effective way.

These elements include:

1. Knowledge Graphs,
2. Visualizations of Dynamic Competence Maps (DCMs) as tools for progress tracking,
3. Language Model-generated flashcards and assessments,
4. Flashcard-style learning, and
5. QA review and feedback implemented through a star rating system.

3.2 Research Questions

The following research questions guide our investigation:

- **RQ1:** What changes in the cost/benefit ratio occur with the introduction of LLM-generated content that is quality-enhanced through a cost/benefit optimizing workflow, as outlined in Sect. 3.3?
- **RQ2:** How does providing individualized and adaptive learning paths based on such assessments, as proposed, affect the learning experience of individual learners?
- **RQ3:** What insights and quality improvement approaches are possible based on the empirical data that is gathered using this approach?

3.3 Contributions

The novel idea of our research is to combine well-known TEL approaches, such as Personalized Learning, Learning Management Systems, and Adaptive Learning Technologies, with LLMs in a cost/benefit and quality-optimizing way. Our research aims to make the following contributions to the fields of the Semantic Web and technology-enhanced learning:

Semi-automated Semantification of Learning Content The RWTH Aachen University i5 chair for Database and Information Systems (DBIS) Lecture Sem antic Mediawiki[2] demonstrates the principle of taking input from PowerPoint and enriching it with metadata that enables cross-linking learning content. This Semantic Mediawiki contains the learning content of the lecture as a knowledge graph. The semantified form of the lecture has been curated from PowerPoint presentations, Moodle content, and a spreadsheet that provides metadata such as links between the items:

- 8 Presentation Pages derived from the original PowerPoint material files
- 11 Chapters derived from the 11 lecture sessions
- 550 Slide pages derived from the PowerPoint slides
- 95 Learning Goal pages
- 169 Keyword pages
- 26 Publication pages

The core entities are represented by the Semantic Mediawiki Concepts Presentation, Chapter, Slide, Learning Goal, Keyword, and Publication, which capture the metadata attributes and relations of the learning content and are computer-readable and queryable.

Dynamic Competence Map Visualization. The visualization of learning progress is often achieved using Skills Wheels[3] or Radar Charts. The Dynamic Competence Maps (DCM) Visualization as depicted in Fig. 1 has been implemented as part of the BMBF-funded TrainSpot2 project (Grant 16INB2062B) in the dcm GitHub[4] open-source project to supply both visualizations in SVG format based on computer-readable Syllabus and Learner Achievement inputs. This visualization is used for progress feedback of individual learners and for maintaining a flashcard-style trace of learning content items already visited. The frequency of repetition is initially adjusted to the learners' self-assessment and, with each assessment, adapted to their performance.

LLM-Generated Personalized Learning and Assessment Content. A first step is collecting learners' individual background details with a few interview questions about their current role, educational background, prior knowledge, expectations, and aspired achievements. Combining this personal background information with the learning material knowledge graph allows supplying the learner

[2] http://dbis-vl.wikidata.dbis.rwth-aachen.de/index.php/Main_Page.
[3] https://wiki.bitplan.com/index.php/Skills_Wheel.
[4] https://github.com/WolfgangFahl/dcm.

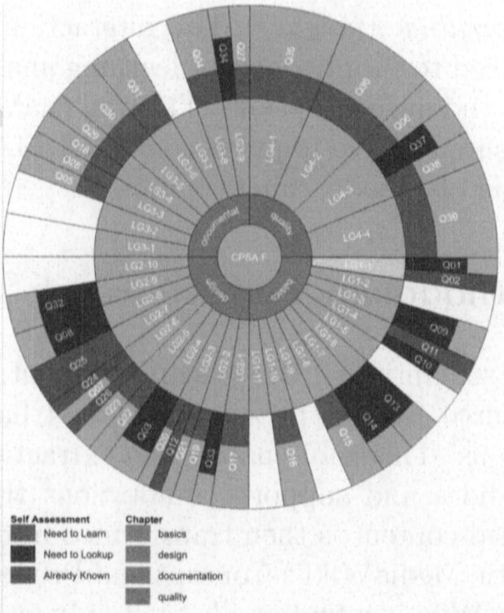

Fig. 1. Dynamic Competence Map Visualization

with individualized content generated by an LLM based on this input. A small ChatGPT-4 experiment[5] showcases the potential.

Cost/Benefit Optimized Content Quality Assessment Workflow. The diagram in Fig. 2 illustrates the workflow of the star rating system with peer review used for assuring and improving the quality of the learning content. The roles LLM, Learner, Assistant and Teacher are assigned different rating rights based on the assumed cost involved with each role.

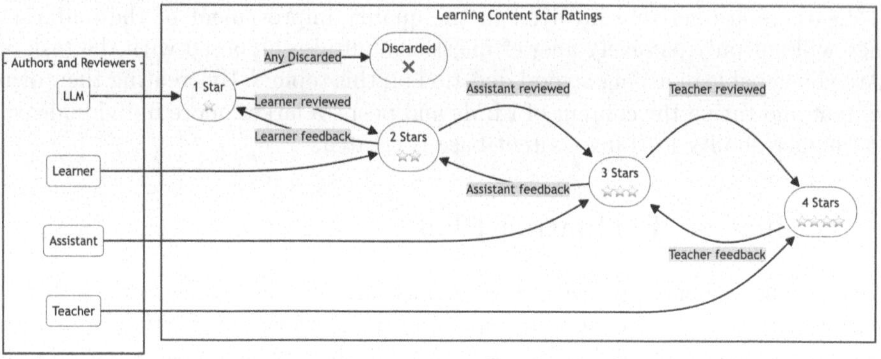

Fig. 2. Star Rating System with Peer Review Workflow (UML State diagram)

[5] https://cr.bitplan.com/index.php/Workdocumentation_2024-02-02.

Empirical Data for Learning Analytics. The interaction of students with the TEL system will be traced to supply data for learning analytics, focusing on students' individual needs and misconceptions. This will enable continuous improvement (CI)/define-measure-analyze-improve-control (DMAIC) quality improvement cycles to be applied to the learning content.

4 Research Methodology and Approach

The first step involves semantifying the teaching content. For this purpose, the Python-based open-source project pySemanticSlides[6] has been developed for PowerPoint presentations. This tool enables the extraction of text and graphics from PowerPoint slides and supports annotations that provide additional metadata. The extracted content is then transformed into Semantic MediaWiki pages, utilizing Semantic MediaWiki's Concept and Property elements to form a Knowledge Graph. The Wiki is intentionally read-only and is not open for direct student use. Instead, frontends are applied.

One frontend collects personal background data from learners, such as their role, previous education, current environment, prior knowledge, expectations, and interests. It then provides a visual representation of a Dynamic Competence Map (DCM), assessing the learner's current knowledge level. Leveraging this input, an LLM-based interactive learning platform enhances the richly linked wiki content. Using the "Zettelkasten" method, the LLM generates individualized quiz cards, exam questions, and exercises based on standard material, tailored to the learner's background and current knowledge as tracked by the DCM visualization.

A second frontend delivers the actual learning experience by monitoring navigation through content links and offering self-assessments and repetition based on the learner's path.

Learners are actively involved in the quality improvement of the material-they will not only passively answer questions but also be posed with the task of "Are you capable of asking a good question on this topic?". By creating their own content and rating the content of LLMs and peers, a larger, more individualized, and higher-quality learning content base is created.

5 Evaluation/Evaluation Plan

Engagement Evaluation: We intend to measure learner engagement with the platform. Metrics will include time spent on the platform, interaction rates with the learning materials, and progression through the Dynamic Competence Maps in comparison with the self-assessment results. A focus will be on identifying misconceptions and clustering groups of learners with similar individual needs.

Learning Outcomes: Although we acknowledge the challenges highlighted by Reich in measuring significant objective differences between traditional methods

[6] https://github.com/WolfgangFahl/pySemanticSlides.

and technology-enhanced learning solutions, we intend to interview learners to gather insights into how they perceive the impact of our framework on their motivation, satisfaction, and overall learning experience.

The systems under development shall be scientifically evaluated in the RWTH Aachen i5 course database and information systems, with volunteers recruited from some 600 students per semester. As the chief trainer of BITPlan GmbH and initiator of the International Software Architecture Qualification Board (iSAQB) e.V.[7], the author intends to propose the application of the DCM feedback mechanism to that association. The iSAQB e.V. is responsible for the syllabus "Certified Professional for Software Architecture (CPSA-F)." There is a strict separation of responsibility in the certification workflow between syllabus creation, training, and certification, which are done by independent organizations - therefore, the members' meeting needs to decide on this move. Participants of CPSA-F trainings may be offered access to the system and interviewed, depending on the acceptance of the proposal.

6 Results

At this stage, only preliminary results are available, which demonstrate the technical feasibility of the GraphWiseLearn approach. For example, the wiki content has been cross-checked to ensure the integrity of the provided metadata and content aligns with the original learning material. The Cross-check results[8] show 20 deviations out of over 2000 checks that have been performed, indicating a much higher consistency than would have been the case with manual curation.

The KG based approach for the learning material has been proven to be effective for some 750 participants of software architecture trainings in the past. The main advantage being the straightforward connection between learning goals, learning content, and self-assessment elements such as quiz cards.

In one of the author's software architecture trainings, ten participants used a self-assessment tool that is based on the DCM visualization. During the training, the focus on learning goals with statistical relevance was well received.

7 Conclusions/Lessons Learned

In Summer Semester 2022 the semantified DBIS Lecture has been offered as a learning tool for students for the first time. There has been no scientific evaluation during that semester. Since their was no frontend the individual interactions of the students could not be traced.

Traditionally, teaching resources, including slides, videos, exercises, and exams, constitute a stable fund of material. While the foundational content remains relatively constant, exercises and exams require regular updates to stay relevant for each new lecture iteration.

[7] https://www.isaqb.org.

[8] http://dbis-vl.wikidata.dbis.rwth-aachen.de/index.php/List_of_Checks.

Our approach offers a viable way to shift towards knowledge graph-based digitization, thereby enabling the application of technology-enhanced learning.

This transition facilitates the dynamic evolution of educational content by leveraging empirical data on student needs and misconceptions, which was previously unattainable.

Integrating content and assessments generated by Large Language Models (LLMs) with crowd-sourced human review cycles offers a promising strategy. This method establishes a continuous cycle of improvement for training materials, enabling the iterative refinement of teaching content based on actionable insights gained from learner interactions. This route promises a cost-effective way of personalizing teaching with a much larger fund of material targeted at the needs and misconceptions of learners.

References

1. Anderson, L.W., et al.: A Taxonomy for Learning, Teaching, and Assessing. Pearson, Upper Saddle River (2000)
2. Bloom, B.S. (ed.): Taxonomie von Lernzielen im kognitiven Bereich, 5th edn. Beltz Studienbuch, Julius Beltz, Weinheim, Germany (1976)
3. Carnovale, S., Allen, C., Pullman, M., Wong, D.: Using continuous improvement in online program design: DMAIC as a tool for assurance of learning assessments. Decis. Sci. J. Innov. Educ. **14**(2), 128–153 (2016). https://doi.org/10.1111/dsji.12094
4. Durand, G., Belacel, N., LaPlante, F.: Graph theory based model for learning path recommendation. Inf. Sci. **251**, 10–21 (2013). https://doi.org/10.1016/j.ins.2013.04.017
5. Erler, W., Gerzer-Saß, A., Nußhart, C., Saß, J.: Die kompetenzbilanz - ein instrument zur selbsteinschätzung und beruflichen entwicklung. In: Erpenbeck, J., Rosenstiel, L.V. (eds.) Handbuch Kompetenzmessung, pp. 339–352. Schäffer-Poeschel Verlag, Stuttgart (2003)
6. Heffler, B.: Individual learning style and the learning style inventory. Educ. Stud. **27**(3), 307–316 (2001). https://doi.org/10.1080/03055690120076583
7. Heist, N., Haase, P.: Flexible and extensible competency management with knowledge graphs. In: Seneviratne, O., Pesquita, C., Sequeda, J., Etcheverry, L. (eds.) Proceedings of the ISWC 2021 Posters, Demos and Industry Tracks: From Novel Ideas to Industrial Practice co-located with 20th International Semantic Web Conference (ISWC 2021), Virtual Conference, 24–28 October 2021. CEUR Workshop Proceedings, vol. 2980. CEUR-WS.org (2021). https://ceur-ws.org/Vol-2980/paper412.pdf
8. Ilkou, E.: Personal knowledge graphs: use cases in e-learning platforms. In: Companion Proceedings of the Web Conference 2022, WWW 2022. ACM, April 2022. https://doi.org/10.1145/3487553.3524196
9. Leitner, S.: So lernt man lernen. Herder Spektrum, Verlag Herder, Freiburg, Germany, 18th edn., February 2011
10. Malashenko, G.T., et al.: A digital model of full-cycle training based on the Zettelkasten and interval repetition system. Emerg. Sci. J. **7**, 1–15 (2023). https://doi.org/10.28991/esj-2023-sied2-01

11. Miller, G.E.: The assessment of clinical skills/competence/performance. Acad. Med. **65**(9), S63-7 (1990). https://doi.org/10.1097/00001888-199009000-00045
12. Preißer, R., Völzke, R.: Kompetenzbilanzierung - hintergründe, verfahren, entwicklungsnotwendigkeiten. REPORT Zeitschrift für Weiterbildungsforschung **2007**(1), 62–71 (2007). http://www.die-bonn.de/id/3549. Accessed 14 Feb 2024
13. Reich, J.: Failure to Disrupt. Harvard University Press, London (2022)
14. Reich, J., Ruipérez-Valiente, J.A.: The MOOC pivot. Science **363**(6423), 130–131 (2019). https://doi.org/10.1126/science.aav7958
15. Shemshack, A., Kinshuk, Spector, J.M.: A comprehensive analysis of personalized learning components. J. Comput. Educ. **8**(4), 485–503 (2021). https://doi.org/10.1007/s40692-021-00188-7
16. Triebel, C.: Kompetenzbilanzierung als psychologische Intervention: Wirkfaktoren und Wirkprinzipien in Laufbahnberatung und Coaching. Dissertation, Universität der Bundeswehr München, Munich, Germany (2009). https://d-nb.info/999369652/34, Doktors der Philosophie (Dr. phil.)
17. Yang, Y., Lin, J., Zhang, X., Wang, M.: PKG: a personal knowledge graph for recommendation. In: Proceedings of the 45th International ACM SIGIR Conference on Research and Development in Information Retrieval, SIGIR 2022. ACM (2022). https://doi.org/10.1145/3477495.3531671
18. Yin, Y.: Integration of a Moodle Chatbot into Online Courses utilizing State-of-the-Art NLP Techniques. Bachelorarbeit, Advisor: Alexander Tobias Neumann, RWTH Aachen University, Aachen (2023). https://publications.rwth-aachen.de/record/977904, Bachelorarbeit, RWTH Aachen University, 2023

AIREG: Enhanced Educational Recommender System with Large Language Models and Knowledge Graphs

Fatemeh Fathi(✉)

RWTH Aachen University, Aachen, Germany
fathi@dbis.rwth-aachen.de

Abstract. In the nowadays modern digital era, the overwhelming amount of available online data has established challenges for individuals seeking personalized educational and career pathways with relevant skill dependencies, especially when surfing e-learning and online recruitment platforms. This challenge emphasizes the need for novel advancements in knowledge-enhanced Recommender Systems, offering more personalized, accurate, and timely recommendations. Recently, the rapid development of Large Language Models (LLMs) with their broad knowledge and complex reasoning skills, has significantly enhanced the ability of these systems to offer precise and knowledge-based suggestions. It highlights their potential to enrich these systems using their vast amount of knowledge and sophisticated reasoning capabilities, to leverage them as an alternative to structured knowledge bases like knowledge graphs (KGs). However, LLMs have still limitations for knowledge-based content generation, especially when it's a domain-specific case. To address this issue, researchers propose to enhance the system with explicit factual knowledge from KGs. This research aims to explore advanced technological developments in knowledge-enhanced conversational Recommender Systems to propose a novel system, named **AIREG** for the educational and career development sectors.

Keywords: Recommender System · Large Language Model · Knowledge Graph · Knowledge Extraction

1 Introduction

In the evolving educational technology landscape, with the rapid expansion of digital education and career development, Recommender Systems plays a vital role in providing relevant and personalized learning materials and career pathways [13]. For instance, consider a scenario where a learner is exploring topics in software development for upskilling or reskilling according to their current resume and some additional background information they provide through an interaction with the system to find a suitable learning or career path. Traditional Recommender Systems mostly recommend resources based on their popularity or keyword matching and rely on conventional machine-learning techniques [22]. These systems often provide general recommendations that may not be aligned

A. Meroño Peñuela et al. (Eds.): ESWC 2024, LNCS 15345, pp. 84–93, 2025.
https://doi.org/10.1007/978-3-031-78955-7_9

with the unique interests or demands of the user since they fail to take into account the semantics of user interactions or current available educational and job opportunities.

The rapid evolution of the job market and the increasing demand for digital and online learning platforms, digital certificates and online submitting documents, all pose significant challenges in career development, necessitating effective and standard methods [10]. However, current Recommender Systems fall short of dynamically integrating structured data such as interactions data, about evolving education opportunities, career paths, and individual user profiles. This limitation prevents personalized, proactive career guidance and educational recommendations, emphasizing the need for an advanced approach that combines the capabilities of Large Language Models (LLMs) and knowledge Graphs (KGs), with user's profile and their interaction data to enhance Recommender Systems' effectiveness in navigating the complexities of career advancement and continuous learning. This gap emphasizes the importance of developing innovative approaches that leverage the latest advancements in artificial intelligence (AI).

The emergence of LLMs and KGs, and their integration into Recommender Systems, can significantly improve the accuracy and relevance of educational recommendations. LLMs, with their deep understanding of context and user-generated content [2], along with KGs that provide a semantic web of interconnected data, can significantly enhance the personalization and accuracy of recommendations delivered to users. However, many current approaches consider KGs as static entities, unable to update their knowledge base dynamically [6].

The combination of LLMs and KGs unlocks these limitations. In addition to providing a deep understanding of natural language, user intentions, and preferences, LLMs can provide structured data from unstructured one. On the other hand, KGs will validate and check the feasibility of the extracted information through their reasoning ability. This integration enables Recommender Systems to not only understand the latent and nuanced educational needs of learners but also to align their needs with the most appropriate educational material and resources based on the learner's learning journey and style [17]. Meanwhile, integrating other AI approaches such as Generative adversarial networks (GANs) models improves the system's performance significantly [20]. Together, these technologies empower the system to provide recommendations that are not only personalized but also aligned with the latest developments in education and industry. However, integrating these technologies to develop an effective Recommender System poses significant challenges, including the dynamic updating of KGs with real-time data, optimizing user interaction data for more relevant recommendations, and ensuring the system's adaptability to diverse user needs and market conditions. In this study, we focus on both educational and career domains due to the interconnected nature of these domains. Hence, we propose the *AIREG* designed for both domains. This dual focus of the system represents the system's ability to adapt and provide in-line recommendations with both learning objectives and long-term career goals.

This research aims to explore these challenges and propose a novel Recommender System framework that makes the way easy for people to choose their educational and career paths, improving accessibility, individualization, and alignment with the changing labor market for career growth and lifelong learning. Section introduces the proposed Recommender System, *AIREG*, which combines the AI capabilities of LLMs with KGs.

The rest of the paper is organized as follows: Sect. 2 introduces the background and related works to provide insights into the integration of Recommender Systems with LLMs and KGs, and explores the enhanced educational Recommender Systems (AIREG), designed especially in education. Section 3 defines the problem and outlines the contributions of this research. Section 4 delves into the methodology, detailing the innovative approaches and technologies employed. Section 5 presents our experimental evaluation plan and metrics to assess the effectiveness of the proposed system. Finally, Sect. 6 summarizes the proposed approach, and provides insights into our plan for this Ph.D. thesis.

2 State of the Art

Since the topic covers a broad range of subtopics and studies, we organize this section by going firstly through KG construction studies. Then we introduce key point papers on integrating LLMs with KGs. One step forward, we explore conducted studies on integrating KGs and LLMs for recommendation tasks. As the last step, we review some key papers using mentioned advanced approaches in the educational and career pathways and resource recommendations.

In the KG construction area, recent studies explored novel approaches for creating KGs from massive unstructured data sources using machine learning and NLP techniques. For instance, [8] used advanced NLP approaches to structure scholarly subject information into knowledge graphs, providing the groundwork for context-aware recommendation systems. Similarly, [15] introduced Text2kgbench, a benchmark for evaluating ontology-driven KG generation from text. Another study by [11] demonstrates the potential of web mining techniques to extract valuable insights from German Labor online resources to provide a rich source of real-time data to construct up-to-date KG through provided APIs.

Nevertheless, while LLMs are performing very well in understanding and processing natural language and mimicking human behavior, they still have issues in recalling some facts while generating knowledge-based contents [21]. To bridge this gap, the integration of LLMs with KGs emerged as a promising approach. Recent studies such as the one conducted by [18] present an overview of integrating LLMs and KGs, which can be considered as a groundwork for the new generation of AI-driven educational tools to provide more accurate, dynamic, and personalized recommendations. They propose a road map in which they discuss how to utilize the combination capabilities of LLMs and KGs for improved inference, knowledge representation, and reasoning. These systems aim to use the extensive knowledge encoded in LLMs and explicit relations in KGs to enhance

Recommender Systems' performance [19]. Furthermore, a comparative analysis of knowledge injection methodologies for LLMs in the scholarly domain conducted by [7] demonstrated that the knowledge injection improves content suggestion accuracy. In a study by [4], the authors demonstrated that using LLMs, such as ChatGPT, they can generate text from KG data, which shows the ability of LLMs to convert structured knowledge into human-readable text. Also, an experiment conducted by [14], investigates how LLMs, such as ChatGPT, can facilitate KGEs by contributing to the development and management of KGs.

Moreover, The incorporation of recent advanced techniques such as Retrieval-Augmented Generation (RAG) approaches, as surveyed by [23], has shown significant results in augmenting LLMs' content generation with structured KG and their information retrieval ability, and improving the personalization and relevancy of recommendations. The development of explainable Recommender Systems using KGs to provide transparency in the recommendation process is also gaining attraction in this research area. Such systems help users understand the reason behind recommendations, which increases their trust and engagement with the system. A study by [5], explores the development of Recommender Systems that utilize KGs to enhance the explainability of their recommendations. They also discuss how KGs can be effectively used to improve the trustworthiness and acceptance of Recommender Systems by users through better explainability. According to this article, by integrating KGs, the system can provide users with clear and logical reasons for its suggestions, which makes the recommendation process more transparent and understandable.

A recent study by [21], proposed the idea of integrating explicit factual knowledge from KGs into pre-trained LLMs (PLMs), which led to the creation of KG-enhanced large language models (KGLLMs). The study also investigates the integration of LLMs into Automatic Speech Recognition (ASR) systems to improve transcription accuracy. Another study conducted by [12], proposes the CHAT-REC framework, an LLM-Augmented Recommender System, which converts user profiles and historical interactions into prompts to enable in-context learning and improve the performance of the system. CHAT-REC also manages cold-start scenarios with new items through prompt-based injection of information into LLMs.

In the education and e-learning domain, [3] proposes the development of a system that improves e-learning experiences by helping students discover courses that match their interests and academic needs more effectively. The development of explainable Recommender Systems using KGs to provide transparency in the recommendation process is also gaining attraction in this research area. A further step forward in the educational domain is the development of KGs and Recommender Systems for suggesting reskilling and upskilling options aligned with the Career domain. An experiment by [20] explores the development of KGs and Recommender Systems to assist individuals in identifying online possibilities for reskilling and upskilling. The RS can offer personalized learning pathways based on users' skill gaps and career goals. A study conducted by [1], proposes a multi-objective fused personalized recommendations for educational resources to improve recommendations' diversity and accuracy. The system employs a recommendation layer including SOM-CNN and ITEM-SOM models to provide a recommendation list based on learner users' presentation features and education resources' representation features. To improve the user experience by providing more relevant and varied educational content, this approach represents a significant advancement in recommending personalized educational resources.

3 Problem Statement and Contributions

This thesis aims to explore and address the challenges of effectively integrating several advanced technologies, such as LLMs, KGs, and Generative adversarial networks (GANs), to provide more enhanced recommendations for both educational pathways and job market opportunities. By leveraging the capability of KGs for structured knowledge representation, LLMs for their natural language processing and deep understanding and content generation abilities, and GANs for simulating and predicting job market trends, in this study we propose the AIREG recommender system which provides personalized, accurate, and timely recommendations.

3.1 Research Questions

To explore and investigate the defined problem and its challenges, this research will focus on addressing the following research questions:

RQ1: Does the integration of external knowledge bases such as KGs enhance the performance of LLM-based Recommender Systems in providing personalized recommendations for employees and learners, while ensuring a high level of personalization and accuracy?

RQ2: What methodologies could be deployed to dynamically update KGs and LLMs with real-time job market data and user interactions?

RQ3: How can AIREG leverage user feedback to dynamically refine and enhance the personalization and accuracy of recommendations?

3.2 Main Contributions

The main contribution of this research is the integration of cutting-edge technologies, such as KGs, LLMs, and GANs within the semantic web framework to implement a highly adaptive recommender system, named AIREG, tailored for both career and educational pathways. Furthermore, to be aligned with the European regulatory standards, we aim to leverage detailed regional structures and domain-specific competencies by integrating the German Labor Market KG through a study conducted by [11]. With this approach, our system aims to overcome the limitations of the ESCO-as a European classification of skills, competencies, and Qualifications[1]- based recommender systems in this research area. We hypothesize that this integration not only enhances the system's ability to provide personalized and accurate recommendations but also introduces a dynamic framework for continuously updating the system with real-time job market and educational data.

4 Methodology

In this section, we delve into the details of the proposed AIREG system and its components. As shown in Fig. 1, AIREG has the following five main components:

1. **User profile enhancement:** To complete and improve the quality of the user's resumes, we utilize a prompting approach leveraging the LLM's knowledge and ability in natural language processing based on the [10] benchmark. With some adjustments in their approach, we also establish two different ways to enhance user's resume as follows:
   - **Interactive resume completion** To enhance the quality of the user's resume, we use both the user's self-description text as their resume and some additional background information by selecting some additional skills via a provided skill list associated with the European regulations like GLMO [9]. We leverage the LLM with a designed prompt associated

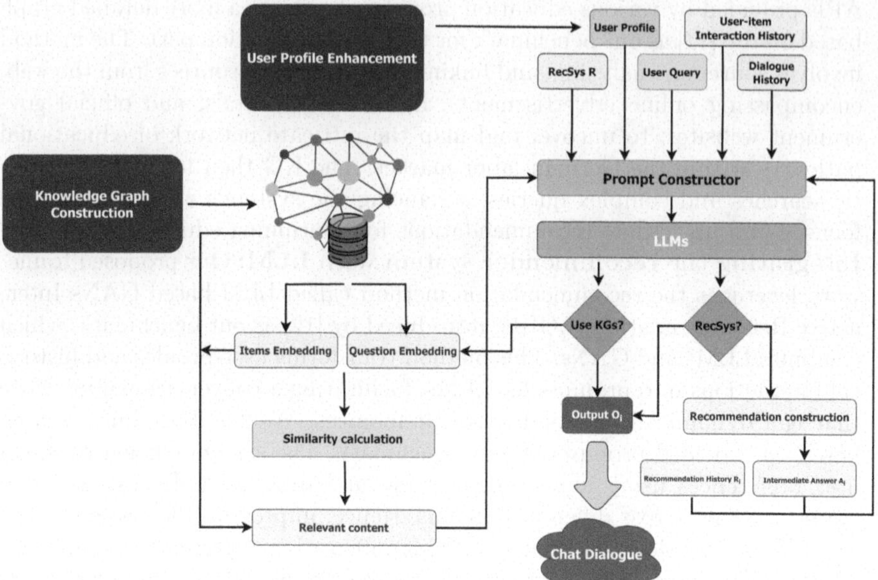

Fig. 1. The architectural design of the AIREG system

[1] https://esco.ec.europa.eu/en.

with the recommendation field to provide educational or job-related recommendations based on the user's resume and the additional background information provided by the user. Utilizing the interactive behavior of the user through providing additional background information, we aim to alleviate the fabricated and hallucinated generation of LLMs. In this approach, we also aim to fill gaps and suggest additions or improvements in the user's resume that are compatible with current industry standards.
 - **Resume quality alignment (GANs-based model)** To improve the representations of low-quality resumes, we'll make use of a GAN model based on the [10] benchmark to align low-quality generated resumes with high-quality ones by improving the representations of low-quality resumes. However, this benchmark considers a wrong assumption which indicates few-shot and many-shot users provide low and high-quality resumes respectively-an assumption that AIREG addresses by manually verifying the quality of resumes. The GAN model comprises a generator and a discriminator, where the generator aims to enhance resume representations to make them indistinguishable from the discriminator, which in turn attempts to differentiate between refined representations and high-quality ones. Through continuous iterative training, the generator's ability to improve resume quality will be significantly enhanced, which leads to more accurate educational and career pathway recommendation results.

2. **The Knowledge Graph:** The KG construction involves scrawling data using APIs provided by various education providers to create a more detailed graph based on the [11] as our benchmark for the KG construction part. The method involves sourcing, analyzing, and linking disparate data sources from the web, encompassing online advertisements, information portals, and official government websites, to uncover and map the intricate network of educational pathways within the German labor market. The KG then facilitates semantic searches and complex queries, enhancing the system's ability to provide focused and up-to-date recommendations for continuing education.
3. **Integrating the recommender system with LLM:** Our proposed framework leverages the recommendation method called LLM-based GANs Interactive Recommendation (LGIR), introduced by [12] as our benchmark, which combines LLMs and GANs. This method transforms user-profiles and historical interactions into prompts for LLMs, facilitating a conversational interface that can dynamically adapt to user preferences. We'll initiate our research based on provided prompts by our benchmark. The system efficiently learns user preferences using in-context learning and provides individualized recommendations across different domains. Hence, improving the system's ability to manage cold-start scenarios. This integration represents a significant advancement in recommender systems technology providing a more engaging and user-centric experience. We adopt LLMs such as Misteral and GPT-4 OpenAI as the LLM model in this study.

   As shown in Fig. 1, the model takes as input user-item history interactions, user profile, user query, and history of dialogue before the current query and incorporates all in a designed prompt through the prompt constructor module which triggers the LLM. The LLM then interfaces with any recommender system R. As the user profile, we use the enhanced user profile provided by the user profile enhancement process. The proposed framework introduces how to use the external information about education providers along with ESCO information to enrich the model with more information about educational requirements, hence, mitigating cold-start scenarios.

5 Evaluation Plan

To implement the proposed integrated approach effectively, many datasets, and evaluation metrics based on the baselines would be essential. In this section, we describe the plan for evaluating the performance and effectiveness of the AIREG system based on different datasets and evaluation metrics.

5.1 Datasets

- For this thesis, we will leverage multiple datasets to construct the KG, enhance user profiles, and evaluate the recommender system's performance. These datasets are essential to ensure that the AIREG system can provide accurate, personalized, and timely recommendations for users aiming for reskilling and upskilling opportunities.
- **Knowledge Graph Construction:** In case we don't have any access to the KG construction approach introduced by [11], we'll use the list of introduced APIs in their study to construct our own KG, and online course platforms such as Udemy, and Coursera.
- **User Profile Enhancement:** enhancing the user's profile relies on datasets containing information from historical user interaction data with Recommender Systems (like real online interaction logs for job recommendation), and user-provided information such as resumes, educational backgrounds, and job experiences).
- **Career Path Recommendation:** To evaluate the career path recommendations, we can use the publicly available CareerCoach 2022 gold standard dataset.

5.2 Proposed Evaluation

To evaluate the performance of the proposed system, we will consider a multi-facet evaluation plan:

Qualitative Evaluation: To evaluate the performance of the component in enhancing user engagement, we employ the Usability evaluation approach [16], which investigates metrics such as Learnability, Efficiency, Memorability, Errors, and Satisfaction. This evaluation will include participants from students and learners, and career-oriented individuals to evaluate the designed system.

Quantitative Evaluation:

1. Top-K recommendations metrics, using widely used metrics such as Precision, Recall, F1-score, Normalized Discounted Cumulative Gain (NDCG), mean average ranking precision (MAP), and mean reciprocal rank (MRR) to evaluate the Top-K recommendations of the system.
2. Ranking prediction metrics, such as Root Mean Squared Error (RMSE), and Mean Absolute Error (MAE) to evaluate the ranking of provided recommendations.
3. Investigating the performance of the system with different LLMs and recommendation methods
4. Knowledge Graph Construction, assessment using popular metrics such as Precision, Recall, and F1-score.

6 Conclusion

This symposium paper explores the challenges of integrating state-of-the-art technologies such as Large Language Models (LLMs) and Knowledge Graphs (KGs) to develop a new kind of Recommender Systems within the realms of education and career. The objective is to tackle the limitations of existing Recommender Systems by leveraging the unique capabilities of these technologies to provide more personalized, accurate, and timely educational and career pathways. The proposed Recommender System, AIREG, which combines the AI capabilities of LLMs with KGs and associated components was discussed in (Sect. 4). Given that we are at an early stage of the entire thesis research and the conceptualized AIREG system, the datasets and evaluation criteria might change, we are looking forward to discussing this research with our mentor and the possibility of establishing long-term collaboration with our institute in the field of Semantic Web and KG.

References

1. Multi-objective fused educational resource personalized recommendation system and method (2020)
2. Allen, B.P., Stork, L., Groth, P.: Knowledge engineering using large language models. arXiv preprint arXiv:2310.00637 (2023)
3. Amane, M., Aissaoui, K., Berrada, M.: A multi-agent and content-based course recommender system for university e-learning platforms. In: Motahhir, S., Bossoufi, B. (eds.) ICDTA 2021. LNNS, vol. 211, pp. 663–672. Springer, Cham (2021). https://doi.org/10.1007/978-3-030-73882-2_60
4. Axelsson, A., Skantze, G.: Using large language models for zero-shot natural language generation from knowledge graphs. arXiv preprint arXiv:2307.07312 (2023)
5. Balloccu, G., Boratto, L., Fenu, G., Marras, M.: Hands on explainable recommender systems with knowledge graphs. In: Proceedings of the 16th ACM Conference on Recommender Systems, pp. 710–713 (2022)
6. Biswas, R., et al.: Knowledge graph embeddings: open challenges and opportunities. Trans. Graph Data Knowl. **1**(1), 4–1 (2023)

7. Cadeddu, A., et al.: A comparative analysis of knowledge injection strategies for large language models in the scholarly domain. Eng. Appl. Artif. Intell. **133**, 108166 (2024)
8. Dessì, D., Osborne, F., Recupero, D.R., Buscaldi, D., Motta, E.: Generating knowledge graphs by employing natural language processing and machine learning techniques within the scholarly domain. Futur. Gener. Comput. Syst. **116**, 253–264 (2021)
9. Dörpinghaus, J., Binnewitt, J., Winnige, S., Hein, K., Krüger, K.: Towards a German labor market ontology: challenges and applications. Appl. Ontol. (Preprint), 1–23 (2023)
10. Du, Y., et al.: Enhancing job recommendation through LLM-based generative adversarial networks. In: Proceedings of the AAAI Conference on Artificial Intelligence, vol. 38, pp. 8363–8371 (2024)
11. Fischer, A., Dörpinghaus, J.: Web mining of online resources for German labor market research and education: finding the ground truth? Knowledge **4**(1), 51–67 (2024)
12. Gao, Y., Sheng, T., Xiang, Y., Xiong, Y., Wang, H., Zhang, J.: Chat-REC: towards interactive and explainable LLMs-augmented recommender system. arXiv preprint arXiv:2303.14524 (2023)
13. Lahoud, C., Moussa, S., Obeid, C., Khoury, H.E., Champin, P.A.: A comparative analysis of different recommender systems for university major and career domain guidance. Educ. Inf. Technol. **28**(7), 8733–8759 (2023)
14. Meyer, L.P., et al.: LLM-assisted knowledge graph engineering: experiments with ChatGPT. In: Zinke-Wehlmann, C., Friedrich, J. (eds.) Working conference on Artificial Intelligence Development for a Resilient and Sustainable Tomorrow, pp. 103–115. Springer, Cham (2023). https://doi.org/10.1007/978-3-658-43705-3_8
15. Mihindukulasooriya, N., Tiwari, S., Enguix, C.F., Lata, K.: Text2KGBench: a benchmark for ontology-driven knowledge graph generation from text. In: International Semantic Web Conference, pp. 247–265. Springer, Cham (2023). https://doi.org/10.1007/978-3-031-47243-5_14
16. Nielsen, J., Molich, R.: Heuristic evaluation of user interfaces. In: Proceedings of the SIGCHI Conference on Human Factors in Computing Systems, pp. 249–256 (1990)
17. Pan, J.Z., et al.: Large language models and knowledge graphs: opportunities and challenges. arXiv preprint arXiv:2308.06374 (2023)
18. Pan, S., Luo, L., Wang, Y., Chen, C., Wang, J., Wu, X.: Unifying large language models and knowledge graphs: a roadmap. IEEE Trans. Knowl. Data Eng. (2024)
19. Wang, J., Shi, Y., Yu, H., Yan, Z., Li, H., Chen, Z.: A novel KG-based recommendation model via relation-aware attentional GCN. Knowl.-Based Syst. **275**, 110702 (2023)
20. Weichselbraun, A., Waldvogel, R., Fraefel, A., van Schie, A., Kuntschik, P.: Building knowledge graphs and recommender systems for suggesting reskilling and upskilling options from the web. Information **13**(11), 510 (2022)
21. Yang, L., Chen, H., Li, Z., Ding, X., Wu, X.: ChatGPT is not enough: enhancing large language models with knowledge graphs for fact-aware language modeling. arXiv preprint arXiv:2306.11489 (2023)
22. Zhang, S., Yao, L., Sun, A., Tay, Y.: Deep learning based recommender system: a survey and new perspectives. ACM Comput. Surv. (CSUR) **52**(1), 1–38 (2019)
23. Zhao, P., et al.: Retrieval-augmented generation for AI-generated content: a survey. arXiv preprint arXiv:2402.19473 (2024)

Explaining Misleading Claims Using Graphs of Entities

Kateřina Haniková(✉)

Faculty of Informatics and Statistics, Prague University of Economics and Business, nám. W. Churchilla 1938/4, Prague, Czech Republic
katerina.hanikova@vse.cz

Abstract. This early-stage PhD paper introduces the intended research of the author's PhD study. The research is focused on explaining misleading claims, which have been fact-checked, using graphs of entities. This approach combines argumentation modeling with the fact-checking domain. Existing work seems to focus more on whole sentences concerning argumentation, while this research aims to go deeper at the level of entities and relationships between them. Preliminary studies have already revealed some repetitive argumentation elements that are based on an entity graph. The results from this study should help us understand the misleading claims better and suggest how knowledge behind unstructured data (meaning texts) can be expressed in formal representation.

Keywords: Explaining misinformation · Entity graph · Fact-checking · Argumentation

1 Introduction

Fact-checking is an activity of checking claims that are spread through a public space. This activity is done by fact-checkers, such as PolitiFact.com, FullFact.org, LeadStories.com, or less-spoken-language one, the Czech Demagog.cz.[1] The task of the fact-checkers is to provide arguments supported by trustworthy resources, such as research papers by subject-matter experts, laws, etc., to verify if a claim is true, false, or a mixture of both (specific categories may vary depending on a fact-checker). Fact-checking reports tend to be detailed and thus long. Many readers do not want to read a full report. Therefore, some platforms include summarising parts (e.g., PolitiFact.com). Sometimes, it can be challenging to understand fact-checking reports and what is wrong with the claim. Modeling the core of fact-checked claims can reveal inaccurate information in a claim and help explain it better.

Fact-checked reports can also be a "fount of wisdom." Fact-checkers elaborate on a detailed argumentation that can be used for studying the underlying patterns and concepts. This can contribute to building some formal knowledge, which can then be incorporated into ontologies. Additionally, we can learn more

[1] The International Fact-Checking Network (IFCN) coordinated by Poynter.org provides a list of verified signatories of the IFCN code of principles, which is available at: https://ifcncodeofprinciples.poynter.org/signatories.

A. Meroño Peñuela et al. (Eds.): ESWC 2024, LNCS 15345, pp. 94–103, 2025.
https://doi.org/10.1007/978-3-031-78955-7_10

about argumentation techniques by decomposing fact-checkers' argumentation into argumentative elements.

Finally, this research builds a connection between knowledge graphs and psychology. The idea is to teach people critical thinking by explaining the core argumentation and misleading structures used in the fact-checked claims (leveraging on knowledge graphs). This follows on from the Inoculation theory [14], which was later applied to the misinformation domain [19] (more described in Sect. 2.1). This work hypothesizes that knowledge graphs can be effective inoculation tools.

2 State of the Art

2.1 Foundations of Inoculation Theory

Many researchers from various fields try to find ways to stop the dissemination of misinformation. A background theory for this research is the Inoculation theory, introduced in the 1960s by William J. McGuire [13,14]. Inoculation theory uses a biological metaphor referring to the phenomenon that when we are vaccinated by some weakened virus, our body develops immunity to face even stronger exposure to this virus. Analogically, when we want to build immunity against persuasive attacks, we should first "inject" people with small doses of such persuasive attacks [14]. This theory became popular, especially in countering the spread of misinformation.

One of the current experts on inoculation theory applied to misinformation is Sander van der Linden. He addresses the main trends such as *Inoculating against fake news about COVID-19* [12] or *Inoculating the public against misinformation about climate change* [11]. Traberg et al. [19] then focus on preventing misinformation from influencing people. They argue that prevention is the best protection against a virus (whether we talk about pandemics or infodemics). Fact-checkers are focused more on *debugging* misinformation – meaning that they verify claims *after* they are spread in public space. However, it seems more effective to teach people to think critically and recognize some misinformation techniques so that they avoid sharing potentially harmful content without verifying it first. Recently, the inoculation theory was also applied through different games. The most recent review on *tackling misinformation with games* [9] showed that this is a relatively new area, and articles on this topic started to be published in 2019.

To summarise, this PhD research hypothesis is that knowledge graphs can also be used as psychological "vaccines" to build resilience against misinformation.

2.2 Argumentation in the Fact-Checking Domain

Different fact-checkers use different scales of verdicts or typologies of misinformation, which can lead to confusion because there is no harmonization or unified methodology. An approach considered in this PhD research is focused on the analysis and classification of fact-checked misleading claims with the help of graph structures, which provides a new perspective on how to look at those claims. The aim is to develop a formal ontological model that would allow to capture the argumentation of fact-checkers and also support explaining misleading claims. The following paragraphs are directed at an overview of existing work in this area, starting from argumentation models and continuing with models about fact-checking.

One of the ontological models from the domain of argumentation is the Argument Interchange Format (AIF) [3]. This model is focused primarily on the interchange of argumentation data between different software systems. The aim differs from this PhD project because it is not focused on end-users (people) but rather on machines. Another ontology is the Argument Model Ontology (AMO) [6]. The AMO builds upon Toulmin's theory[2] that defines six elements: claim, warrant, data (evidence), backing, qualifier, and rebuttal.

In the fact-checking domain, probably the most widely used model is ClaimReview[3]. The Duke University Reporters' Lab developed this model in cooperation with Schema.org.[4] The main three classes are *ClaimReview*, *Claim* and *Rating*. Additionally, many properties can be reused from Schema.org, allowing for the creation of interesting datasets – for example, ClaimsKG [18] uses ClaimReview.

Another model – The Open Claims conceptual model [1] elaborates more about different components of a claim. This model is based on three main classes: claim proposition, claim utterance, and claim context. The interesting part that this paper considers is a representation of the claim proposition. This representation can be textual or more formal. This is closely related to this PhD research. It is also focused on capturing claims in more formal representation. However, the research aims to go even further to study an argumentation provided by a fact-checker at the same formal level.

This research aims to connect the argumentation and fact-checking domains since they are closely related. The aim is to capture the core of fact-checking reports at a more granular level than current models offer.

2.3 Argumentation Mining

Another area of the research is the automated identification of argument components, which is a task of argumentation mining (AM). Argumentation mining aims at an automated extraction of structured arguments from unstructured information (such as textual documents) [10]. In this context, the subject of this PhD research can be classified as the extraction of the argumentation structure of a monologue [2], meaning there is an argumentative text from one side (provided by fact-checkers) and not a dialogue. Recent research highlights the

[2] Work describing Toulmin's theory [8].
[3] https://www.claimreviewproject.com/.
[4] https://schema.org/.

promising role of deep learning in the argumentation mining field, particularly transformer-based architectures like BERT [4]. For example, the study [7] used BERT and the argumentation context to classify argumentation components. All cited studies can serve as an inspiration for the task of automated classification of argumentation elements.

3 Problem Statement and Contributions

Fact-checkers' reports tend to be long, and people not involved in the topic covered by reports can have problems with understanding. Categorizing claims just by saying they are false or misleading does not say much about what is wrong with the claim. This research aims to improve critical thinking by transforming the argumentation developed by fact-checkers into graph structures. The main research questions are:

RQ1 Are there any repetitive patterns behind claims and argumentation developed by fact-checkers?
RQ2 How can we formalize argumentation developed by fact-checkers at the level of entities and relationships?
RQ3 How do people perceive and understand explanations based on graphs?
RQ4 Can machines learn to recognize argumentation elements in misleading claims?

RQ1 aims to explore whether there are some repetitive patterns behind fact-checked claims. The emphasis is on false or misleading claims and representing these claims in semi-formal models (graphs of entities). This is followed by the next question, RQ2, which aims to develop a formal representation of argumentation as a new kind of argumentation ontology. RQ3 tests whether explanations based on graphs can improve the understanding of fact-checked claims and if people can learn to think about claims in a more structured way. Answering RQ4 will have to rely on research in the domain of machine learning, namely, verifying whether machines can learn to recognize specific kinds of argumentation elements.

4 Research Methodology and Approach

With respect to the order of the research questions, the research will proceed as follows:

1. *Empirical research.* The research will start with manually analyzing fact-checked claims from different portals. The task is to represent the claims as semi-formal models and gather some repetitive argumentation patterns. Expected outcomes are an annotated dataset of fact-checked misleading claims and some catalog of graph entity models.
   A possible approach to modeling fact-checked misleading claims is to create semi-formal models in a tool called PURO Modeler [5]. PURO Modeler

distinguishes between *particulars* and *universals*, allowing to create models at the level of instances. Another advantage that can be useful in modeling fact-checked claims is that the tool supports creating n-ary relationships. Most ontology modeling tools allow just binary relationships, which is fine since the Web Ontology Language (OWL) is based on description logics that consider only binary relationships. However, for the first domain analysis and studying structures, it can be helpful not to be limited to binary relationships.
2. *Ontology development.* The semi-formal models will be explored in order to find some main concepts. After a conceptual model is created, the formal ontological model will be designed, considering the use of existing models. A state-of-the-art methodology to be possibly used for ontology development is Linked Open Terms (LOT) [15]. The expected outcome from this phase is a new kind of argumentation ontology tuned for the fact-checking domain.
3. *Cognitive experiments.* The experiments will require the elaboration of sophisticated questionnaires, allowing us to test if a misinformation explanation based on graphs can improve the understanding of misleading claims. The initial idea of the questionnaire is to let it consist of three parts. The first part will consist of claims and textual summaries from fact-checkers, and the participants will be asked questions revealing their degree of understanding. The second set will contain claims and explanations based on graphs of entities with similar questions. And finally, there will be just claims, and the participants will be asked to suggest what they think might be wrong or worth verifying. The expected output from this phase will be the analysis of the questionnaire results.
4. *Machine learning.* The task will be to develop predictive models for specific argumentation elements, most likely based on state-of-the-art LLMs. The annotated dataset from the first phase of this research will be used as training data. The expected outcome of this section is a set of models capable of predicting argumentation elements and experimental results about their application.

5 Evaluation Plan

The new ontology should help explain the misleading claims and suggest how the knowledge behind unstructured data (fact-checked claims) can be expressed in formal representation. The evaluation of the ontology model could be based on the LOT methodology [15] and the NeOn methodological guidelines [16]. Some corresponding evaluation criteria may be:

1. *Domain coverage.* To determine if the model can capture diverse types of fact-checked claims, it will be applied to a set of claims (from different fact-checkers), giving rise to a knowledge graph.
2. *Fit for purpose or application.* This will be determined with a user study verifying if explanations based on the knowledge graphs are more effective/ more understandable compared to explanations in natural language.

3. *Logical consistency checking.* The ontology model should be consistent and without logical errors, which can be partially achieved through reasoners.

Besides those three evaluation criteria, feedback from users, domain experts, and ontology experts will be needed. This feedback needs to be gained continuously as the research proceeds.

Apart from the formal ontological model and the knowledge graph, the other result will be an annotated dataset. The annotated dataset could serve to train a model that would automatically predict some argumentation elements. An evaluation of the prediction model will be based on an accuracy metric computed upon cross-validation on a ground truth corpus and ex-post user evaluation of random samples.

6 Preliminary Results

Preliminary studies started by modeling different examples of fact-checked misleading claims. Let me first show three examples to demonstrate the modeling process. The examples can be seen in Fig. 1. The models were created with PURO Modeler[5] and are at this phase rather semi-formal. The examples are taken from PolitiFact.org from the half-true category.

The first example[6] represents the claim *"The Earth just started spinning faster than ever before and scientists are gravely concerned."* The claim does not specify which scientist, so in the diagram, we can see a *Some objects* node representing an unspecified set of instances of *scientists.*[7] Afterward, there is a green diamond representing the relationship *are concerned about* between the *Some objects* and the event *the Earth is spinning faster.* From the fact-checker's report, we can learn that the event is actually true; however, scientists are *not* concerned about it. This means that the **relationship** is **false**, but the **event** is **true**. In the diagram, these are shown as grey notes.

The second example[8] represents the claim *"In the 1960s, liberals emptied our psych wards."*. In the diagram, we can see again *some objects* that are instances of *liberals.* We also have a relationship *played a role in*, which originates those *Some objects* and leads to the time specification *the 1960s* and *psych wards emptying.* What the fact-checker added is that in this claim, there is missing another group of people *conservatives* (we can call this group as *politicians*). So, in this claim, it was identified as **missing subset**.

The third example[9] represents the claim *"Two years ago this week, 18 million people were out of work needing unemployment benefits. Today, that number is under 1.6 million, the lowest in decades."* In this claim, two values are compared.

[5] https://puromodeler.vse.cz/.
[6] http://tinyurl.com/hd326hwk.
[7] This specific PURO diagram primitive is based on the so-called MISO modeling pattern, addressing the problem of 'multiple indirectly specified objects' [17].
[8] http://tinyurl.com/yexwp7jf.
[9] http://tinyurl.com/4jcf3u5c.

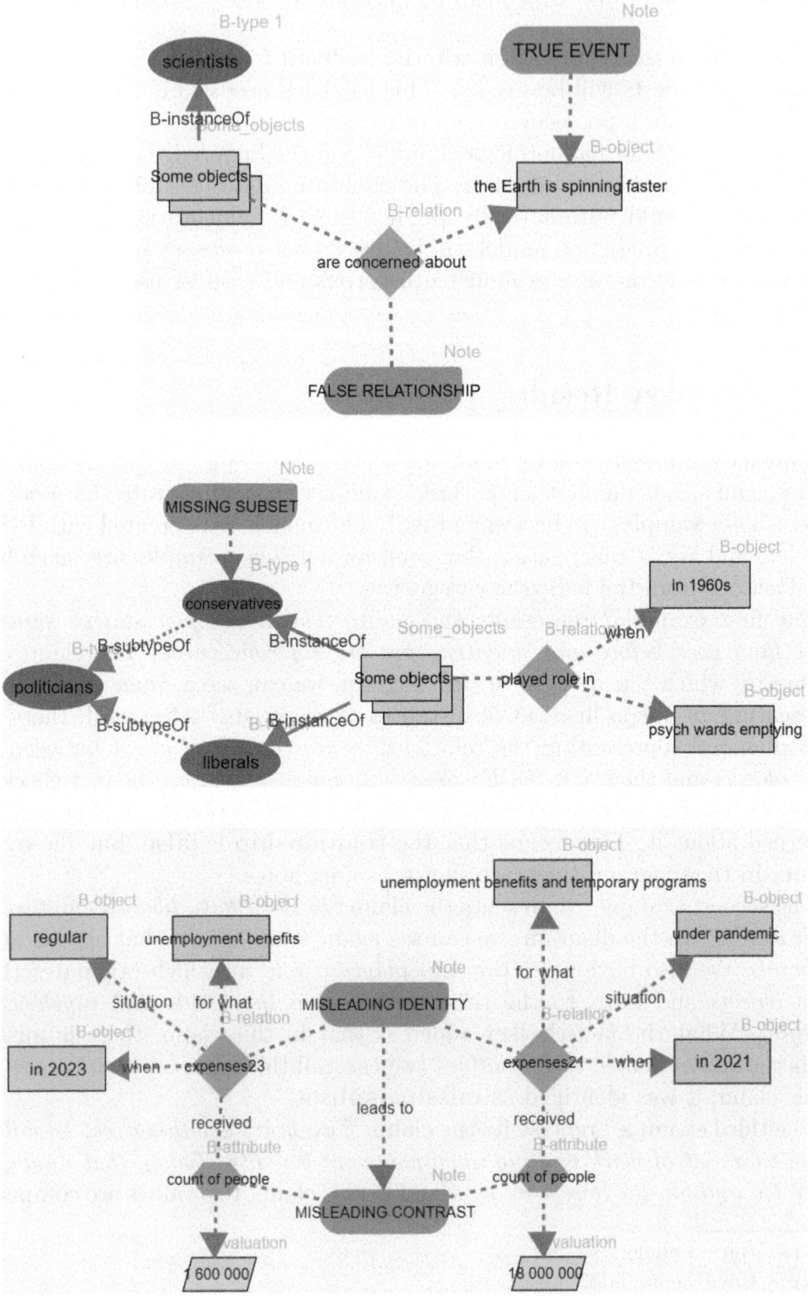

Fig. 1. Example models of misleading claims

However, if we look closer, we can see that those are not as comparable as it was claimed. On the right side of the diagram, there are *expenses* (green diamond) in 2021. On the left side, there are *expenses* in 2023. Now, the situation in 2021 was *under pandemic*, while in 2023 it was *regular*. Expenses in 2021 were for *unemployment benefits and temporary programs*; meanwhile, in 2023, they were just for *unemployment benefits*. So, if we look at both sides, we can see that those *expenses* are not identical, and this **misleading identity** leads to **misleading contrast**.

After explaining the examples, let us look at what has been discovered so far. Behind misleading claims that have been fact-checked, we can find some repetitive patterns, which can be expressed through argumentation elements. Those argumentation elements are tied to entity graphs (as shown in Fig. 1). Two types of argumentation elements can be recognized: 1) verdict argumentation elements (those in UPPER CASE) and 2) auxiliary argumentation elements (would be in Sentence case).

Verdict argumentation elements are created as a noun phrase (adjective and noun). The noun mainly refers to graphical primitives as 'relationship', 'object', 'type', 'attribute', and 'value'. There are also additional nouns not directly related to graphical primitives, such as 'identity' or 'contrast' in the third example. Six adjectives have also been defined: 'misleading', 'missing', 'false', 'unsubstantiated', 'exaggerated', and 'true'. The noun specifies *what* is wrong in the claim, and the adjective *how* it is wrong.

Sometimes, auxiliary argumentation elements are also needed to explain the claim. These were not in the presented examples. Often, they amount to notions such as 'Presumed justification' or 'Denial justification', representing evidence that supports the claim or evidence that refutes the claim. The preliminary studies were focused on 'half-true' claims. Some claims from this category can be true based on one viewpoint. However, the fact-checker adds another, less biased view, which denies the claim.

To conclude, up to this point, it was proved that misleading claims that have been fact-checked could be reformulated into graph structures, and via aggregating those graph structures, some repetitive argumentation elements can be found. The work will continue with an experiment to see if people already familiar with those argumentation verdict elements can, with some success, estimate them without having the fact-checker's explanation itself at their disposal, or, at least, if they can learn to think about claims in a more structured way through the graph-based thinking. So, they will be provided with some misleading claims, and the task will be to suggest what could be wrong in the claim based on their previous experience. The aim will be to capture just the *nouns* like relationship, value, subset, etc. If this experiment is successful and proves that people can learn to think about the claims in this way, we could possibly find a way to teach a machine (precisely speaking, some LLM) to perform the same task, namely, at least to suggest some Y/N questions that would lead the user to check the veracity of particular parts of the claim.

7 Conclusions

This study presents a novel view of misleading claims that have been fact-checked – a graph view. The preliminary results showed that the fact-checked claims can be transformed into entity graphs. These entity graphs can expose which part of the claim is wrong, misleading, or whether the claim is silent about some important piece of information that would affect its veracity. This research can reveal some interesting insights, either with respect to the misinformation domain or to the argumentation theory/ontology perspective. The claims are modeled in a structured way, so they should be independent of fact-checkers' verdict categorization. Here, emphasis is put directly on *what* is wrong rather than on the rate of truthfulness.

The main result should be the formalization of the knowledge gained from the study of graph structures behind fact-checked claims. This knowledge will be expressed as an ontological model. Apart from the formal ontological model, other results will be an annotated dataset and a knowledge graph. Both could be used with a combination of large language models to support explaining misinformation.

In conclusion, this research's findings should help explain misinformation and help people develop critical thinking by decomposing the argumentation behind fact-checked misleading claims into graph structures.

Acknowledgments. Special thanks go to my supervisor, Vojtěch Svátek, for his support and valuable feedback. The research is partially supported by CHIST-ERA within the CIMPLE project (CHIST-ERA-19-XAI-003).

Disclosure of Interests. The author has no competing interests to declare that are relevant to the content of this article.

References

1. Boland, K., Fafalios, P., Tchechmedjiev, A., Dietze, S., Todorov, K.: Beyond facts - a survey and conceptualisation of claims in online discourse analysis. Semant. Web **13**(5), 793–827 (2022). https://doi.org/10.3233/SW-212838
2. Cao, L.: AutoAM: An End-To-End Neural Model for Automatic and Universal Argument Mining, September 2023. http://arxiv.org/abs/2309.09300
3. Chesñevar, C., et al.: Towards an argument interchange format. Knowl. Eng. Rev. **21**(4), 293–316 (2006). https://doi.org/10.1017/S0269888906001044
4. Choudhary, K., et al.: Recent advances and applications of deep learning methods in materials science. NPJ Comput. Mater. **8**(1), 1–26 (2022). https://doi.org/10.1038/s41524-022-00734-6
5. Dudáš, M., Svátek, V., Vacura, M., Zamazal, O.: Starting ontology development by visually modeling an example situation - a user study. In: Proceedings of the Second International Workshop on Visualization and Interaction for Ontologies and Linked Data, pp. 114–119 (2016)
6. Vitali, F., Peroni, S.: The Argument Model Ontology, May 2011. https://sparontologies.github.io/amo/current/amo.html

7. Hidayaturrahman, Dave, E., Suhartono, D., Arymurthy, A.M.: Enhancing argumentation component classification using contextual language model. J. Big Data **8**(1), 103 (2021). https://doi.org/10.1186/s40537-021-00490-2
8. Karbach, J.: Using Toulmin's model of argumentation. J. Teach. Writ. **6**(1), 81–92 (1987)
9. Kiili, K., Siuko, J., Ninaus, M.: Tackling misinformation with games: a systematic literature review. Interact. Learn. Environ. 1–16 (2024). https://doi.org/10.1080/10494820.2023.2299999
10. Lawrence, J., Reed, C.: Argument mining: a survey. Comput. Linguist. **45**(4), 765–818 (2020). https://direct.mit.edu/coli/article/45/4/765/93362/Argument-Mining-A-Survey
11. van der Linden, S., Leiserowitz, A., Rosenthal, S., Maibach, E.: Inoculating the public against misinformation about climate change. Global Chall. **1**(2), 7 (2017). https://doi.org/10.1002/gch2.201600008
12. van der Linden, S., Roozenbeek, J., Compton, J.: Inoculating against fake news about COVID-19. Front. Psychol. **11** (2020). https://doi.org/10.3389/fpsyg.2020.566790
13. McGuire, W.J.: The effectiveness of supportive and refutational defenses in immunizing and restoring beliefs against persuasion. Sociometry **24**(2), 184–197 (1961). https://doi.org/10.2307/2786067
14. McGuire, W.J.: Some contemporary approaches. In: Advances in Experimental Social Psychology, vol. 1, pp. 191–229. Academic Press, January 1964. https://doi.org/10.1016/S0065-2601(08)60052-0
15. Poveda-Villalón, M., Fernández-Izquierdo, A., Fernández-López, M., García-Castro, R.: LOT: an industrial oriented ontology engineering framework. Eng. Appl. Artif. Intell. **111**, 104755 (2022). https://doi.org/10.1016/j.engappai.2022.104755
16. Sabou, M., Fernandez, M.: Ontology (Network) Evaluation, pp. 193–212. Springer, Heidelberg (2012). https://doi.org/10.1007/978-3-642-24794-1_9
17. Svátek, V., Kluka, J., Vacura, M., Homola, M., Dudáš, M.: Patterns for referring to multiple indirectly specified objects (MISO): analysis and guidelines. In: Advances in Pattern-Based Ontology Engineering, the Workshop on Ontology Design and Patterns (WOP). Studies on the Semantic Web, vol. 51, pp. 1–24. IOS Press (2021). https://doi.org/10.3233/SSW210004
18. Tchechmedjiev, A., et al.: ClaimsKG: a knowledge graph of fact-checked claims. In: Ghidini, C., et al. (eds.) ISWC 2019 - 18th International Semantic Web Conference, pp. 309–324. Springer, Heidelberg (2019). https://doi.org/10.1007/978-3-030-30796-7_20
19. Traberg, C.S., Roozenbeek, J., van der Linden, S.: Psychological inoculation against misinformation: current evidence and future directions. Ann. Am. Acad. Pol. Soc. Sci. **700**(1), 136–151 (2022). https://doi.org/10.1177/00027162221087936

Enabling Efficient and Semantic-Aware Constraint Validation in Knowledge Graphs

Jin Ke(✉)

Technical University of Munich, Munich, Germany
jin.ke@rub.de

Abstract. As the usage of RDF knowledge graphs (KGs) becomes more pervasive in practical applications, there is a burgeoning need for high-quality RDF data. The SHApes Constraint Language (SHACL) enables precise constraint expression on RDF graphs, ensuring data structure compliance. However, a SHACL validation that overlooks the crucial implicit information encoded in the ontology of the KG may result in unsound results. Semantic-aware SHACL validation addresses this by considering implicit information in RDF graphs, thus enabling thorough and accurate data validation. Current methods that incorporate entailment into SHACL validation often face efficiency challenges due to the resource-intensive nature of applying inference rules across entire datasets. In this doctoral work, we explore methods to enhance the efficiency of semantic-aware SHACL validation, presenting the problem statement, research questions, hypotheses. The paper concludes by our proposed method and sharing preliminary results from our research.

Keywords: SHACL · RDF · Data Quality · Reasoning · Constraints

1 Introduction

SHACL (SHApes Constraint Language) has been recommended by the W3C for the validation of knowledge graphs (KGs) modelled in RDF. As a language for expressing constraints on RDF graphs, SHACL enables the definition of RDF data structures, such as required properties, acceptable datatypes, and allowable values for specific properties. The process of SHACL validation acts as a safeguard, ensuring adherence to predefined schemas within RDF graphs, thereby enhancing the quality and interoperability of data [30], and paving the way for the development of advanced automated applications [21,24].

Semantic-aware SHACL validation refers to the process of using the SHACL framework to validate RDF graphs under the context of semantics and inference. The incorporation of entailment enables SHACL engines to identify implicit relationships between entities, properties, and classes, thus achieving a thorough and accurate data validation. However, Corman et al. [7] have shown that the validation of RDF graphs against SHACL constraints, especially when involving recursion, is an NP-hard problem. Incorporating reasoning on top of SHACL validation adds another layer of complexity. Furthermore, SHACL lacks native support

Jin Ke—Early Stage Ph.D.

A. Meroño Peñuela et al. (Eds.): ESWC 2024, LNCS 15345, pp. 104–114, 2025.
https://doi.org/10.1007/978-3-031-78955-7_11

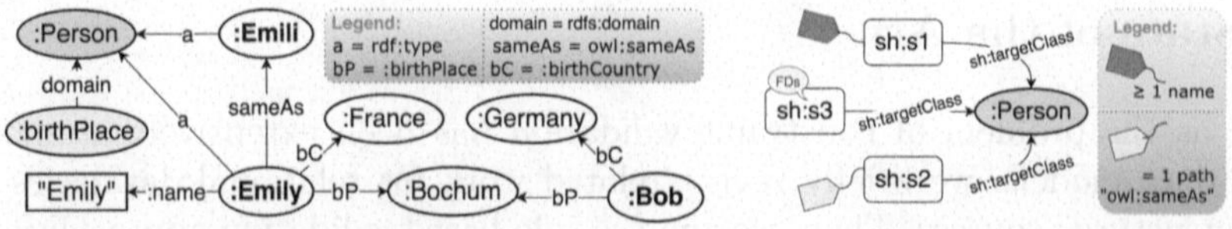

(a) Data graph (b) Shapes graph

```
SELECT * WHERE { $e1 :bP ?p ; :bC ?c1 . ?e2 :bP ?p ; :bC ?c2 . FILTER (?c1 != ?c2) }
```

(c) SPARQL query for expressing the functional depency of `sh:s3`

Fig. 1. Motivating example. Shape `sh:s1` states every person should have at least one `:name`; and `sh:s2` states every person should have exactly one `owl:sameAs` property.

for certain highly expressive constraint types, such as functional dependencies (FDs), making their implementation in SHACL less efficient. FDs state that some properties values are determined by the values of another set of properties. For instance, consider the example in Fig. 1, we verify for all `:Person` instances that `:birthPlace` → `:birthCountry` in `sh:s3`, i.e., if two people share the same birthplace, their birth countries should be the same. To achieve this, we have to implement SHACL validation using a SPARQL query in Fig. 1(c). Additionally, shapes graphs obtained with mining processes [27] often include numerous logically redundant constraints, leading to unnecessary repetitions in the validation process and consuming excessive computational resources. Besides, enabling entailment can lead to undesired behaviours. These issues often stem from the inherent reflexive nature of certain properties within the entailment framework, for instance, when following the *non-Unique Name Assumption (nUNA)* with `owl:sameAs` in KGs. To illustrate the effects of entailment, consider the example in Fig. 1. Without OWL reasoning, `:Bob` conforms to `sh:s1`, as it is not an instance of the `:Person` class. Yet, this is interpreted as a *false positive*, as when considering the domain of `:birthPlace`, it is entailed that this entity should be targeted by this shape. Therefore, with reasoning, the conclusion is that `:Bob` violates `sh:s1`. Moreover, reflexive properties can produce *spurious* validations with reasoning. Without reasoning, `:Bob` does not conform to `sh:s2`. This result is correct. However, with reasoning, due to the reflexivity of the `owl:sameAs` property, we entail the triple `(:Bob,owl:sameAs,:Bob)`, for which `:Bob` now conforms to `sh:s2`. This result can be considered *spurious*, as the conformance of the shape is due to redundant data entailed during the reasoning process and not due to the actual structure of the data graph. Besides, because of the nUNA, the violations found for `:Emily` are also reported for `:Emili`, which quickly inflates the validation reports with duplicate results. These show the importance of considering semantics to produce accurate results.

This doctoral dissertation is focused on tackling unresolved issues to enhance the efficiency of semantic-aware SHACL validation. Specifically, it delves into: *(i)* devising efficient strategies for integrating FDs within SHACL, *(ii)* reducing redundancy in shapes graphs to prevent repetitive validations, and *(iii)* investigating approaches to efficiently incorporate reasoning into SHACL validation.

2 State of the Art

First, as the problem of constraint validation has been extensively studied in other data models, we briefly revisit related work for relational databases and semi-structured sources. Then, we analyse rule-based validation approaches over KGs which is closely related to this thesis. Lastly, we position our work w.r.t. state-of-the-art SHACL validators over KGs that do not incorporate entailment.

Validation over Other Data Models. The problem of constraint validation has been widely investigated in the context of data quality over the relational model and XML. The techniques for the relational model and databases focus on the discovery of different types of constraints, namely, functional dependencies (FDs), conditional FDs, pattern FDs, edit rules, denial constraints (e.g. [4,8,10,26]). Most of these works present techniques to efficiently validate whether relations conform to the specified constraints. Other solutions present techniques to repair violations of these constraints (e.g. [2,16,20]). Although SHACL Core can express edit rule constraints well, it does not provide built-in constraint types for FDs constraints. Real-world scenarios require more complex shapes and SPARQL-based constraints (`sh:sparql`) to accurately implement and enforce FDs in RDF data using SHACL [15]. In comparison to these works, we do not present a validation or repair engine, but rather the strategies to apply targeted reasoning to the RDF graph and the shapes graph (with the constraints) to incorporate the semantics of ontologies using entailment regimes. Also, the aspect of reasoning in our work is not the same as the notion of "reasoning over functional dependencies" [8] also studied in databases. The latter typically involves applying Armstrong's axioms (reflexivity, augmentation, transitivity), computing the closure of attribute sets and analyzing normalization to ensure a well-designed database. Similarly to the literature on the relational model, several works have focused on the validation of semi-structured data models [17] and XML documents [3,9] with different types of constraints, including keys, foreign keys, integrity constraints, functional dependencies, and embedded dependencies.

Rule-Based Validation over KGs. Several approaches support the inclusion of rules for SHACL validation. These rules can be defined in entailment regimes (e.g., RDFS, OWL) or in (domain-specific) inference rules. These approaches follow mainly two types of validation strategies, which extend the data graph or the shapes graph to incorporate the rules. Then, the actual validation process can be carried out with an off-the-shelf validator using the extended structures. One of these strategies relies on materializing the closure G^* of the data graph G for the set of rules; this strategy can be applied only in the presence of rules that do no introduce the existence of nodes that are not explicit in the original graph G. This strategy is implemented by pySHACL [29], which currently supports the entailment regimes RDFS [14] and OWL 2 RL [23]. The main drawbacks of this strategy are that G^* can be expensive to compute, and it contains a large number of redundant, inferred triples, exacerbating the performance of the validation process. A second strategy relies on rewriting the shapes graph $\mathcal{S}$ into a graph $\mathcal{S}'$, which extends the shapes to incorporate the information encoded in the inference rules. The works by Ahmetaj et al. [1] and Savković et al. [28] provide formal shapes re-writings to incorporate the OWL 2 QL entailment regime into SHACL validation. These works provide guarantee the correcteness of SHACL validation with OWL 2 QL entailment. However, these works do not handle the semantics of the `owl:sameAs` predicate, as more expressive fragments of OWL 2 are required for this. Thus they cannot address the challenges posed by the nUNA in real-world scenarios. Validatrr [22] also applies shapes rewriting to support certain OWL features during SHACL validation. The main limitation of this work is that it does not provide theoretical guarantees, therefore, some OWL constructs may generate an exponential number of possible rewritings. To mitigate the issues of the two aforementioned strategies, a hybrid strategy can be applied where the inference and shapes rewriting is carried out in a targeted manner. For instance, the solution by Pareti et al. [24,25] extends the data graph schema and rewrites the target queries and the constraints to incorporate inference rules. Another way of incorporating entailment regimes in validation is to decide SHACL shape containment. Leinberger et al. [19] explored how to determine SHACL shape containment using description logic reasoning, providing a formal approach to constraint validation in RDF data graphs. In this doctoral work, we will use these results to rewrite SHACL constraints into simpler, equivalent ones (without redundancy) that can be validated efficiently.

Validation without Entailment over KGs. Other approaches [5,11,29] focus on the problem of efficient SHACL validation directly over the data graph, without considering the semantics of ontologies and entailment regimes. In contrast to these approaches, we propose solutions that enhance the shapes and data graph to remove redundancies and account for entailment regimes, before the actual validation is carried out. Therefore, our solution can be used in combination with any state-of-the-art SHACL validator.

3 Problem Statement and Contributions

SHACL validation requires two inputs, formally defined as follows [6,7]: the *data graph* G is an RDF graph to be validated, and the *shapes graph* $\mathcal{S}$ which is a set of shapes defined as a triple $\langle s, targ_s, \varphi_s \rangle$, where s is a shape name, $targ_s$ is a (possibly empty) monadic query to a shape to retrieve the focus nodes, and φ_s is a constraint formula for s. The validation of $\mathcal{S}$ over G is denoted $[\![\mathcal{S}]\!]^G$ [7].

The semantic-aware SHACL validation checks the conformance of the data graph G following an entailment regime $\mathcal{E}$ to a shapes graph $\mathcal{S}$. In this case, the implicit information in G entailed by $\mathcal{E}$ can be taken into account in the validation process. We denote with $[\![\mathcal{S}]\!]^{G,\mathcal{E}}$ the validation of $\mathcal{S}$ over G under $\mathcal{E}$.

In practice, the computation of the validation result is executed by a validation strategy. We denote a SHACL validation strategy by $\mathbb{S}$ and the universe of strategies by $\mathfrak{S}$. To generate a validation result, a strategy $\mathbb{S}$ is executed on a given data graph G under the entailment regime $\mathcal{E}$ against the given shapes graph $\mathcal{S}$, which we denote by $\mathbb{S}(\mathcal{S}, G, \mathcal{E})$. Then, we use the execution runtime of the strategy $time\big(\mathbb{S}(\mathcal{S}, G, \mathcal{E})\big)$ to evaluate its efficiency. Therefore, we formalize our problem statement as the following optimization problem:

Problem Statement (Efficient SHACL Validation Under Entailment): Given a data graph G, a shapes graph $\mathcal{S}$, and an entailment regime $\mathcal{E}$. The problem of efficient SHACL validation under entailment is defined as devising a validation strategy $\mathbb{S} \in \mathfrak{S}$ that minimizes the execution runtime while devising all violations to the shapes graph $\mathcal{S}$ over the data graph G under the entailment regime $\mathcal{E}$:

$$\arg\min_{\mathbb{S}\in\mathfrak{S}} \Big(time\big(\mathbb{S}(\mathcal{S}, G, \mathcal{E})\big)\Big), \text{ subject to } \mathbb{S}(\mathcal{S}, G, \mathcal{E}) = [\![\mathcal{S}]\!]^{G,\mathcal{E}}.$$

Contributions. To tackle this research problem, our novel contributions rely on the investigation of the following research questions:

RQ1 Expressiveness of SHACL Constraints:

- What is the expressivity of SHACL constraints w.r.t. constraints in other data models (e.g., edit rules or denial constraints)?
- How to validate expressive constraints (e.g., functional dependencies) efficiently in SHACL?

RQ2 Elimination of Redundancy in the Shapes Graph:

- How to remove duplicate constraints in the shapes graph when the validation does not consider reasoning?
- How to eliminate redundant constraints in the shapes graph when the validation includes reasoning?

RQ3 Efficient Reasoning over Data Graphs for Validation:

- How to reason over data graphs to improve the efficiency of SHACL validation with entailment?
- How to cope with the possible negative impact of nUNA on SHACL validation when enhancing RDF graphs through reasoning in OWL?

These research questions lead to our following hypothesis:

H1 Implementing highly expressive constraints such as FDs in SHACL typically requires the use of SPARQL expressions. Still, these constraints can be realized in SHACL without SPARQL by enhancing the data and shapes graphs.

H2 Shape rewriting can eliminate redundancy within the shapes graph while maintaining the expressiveness of the original one.

H3 Constraint-guided reasoning over the data graph allows for incorporating the semantics encoded in the ontology, while quickly producing a materialized graph that can be validated efficiently.

4 Research Methodology and Approach

The upcoming research and contributions aim to address the research questions posed by enhancing the data graphs and shapes graphs before validation. The methodology implemented for this doctoral research is structured as follows:

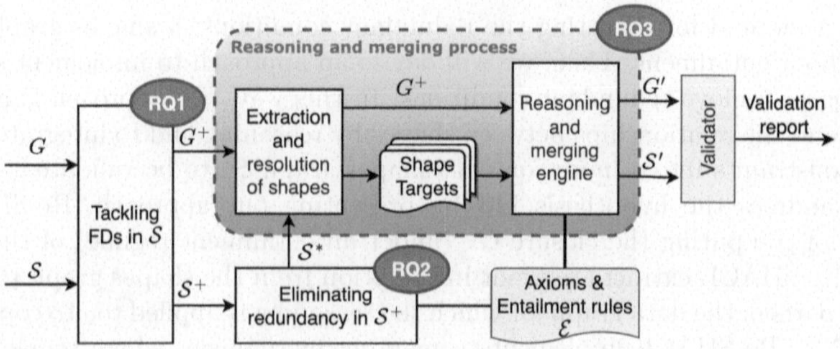

Fig. 2. Overview of our approach.

1. *Exploration of state-of-the-art techniques.* This involves a thorough review of existing literature pertinent to the problem at hand, focusing on constraints validation within the realms of Databases and Semantic Web.
2. *Research questions and hypotheses formalization.* The research problem is clearly defined, leading to the formulation of specific research questions and hypotheses to guide the investigation.
3. *Devising the solutions.* Solutions are conceptualized to address the formulated hypotheses, focusing on the innovative aspects that these solutions bring to improve the efficiency of SHACL validation.
4. *Theoretical and empirical analyses.* The proposed solutions are analyzed rigorously in terms of their theoretical properties and performance in practice. This includes a detailed examination of the solutions' theoretical complexity to ensure their feasibility, and a comparative experimental evaluation against the state of the art to assess our solutions practical performance. The experimental steps are: *(i)* selecting the datasets, baseline methods and metrics to be used, *(ii)* developing experimental plans and evaluation strategies for the research questions, adapting existing benchmarks and evaluation metrics as needed, *(iii)* running our approaches and baseline methods according to the experimental plan, and *(iv)* analyzing experimental results to draw meaningful conclusions about the effectiveness and efficiency of the solutions.

We will propose corresponding approaches for each of our stated research questions. Figure 2 depicts an overview of these approaches and labels the corresponding research questions. Regarding **H1**, we would like to study and compare the expressiveness of different types of constraints in different data models. Especially, we are interested in methods to implement FDs within SHACL. Since FDs target several nodes at the same time, it is only possible to express FDs using SPARQL-based constraints (`sh:sparql`) in SHACL, which are time consuming to execute. Instead, our approach will analyze the given FDs and generate G^+ where groups of target nodes are folded based on the attribute-value pairs to be validated in the FDs. Then, our approach obtains the rewritten shapes graph $\mathcal{S}^+$ by rewriting the SPARQL-based constraints as built-in SHACL constraints against the folded nodes. These techniques will allow for checking FDs efficiently.

We are inspired to study **H2** from works [19,24,25] and propose a rewriting solution for shapes graphs to eliminate the redundancy in them. First, we will present a method for detecting the redundant conditions in shapes graph with and without entailment. Then, we will devise an approach to implement shapes rewriting to remove redundant conditions. In this way, our approach is able to understand the relationships between shapes by reasoning and to integrate these shape constraints into a more compact shapes graph $\mathcal{S}^*$ to be validated.

We address the hypothesis **H3** by presenting our approach, Re-SHACL. Instead of computing the closure G^* (under an entailment regime) of the data graph, Re-SHACL extracts relevant information from the shapes graph to identify the parts of the data graph for which the reasoning is applied to. To cope with the nUNA, Re-SHACL implements a merging mechanism, where semantically equivalent entities are consolidated into a single, unified representation in the data graph G'. Because of this merging, Re-SHACL rewrites the shapes graph to $\mathcal{S}'$ to replace the identifiers of the merged entities that occur in the shapes graph. The combination of the targeted reasoning and the entity merging, allows Re-SHACL to obtain concise, semantically enhanced data graphs, which can be efficiently evaluated using any SHACL validator without entailment.

5 Evaluation Plan

We plan to theoretically and experimentally evaluate the proposed methods. To provide theoretical guarantees for our methods, we will study their complexity and prove their correctness. Regarding the experimental evaluation, we will perform experiments and then analyze the results of different methods.

Benchmarks and Datasets. We will use synthetic data graphs (e.g., LUBM [13]) and real-world datasets (e.g., DBpedia [18] and Wikidata [31]). For the synthetic dataset, we have the flexibility to control the size of the generated dataset when synthesizing the database, which is helpful to fully analyze the effect of dataset dimensions on the experimental results. Real-world datasets contain real data obtained directly from real environments that do not follow the Unique Name Assumption (UNA). Therefore, the real-world datasets provide an important set up for assessing the studied methods. Regarding the shapes graphs, related works [11,27] have published some shapes graphs designed for the dataset we have chosen. We will reuse and adapt these shapes graphs as much as possible.

Baselines. We will compare to approaches that support entailment regimes (e.g., pySHACL [29]), to measure the entailment regimes' impact on runtime and the number and type of violations that can be detected with reasoning. We will also use off-the-shelf validators (e.g., [5,6,11]) to show how our techniques can enhance the performance of state-of-the-art SHACL validators.

Metrics. To measure the performance of our methods, we will use several evaluation metrics, including the *execution time* of the approaches and *the number of violations* in the validation report. In the studies that handle the shapes graphs (i.e., for **H1** and **H2**) we also report on metrics about the shapes graph and the rewritten shapes graph, such as the *number of shapes* and *number of property constraints* in the graph. For the methods of enhancing data graphs (i.e., **H3**),

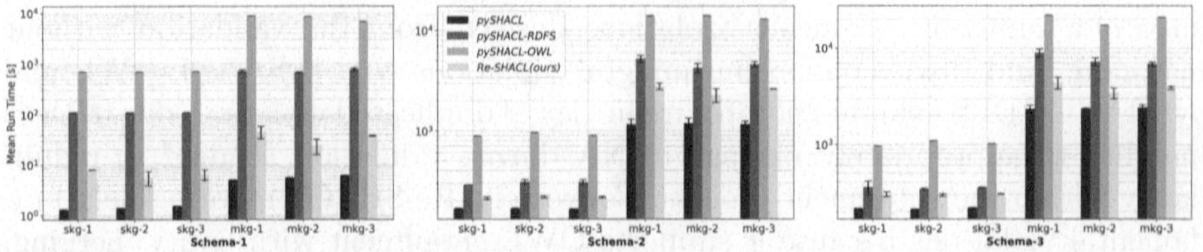

Fig. 3. Preliminary results over LUBM datasets using three shapes graphs.

we will also consider the metrics of *generation time* of the materialized graphs and their *size*. Studying these metrics helps us to better analyze the results of experiments, and to investigate which factors affect validation performance.

6 Preliminary Results

We have delved into **H3** and propose Re-SHACL, an approach based on materialization and shape rewriting that considers the targets in the shapes to carry out targeted reasoning and merging to perform efficient validation with OWL LD entailment regime [12]. It follows a hybrid strategy with two main novelties: *(i)* it is tailored to entailment regimes and mitigates the undesired results obtained due to reflexive properties defined in RDFS and OWL and due to the nUNA followed in data graphs; and *(ii)* our shapes graph rewritings correspond to simple substitutions, which makes our solution efficient.

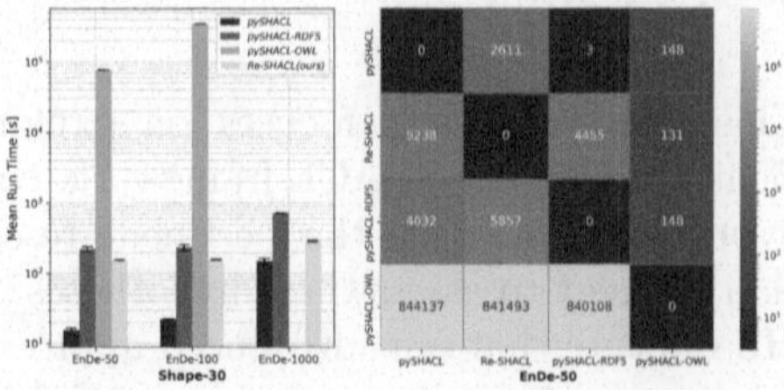

(a) (b)

Fig. 4. Preliminary results over DBpedia subsets with real-world shapes graphs: (a) Runtime (reasoning + validation). (b) Analysis of validation reports for the DBpedia subset EnDe-50. These values reflect how many violations appeared in the report R_y in the approach of the y-axis but not in the report R_x in the approach of x-axis.

We conducted experiments using six synthetic datasets LUBM generated by Figuera et al. [11] and three real-world subsets obtained from DBPedia. We use pySHACL as the validator for Re-SHACL, and compare to pySHACL with no/RDFS/OWL 2 RL entailment. Figure 3 and Fig. 4(a) show the runtimes. Clearly the fastest approach is pySHACL without entailment. Re-SHACL exhibits a considerably lower runtime than pySHACL-RDFS in most configurations, despite that OWL LD reasoning (implemented by Re-SHACL) is more expressive than RDFS. In comparison to pySHACL-OWL, Re-SHACL is orders of magnitude faster in all datasets, especially in DBpedia. The LUBM results show that the runtime is affected by both the data and shapes graphs.

Figure 4(b) represents the difference between the validation reports obtained with the different approaches. By analyzing the differences in the validation reports, we draw the following conclusions: *(i)* Using reasoning can effectively filter out numerous erroneous violations derived from the validation without reasoning, and discover more meaningful violations. *(ii)* pySHACL-OWL and pySHACL-RDFS exhibit a notable frequency of duplicated violations due to their inability to appropriately manage nUNA during validation, leading to redundancy within the entailment process. Conversely, Re-SHACL reports solely fundamental violations because it supports OWL entailment with entity merging, thereby eliminating the repetition of violation reports. *(iii)* When dealing with reflexive properties, pySHACL-OWL may generate false positive violations due to OWL entailment causing every individual `e` in the data graph to imply the triple `(e,owl:sameAs,e)`, which conflicts with `sh:minCount` and `sh:maxCount` restrictions, leading to overlooked or incorrect validation outcomes.

Summarizing, our results show that Re-SHACL outperforms orders of magnitude existing approaches that support RDFS and OWL entailment.

7 Conclusions

This doctoral thesis focuses on exploring how to validate RDF data efficiently within the SHACL framework, considering entailment. We develop three hypotheses to tackle the pertinent research questions and outline an evaluation strategy to assess these hypotheses' viability. Initial findings for Hypothesis **H3** indicate that our introduced approach, Re-SHACL, employing shape-based inference and merging techniques, effectively supports entailment during validation. This preliminary result affirms our direction and gives us confidence in the ongoing research related to **H1** and **H2**.

Future work for H3 involves enhancing the method to support OWL 2 RL and advanced features in SHACL. Our subsequent focus will be on examining the other two hypotheses, **H1** and **H2**. Finally, we will discuss how to integrate the solutions derived from all three hypotheses to optimize validation efficiency.

Acknowledgement. I would like to thank my supervisor Prof. Dr. Maribel Acosta for her strong support and insightful feedback.

References

1. Ahmetaj, S., Ortiz, M., Oudshoorn, A., Šimkus, M.: Reconciling shacl and ontologies: semantics and validation via rewriting. In: ECAI, pp. 27–35 (2023)
2. Bronselaer, A., Acosta, M.: Parker: data fusion through consistent repairs using edit rules under partial keys. Inf. Fusion **100**, 101942 (2023)
3. Buneman, P., Fan, W., Simeon, J., Weinstein, S.: Constraints for semistructured data and xml. ACM SIGMOD Rec. **30**(1), 47–54 (2001)
4. Chu, X., Ilyas, I.F., Papotti, P.: Discovering denial constraints. Proc. VLDB Endow. **6**(13), 1498–1509 (2013)
5. Corman, J., Florenzano, F., Reutter, J.L., Savkovic, O.: Shacl2sparql: validating a sparql endpoint against recursive shacl constraints. In: The Semantic Web-ISWC, vol. 2456. CEUR Workshop Proceedings, pp. 165–168 (2019)

6. Corman, J., Florenzano, F., Reutter, J.L., Savković, O.: Validating SHACL Constraints over a SPARQL Endpoint. In: Ghidini, C., et al. (eds.) ISWC 2019. LNCS, vol. 11778, pp. 145–163. Springer, Cham (2019). https://doi.org/10.1007/978-3-030-30793-6_9
7. Corman, J., Reutter, J.L., Savković, O.: Semantics and validation of recursive SHACL. In: Vrandečić, D., et al. (eds.) ISWC 2018. LNCS, vol. 11136, pp. 318–336. Springer, Cham (2018). https://doi.org/10.1007/978-3-030-00671-6_19
8. Fan, W., Geerts, F., Jia, X., Kementsietsidis, A.: Conditional functional dependencies for capturing data inconsistencies. ACM TODS **33**(2), 1–48 (2008)
9. Fan, W., Siméon, J.: Integrity constraints for xml. In: Proceedings of the ACM SIGMOD-SIGACT-SIGAI Symposium on PODS, pp. 23–34. ACM (2000)
10. Fellegi, I.P., Holt, D.: A systematic approach to automatic edit and imputation. J. Am. Stat. Assoc. **71**(353), 17–35 (1976)
11. Figuera, M., Rohde, P.D., Vidal, M.: Trav-shacl: efficiently validating networks of SHACL constraints. In: WWW, pp. 3337–3348. ACM/IW3C2 (2021)
12. Glimm, B., Hogan, A., Krötzsch, M., Polleres, A.: OWL: yet to arrive on the web of data? In: LDOW, vol. 937. CEUR Workshop Proceedings (2012)
13. Guo, Y., Pan, Z., Heflin, J.: LUBM: a benchmark for OWL knowledge base systems. J. Web Semant. **3**(2–3), 158–182 (2005)
14. Hayes, P.J., Patel-Schneider, P.F.: RDF 1.1 Semantics (2014). https://www.w3.org/TR/rdf11-mt/#rdf-interpretations, W3C Recommendation
15. Knublauch, H., Kontokostas, D.: Shapes Constraint Language (SHACL) (2017). https://www.w3.org/TR/shacl-js/, W3C Recommendation
16. Kolahi, S., Lakshmanan, L.V.: On approximating optimum repairs for functional dependency violations. In: ICDT, vol. 361, pp. 53–62. ACM (2009)
17. Korn, F., Saha, B., Srivastava, D., Ying, S.: On repairing structural problems in semi-structured data. Proc. VLDB Endow. **6**(9), 601–612 (2013)
18. Lehmann, J., et al.: Dbpedia - a large-scale, multilingual knowledge base extracted from wikipedia. Semantic Web **6**(2), 167–195 (2015)
19. Leinberger, M., Seifer, P., Rienstra, T., Lämmel, R., Staab, S.: Deciding SHACL shape containment through description logics reasoning. In: Pan, J.Z., et al. (eds.) ISWC 2020. LNCS, vol. 12506, pp. 366–383. Springer, Cham (2020). https://doi.org/10.1007/978-3-030-62419-4_21
20. Livshits, E., Kimelfeld, B., Roy, S.: Computing optimal repairs for functional dependencies. ACM TODS **45**(1), 1–46 (2020)
21. Mäkelburg, J., John, C., Acosta, M.: Automation of electronic invoice validation using knowledge graph technologies. In: Proceedings of ESWC (2024). (to appear)
22. Meester, B.D., Heyvaert, P., Arndt, D., Dimou, A., Verborgh, R.: RDF graph validation using rule-based reasoning. Semantic Web **12**(1), 117–142 (2021)
23. Motik, B., Grau, B.C., Horrocks, I., Wu, Z., Fokoue, A., Lut, C.: OWL 2 Web Ontology Language Profiles (2012) W3C Recommendation
24. Pareti, P., Konstantinidis, G.: A review of SHACL: from data validation to schema reasoning for RDF graphs. In: Reasoning Web, pp. 115–144 (2021)
25. Pareti, P., Konstantinidis, G., Norman, T.J., Şensoy, M.: SHACL constraints with inference rules. In: Ghidini, C., et al. (eds.) ISWC 2019. LNCS, vol. 11778, pp. 539–557. Springer, Cham (2019). https://doi.org/10.1007/978-3-030-30793-6_31
26. Qahtan, A.A., Tang, N., Ouzzani, M., Cao, Y., Stonebraker, M.: Pattern functional dependencies for data cleaning. Proc. VLDB Endow. **13**(5), 684–697 (2020)
27. Rabbani, K., Lissandrini, M., Hose, K.: Extraction of validating shapes from very large knowledge graphs. Proc. VLDB Endow. **16**(5), 1023–1032 (2023)

28. Savković, O., Kharlamov, E., Lamparter, S.: Validation of SHACL constraints over KGs with OWL 2 QL ontologies via rewriting. In: Hitzler, P., et al. (eds.) ESWC 2019. LNCS, vol. 11503, pp. 314–329. Springer, Cham (2019). https://doi.org/10.1007/978-3-030-21348-0_21
29. Sommer, A., Car, N., Yu, J.: pySHACL (2018). https://pypi.org/project/pyshacl/0.9.5/, A Python validator for SHACL
30. Stolk, S., McGlinn, K.: Validation of ifcowl datasets using SHACL. In: LDAC, vol. 2636. CEUR Workshop Proceedings, pp. 91–104. CEUR-WS.org (2020)
31. Vrandecic, D., Krötzsch, M.: Wikidata: a free collaborative knowledgebase. Commun. ACM **57**(10), 78–85 (2014)

Knowledge Graph-Enhanced Vision-to-Language Multimodal Models for Radiology Report Generation

Yongli Mou(✉)

RWTH Aachen University, Ahornstr. 55, 52074 Aachen, Germany
mou@dbis.rwth-aachen.de

Abstract. Current deep learning models for automated radiology report generation leverage architecture that comprises a visual encoder and a text decoder, but often lack the semantic depth and contextual understanding necessary for producing clinically relevant, easy-to-read, and accurate reports. The situation is even more challenging due to the complex nature of medical imaging and the specialized language and medical terminologies in radiology reports. The gap in domain-specific knowledge in current deep learning models underscores the necessity for approaches that integrate specialized radiological expertise into advanced language models. In this research, we propose a knowledge graph-enhanced vision-to-language multimodal model for radiology report generation, that leverages existing medical and radiological knowledge graphs. We explore contrastive learning approaches for pre-training multimodal models to learn the joint embeddings of modalities including images, graphs and texts. Our research not only contributes to the field of semantic web research by demonstrating the potential of knowledge graphs in enhancing deep learning models but also aims to revolutionize the radiology reporting process by automating it with greater accuracy, thereby reducing the workload of radiologists and mitigating the risk of human error.

Keywords: Radiology report generation · Multimodal learning · Knowledge graphs

1 Introduction

Radiology is a vital component of modern medical practice and plays a crucial role in medical diagnosis, treatment planning, and monitoring of diseases, which involves the interpretation of various medical imaging modalities such as X-rays, CT scans and MRI. From detecting fractures and tumors to monitoring the progression of chronic diseases, radiology is integral to both acute and long-term patient care. The current radiology report generation process predominantly relies on radiologists' verbal descriptions and subjective interpretations based on radiographs, which remains a largely manual and labor-intensive process. Radiologists often face a substantial workload and the generation of detailed

A. Meroño Peñuela et al. (Eds.): ESWC 2024, LNCS 15345, pp. 115–124, 2025.
https://doi.org/10.1007/978-3-031-78955-7_12

accurate reports can be time-consuming. This situation is amplified by the global shortage of skilled radiologists and the variability in report quality due to human factors such as fatigue and cognitive biases [22]. Errors or inconsistencies in radiology reports can have significant consequences on patient care and outcomes, which drive the need for accurate and automated solutions for radiology report generation (RRG), a complex cross-modal text generation task.

The integration of artificial intelligence (AI) in medical imaging has revolutionized the field of radiology. In recent decades, medical image analysis has achieved tremendous advancements in a variety of tasks such as classification and segmentation enhancing the ability of clinicians to interpret complex imaging data with greater accuracy and efficiency, which is primarily driven by the rapid development of deep learning [3]. Recently, vision-language pre-training approaches such as CLIP [21] and BLIP [10,11] have achieved tremendous success on various multimodal downstream tasks including image caption [23], visual question [17], etc. Similarly, automated RRG aims to generate descriptive text from a set of radiographs. The current state-of-the-art deep learning models for RRG are built on the multimodal (vision-to-language) encoder-decoder architecture. However, they are still subject to several significant challenges when applied to RRG. One of the key challenges is that radiology reports are often rich in specialized complex medical terms, abbreviations and expressions that describe the anatomy and any abnormalities or changes observed, and sometimes suggest potential diagnoses. This requires that the deep learning models are extensively trained on medical texts. Domain-specific knowledge is crucial for accurate and contextually relevant radiology report generation. This gap highlights the need for a specialized approach that combines the strengths of advanced vision-language multimodal models and domain-specific knowledge in radiology. Knowledge Graphs (KGs) are designed to accumulate and convey factual knowledge of the real world, which organize and represent knowledge in the form of graphs, where the nodes represent entities of interest or attributes and edges represent relations between these entities and attributes [20]. In the medical domain, KGs have emerged as a powerful tool in organizing and representing complex healthcare data and medical knowledge. RadGraph is a knowledge graph dataset, whose entities and relations are extracted from full-text radiology reports [7]. One notable feature of radiology reports is their highly structured nature. Typically, physicians adhere to specific sentence patterns when describing diseases and organs, and employ consistent templates to construct the entire report [15]. Leveraging relevant entities and relations, LLM-augmented KG-to-text methods [19] can generate high-quality texts that accurately and consistently describe the knowledge graph information.

In this research, we explore multimodal learning approaches for learning joint embedding of modalities including images, graphs and texts. Leveraging existing medical and radiological knowledge graphs, we propose a knowledge graph-enhanced vision-to-language multimodal model for radiology report generation. This research aims to contribute meaningfully to Semantic Web research, showcasing its potential to enhance the semantic richness of domain-specific knowledge for deep learning model training. Central to this endeavor is the utilization of medical knowledge graphs that link from various sources such as clinical data, research, drug information, etc., and provide a comprehensive understanding of domain knowledge.

2 State of the Art

Contrastive pre-training has received tremendous success in multimodal learning, especially in vision-language pretraining. Contrastive Language-Image Pre-training (CLIP) [21] involves a simple pre-training task that leverages the vast amount of text paired with images available on the internet. Utilizing loss such as InfoNCE [18], CLIP pulls image embedding and corresponding text embedding closer and pushes unpaired image and text farther in the embedding space. It can scale to achieve competitive zero-shot performance across a variety of image classification datasets. Following the idea of CLIP [21], You et al. [28] propose CXR-CLIP multi-view supervision [13] combining with image contrastive loss and text contrastive loss for enhancing the learning of study-level features of medical images and reports. Similarly, Li et al. [12] adopt BLIP [10,11] for image-language multimodal learning, which employs a multimodal mixture of encoder-decoder architecture and utilizes the image-text contrastive loss to align the vision and language representations, image-text matching loss to learn cross-attention features between positive and negative image-text pairs, and finally language modeling loss for generating reports.

Knowledge injection approaches have recently emerged to address the lack of domain-specific knowledge and hallucination problems of language models [19]. Xu et al. propose KILM that injects entity-related knowledge into encoder-decoder pre-trained language models by incorporating knowledge-infilling into training objectives [26]. Zhang et al. propose GreaseLM layers that fuse encoded representations from pre-trained language models and graph neural networks over modality interaction operations [29]. Liu et al. utilize a pre-constructed knowledge graph as posterior knowledge to enhance RRG [16]. To address the limitation of approaches based on predicted knowledge graphs such as incomplete information, Li et al. [12] utilize a pre-constructed knowledge graph to assist the report generation process, however, their approach faces knowledge noises involved during the dynamic graph construction process caused by retrieved reports.

3 Problem Statement and Contributions

3.1 Problem Statement

The overarching goal of this research is to develop a model capable of generating accurate, coherent, and clinically relevant radiology reports from radiographs. The central problem to be addressed in this research is the lack of domain-specific knowledge of current state-of-the-art deep learning models. In this research, we leverage existing knowledge graphs such as SNOMED CT and RadGraph and explore the concept of knowledge graph-enhanced vision-to-language multimodal models specifically designed for radiology report generation. Incorporating advanced AI techniques, particularly those involving multimodal learning and knowledge fusion, promises to not only streamline this process but also enhance the consistency and quality of radiology reports.

Research Questions. To address this problem, the research is guided by the following questions:

- RQ1: How should we train the multimodal models that learn a joint embedding across different modalities, i.e., images, graphs and text?
- RQ2: How can we extract knowledge from the visual representation of radiographs?
- RQ3: How can we model and fuse the knowledge for enhanced report generation?

Research Hypothesis. Based on these questions, the research hypothesis is formulated as follows: "*The integration of knowledge graph into the transformer-based vision-to-language multimodal model can improve the accuracy, consistency and clinical relevance of automated radiology report generation*". This hypothesis is based on the assumption that transformer-based crossmodal models are capable of synergizing the embeddings of visual features (radiology images) and structured knowledge (ontologies, medical lexicons, etc.) to produce more accurate, consistent, semantic richness, and clinically relevant radiology.

3.2 Contributions

A novel aspect of this research is the integration of semantic web technologies, in particular knowledge graphs, into the multimodal deep learning model, which enhances the model's capacity to utilize complex medical terminologies and relations and enrich the semantic quality of radiology reports. A significant part of this research will involve a thorough empirical evaluation of the model against traditional and existing automated methods, focusing on clinical relevance and accuracy. By applying knowledge graphs to a practical healthcare domain, this research aims to contribute meaningfully to Semantic Web research, showcasing its potential to enhance data interpretation and utility in medical contexts.

4 Research Methodology and Approach

After reviewing relevant literature, we have identified the research gap we are going to tackle in this research, i.e., the lack of domain-specific knowledge in the current deep learning-based approaches, which also leads to the formulation of research questions to guide the research. In this section, we outline the

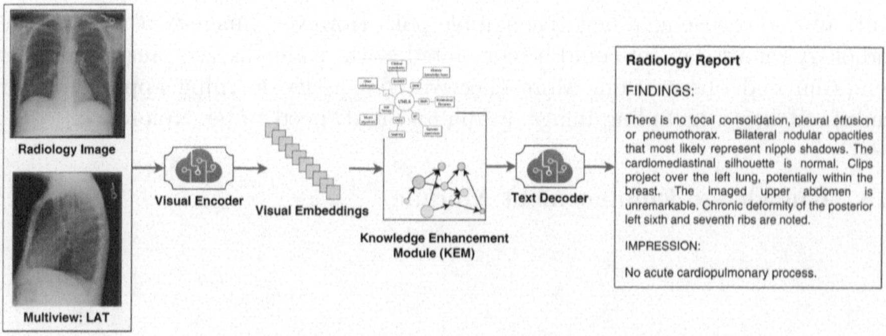

Fig. 1. Architecture overview of knowledge-enhanced image-to-language multimodal model for radiology report generation.

methodology employed in developing the proposed knowledge graph-enhanced image-to-language multimodal model for radiology report generation. Drawing from insights garnered during the literature review, we design our architectural framework depicted in Fig. 1. Central to this architecture is the incorporation of a Knowledge Enhancement Module (KEM) as shown in Fig. 2, aimed at extracting and integrating relevant domain knowledge into the model.

4.1 Architecture Overview

As shown in Fig. 1, we adopt an encoder-decoder architecture that is widely used in current state-of-the-art approaches [15] and introduce a Knowledge Enhancement Module (KEM) for knowledge extraction, processing and fusion. Formally, the model employs a visual encoder f_v to extract visual features $\mathcal{H}^v = f_v(\mathcal{I})$ from a radiograph $\mathcal{I}$. The KEM module takes visual embedding as input and extracts, processes and fuses the knowledge into the joint embedding $\mathcal{K} = KEM(H^v)$. Finally, a text decoder f_t translates the fused features into report texts $\hat{\mathcal{R}} = f_t(\mathcal{K})$. Deep learning-based approaches utilize radiology reports $\mathcal{R}^*$ written by professional radiologists as the reference for the corresponding radiographs and the objective is to minimize the discrepancies of the output of the model $\hat{\mathcal{R}}$ and the reference report $\mathcal{R}^*$.

4.2 Multimodal Model Training

To address RQ1, we will investigate various training strategies to optimize the effectiveness of multimodal models for radiology report generation. We leverage recent advancements in multimodal learning and contrastive learning techniques, such as [5,30], to learn a joint embedding across different modalities, i.e., images, graphs and text, and to bridge the modality gap, enhancing the interchangeability of embeddings. Contrastive learning can drive a variety of pretext tasks, however, most studies follow instance discrimination tasks, which consider a query and a key as a positive pair if they originate from the same image-text pair, and otherwise as a negative sample pair. However, image-text pairs in the radiology report dataset could be correlated as the same disease causes the same symptom and observation. More effective contrastive learning approaches for multimodalities, including image, graph and text, need to be explored.

4.3 Knowledge Enhancement Module

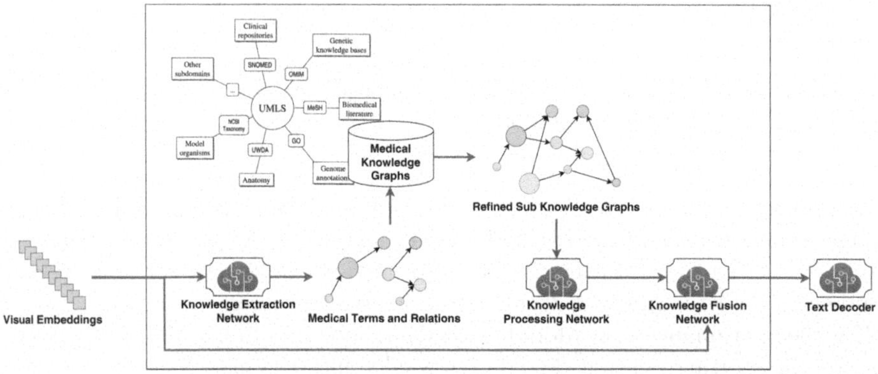

Fig. 2. Knowledge Enhancement Module (KEM) for knowledge extraction, processing and fusion.

To enrich the semantics of the extracted visual features, we propose the knowledge enhancement module for extraction, processing, and fusion of domain-specific knowledge as shown in Fig. 2.

Sub-Knowledge Graph Construction and Refinement. A knowledge extraction network f_{ke} is employed to predict included knowledge $\mathcal{G}^m = f_k(H^v)$ such as medical terms and relations, then the extracted knowledge is refined and used to construct a sub knowledge graph $\mathcal{G}_{sub}$ from large scale medical knowledge graphs such as UMLS. To address RQ2, we will employ various techniques for extracting domain-specific knowledge from the visual representation of radiographs. This may include but is not limited to the utilization of attention mechanisms to identify salient regions and features within the radiographs and the incorporation of domain-specific rules and heuristics to guide the feature extraction process.

Knowledge Processing and Fusion. Addressing RQ3 involves devising effective strategies to model and fuse the extracted knowledge (in the form of graphs) for enhanced report generation. Traditional embedding methods can not well model such kind of multi-relational data. We employ the variants of graph attention network [24] from [27] for modeling and processing knowledge graphs. Similar to GreaseLM [29], we utilize a cross-modal fuser $\mathcal{K} = f_f(\mathcal{H}^v, f_g(\mathcal{G}_{sub}))$ to integrate the embeddings of visual and knowledge graph features.

5 Evaluation Plan

For the validation of the hypothesis and the evaluation of the effectiveness of our proposed approaches for RRG, we describe our evaluation plan in this section, which is designed to measure the accuracy, consistency, and clinical relevance of the reports generated by our proposed models, comparing them with other state-of-the-art models.

5.1 Datasets

The success of any deep learning model heavily relies on the quality and quantity of the data used for training and testing. In this research, we will collect a diverse dataset of radiographs along with their corresponding expert-generated radiology reports or annotations, as well as medical knowledge graphs that models acquire domain-specific knowledge.

Radiograph Datasets. Essential to our model's training and evaluation are extensive datasets comprising radiographs and corresponding reports. The datasets selected include MIMIC-CXR [8,9], IU X-Ray [4], NIH ChestX-ray [25], Chexpert [6], and for multilingual capabilities, datasets like CX-CHR [14] and PadChest [2].

Medical Knowledge Graphs. Our models not only rely on image and text data but also integrate substantial medical knowledge from various sources, such as knowledge graphs. The integration of knowledge graphs aims to enhance the clinical accuracy and relevance of the generated reports. The key knowledge graphs we are incorporating are UMLS [1] and RadGraph [7].

5.2 Metrics

Our evaluation plan employs a multifaceted set of metrics to measure the accuracy, consistency, and clinical relevance of the reports generated by our models, offering a comprehensive comparison with traditional manual methods and state-of-the-art models. In general, our chosen metrics for RRG are categorized into three types based on the target granularity, namely, entity level, graph level, and report level. The evaluation metrics are detailed as follows:

1. **Entity Recognition and Graph Construction**: Metrics such as accuracy, recall, precision, and F_1 score are used to evaluate the clinical entity recognition. To ensure the clinical utility of the generated reports, we also calculate the accuracy of the diagnoses provided in the generated reports compared to the diagnoses concluded from the reference standard. We evaluate graph construction by using metrics including F_1 score and ROUGE-2, similar to the Tianchi knowledge graph construction competition[1].
2. **Report Accuracy and Consistency**: We use metrics from natural language generation and image caption tasks to evaluate the report accuracy and consistency compared to the reference reports, including BLUE, METEOR, ROUGE, CIDEr and BERTScore.

Besides, we plan to conduct a proper user study in collaboration with the radiology department and pathology department at University Hospital Aachen, as those metrics from traditional natural language processing tasks still have their limits and do not provide qualitative results. Expert assessment of the generated reports can be more reasonable but expensive and time-consuming.

6 Results

As this paper is part of an early-stage Ph.D. symposium, we are currently in the process of running baseline models. Consequently, we do not yet have any results to report at the time of writing. However, we can refer to the results in reference [15], which indicate that knowledge enhancement and cross-modal approaches have a positive impact compared to image caption methods.

7 Conclusions/Lessons Learned

In conclusion, this paper has explored the challenges and limitations that current approaches are facing for radiology report generation, highlighting the critical issue of the lack of domain-specific knowledge in existing vision-language multimodal models. To address this research gap, we propose the integration of a knowledge enhancement module into existing vision-language multimodal models. The KEM module aims to extract and incorporate domain-specific knowledge from the visual embedding of radiograph features and medical knowledge graphs, enhancing the model's understanding of medical concepts and improving the quality of generated reports. By leveraging advanced AI techniques such as multimodal learning and knowledge fusion, the proposed approach seeks to overcome the limitations of current methods and pave the way for more effective and clinically useful radiology report generation systems. However, since this research is at an early stage, we are looking forward to discussing the research challenges we try to address in this paper and other challenges we may not be aware of, possible improvements to our proposed architecture and modules (Figs. 1 and 2), as well as the implementation of an effective plan to evaluate our research.

[1] https://tianchi.aliyun.com/competition/entrance/532080/information.

References

1. Bodenreider, O.: The unified medical language system (umls): integrating biomedical terminology. Nucleic Acids Res. **32**(suppl_1), D267–D270 (2004)
2. Bustos, A., Pertusa, A., Salinas, J.M., De La Iglesia-Vaya, M.: Padchest: a large chest x-ray image dataset with multi-label annotated reports. Med. Image Anal. **66**, 101797 (2020)
3. Chen, X., et al.: Recent advances and clinical applications of deep learning in medical image analysis. Med. Image Anal. **79**, 102444 (2022)
4. Demner-Fushman, D., et al.: Preparing a collection of radiology examinations for distribution and retrieval. J. Am. Med. Inform. Assoc. **23**(2), 304–310 (2016)
5. Girdhar, R., et al.: Imagebind: one embedding space to bind them all. In: Proceedings of the IEEE/CVF Conference on Computer Vision and Pattern Recognition, pp. 15180–15190 (2023)
6. Irvin, J., et al.: Chexpert: a large chest radiograph dataset with uncertainty labels and expert comparison. In: Proceedings of the AAAI Conference on Artificial Intelligence, vol. 33, pp. 590–597 (2019)
7. Jain, S., et al.: Radgraph: Extracting clinical entities and relations from radiology reports. arXiv preprint arXiv:2106.14463 (2021)
8. Johnson, A.E., et al.: Mimic-cxr, a de-identified publicly available database of chest radiographs with free-text reports. Sci. Data **6**(1), 317 (2019)
9. Johnson, A.E., et al.: Mimic-cxr-jpg, a large publicly available database of labeled chest radiographs. arXiv preprint arXiv:1901.07042 (2019)
10. Li, J., Li, D., Savarese, S., Hoi, S.: Blip-2: bootstrapping language-image pre-training with frozen image encoders and large language models. arXiv preprint arXiv:2301.12597 (2023)
11. Li, J., Li, D., Xiong, C., Hoi, S.: Blip: bootstrapping language-image pre-training for unified vision-language understanding and generation. In: International Conference on Machine Learning, pp. 12888–12900. PMLR (2022)
12. Li, M., Lin, B., Chen, Z., Lin, H., Liang, X., Chang, X.: Dynamic graph enhanced contrastive learning for chest x-ray report generation. In: Proceedings of the IEEE/CVF Conference on Computer Vision and Pattern Recognition, pp. 3334–3343 (2023)
13. Li, Y., et al.: Supervision exists everywhere: A data efficient contrastive language-image pre-training paradigm. arXiv preprint arXiv:2110.05208 (2021)
14. Li, Y., Liang, X., Hu, Z., Xing, E.P.: Hybrid retrieval-generation reinforced agent for medical image report generation. Adv. Neural Inform. Process. Syst. **31** (2018)
15. Liu, C., Tian, Y., Song, Y.: A systematic review of deep learning-based research on radiology report generation. arXiv preprint arXiv:2311.14199 (2023)
16. Liu, F., Wu, X., Ge, S., Fan, W., Zou, Y.: Exploring and distilling posterior and prior knowledge for radiology report generation. In: Proceedings of the IEEE/CVF Conference on Computer Vision and Pattern Recognition, pp. 13753–13762 (2021)
17. Liu, H., Li, C., Wu, Q., Lee, Y.J.: Visual instruction tuning. arXiv preprint arXiv:2304.08485 (2023)
18. Oord, A.v.d., Li, Y., Vinyals, O.: Representation learning with contrastive predictive coding. arXiv preprint arXiv:1807.03748 (2018)
19. Pan, S., Luo, L., Wang, Y., Chen, C., Wang, J., Wu, X.: Unifying large language models and knowledge graphs: A roadmap. IEEE Trans. Knowl. Data Eng. (2024)
20. Peng, C., Xia, F., Naseriparsa, M., Osborne, F.: Knowledge graphs: opportunities and challenges. Artifi. Intell. Rev. 1–32 (2023)

21. Radford, A., et al.: Learning transferable visual models from natural language supervision. In: International Conference on Machine Learning, pp. 8748–8763. PMLR (2021)
22. Singh, S., Karimi, S., Ho-Shon, K., Hamey, L.: Show, tell and summarise: learning to generate and summarise radiology findings from medical images. Neural Comput. Appl. **33**(13), 7441–7465 (2021). https://doi.org/10.1007/s00521-021-05943-6
23. Stefanini, M., Cornia, M., Baraldi, L., Cascianelli, S., Fiameni, G., Cucchiara, R.: From show to tell: a survey on deep learning-based image captioning. IEEE Trans. Pattern Anal. Mach. Intell. **45**(1), 539–559 (2022)
24. Velickovic, P., Cucurull, G., Casanova, A., Romero, A., Lio, P., Bengio, Y., et al.: Graph attention networks. Stat **1050**(20), 10–48550 (2017)
25. Wang, X., Peng, Y., Lu, L., Lu, Z., Bagheri, M., Summers, R.M.: Chestx-ray8: hospital-scale chest x-ray database and benchmarks on weakly-supervised classification and localization of common thorax diseases. In: Proceedings of the IEEE Conference on Computer Vision and Pattern Recognition, pp. 2097–2106 (2017)
26. Xu, Y., Namazifar, M., Hazarika, D., Padmakumar, A., Liu, Y., Hakkani-Tür, D.: Kilm: knowledge injection into encoder-decoder language models. arXiv preprint arXiv:2302.09170 (2023)
27. Yasunaga, M., Ren, H., Bosselut, A., Liang, P., Leskovec, J.: Qa-gnn: reasoning with language models and knowledge graphs for question answering. arXiv preprint arXiv:2104.06378 (2021)
28. You, K., et al.: Cxr-clip: toward large scale chest x-ray language-image pre-training. In: International Conference on Medical Image Computing and Computer-Assisted Intervention, pp. 101–111. Springer (2023). https://doi.org/10.1007/978-3-031-43895-0_10
29. Zhang, X., et al.: Greaselm: graph reasoning enhanced language models. In: International Conference on Learning Representations (2021)
30. Zhang, Y., Sui, E., Yeung-Levy, S.: Connect, collapse, corrupt: learning cross-modal tasks with uni-modal data. arXiv preprint arXiv:2401.08567 (2024)

AI Supported Knowledge Graph Design and Generation

Marco Ratta(✉)

The Open University, Walton Hall, Milton Keynes, UK
marco.ratta@open.ac.uk

Abstract. Knowledge Graphs (KG) have risen to be a powerful mechanism to represent data. Despite this most data sources are generally still represented via heterogeneous non-graph data structures. Converting these into KGs necessitates considerable effort from experts, proving this to be a time consuming process. While tools have been developed to aid KG builders, a gap still exists in terms of technologies that support the automation of designing KG building pipelines. Addressing this gap motivates this research. The aim is to first understand the problem at the knowledge level and, inspired by the recent release of generative tools such as *GPT-Engineer*, to put forward a conversational agent aimed at assisting the user in building their pipelines. We report on the preliminary findings that we have so far reached during the first year of research in deriving the requirements for building KG generating pipelines from the literature.

Keywords: Knowledge Graph Generation · Knowledge Graph Design · Artificial Intelligence · Knowledge Graph Refinement

1 Introduction and Motivation

Knowledge Graphs [13] have risen to be a powerful mechanisms to represent data and have been shown to play an important role for many applications, including conversational agents, data integration, and recommender systems [28].

However, most data sources come in heterogeneous non-graph data structures, schemes, and formats [6]. Converting these sources into KG representations involves a range of specific tasks. These span from mapping tasks, such as mapping a specific data type to its specific URI format, through to ontology engineering tasks such as aligning data specific vocabulary with known vocabularies. A central problem is also the organisation of these tasks into a pipeline whereby one is able to go from the original data to the KG. This process necessitates a considerable effort from both KG engineers and domain experts, showing this to be an often time consuming and complicated process [2].

While advances have been made in terms of supporting KG engineers in their work, "existing techniques offer [...] solutions, each covering a specific aspect of KG construction, but automatically orchestrating [...] the whole construction process remains the challenge" [14]. Addressing this challenge poses questions such as, for example, given data sources and a target ontology can a pipeline from

A. Meroño Peñuela et al. (Eds.): ESWC 2024, LNCS 15345, pp. 125–134, 2025.
https://doi.org/10.1007/978-3-031-78955-7_13

the sources to the target KG be generated automatically? If human intervention is required, what is the nature and extent of this input? And what is the role and extent of background knowledge? Addressing this challenge and questions is the motivation behind this research.

To accomplish this, we first aim to understand the problem of KG design and generation at the knowledge level, beginning with a review of the relevant literature to look at how KGs have concretely been built. The purpose is to abstract the required KG tasks and operations that ought to be supported, and from these to build a systematic model of the same and to combine them into pipelines inspired by problem solving methods. Influenced by recent generative tools such as *GPT-Engineer*[1], where the user interacts conversationally with the agent to develop code, the final aim is to build a conversational agent that leads a user through a problem-solving tree on the basis of its own knowledge base and the information provided by the user at each step. This whilst employing "under the hood" either rule-based or generative AI based techniques and/or tools to solve the required tasks and at the end outputs a KG view of the input source data.

Thus, our objectives are: (i) enriching the theoretical understanding of KG design and generation by looking into the existence of abstractable KG building tasks (i.e. that go beyond a single use-case) and using these to formulate abstract high-level tasks, (ii) extending the application domain of AI to the design of KG generating pipelines through the orchestration of tasks and (iii) supporting the community of practitioners by releasing novel methods for designing and organising KG building.

The remainder of the paper is structured as follows. First, we delve into the state of the art, then we state our research questions and contribution. Subsequently we proceed to describe our intended methodology and the evaluation approach. Finally we report on the early findings that we have so far achieved in the abstraction of general KG construction tasks from the literature during this first year of research.

2 State of the Art

As it is not assumed that the required tasks and the methods for solving them are known beforehand, we take a knowledge engineering approach to tackling our problem. This entails that the practice of KG engineers and creators is taken as "a source of knowledge that cannot be obtained from anywhere else" [22]. Central to a knowledge engineering approach are also problem solving methods (PSMs) [9], which are domain-independent reasoning components specifying reusable patterns of behaviour. Furthermore, when we speak of automation we usually refer to the automation of a process at the knowledge level, where we consider a solution to the problem via the design of actions, goals and body of a hybrid symbolic-generative agent.

[1] https://github.com/gpt-engineer-org/gpt-engineer.

The application domain of this research falls under the umbrella of data integration processes. Lenzerini [17] formalises such a process. This combines data from heterogeneous sources into a single unified view available to a user or client. Its basic components are the heterogeneous data sources, a global schema acting as a mediator and view of this underlying data and the mappings that connect the information contained in the sources to the schema of the global view. For us this global view is a KG.

By KG we understand a graph intended to accumulate and convey knowledge of an object whose nodes represent entities of interest and whose edges represent relations between these entities [13]. A number of approaches and tools have been developed to aid KG engineers in their work. Central to the task of KG construction has been the effort put into the development of W3C recommended R2RML/RML mapping languages for the creation of RDF mappings [7] and the tools that materialise them [6] [1]. Further technologies include methods for resolving data heterogeneity such as Ontology Based Data Access (OBDA) [4] [3], Extract Transform Load (ETL) based tools [25], and SPARQL based tools [16]. Further, there are also multi-agency [21] and deep-learning [27] approaches for schema matching and ontology mapping, and a variety of fuzzy logic, probabilistic soft logic and machine/deep learning methods [14].

One of our hypotheses is that we can frame the problem of designing KG generation pipelines as one of graph-to-graph manipulation. The *Facade-X* methodology [2] is therefore one of the starting points of the artifact development process as it can resolve from the start the heterogeneity of the data sources into graphs. This methodology assumes a two-phase iterative process: (a) re-engineering, where the task is to resolve the heterogeneous formats of the sources into a graph, and (b) re-modelling, where the main objective is to add semantics [5]. High-level tasks undertaken during these include: (i) specifying a representative ontology for the sources, (ii) extracting the information, (iii) generating the graph from the mappings and (iv) KG evaluation and quality assessment. Crucially, this hypothesis and starting point allows to connect our approach with possible implementations from the field of graph transformation, which focuses on geometrical and rule based methods for graph to graph manipulations [11], from ontology matching and alignment [24] [15]from knowledge graph refinement [23] and from ontology design patterns [8] and engineering [10].

Recently a lot of the attention has focused on large language models (LLMs) as possibly universal means for the development of AI and real-world programming tasks [26], although not without debate in the community [20]. Other than the previously mentioned *GPT-Engineer*, *PandasAI*[2] provides another example of using a conversational agent for working with databases. The use of LLMs for the generation of KGs has also been the object of investigation by the academic community [19].

Finally, we aim to implement a methodology based on the principles of design science [12]. This is an iterative process that can be viewed as three closely related cycles of activities that are happening simultaneously: the relevance cycle,

[2] https://github.com/Sinaptik-AI/pandas-ai.

the rigor cycle and the design cycle. The relevance cycle is concerned with the introduction of input requirements from the contextual environment into the development process and introducing the research artifacts into environmental field testing. The rigor cycle aims to ensure the proper theoretical grounding of our development work. The design cycle aims at generating design alternatives and evaluating them against the requirements provided by the other cycles.

3 Problem Statement and Contributions

The overarching research question of the project is the following:

(RQ1) How can the development of Knowledge Graph generating processes from structured and semi-structured data sources be automated?

The answer to this question can be broken into two interconnected parts, each with their own sub-questions. For the first part, concerned with requirements and theoretical rigor, we ask:

(RQ2) are there general features, specifically tasks, in Knowledge Graph generation pipelines that are shared and that can be abstracted?

(RQ3) how can we systematise our findings into a model of the process of designing Knowledge Graph generating pipelines at the knowledge level?

For the second part, concerned with implementation, our target is that given a set of data sources and a set of ontologies, the system aids in the designing of a KG generating pipeline derived from the given inputs. Our assumption is that this can be achieved through a hybrid symbolic and generative AI system, supported by breaking down the problem into tasks that can be addressed by PSMs that are to be applied to graph-to-graph transformations. But is this actually required and is it beneficial with respect to an approach based say solely on using an LLM and prompt engineering? Therefore,

(RQ4) Does the breaking down of the problem into tasks and methods help with the creation of KG generating pipelines?

(RQ5) Can the process of converting and integrating structured and semi-structured sources be adequately modelled as a problem of graph-to-graph transformations?

It is also the case that, for example, in a task of entity alignment where the same entity is referenced by name in one source and by an identification number in a second sources requires a background knowledge that only a user acquainted with the sources can provide. Thus, it can be asked

(RQ6) how much of the process of KG design and generation can be automated?

(RQ7) Which parts of the process require necessary human intervention (e.g. providing background knowledge)? What is the nature and extent of this intervention?

(RQ8) What is the impact of this intervention on the generated pipelines? Can these be linear from source to target or must they include iterative problem solving structures?

4 Research Methodology and Approach

To carry out the research programme we intend to implement a methodology based on the principles of design science as follows.

The first step is to conduct a literature review of relevant sources. As parts of the relevance cycle and the rigor cycle are concerned with introducing requirements into the development process, the plan is to collect these empirically by looking at how KG builders have operated concretely. The target is then twofold. We look first for the KG task required to answer the research questions of the first part (RQ1-3) and we collect a variety of other data related to concrete KG pipelines. This includes for example the provenance of the sources (i.e. numerical, textual, etc.), their formats (csv, xml, etc.), the producing stakeholders of the graphs (semantic web researchers, government institutions, etc.) or the tools that have been used to generate the graphs. As this PhD is in its first year this step is being carried out at the moment.

The second step is to classify and systematise the tasks abstracted in the first to build the knowledge level model that will contain the answers to the research questions of the first part of the PhD (RQ1-3). Following this is the development on the basis of this model of a series of problem solving methods. These initial three steps are required in order to complete the theoretical background of the rigor cycle.

Once the requirements have been formalised, the next step is to begin to implement the design cycle and the application of the problem solving methods that have been developed to graph-to-graph transformations. Within this a number of crucial design choices will also require implementation. These include, for example, determining the distribution of the tasks between the artifact and the user (RQ6), the specification of the role of the user interacting with the system and the necessary background knowledge (RQ7-8) and the task distribution model between symbolic and generative AI methods.

Finally, to conclude the relevance and design cycle, we plan to implement an evaluation of the artifact produced through a compare and contrast approach, using a dataset of KGs that have been built with already tried and tested methods and thus also evaluating some of our initial assumptions (RQ4-5).

5 Evaluation Plan

We provide below a high-level description of how we plan to evaluate the work.

The plan is to perform a final-state based evaluation of the outcomes *(EV1)* and a fine-grained evaluation of the process leading to those outcomes *(EV2)*.

In terms of outcomes, we consider the final KG output *(EV1.1)* and the KG building pipeline that the system plans *(EV1.2)*. For *(EV1.1)* we plan on using a selection of (i) quantitative metrics [18] and (ii) competency questions. For *(EV1.2)* we plan on evaluating (i) functional correctness (ii) pipeline execution feasibility and (iii) pipeline generation efficiency, i.e. the time taken for this generation to occur and whether it is sustainable for a user workflow.

For the fine-grained evaluation of the process *(EV2)*, this means evaluating the recommended transformation tasks to perform, the recommendations (vocabulary terms, types, relations, extension actions, etc.) that the system provides for these actions, the ability to break each of them down into cognitively meaningful steps (explainability), the extent to which the user is capable of tailoring the behaviour of the system and the ability to generate correct and executable code. To measure this we plan on relying on precision and recall metrics and an expert based evaluation looking for (i) accuracy, (ii) quality, (iii) effort, (iv) explainability and (v) user agency, understood as the ability of the user to be in control of the process.

We plan on implementing our evaluation work by instantiating the following KG building scenarios:

(S1) Given the data sources and multiple ontologies, select the subset of representative ontologies and generate the KG building pipeline.

(S2) Given the data sources and the target ontology, generate the KG building pipeline.

(S3) Given applicable tasks and data sources, build a KG graph generating the relevant semantics.

To do so we plan on making use of benchmarks already published by the Semantic Web community, such as *GTFS-Madrid*[3], *LUBM*[4], *BSBM*[5] and *NPD*[6] and a selection of the KGs surveyed for the literature review for which a published expert manual/semi-automatic/automatic solution for the KG exists.

Following FAIR[7] open science practices, we plan on releasing the whole source code on *GitHub* to make it available for reproducibility.

6 Preliminary Findings

We now report on the early findings from the literature review. This is being conducted on a selection of papers from four publications, the *Semantic Web Journal*[8], the *Journal of Web Semantics*[9] and the conference proceedings from the *Extended Semantic Web Conference* and the *International Semantic Web Conference*. These have been selected as the main venues of Semantic Web research. Isolating a small sample of relevant papers deemed relevant, we constructed a keyword search[10] which we ran on the databases over the period 2013–2024. We ordered the results using the publications' search functions for relevance and have gone through the first 100 hits of each search. By reading the title and

[3] https://github.com/oeg-upm/gtfs-bench.

[4] https://swat.cse.lehigh.edu/projects/lubm/.

[5] http://wbsg.informatik.uni-mannheim.de/bizer/berlinsparqlbenchmark/.

[6] https://github.com/ontop/npd-benchmark.

[7] https://www.go-fair.org/fair-principles/.

[8] https://www.semantic-web-journal.net/.

[9] https://www.sciencedirect.com/journal/journal-of-web-semantics.

[10] ("data transformation" OR "data transformations") AND ("knowledge graph" OR "knowledge graphs" OR "linked open data" OR "linked data").

Table 1. KG building tasks

Task ID: Name	Task Description
T1: URI design	Constructing an expression pattern for a URI
T2: URI mapping	Mapping an element's type to its specific URI pattern
T3: Prefix mapping	Mapping a URI to its target prefix
T4: Type mapping	Mapping a data type of the sources to the corresponding target type of the ontology
T5: Entity linking	Mapping an entity/object in the source to the corresponding entity in an existing taxonomy/graph
T6: Entity resolution	Establishing whether multiple objects refer to the same object
T7: Domain ontology selection	Selecting ontologies that are relevant to the domain
T8: Ontology feature selection	Selecting the parts of an ontology that are descriptively relevant
T9: Ontology composition	Assembling a plurality ontology parts into a single domain model
T10: Ontological requirements specification	Specifying the ontological requirements for representing the underlying sources
T11: Database interlinking	Generating triples that link a RDF graph to another
T12: Ontology extension	Constructing a custom extension of an ontology
T13: Schema validation	Checking a graph conforms to the given schema or ontology
T14: Content validation	Validating the semantic content of a graph
T15: Syntax validation	Validating the syntactic content of a graph
T16: Graph syntax selection	Selecting the syntax in which to express a graph
T17: Source to RDF mapping	Mapping source components to their respective RDF terms
T18: Language tagging	Adding language tags to literals
T19: Links explicitation	Rendering implicit links in the sources explicit via triples
T20: Subclassing	Mapping a source class to an ontology class via rdfs:subClassOf
T21: Subpropertying	Mapping a source property to an ontology property via rdfs:subPropertyOf
T22: Ontology alignment	Linking a class/property of the ontology to a class and/or property of another ontology via a specific triple
T23: Internal linking	Linking unconnected data in the sources with one another via a triple
T24: External linking	Linking resources to their representations in external datasets
T25: Data format modification	Modifying the format of a piece of data in the sources to another one in the graph
T26: Data model transformation	Mapping RDF data in one data model to a different one

abstracts we targeted papers that describe an actual KG construction pipeline built from any source and excluded papers describing tools, systems or ontologies without any use in an actual KG construction process. 67 papers have been selected to go to a further screening process where, applying the same criteria that a paper must describe an actual KG building process. 65 of them have been selected for reading.

The goal of the literature review is to provide an empirical ground, based on the published KGs in the scientific literature, to the tasks that a system built for producing a KG from given sources ought to be able to perform. Furthermore, we collect a number of other data related to the process of building KGs (e.g. ontologies re-used, tools used, custom solutions, etc.). After reviewing 25% of the papers, we have collected a number of statistics and abstracted a series of tasks (Table 1). An interesting datum is that so far in 62.5% of the papers reviewed the authors explicitly mention the use of custom scripts and solutions for either performing tasks or for orchestrating the whole pipeline, which we interpret as evidence for the existence of the problem that we wish to tackle.

As the review is still ongoing the above list does not intend to be exhaustive. Once finished, the next step is to analyse and systematise them into a knowledge level model. This includes categorising them in terms of thematic groups, identifying which tasks can be considered concrete or abstract, or which specialise or are parts of others. Furthermore, as possible future work stemming from this research, it would be of interest to compare the results obtained with the tasks highlighted by known published methodologies and to find possible overlaps and differences.

7 Conclusion

In this work I have proceeded to expose my early stage (first year) PhD research on the yet open problem of theorising and applying the methods and tools of artificial intelligence to the problem of automating the designing KG generating pipelines.

To conclude, a brief discussion of some of the challenges that may be faced is required. A risk with what has been proposed is the possibly vast scale of the endeavour, the mitigation of which could lead to require some scope narrowing as we will begin to attempt to move from the knowledge level representation of our object to the building of its implementation. The early stage nature of this project also still leaves a number of open questions. A central one that may affect the final results and related to the assumptions that have been taken is the extent to which automation can be achieved. That is, how many of the overall tasks to be performed can be safely allocated to an agent and how many to the user, either by design or by necessity, cannot be answered at this stage. Providing an answer to these questions will indeed play a part in the future development of this PhD project.

Acknowledgements. This research was supported by the UK EPSRC Doctoral Training Partnership 2022-2024 Open University and partly by the EU-funded project Polifonia: a digital harmoniser of musical cultural heritage (Grant Agreement N. 101004746), https://polifonia-project.eu.

Supervisors: Dr. Enrico Daga and Dr. Paul Mulholland.

References

1. Arenas-Guerrero, J., Chaves-Fraga, D., Toledo, J., Pérez, M.S., Corcho, O.: Morph-KGC: scalable knowledge graph materialization with mapping partitions. Semantic Web **15**(1), 1–20 (2024). https://doi.org/10.3233/SW-223135
2. Asprino, L., Daga, E., Gangemi, A., Mulholland, P.: Knowledge graph construction with a façade: a unified method to access heterogeneous data sources on the web. ACM Trans. Internet Technol. (2022)
3. Buron, M., Goasdoué, F., Manolescu, I., Mugnier, M.L.: Obi-wan: ontology-based rdf integration of heterogeneous data. Proc VLDB Endowment **13**(12), 2933–2936 (2020)
4. Corcho, O., Priyatna, F., Chaves-Fraga, D.: Towards a new generation of ontology based data access. Semantic Web **11**(1), 153–160 (2020)
5. Daga, E., Asprino, L., Mulholland, P., Gangemi, A.: Facade-x: an opinionated approach to sparql anything. Stud. Semantic Web **53**, 58–73 (2021)
6. Dimou, A., Chaves-Fraga, D.: Declarative description of knowledge graphs construction automation: Status & challenges. In: Proceedings of the 3rd International Workshop on Knowledge Graph Construction (KGCW 2022) co-located with 19th Extended Semantic Web Conference (ESWC 2022), vol. 3141 (2022)
7. Dimou, A., Vander Sande, M., Colpaert, P., Verborgh, R., Mannens, E., Van de Walle, R.: Rml: a generic language for integrated rdf mappings of heterogeneous data. Ldow **1184** (2014)
8. Falbo, R.d.A., Guizzardi, G., Gangemi, A., Presutti, V.: Ontology patterns: clarifying concepts and terminology. In: Proceedings of the 4th Workshop on Ontology and Semantic Web Patterns, vol. 1188 (2013)
9. Fensel, D., Motta, E.: Structured development of problem solving methods. IEEE Trans. Knowl. Data Eng. **13**(6), 913–932 (2001)
10. Fernández-López, M., Gómez-Pérez, A., Juristo, N.: Methontology: from ontological art towards ontological engineering (1997)
11. Heckel, R.: Graph transformation in a nutshell. Electronic Notes In Theoretical Computer Science, vol. 148(1), pp. 187–198 (2006)
12. Hevner, A., Chatterjee, S., Hevner, A., Chatterjee, S.: Design science research in information systems. Design Res. Inform. Syst. Theory Pract., 9–22 (2010)
13. Hogan, A., et al.: Knowledge graphs. ACM Comput. Surv. (CSUR) **54**(4), 1–37 (2021)
14. Hur, A., Janjua, N., Ahmed, M.: A survey on state-of-the-art techniques for knowledge graphs construction and challenges ahead. In: 2021 IEEE Fourth International Conference on Artificial Intelligence and Knowledge Engineering (AIKE), pp. 99–103. IEEE (2021)
15. Jiménez-Ruiz, E., Grau, B.C., Zhou, Y., Horrocks, I.: Large-scale interactive ontology matching: algorithms and implementation. ECAI **242**, 444–449 (2012)
16. Lefrançois, M., Zimmermann, A., Bakerally, N.: A SPARQL extension for generating rdf from heterogeneous formats. In: Blomqvist, E., Maynard, D., Gangemi, A., Hoekstra, R., Hitzler, P., Hartig, O. (eds.) ESWC 2017. LNCS, vol. 10249, pp. 35–50. Springer, Cham (2017). https://doi.org/10.1007/978-3-319-58068-5_3
17. Lenzerini, M.: Data integration: a theoretical perspective. In: Proceedings of the twenty-first ACM SIGMOD-SIGACT-SIGART Symposium on Principles of Database Systems, pp. 233–246 (2002)
18. Lourdusamy, R., John, A.: A review on metrics for ontology evaluation. In: 2018 2nd International Conference on Inventive Systems and Control (ICISC), pp. 1415–1421. IEEE (2018)

19. Meyer, L.P., et al.: Llm-assisted knowledge graph engineering: Experiments with chatgpt. arXiv preprint arXiv:2307.06917 (2023)
20. Mitchell, M., Krakauer, D.C.: The debate over understanding in ai's large language models. Proc. Natl. Acad. Sci. **120**(13), e2215907120 (2023)
21. Nagy, M., Vargas-Vera, M.: Towards an automatic semantic data integration: Multi-agent framework approach. Semantic Web, 107–134 (2010)
22. Newell, A.: The knowledge level. Artifi. Intell. **18**(1), 87–127 (1982)
23. Paulheim, H.: Knowledge graph refinement: a survey of approaches and evaluation methods. Semantic Web **8**(3), 489–508 (2017)
24. Shvaiko, P., Euzenat, J.: Ontology matching: state of the art and future challenges. IEEE Trans. Knowl. Data Eng. **25**(1), 158–176 (2011)
25. Sreemathy, J., Nisha, S., RM, G.P., et al.: Data integration in etl using talend. In: 2020 6th International Conference on Advanced Computing and Communication Systems (ICACCS), pp. 1444–1448. IEEE (2020)
26. Vaithilingam, P., Zhang, T., Glassman, E.L.: Expectation vs. experience: evaluating the usability of code generation tools powered by large language models. In: CHI Conference on Human Factors in Computing Systems Extended Abstracts, pp. 1–7 (2022)
27. Zhang, J., Shin, B., Choi, J.D., Ho, J.C.: SMAT: an attention-based deep learning solution to the automation of schema matching. In: Bellatreche, L., Dumas, M., Karras, P., Matulevičius, R. (eds.) ADBIS 2021. LNCS, vol. 12843, pp. 260–274. Springer, Cham (2021). https://doi.org/10.1007/978-3-030-82472-3_19
28. Ze, X.: A survey on application of knowledge graph. J. Phys: Conf. Ser. **1487**, 012016 (2020)

Hybridization of Description Logics and Logic Programming

Arun Raveendran Nair Sheela[1,2(✉)]

[1] Clermont Auvergne University, Clermont-Ferrand, France
[2] Thales Group, Paris, France
Arun.RAVEENDRAN_NAIR_SHEELA@doctorant.uca.fr,
arun.raveendran-nair-sheela@thalesgroup.com

Abstract. Thales aims to develop a virtual assistant to support pilots during flights, with a central component being the knowledge base. This knowledge base is built using a knowledge representation (KR) and reasoning system, encompassing various knowledge types including static and dynamic. However, existing KR systems present some limitations which include expressiveness and reasoning performance. The problem of expressiveness can be addressed by integrating two distinct KR concepts: Rules and Ontologies.

Ontologies offers a framework for formalizing concepts, properties, and relationships, whereas rules express knowledge through IF-Then constructs. Integrating these approaches enriches knowledge representation and reasoning systems in many ways and helps to achieve completeness. However, this integration poses challenges, such as the difficulty of aligning their semantics and addressing issues of decidability. This thesis focuses on defining a methodology to combine rules and ontologies to overcome these challenges and build an optimized reasoner to execute the reasoning tasks of the virtual assistant ensuring good performance.

Keywords: Description Logic · Rules · Logic Programming · Hybrid Knowledge Base

1 Introduction

Artificial Intelligence (AI) exhibits various applications in the aviation industry such as virtual assistants. Deploying a virtual assistant during flights enhances pilot proficiency and ensuring the seamless execution of flight operations. In this context, Thales plans to construct a virtual assistant using a symbolic AI system, which falls under the domain of AI. The entirety of information within the virtual assistant is systematically represented in its knowledge base using a KR language. Utilizing this knowledge base with other components, the virtual

Early Stage Ph.D. - Work Started From September 2023.
https://www.thalesgroup.com/.

A. Meroño Peñuela et al. (Eds.): ESWC 2024, LNCS 15345, pp. 135–145, 2025.
https://doi.org/10.1007/978-3-031-78955-7_14

assistant guides pilots through the execution of varied tasks, facilitated by a sophisticated reasoner.

Some use cases of this virtual assistant include fault detection and troubleshooting, providing suggestions to pilots for improving flight performance, answering queries, and assisting in the decision-making process during critical situations. To execute these use cases, knowledge engineers represent contextual information along with instantaneous knowledge such as flight machinery data, meteorological data, and information from air traffic controllers in the knowledge base. This knowledge can be classified into three different types: static knowledge, which remains unchanged during flight; dynamic knowledge with infrequent updates and dynamic knowledge with periodic updates which changes during flights.

For the effective construction of a knowledge base, essential features include the Closed-World Assumption (CWA) means assuming false if something cannot be derived as true, beneficial for tasks like representing a list of airports, and the Open-World Assumption (OWA) means no conclusions is made from the absence of information, useful for use cases related to weather information. Also, we need to represent some procedural rules that help with fault detection and rectification. Additionally, Non-monotonic Reasoning, entails that new knowledge will invalidate the previously drawn conclusion, is required to perform reasoning over dynamic knowledge, which changes over time. A comprehensive solution to include all these features is to integrate two major KR concepts: Ontologies and Rules.

Ontologies are structured representations of knowledge within specific domains, that defines the type of entities that exist, properties that can be used to describe them, and relationships among those [28]. Description Logic (DL)s, a decidable variant of first-order logic is a widely accepted ontology language [1].

Rules capture knowledge about the world by expressing the IF-Then relationship, There are many varieties of rule languages. But in general, they can be divided into Production systems and Logic Programming (LP) systems [9]. Production systems express knowledge using conditional statements with a specific control flow and the Logic Programming system uses a declarative style which means modelling what should be achieved instead of how to achieve it.

LP and DLs have many distinct features. So combining both approaches will enhance the capabilities of a knowledge representation and reasoning system. In [27], define several benefits of LP over DLs. LP facilitates the representation of non-tree-like relationships, offering a more flexible and dynamic approach to expressing complex connections within a knowledge domain and operates under the CWA and is non-monotonic. N-ary predicates, ability to represent integrity constraints, and exception modeling are some of the other benefits of LP. Furthermore, the availability of highly optimized reasoners enhances the efficiency of reasoning processes.

Contrarily, DLs offers a rich set of constructors for complex entity connections and allow reasoning over abstract relationships without requiring concrete instances, known as Terminological Reasoning. Reasoning with DL is based on OWA and it is monotonic which means new knowledge doesn't invalidate the previously drawn conclusion. Various DLs can be defined based on the combination of different constructors offering flexibility to choose a language that matches the required expressivity. Moreover, DLs enable Open-domain Reasoning, accommodating an infinite number of anonymous individuals within their reasoning framework.

Overall, LPs are suited for data-centric reasoning tasks like query answering, while DLs stand out for their terminological reasoning capabilities and hierarchical representation style. Despite the benefits, there are several challenges we need to face while combining DLs and LP due to inherent differences in the semantics of both approaches [13,31]. This includes managing default assumptions such as CWA and OWA, monotonicity, treatment of equality, domain, and negation choices (Weak Negation for LP and Explicit Negation for DLs). Furthermore, decidability is another concern during this reconciliation. However, several works are being published that address the aforementioned challenges and give solutions to solve them (explained in Sect. 2.3).

2 State of the Art

This section is split into three parts, covering the languages and reasoners for LP systems and DLs separately, and also delving into works that combine both approaches.

2.1 Reasoning in Description Logics

The current standard for ontologies is the Web Ontology Language (OWL), rooted in DLs. OWL offers a range of variants offering diverse constructors, each with distinct computational complexities tailored for specific use cases. At one end, there's the most expressive variant, OWL Full [34], allowing for rich and complex modeling but undecidable, OWL 2 introduced more tractable variants, such as OWL 2 RL (Rule Language), OWL 2 EL (Existential Language), and OWL 2 QL (Query Language) [6]. Listing 1.1 defines a small Description Logic (DL) with a Terminological Box (TBox) that delineates the abstract relationship among classes and properties, and an Assertional Box (ABox) specifies instances of these classes and properties. Equivalent OWL syntax of this is mentioned in Listing 1.2.

Listing 14.1. Example DL ontology

```
<!-- Axioms/Terminological Box/TBox -->
TBox = {Parent subClass Human }.
<!-- Assertional Box/ABox/Instances -->
ABox = {Parent(individual_a)}.
#Reasoning Tasks
<!-- Subsumption Checking -->
?- subClass(Human,Parent). - Result: Yes.
<!-- Instance Checking -->
?- Human(individual_a). - Result:Yes.
<!-- Instance Retrivel -->
?- Human(X). - Result:individual_a.
```

Listing 14.2. Equivalent OWL Syntax

```
<!-- Axioms/Terminologies/TBox -->
<owl:Class rdf:about="#Human"/>
<owl:Class rdf:about="#Parent">
  <rdf:subClassOf rdf:resource="#Human"/>
</owl:Class>
<owl:Class rdf:about="#Father">
  <rdf:subClassOf rdf:resource="#Parent"/>
</owl:Class>
<!-- Assertions/ABox/Instances -->
<owl:NamedIndividual rdf:about="#individual_a">
  <rdf:type rdf:resource="#Human"/>
</owl:NamedIndividual>
```

In OWL languages, key reasoning tasks include consistency checking ensures logical coherence, instance checking verifying individual membership in specified concepts, subsumption checking for assessing concept hierarchy relationships and instance retrieval involves extracting relevant instances based on defined criteria. Several DL reasoning methodologies, such as Tableau-based algorithms, Classification, Rule-based DL reasoning, First-order Theorem prover-based DL reasoning, and DLE framework-based reasoning, are commonly employed to execute the mentioned reasoning tasks. Tableau-based reasoning is a method that constructs proof trees to ascertain the consistency of DL ontologies employed by well-known reasoners such as Pellet [15] and HermiT [35]. ELK is a reasoner that utilizes classification, the process of determining the subsumption relationships between concepts within an ontology by applying inference rules [43]. Additional reasoning methods include rule-based DL reasoners by taking advantage of rule engines to perform efficient reasoning over very large ABox (RDFox), by using first-order theorem provers (Surnia [18], Hoolet [3] using Vampire Theorem Prover) and Description Logic Entailement (DLE) framework by combining the benefits of tableau algorithm for effective TBox reasoning and rule engines for ABox reasoning [26] (DLE-Jena).

2.2 Reasoning in Logic Programming

Different LP systems include Answer Set Programming (ASP) [24], General Logic Programming [33], F-logic [21], and Constraint Logic Programming [38]. Notably, these declarative languages primarily focus on query answering as the principal reasoning task, except ASP, which encompasses tasks such as brave and cautious reasoning, and answer set checking. ASP focuses on generating answer sets, while other languages often utilize a backward chaining approach, attempting to prove the query by tracing back from known evidence. For General Logic Programming, reasoning engines such as SWI-Prolog, XSB Prolog, and B-prolog are commonly employed. In ASP, dedicated reasoning engines such as Clingo, DLV, S-Models and F-logic rely on engines like Florid and Flora2.

2.3 Combining DLs and LP System

Numerous research endeavours have explored the amalgamation of DLs and LP, leading to a categorization of below integration methods based on the intended semantics of the combined language, its expressivity, and the nature of the interaction between them. Broadly, the integration strategies can be distilled into two overarching approaches based on the semantics of the integrated languages: the Homogeneous Approach and the Hybrid Approach [11, 14].

Homogeneous Integration utilized a unified language with a single semantics that embedded both DLs and rules. Based on the expressivity, we can further classify Homogeneous integration into monotonic and quasi-monotonic approaches (also called Full Integration or Embedding Approach).

Monotonic Approach is mainly focused on first-order semantics and employs only open-world assumption. Semantic Web Rule Language (SWRL) [20], a union of DLs and Horn Logic is considered as a language of this approach. But in general, SWRL is considered undecidable, so various tractable forms were invented which include Description Logic Program (DLP) [4], Description Logic Rules [22], DL Safe Rules [22], and Existential Logic Program (ELP) [22]. There are mainly three ways to construct a reasoner for this approach: using a first-order theorem prover, an OWL reasoner, or a rule engine. In all these cases, we need to use a translator to convert either rules or DLs or both to the language accepted by the reasoner.

Quasi-monotonic Approach extends the above approach by adding non-monotonic features by utilizing the extensions of first-order logics such as circumscription, default logic, and defeasible logic. In this approach, both open-world and closed-world assumptions are employed to execute the reasoning tasks. MKNF+ [7] and Hybrid MKNF [25], based on auto-epistemic logic and DR-logic [5] based on defeasible logic are some of the existing languages for this approach. Also, open-answer set [36] and first-order stable model semantics [29] can serve as unifying logic system to embedded both LP and DLs. Some works includes Extended Forest Logic Program and Guarded Hybrid Knowledge base [19] can illustrate this. We can construct a reasoner for this approach by using meta programming with a rule engine to guarantee the semantics of the language. NoHr Reasoner is a query answering tool based on Hybrid MKNF, which uses XSB Prolog as the backend and uses a direct translator for OWL to LP conversion [41]. NoHr supports the tractable forms of OWL such as OWL 2 RL, OWL 2 EL, and OWL 2 QL. Also, there exists a prototype implementation of DR-Prolog, which uses the same XSB Prolog as backend.

In **Hybrid Integration**, two distinct semantics coexist, one dedicated to DLs and the other tailored to LP. Based on how DL and LP interact, we can further classify the hybrid integration into two types, Loose and Tight Integration [12].

In **Loose Integration**, the DL and LP components are treated as distinct entities that share knowledge by exchanging the logical consequences derived from each other. DL-Program employs loose integration that use DL queries in the body of the rules that interact with the DL component [40]. Several implementations such as NLP-DL [39], a web interface using Racer and DLV, DReW System [17] utilizing DLV and DL to LP translator and F-Logic# [37] appointing onto-broker engines (both f-logic and DL), are built on DL-programs. DLV-Hex, built upon the Hex system, can also be regarded as a reasoner for DL-Programs.

In **Tight Integration**, the interaction between LP and the DL part occurs at the level of the semantics of both components. In this approach, a shared model for both LP and DL is established and computed by deriving a model for DL under first-order semantics. Subsequently, the model of LP is computed by employing either well-founded semantics or stable-model semantics after eliminating the DL atoms by utilizing the initially derived DL model. So for each DL model, there exists a corresponding LP model. DL-Log under stable model semantics [30] and HD-Rules under well-founded semantics [42] are some of the existing languages that use tight integration. Also, there exists a prototype reasoner for HD-Rules as a web interface that uses Pellet and XSB Prolog as the backend. Additionally, there is an extension for DL-Log called Clopen knowledge, which introduces the capability to employ CWA within DLs [23].

In addition to this, within Hybrid Integration, there is a third approach that blends the characteristics of loose and tight coupling which can be called **Flexible Integration**. Resilient Logic Program is an example of this kind of approach [32].

3 Problem Statement

The prerequisites for the deployment of a Semantic Web system are explained in [8]. Essential components include declarative rules, enabling the generation of new data from pre-existing datasets, integrity constraints to ensure data consistency, ontologies for defining concepts and their interrelations, and procedural rules, which specify how the data can be modified depending on the current state. Furthermore, we need monotonic and non-monotonic negation.

The Monotonic approach, while a straightforward methodology, lacks certain features such as non-monotonic negation and integrity constraints. DL-program and DL+Log cannot express integrity constraints [10], reactive rules and cannot express CWA inside DLs. While DLV-Hex, a reasoner for Hex language, offers the capability to express reactive rules through external plugins (for example, using a Python plugin). However, its efficiency diminishes with larger knowledge bases due to inherent architectural constraints. Moreover, quasi-monotonic approaches like MKNF, though promising, present challenges. But the semantics of such approaches are difficult for knowledge engineers to grasp. Also, we need syntactic restrictions and limit the expressivity to build a practical reasoner due to decidability issues. So the pursuit of a practical reasoner with the aforementioned functionalities remains ongoing, signifying a critical area for advancement in semantic web systems.

Our objective is to develop a practical reasoner that not only incorporates the aforementioned features but also addresses additional requirements needed for the virtual assistant. To guide our research efforts effectively, we have formulated the following research question, delineating the specific areas under investigation:

RQ1 - How to combine DLs with LP system? This research question will be addressed by exploring four sub-research questions defined below:

RQ1.1 -What functional and non-functional requirements does the application domain expect from the integrated KR system? Functional requirements address expressivity, information flow, the default assumptions for a rule, and DL predicates, emphasizing theoretical aspects. Non-functional requirements define characteristics such as query-answering performance, scalability, efficiency, and real-time reasoning performance, predominantly at the reasoner implementation level.

RQ1.2 - Which kind of knowledge is better suited for modelling with DL, conversely, which one is more effectively represented through LP? Carefully evaluating specific criteria is crucial when deciding whether to employ rules, Description Logic (DL), or both to model a particular use case.

RQ1.3 - What are the existing methods to integrate DLs with LP? For each method, answer the two sub-research questions defined below:

RQ1.3.1 - Any implementations are available?

RQ1.3.2 - Will this approach satisfy all the needed requirements?

RQ2 - How to define the semantics of a language that integrates LP and DL to fulfil the functional requirements of this application domain? The answer to this research question depends upon RQ1 (specifically, SRQ3) to identify or invent suitable semantics to combine LP and DL. This research question also aims to study the decidability and tractability of the language and discusses the constraints to enable it.

RQ3 - How to perform essential reasoning tasks such as query answering? This question aims to build a reasoner that adheres to the defined declarative semantics of the language.

RQ3.1 - What architecture and algorithms are most appropriate for this? Two approaches exist for constructing a reasoner for the integrated language: a single rule reasoner or a coupled two-reasoner setup. And when it come to algorithms, options include there forward chaining and backward chaining systems. So identifying an effective methodology to construct the reasoner is pivotal.

RQ3.2 - Is it possible to utilize existing tools for implementation, and if so, which one is the most suitable? Identifying the most efficient tool for implementing the operational semantics to execute the required reasoning task.

How to optimize the execution of reasoning tasks to achieve optimal results? Optimization techniques at both the algorithmic and implementation levels are explored to meet the non-functional requirements of the application domain.

4 Research Methodology

This research is structured into three distinct phases to address the aforementioned research questions: the State of the Art Phase, Experimentation Phase, and Evaluation phase. The objective of the state-of-the-art phase is to explore existing methods that combine LP and DLs. This includes grasping the theory behind each approach and testing them at both theoretical and practical levels to uncover any limitations with respect to the functional requirements of the virtual assistant. Subsequently, we aim to pinpoint necessary improvements to enhance these approaches to meet the requirements of a virtual assistant. During the experimentation phase, we leverage insights from the previous stage to devise a methodology that addresses the identified limitations. This involves constructing an optimized reasoner obeying non-functional requirements. Finally, in the evaluation phase, we conduct a thorough comparison between our methodology and existing approaches to validate whether our objectives have been met. This rigorous evaluation ensures that our proposed methodology satisfies the needs of the virtual assistant effectively.

5 Evaluation Plan

We need to evaluate the result of this thesis theoretically by implementing the use cases to ascertain the fulfilment of the functional requirements. Key parameters for assessment include **Expressivity** (as described in Sect. 3), **Information Flow**, **Domain**, and **Negation choices for DL and LP Predicates**. As requirements evolve, additional parameters will be integrated.

Besides this, we need a quantitative evaluation to analyze the non-functional requirements. We decided to use existing OWL benchmarks incorporating a rule base with it. To do the initial testing, we utilize OWL2Bench, a dataset capable of generating a DL knowledge base and an extension of University Ontology Benchmark (UOBM) with a TBox encompasses four OWL languages (OWL 2 RL, OWL 2 QL, OWL 2 EL, OWL 2 DL) with all possible constructors and an ABox generator of variable size [16]. Selected parameters to evaluate non-functional requirements include **Query Answering Performance**, **Scalability**, **Query Result Comparison** using the Jaccard Similarity index [2], **Real-time Reasoning Performance and Timeliness**, and **Efficiency**. If existing benchmarks prove inadequate, there is a plan to develop an in-house benchmark that integrates both DL and LP to perform the evaluation.

6 Preliminary Result

Answering RQ1.1, the functional requirement involves defining a Knowledge Representation language capable of expressing various virtual assistant use cases, where certain scenarios require evaluation under an open-world assumption and others under a closed-world assumption. Additionally, there is a need for bidirectional information exchange between these cases. Also, the KR system must be able to capture and reason with the real-time data generated in flight. However, additional requirements including expressivity and specific reasoning tasks required for operational use-cases of the virtual assistant are yet to be defined. Also, the reasoner must be capable of providing explanations regarding how inferences are derived. Addressing non-functional requirements, the KR system must exhibit good reasoning performance, scalability, real-time reasoning capabilities, and efficiency in terms of resource consumption. **RQ1.3** is addressed in Sect. 2.3 and Table 1 illustrates the general features of methods to combine LP and DLs (Row 1), including semantics (Row 2), the interaction between LP and DL components (Row 3), default assumptions (Row 4), the domain consideration (Row 5), and a review of existing works (Row 6).

We planned to start working with a Loose integration approach, which is a very simple way to integrate LP and DLs. DL-program which is a promising work based on loose integration and also, there are some prototype reasoners available. Test them to understand their limitations, and subsequently decide on improvements or explore alternative integration types.

Table 1. Different ways to integrate Rules and DL

Homogeneous - Monotonic	Homogeneous - Quasi-Monotonic	Hybrid - Loose Integration	Hybrid - Tight Integration
First-order(FO) Semantics	FO Non-Monotonic Semantics	DL under FO Semantics, Rules under NM semantics	DL under FO Semantics, Rules under NM semantics
Intralingual	Intralingual	Logical Consequences	Model-Based
Only OWA	OWA and CWA for Rules and DL atoms	OWA for DL atoms, CWA for Rule atoms	OWA for DL atoms, CWA for Rule atoms
Both rule and DL atoms are open	Open and closed atoms are allowed in both rules and DL	DL atoms are open, Rule atoms are closed	DL atoms are open, Rule atoms are closed
SWRL	Hybrid MKNF	DL-Program	DL-Log, HD-Rules

7 Conclusion and Future Work

In the above sections, we outlined our research plan to execute this thesis and provided an overview of our initial results. As a first step, we identified the initial requirements needed for this application domain and identified existing methods to combine LP and DLs. From the list, we choose one method for studying and Our chosen framework is the program.

Our next step is to perform evaluations on DL-program concerning identified functional and non-functional requirements. Then recognize the improvement needed for the approach to apply in this context or consider pursuing an alternative approach. Also, illustrate a protocol for knowledge engineers to select either LP or DL while modelling a use case.

Acknowledgments. This research is jointly funded by Thales and National Association of Research and Technology (ANRT), France. I express my sincere thanks to my supervisors: Christophe REY (Clermont Auvergne University), Florence DE GRANCEY (Thales), Victor CHARPENAY (Ecole des Mines de Saint-Étienne), and Farouk TOUMANI (Clermont Auvergne University) for their guidance and assistance thus far.

References

1. The Description Logic Handbook: Theory, Implementation and Applications
2. Jaccard Index. https://en.wikipedia.org/wiki/Jaccard_index
3. Bechhofer, S.: Hoolet (2003). https://owl.man.ac.uk/hoolet/
4. Grosof, B., et al.: Description logic programs: combining logic programs with description logic. In: The Web Conference (2003)
5. Antonis, B., et al.: The DR-Prolog Tool Suite for Defeasible Reasoning and Proof Explanation in the Semantic Web, pp. 345–351 (2008)

6. Motik, B., et al.: Owl 2 web ontology language profiles. In: W3C Recommendation (2012). https://www.w3.org/TR/owl2-profiles/
7. Motik, B., et al.: Reconciling description logics and rules. **57**, 30–62 (2010)
8. Bry, F., Marchiori, M.: Reasoning on the Semantic Web: Beyond Ontology Languages and Reasoners, pp. 317–321 (2005). https://doi.org/10.1049/ic.2005.0749
9. Grosan, C., et al.: Rule Based Expert System, Chap. 7, pp. 149–181.https://doi.org/10.1007/978-8-642-21004-4
10. Cruz-Filipe, L., Nunes, I., Engrácia, P., Gaspar, G.: Achieving tightness in dl-programs (2012). https://api.semanticscholar.org/CorpusID:57065463
11. Odzimierz, D., et al.: Hybrid Reasoning with Rules and Ontologies (2009)
12. Włodzimierz, D., et al.: Hybrid Reasoning with Rules and Ontologies, pp. 1–49 (2009)
13. Thomas, E., et al.: Rules and Ontologies for the Semantic Web, pp. 1–53 (2008). https://doi.org/10.1007/978-3-540-85658-0_1
14. Thomas, E., et al.: Rules and Ontologies for the Semantic Web, vol. 5224, pp. 1–53 (2008). https://doi.org/10.1007/978-3-540-85658-0_1
15. Sirin, E., et al.: Pellet: a practical owl-dl reasoner. J. Web Semant.
16. Singh, G., et al.: Owl2bench: a benchmark for owl 2 reasoners. In: International Workshop on the Semantic Web (2020)
17. Xiao, G., et al.: The drew system for nonmonotonic dl-programs. In: China Semantic Web Symposium (2012)
18. Hawke, S.: Surnia. In: W3c Page (2003). https://www.w3.org/2003/08/surnia/
19. Heymans, S., et al.: Guarded hybrid knowledge bases **8**
20. Horrocks, I., et al.: Semantic web rule langauge. In: W3C (2004)
21. Kifer, M., Lausen, G.: F-logic: a higher-order language for reasoning about objects, inheritance, and scheme. In: ACM SIGMOD Conference (1989)
22. Krotzsch, M.: Description logic rules. In: Phd thesis (2010)
23. Bajraktari, L., et al.: Combining rules and ontologies into Clopen knowledge bases. AAAI Conf. Artif. Intell. (2018)
24. Lifschitz, V.: Answer set programming. In: Answer Set Programming (2019). https://api.semanticscholar.org/CorpusID:61146927
25. Knorr, M., et al.: Local closed world reasoning with description logics under the well-founded semantics. Artif. Intell. **175**(9), 1528–1554 (2011)
26. Meditskos., et al.: Combining a dl reasoner and a rule engine for improving entailment-based owl reasoning. In: The Semantic Web - ISWC (2008)
27. Boris, M., et al.: Can owl and logic programming live together happily ever after? In: The Semantic Web - ISWC 2006, pp. 501–514 (2006)
28. Neuhaus, F.: On the Definition of Ontology (Proceedings of the Joint Ontology Workshops 2017), pp. 1–10 (2017)
29. Ferraris, P., et al.: Stable models and circumscription (2011)
30. Rosati, R.: Dl+Log: Tight Integration of Description Logics and Disjunctive Datalog, pp. 68–78 (2006)
31. Riccardo, R., et al.: Integrating Ontologies and Rules: Semantic and Computational Issues, pp. 128–151 (2006). https://doi.org/10.1007/11837787_5
32. Lukumbuzya, S., et al.: Resilient logic programs: answer set programs challenged by ontologies. In: The Thirty-Fourth Conference on Artificial Intelligence (2020)
33. Schulze, J.: Handbook of logic in artificial intelligence and logic programming (2016). https://api.semanticscholar.org/CorpusID:63249517
34. Bechhofer, S., et al.: Owl 2 web ontology language profiles. In: W3C Recommendation (2004). https://www.w3.org/TR/owl-ref/

35. Rob, S., et al.: Hermit: A Highly-Efficient Owl Reasoner, vol. 432 (2008)
36. Heymans, S., et al.: Open answer set programming for the semantic web. J. Appl. Logic
37. Heymans, S., et al.: F-logic: loosely coupling f-logic rules and ontologies. In: 2010 IEEE/WIC/ACM International Conference on Web Intelligence and Intelligent Agent Technology **1**, 248–255 (2010)
38. Frhwirth, T.W., et al.: Constraint logic programming - an informal introduction. In: Logic Programming Summer School (1992)
39. Eiter, T., et al.: Nlp-dl (2007). https://www.mat.unical.it/ianni/swlp/
40. Eiter, T., et al.: Combining answer set programming with description logics for the semantic web. Artif. Intell. **172**(12), 1495–1539 (2008)
41. Kasalica, V., et al.: Nohr: an overview. Artif. Intell. 1–7 (2020)
42. Drabent, W., et al.: Hd-rules: a hybrid system interfacing prolog with DL-reasoners. In: Applications of Logic Programming to the Web (2007)
43. Kazakov, Y., et al.: Elk reasoner: architecture and evaluation. In: International Workshop on OWL Reasoner Evaluation (2012)

Extended Best Papers from the Workshops

Analysis of Automated Tools for FAIRness Evaluation: A Literature Perspective

Leonardo Guerreiro Azevedo[1(✉)], Gabriel Banaggia[2], Julio Tesolin[3], and Renato Cerqueira[1]

[1] IBM Research, IBM, Avenida República do Chile, 330, 11o. floor, Rio de Janeiro, RJ, 20031-170, Brazil
{lga,rcerq}@br.ibm.com

[2] Department of Social Sciences, PUC-Rio, Rua Marquês de São Vicente, 225, Rio de Janeiro, Rio de Janeiro, 22451-900, Brazil
banaggia@puc-rio.br

[3] PGED/IME, Praça Gal. Tibúrcio, 80, Rio de Janeiro, RJ, 22290-270, Brazil
jcctesolin@ime.eb.br

Abstract. The FAIR Principles were introduced to address data challenges and improve the Findability, Accessibility, Interoperability, and Reusability of digital resources, following several Semantic Web standards. 'FAIRness' corresponds to a percentage grade indicating how close a digital object is to abiding by those principles. Several tools have been developed to assess the FAIRness of data digital objects in support of enacting the FAIR Principles. This work offers an appraisal of tools that evaluate the FAIRness of such objects, focusing on fully automated solutions. We conduct a literature review about existing tools, extract from it a set of requirements they aim to fulfill, and assess how each one fares considering this ensemble. Our results help researchers, developers, and data stewards with an overview of the tools, including an analysis of tools' fulfillment to the elicited requirements, making explicit existing gaps, and giving directions to improvements needed.

Keywords: FAIR principles · FAIRness · FAIRness evaluation · Automated Tools for FAIRness Evaluation · Requirements for FAIRness Automated Tools

1 Introduction

Research data can benefit from infrastructure improvements to support its use and the accrual of generated information and knowledge, which should be discovered and reused for investigations [45].

For authors G. Banaggia and J. Tesolin: ***Work done while at IBM Research.***

A. Meroño Peñuela et al. (Eds.): ESWC 2024, LNCS 15345, pp. 149–166, 2025.
https://doi.org/10.1007/978-3-031-78955-7_15

Enhancing knowledge discovery for human and computational agents is a challenge for data-intensive sciences, involving accessing, integrating, and analyzing task-appropriate data [45]. Wilkinson *et al.* [45] proposed the FAIR principles, a set of 15 recommendations for improving the **F**indability, **A**ccessibility, **I**nteroperability, and **R**eusability of digital resources [24]. The FAIR principles are supposed to be domain-independent, aim to facilitate the reuse of data by both humans and machines [41], and are related to several Semantic Web standards [2,39]. Semantic tools are needed to engage various communities towards FAIRer resources [19]. These principles can be applied not only to data but also to algorithms, vocabularies, tools, workflows, and other data-related services insofar as they are made available as digital objects [45] [33]. Research involving digital objects benefits from applying the FAIR principles to ensure goals like transparency, reproducibility, and reusability [42]. The FAIR principles are thus suggested as a prerequisite for proper data management and stewardship [45].

There are several mechanisms to support data infrastructure architecture in its tasks of planning, designing, building, publishing, and maintaining FAIR data. Such mechanisms include best practices and guidelines, methods, processes, data maturity models, questionnaires, and (semi-)automated tools that aim to evaluate a digital object's so-called 'FAIRness level'. FAIRness corresponds to a percentage grade indicating how close a digital object is to abiding by the FAIR principles' characteristics considered relevant for a community or task. To reach the goals of sustainable and robust progress in research, FAIRness should be considered in the whole process: from planning, through observation or data creation, until publication, rather than late in the data life cycle [3]. Manual and semi-automated mechanisms are essential to improve overall understanding and appreciation of the research life cycle [44]; nevertheless, assessing FAIRness with them is time-consuming, requires experience, carries difficulties when inspection is needed, and does not scale when considering several digital objects [19]. An automated tool is more appropriate to handle these issues. Automated tools perform the FAIRness evaluation without human intervention, resulting in a more objective evaluation and allowing the comparison of distinct digital objects.

This work analyzes tools for FAIRness assessment with a focus on automated solutions. We conducted a literature review to discover the tools and elicited the tools' requirements. None of the surveyed papers systematically present such a requirement list. They characterize and compare tools abstractly and do not use requirements. We examine the tools to verify how they fulfill the requirements and analyze their coverage and existing gaps.

Our main contributions are the aggregated requirements list and the evaluation of the tools. The requirements guide analyzing and developing tools that effectively and automatically evaluate FAIRness. The overview of how existing tools support the requirements aids one in choosing an existing tool to apply in one's scenario or engaging in new tool development.

The remainder of this work is divided as follows. Section 2 presents the literature review, the tools found, and the elicited requirements. Section 3 describes the automated tools for FAIRness evaluation and how they address the requirements.

Section 4 compares the tools considering the requirements catering. Section 5 presents the related work and highlights our contributions appertaining to them. Finally, Sect. 6 presents our conclusions and proposals for future work.

2 Literature Review

Scientific research takes into account the existing literature on a topic as the best evidence for assessing the current state of any particular subject of inquiry. In computer science, evidence-based approaches were developed inspired by methods initially proposed for the social sciences and medicine research, with a strong, evidence-based empirical focus [26]. Evidence is constituted by a synthesis of the best available studies that help answer specific research questions. One of the most important ways of generating that synthesis is by doing a systematic literature review (SLR) [28]. However, SLRs are labor-intensive procedures, and simplified literature reviews can already supply interesting results for reduced teams with narrower questions, although preliminary [8]. This work conducted this type of abbreviated literature review.

2.1 Literature Review Steps

We started with the definition of an abridged literature review protocol, which involved the following two research questions:

Rq1. *What are the existing automated tools for FAIRness evaluation?*
Rq2. *Which requirements do these tools meet?*

To find relevant academic texts to answer these questions, we utilized the PICOC method [32] to establish the criteria (displayed in Table 1) which we used to create a search string to find these resources.

Table 1. PICOC Criteria and chosen terms.

Criteria	Chosen Terms and Synonyms
Population	Tool, Automated (Process/Method)
Intervention	Assessment, Evaluation
Comparison	(not included, as this is not a search against an established tool)
Outcome	FAIRness, FAIRification
Context	FAIR Principles, FAIR Data

```
    ("Tool" OR "Automated")
AND ("Assessment" OR "Evaluation")
AND ("FAIRness" OR "FAIRification")
AND ("FAIR Principles" OR "FAIR Data")
```

Using this string, we executed queries in three different repositories (Scopus[1], IEEE Digital Library[2], and ACM Digital Library[3]), restricting the search options to titles, keywords and abstracts as much as possible to achieve a manageable and meaningful total number of results.

There were 32 unique hits initially, with the majority coming from Scopus. Inclusion and exclusion criteria were enacted so that we could privilege texts that already dealt with comparative assessment of different automated FAIRness evaluation tools, which are [27,31,38,40]. These works characterize and compare tools abstractly and do not propose or use requirements in their analysis. From these works, we found the tools listed in Table 2, where FAIR-Checker, F-UJI, and FAIR Evaluator are pointed out as automated. We confirmed that by reading the tools documentation. Looking for a reference to FAIRenough listed by [27], we found a tool with a similar name (FAIR Enough) that is automated and based on F-UJI and FAIR Evaluator. We included this tool in the analysis.

Table 2. Tools found during the literature review.

Tool name and reference for the tool	Automated?	Found at
F-UJI [13,14]	Yes	[31,40]
FAIR Evaluator [43,44]	Yes	[27,31,40]
FAIR Enough [21]	Yes	
FAIR-Checker [19,36]	Yes	[40]
ARDC's FAIR Data Self Assessment Tool [5]	No	[27,38]
Checklist for Evaluation of Dataset Fitness for Use [4]	No	[31]
CSIRO's 5* Oz Data tool (link is broken)	No	[38]
DANS's SATIFYD [11]	No	[27,38]
Data Stewardship Wizard [29,30]	No	[27]
EUDAT's Checklist [25]	No	[38]
FAIRdat [1]	No	[27]
FAIRenough	No	[27]
FAIRshake [9,10]	No	[27,31]
GARDIAN	No	[27]
RDA's Simple Grid [12]	No	[27,38]
Semi-automated workflow for FAIR maturity indicators [6,7]	No	[27]

FAIR Enough was not found in the surveyed papers. It was included in the evaluation due to be a free automated tool based on F-UJI and FAIR Evaluator.
http://oznome.csiro.au/5star/
A survey-based tool that is not accessible since 2021 [27].
https://bigdata.cgiar.ocrg/resources/gardian/ (link is broken)

[1] https://www.scopus.com.
[2] https://ieeexplore.ieee.org.
[3] https://dl.acm.org/dl.cfm.

2.2 Elicited Requirements

To appraise the tools, we elicited the requirements presented in Table 3 by reading the papers found in the literature review and the works describing the automated tools. The former papers elected different parameters and focal points for appraising the tools for FAIRness assessment, but none present or use a list of requirements in their analysis. We created a requirement for any mention of a desirable feature for an automated tool. The purpose of the requirements is to guide the appraisal and development of tools that effectively and automatically evaluate FAIRness. These requirements are crucial for making objective FAIRness evaluations and improving digital objects.

To facilitate the requirements presentation, we grouped them into categories using a bottom-up approach according to their similarities. We present the categories' descriptions and why each requirement matters.

- **General**: Requirements that deal with basic needs the tools have to fulfill. *Reasons*: R1: Without supplying a fully automated solution, FAIRness evaluation does not scale. R2: Without a numeric score, it is difficult to objectively compare results of FAIRness evaluation executed in the same contexts (*e.g.*, FAIR aspects considered, and configurations of metrics and tests used in the evaluation). A maturity level is another kind of FAIRness grade, *e.g.*, the RDA FAIR Data Maturity Model [33] propose maturity levels from 0 to 5 to indicate "how a resource under evaluation performs on meeting the indicators across the FAIR areas". R3: Without being fully autonomous, evaluation is limited in scope to specific repositories and their restrictions. R4: Without referencing the FAIR principles, users cannot follow how they were interpreted and implemented. R5: With no mention of the digital object types that can be evaluated, the scope of the principles is diminished.
- **Deployment**: Requirements that deal with decisions taken by developers. *Reasons*: R6 and R7: Without offering the tool both as a Web page and service, it does not meet the FAIR principles of simultaneous human and machine actionability. R8: Without specifying its use license, different use communities cannot adequately employ the tool. R9: Without specifying its development stage, users do not know whether results can vary after new tool versions come out. R10: Without the ability to customize the tool, evaluation is limited to agnostic parameters, *i.e.*, digital objects being evaluated using the same metrics, tests, and weights independent from the community-specific characteristics. R11: Without allowing authentication, tools cannot evaluate protected data. R12: Without a badge, the user does not have the whole assessment in a visual representation. R13: Without specifying the data lifecycle, users do not know in which data management step the tool can be used. R14: Without recourse to FAIR-enabling services, the tools would not benefit from standardized, open, and well-governed services that support long-term data assessment [14]. As an example, the FAIRsharing.org[4] is an initiative that provides such kind of services [37].

[4] https://fairsharing.org/.

Table 3. List of requirements elicited from analyzing the papers returned by the literature review, or through reading the evaluated tools' papers. The latter ones have their IDs marked with a '*'.

ID	Requirement: The tool should...	Source(s)
R1	...be fully **automated**.	[40]
R2	...give a FAIRness **score**/grade.	[2,27,31,38]
R3	...should work autonomously, *i.e.*, it should work **independently** from a specific domain, digital objects, or framework.	[38]
R4	...present **which principles** are being evaluated with each FAIRness test.	[27]
R5*	...specify the **types of digital object** it assesses (*e.g.*, data objects, data repositories, workflows, software).	[14,44]
R6	...expose their services as APIs (*e.g.*, as **RESTful services** [34]).	[40]
R7	...be available as a standalone **web application**	[31,40]
R8	...indicate its usage **license**.	[27]
R9	...state its **development stage** (*e.g.*, in development, in beta, in production).	[27]
R10	...be **customizable** according to the type of digital object and community.	[2,31]
R11	...allow the user supply **authentication** credentials so that (meta)data can be accessed in their repositories for proper evaluation.	[31]
R12*	...provide a visual representation (*e.g.*, a **badge**) of the FAIR assessment results.	[14,19]
R13*	...support all phases of the **data lifecycle**.	[3,14]
R14*	...rely on **FAIR-enabling services** (*e.g.*, FAIRsharing.org, identifiers.org) to perform the assessment.	[14,44]
R15	...offer **guidance** on how it is used (*e.g.*, providing user manual, help, publications, or explanatory tips).	[27]
R16	...require **little expertise** to use.	[27]
R17	...export the result in a **machine-actionable** way.	[31,40]
R18	...disclose its **rating system** (*e.g.*, presenting evidences concerning the algorithm used and the rationale for the scale chosen).	[38]
R19	...be informative, *i.e.*, it should **teach** the user about the FAIR principles.	[38]
R20	...give **recommendations** on how to improve the FAIRness of the evaluated resource.	[27,38]
R21	...export the result fully readable in **natural language**.	[38]
R22	...store the evaluation results in a **searchable** resource.	[31]
R23*	...support **versioning** of FAIRness assessment.	[44]

The FAIRness badge is a generated image that presents an overview of the results of a FAIRness evaluation, *e.g.*, it may be a pie, bar, or radar chart.

- **User experience**: Requirements that relate to how users employ the tool. *Reasons*: R15: Without receiving guidance, users are left to interpret design decisions by themselves, which could lead to misreading its results. R16: Without being open to users with little technical expertise, entire sections of scientific communities would be cast aside from using the tool.
- **Reporting**: Requirements about how evaluation results are reported. *Reasons*: R17: Without machine-actionable, scientific data is not accessible programmatically, and the FAIR principles are not fully realized since one of their main goals is allowing programmatic access to scientific data. R18: Without explaining the rating system, design decisions are made opaque, and the score becomes uninterpretable. R19 and R20: Without teaching users about the FAIR principles (*e.g.*, explaining the principles or referencing documents about them) or giving recommendations (*e.g.*, suggesting recipes or standard schemas to be used for improvements), one misses the opportunity to increase the FAIRness of data. R21: Without reports supplied in natural language, non-technical users are left out of the result. R22 and R23: Without being able to store and search for past results, it becomes impossible to gauge how FAIRness improved over time.

3 Analysis of the Tools

This section describes the tools and analyzes how they meet the requirements. The requirements were evaluated by reading the documentation of the tools (*i.e.*, web pages, GitHub pages, and papers). Table 4 depicts the results. The score "Yes" (✓) means the requirement is supported. "Partially" (◗) is a requirement not entirely fulfilled. "No" (✗) means it is ignored by the tool.

3.1 F-UJI

F-UJI automatically (**R1**:✓) evaluates the FAIRness (**R2**:✓) of research data objects (**R5**:✓) according to FAIRsFAIR metrics[5] [14]. The evaluation can be applied to data digital objects belonging to any domain (**R3**:✓).

The tool's primary entities are Principles, Metrics, and Tests. Each FAIR principle has one or more metrics that are automatically evaluated by tests (**R4**:✓). Each test is executed using a pass-or-fail approach and returns a score and a maturity level to represent an overview of the digital object's fitness to each FAIR principle. The score represents the FAIRness of the digital object. The maturity levels are Incomplete, Initial, Moderate, and Advanced. They are based on CMMI (Capability Maturity Model Integration) maturity levels [23].

F-UJI is available as a RESTful Web service [34] (**R6**:✓), implemented in Python using the Flask framework, and it is described using the OpenAPI[6] specification. The service accepts two inputs: the unique identifier of the data

[5] The version V0.4 of the metrics are available at Zenodo [15].
[6] https://www.openapis.org/.

Table 4. Tools' appraisal considering the elicited requirements, using symbols to represent entire (✓ = Yes), partial (◗ = Partially) or lack of (✗ = No) fulfillment.

Req.	Req. Keyword	F-UJI	FAIR Evaluator	FAIR Enough	FAIR Checker
R1	Automated	✓	✓	✓	✓
R2	Score	✓	◗	◗	✓
R3	Independent	✓	✓	✓	✓
R4	Refer principles	✓	✓	✓	✓
R5	Types of digital object	✓	✓	✓	✓
R6	RESTful services	✓	✓	✓	✓
R7	Web application	✓	✓	✓	✓
R8	License	✓	✓	✓	✓
R9	Development stage	◗	✗	✗	◗
R10	Customizable	◗	◗	◗	◗
R11	Allow authentication	✓	✗	✗	✗
R12	Badge	✓	✗	✗	✓
R13	Data lifecycle	✗	✗	✗	✗
R14	FAIR-enabling services	✓	✓	✓	◗
R15	Guidance	✓	✓	✓	✓
R16	Little expertise	✓	✓	✓	✓
R17	Machine-actionable	✓	✓	✓	✗
R18	Rating system	✓	✓	✓	✓
R19	Teach	◗	◗	◗	◗
R20	Recommendations	✗	✗	✗	✓
R21	Natural language	◗	◗	◗	✓
R22	Searchable	✗	✗	✗	✗
R23	Versioning	✗	✗	✗	✗

object to be evaluated and, if available, the repository that provisions the digital object's metadata.

The F-UJI Web Client (**R7**:✓) renders a FAIRness badge to give a visual representation of the measurements of the evaluated object (**R12**:✓). The service[7] and the Web Client[8] source codes are available on GitHub under the MIT License (**R8**:✓). There is no information in the F-UJI documentation about in what development stage the tool is (**R9**:◗).

The tool is only customizable by implementing new tests or deactivating some by altering the source code, which requires software development skills. There is no configuration option for non-experts (**R10**:◗). F-UJI's documentation does not detail to which data lifecycle stage the tool applies (**R13**:✗).

[7] https://github.com/pangaea-data-publisher/fuji.
[8] https://github.com/MaastrichtU-IDS/fairificator.

F-UJI employs FAIR-enabling services to perform the evaluation (**R14**:✓). F-UJI implements content negotiation to access metadata that may be available through proprietary Web service (**R11**:✓).

The tool has plenty of documentation, including papers and GitHub pages (**R15**:✓). The Web Client is easy to use since the user must pass only the digital object identifier to execute the FAIRness evaluation. However, Web service development skills are required to make use of the RESTful Web API (**R16**:✓).

The evaluation results are returned in JSON with scores, practical tests, inputs and outputs, and the evaluation context for each metric. The results can be processed by computing agents (**R17**:✓). The Web Client presents the results as an HTML page which includes evidence on how the digital object is evaluated (**R18**:✓) and helps the user learn about FAIR concepts. Although the evidence is beneficial, it requires technical skills to be fully understood (**R19**:◗). The tool does not present explicit recommendations to improve the FAIRness of digital objects (**R20**:✗). The results are not so easy to understand by non-IT people, even though they are readable in natural language (**R21**:◗). Besides, they are not stored in a searchable engine (**R22**:✗) and, consequently, F-UJI does not support storing versions of the evaluation results (**R23**:✗).

3.2 FAIR Evaluator

FAIR Evaluator is a framework to automatically (**R1**:✓) evaluate digital objects. It returns the FAIRness of a digital object as the number tests it passed related to the total number of tests (**R2**:◗). The framework has three main components: (a) Maturity Indicators (MI): community-authored specifications delimiting a specific automatically-measurable FAIR behavior; (b) Compliance Tests: services that test digital resources against MIs; (c) Evaluator: a Web application that registers, assembles, and applies community-relevant Compliance Tests against a digital resource, providing a report about what a machine 'sees' when it visits that resource. The framework is not tied to a specific domain (**R3**:✓) and can be adapted to fit community needs, *i.e.*, the stakeholders may participate in the creation of community-specific MIs, develop their compliance tests, and define which tests to use in an evaluation. The tests also refer to the principles they evaluate (**R4**:✓). It can evaluate not only data digital objects but other types as well, like software digital objects, as long as the user configures the MI Collection with the options that make sense for the evaluation (**R5**:✓).

The FAIR Evaluator is primarily designed for mechanized interaction through its RESTful Web Service API (**R6**:✓) and provides a demonstrative user interface [43] for form-based access (**R7**:✓). The client-side interface is implemented in JavaScript using the AngularJS framework. The service is a Ruby on Rails application with four primary components: (a) a registry of known MI Tests and their annotations; (b) a registry of collections of MI Tests ("Collections") and their annotations; (c) an invocation function that creates a pipeline of MI Tests and applies them to a resource; and (d) a registry of evaluation results. The codes of the framework[9] and the front-end[10] are available on GitHub under the MIT license (**R8**:✓). The framework does not present a summary of the evaluation as a visual representation, like a badge (**R12**:✗). There is no information in the documentation about the tool's development stage (**R9**:✗) nor about in which phases of the data lifecycle the framework could be used (**R13**:✗).

The FAIR Evaluator has 15 defined MIs, evaluated by 22 Compliance Tests, that the user can group in a collection according to priorities and needs. This feature allows the user to indicate the context of an evaluation, *i.e.*, which metrics should be considered. For deeper customization, the user should have software development skills, *e.g.*, to create new tests or change existing ones by refactoring the source files (**R10**:◗). We did not find information about authentication features to access restricted data (**R11**:✗).

A set of FAIR standards is used in the documentation and implementation of the framework's tools, mainly based on FAIRsharing services (**R14**:✓). The framework has plenty of documentation, including papers and GitHub pages (**R15**:✓). The front-end Web Client is easy to use since one has to fill a MIs Collection, the digital object identifier, a title for the evaluation, and the user's unique identifier (*e.g.*, ORCID) to execute the FAIRness evaluation. However, Web service development skills are required to make use of the RESTful Web API, which is expected (**R16**✓).

The results generated by the framework are machine-actionable (**R17**:✓). The user can scan the output for details (**R18**:✓) and learn about FAIR concepts, although it is technical information (**R19**:◗). They give no explicit recommendations to improve the FAIRness of resources (**R20**:✗). Although all this information is human-readable, it is technical and not so easily understood by non-IT people (**R21**:◗). The results are not stored in a searchable engine (**R22**:✗), and although results versioning is a crucial highlighted feature [44], we did not find implementation for that (**R23**:✗).

3.3 FAIR Enough

FAIR Enough [21] evaluates resources (**R5**:✓) automatically (**R1**:✓) and returns their FAIRness level as the percentage of the tests the digital objects passed (**R2**:◗). Its implementation is based on FAIR Evaluator and F-UJI tools. The FAIR metrics test APIs can be registered and used as in the FAIR Evaluator. To run an evaluation, the user provides a URL, but DOI and handles are also accepted for some collections of tests. The tool is not domain specific (**R3**:✓). The tests' results refer to the principles (**R4**:✓).

It is available as a RESTful Web service (**R6**:✓) implemented in Python using FastAPI[11] and provides a frontend Web interface (**R7**:✓) implemented using React[12]. The code is available in GitHub[13] under MIT license (**R8**:✓).

9 https://github.com/FAIRMetrics/Metrics.
10 https://github.com/FAIRsharing/FAIR-Evaluator-FrontEnd.
11 https://fastapi.tiangolo.com/.
12 https://react.dev/.
13 https://github.com/MaastrichtU-IDS/fair-enough.

We did not find information about the tool's development stage (**R9**:✗), in which phases of the data lifecycle the framework could be used (**R13**:✗), and authentication features to access restricted data (**R11**:✗). The tool does not present a visual representation summarizing the evaluation results (**R12**:✗).

The tool and the tests are customizable but require technical skills (**R10**:◗). Tests implementation uses FAIRsharing services (**R14**:✓).

There is documentation available in GitHub (**R15**:✓). The Web Client is easy to use in the same way as the FAIR Evaluator. However, Web service development skills are required to make use of the RESTful Web API (**R16**✓).

Results are provided in JSON when calling the RESTful API or can be downloaded when using the Web interface (**R17**:✓). They contain details about how tests are executed (**R18**:✓), which can be used to learn FAIR concepts, but it is very technical (**R19**:◗). There are no explicit recommendations for FAIRness improvements (**R20**:✗). Technical skills are required to understand the results (**R21**:◗). We did not find documentation about the storage of results in a searchable engine (**R22**:✗) and about versioning (**R23**:✗).

3.4 FAIR-Checker

FAIR-Checker automatically (**R1**:✓) evaluates the FAIRness (**R2**:✓) of digital objects focusing on domain-agnostic metadata (**R3**:✓). The tool can evaluate any digital object, as long as they are described by metadata available on a landing page (**R5**:✓). Its goal is to promote the use of embedded metadata in Web pages to facilitate the findability and reuse of digital scientific resources. The tool helps data producers and curators identify improvement areas and take steps toward enhancing the FAIRness of their resources [19].

The tool execution process starts with the user supplying a URL as input. Then, it extracts semantic annotations from the Web page to create the first version of a Knowledge Graph (KG)[14]. Public KGs are queried using SPARQL during the FAIRness evaluation against metrics tailored to the evaluation of computation ontologies, according to the FAIR principles (**R4**:✓).

FAIR-Checker is a Web application (**R7**:✓) developed in Python based on the Flask Web Framework. Recently, a RESTful API (**R6**:✓) has been made available to provide FAIRness evaluation to online client tools. The tool is available on GitHub[15] under the MIT license (**R8**:✓) and can be used on the Web [36]. We did not find explicit information about the tool's development stage (**R9**:◗). In addition to that, there is no information about in which phases of the data lifecycle the tool can be used (**R13**:✗).

The tool customization requires software development skills (**R10**:◗). Currently, the tool does not handle content negotiation (**R11**:✗). The tool uses state-of-the-art semantic Web technologies and standards to perform the evaluation. Still, it does not employ explicit FAIR-enabling services (**R14**:◗).

[14] "A knowledge graph acquires and integrates information into an ontology and applies a reasoner to derive new knowledge" [16].

[15] https://github.com/IFB-ElixirFr/FAIR-checker.

The tool has plenty of documentation, including papers and GitHub pages (**R15**:✓). To use the tool, the user has to submit selected dataset identifiers to FAIR-Checker and compare the returning reports. Regular usage does not require software development skills (**R16**:✓).

The execution log can be downloaded as a CSV file, but it is not machine-readable (**R17**:✗). The results include: (i) descriptions about the running tests and comments (**R18**:✓); (ii) FAIR learning resources; however, they are tied to the implementation and not to the principle's definitions (**R19**:◗); (iii) a set of recommendations for FAIRness improvements with links to training resources, such as FAIR-CookBook [35] (**R20**:✓); (iv) a visual representation summarizing the tests (**R12**:✓). Results are intended to be understandable by non-IT experts (**R21**:✓). They are not stored in a searchable engine (**R22**:✗), and there is no support for storing versions of them either (**R23**:✗).

4 Discussion

This section compares the catering of the requirements (Table 4) by the tools presenting our analysis separated by the requirements categories. We consider values of 1, 0.5, and 0 to complete (✓), partial (◗), and no (✗) fulfillment, respectively, to present the coverage of the requirements by the tools.

General requirements (R1 to R5): Almost all the tools fulfill the general requirements (100%). ***Comparison***: *(R1):* They are automated (which is the focus of our work); *(R2):* They present a FAIRness score, except FAIR-Evaluator and FAIR Enough; *(R3):* They execute independently from any specific domain; *(R4):* Their metrics reference the principles they evaluate; *(R5):* They point out the kind of digital objects they evaluate.

However, none of the tools assesses all of the 15 FAIR principles. F-UJI considers data and metadata having the same identifier, *i.e.*, residing on the same landing page, which requires refactoring the tool to evaluate them independently. Besides, this tool does not evaluate some principles because, *e.g.*, they consider supporting them to be roles of the repository (like data and metadata preservation - Principle A2), or they need further clarification (like the use of FAIR vocabularies - Principle I2). FAIR Evaluator does not have MIs for principles R1.2 (detailed provenance) and R1.3 (compliance with community-specific standards). FAIR Enough does not present explicitly the metrics they have already implemented for each principle. However, they implemented a fair-test Python library that users can employ to define and publish FAIR metrics using the standard described by the FAIRMetrics working group [17]. The metric publication includes a public URL of a service that executes the evaluation regarding the metric specification, which allows FAIR enough users to add the metric tests to the Metric collection used in evaluations. Currently, there are metrics published for all the principles in the FAIR Enough metric repository [22]. FAIR-Checker does not support assessment for principles: A2, because they consider it to be out of the scope of the Semantic Web; F3 (Metadata includes the identifier of the data), because there is no appropriate vocabulary to identify data unambiguously; and I2, stating there is no strategy for this kind of evaluation.

Deployment requirements (R6 to R14): The fulfillment varies: F-UJI (7 of 9, *i.e.*, 78%), FAIR-Evaluator and FAIR Enough (4.5 of 9, *i.e.*, 50%), FAIR-Checker (6 of 9, *i.e.*, 67%). ***Comparison***: *(R6) and (R7)*: All tools provide RESTful Web services and Web applications, respectively, to users. *(R8):* All tools exhibit their licenses, which is MIT for all of them. *(R9):* Although F-UJI and FAIR-Checker present evidence of wide usage, FAIR Evaluator and FAIR Enough do not have such proof. None of them explicitly explain their development stage. *(R10):* FAIR Evaluator and FAIR Enough are customizable by non-expert users when they choose the collections of MIs to run in an evaluation. Still, they do not have customization considering the configuration of the test parameters. All tools can have their code customized by skilled software developers with knowledge of the FAIR principles and Semantic Web technologies and standards. *(R11):* Authentication is only supported by F-UJI. *(R12):* FAIR Evaluator and FAIR Enough do not provide a visual representation that summarizes the evaluation. F-UJI and FAIR-Checker present that as a multi-level pie chart and radar chart, respectively. *(R13):* None of the tools state in which data lifecycle phase they could be applied. *(R14):* F-UJI, FAIR evaluator, and FAIR Enough employ FAIR-enabling services. FAIR-Checker focuses on using Semantic Web technologies. All of them use libraries and standards.

User Experience requirements (R15 to R16): These requirements are met by all the tools (100%). ***Comparison***: *(R15):* They have plenty of documentation, including papers and GitHub pages, with examples of using the tools. The code is open to be cloned, which allows software engineering experts to inspect it and deepen their knowledge. *(R16):* Their Web interfaces are easy to use, requiring one to supply the digital object identifier and a few other pieces of data. However, using their APIs requires technical skills.

Reporting requirements (R17 to R23): The fulfillment varies: F-UJI, FAIR-Evaluator, and FAIR Enough (3 of 7, *i.e.*, 43%), FAIR-Checker (3.5 of 7, *i.e.*, 50%). ***Comparison***: *(R17):* Only FAIR-Checker does not export machine-actionable results. *(R18):* Their reports present evidence and reasoning about the performed evaluation; however, *(R19):* They are very technical, tied to the implementation, and do not teach users about the FAIR principles. *(R20):* FAIR-Checker is the only one that gives explicit recommendations for FAIRness improvements besides *(R21):* the recommendations are fully readable by non-experts. *(R22):* None of the tools store the results. (R23): Consequently, they do not support results versioning, which would help to understand how a digital object's FAIRness evolves.

Overall, the tools are very similar regarding requirement fulfillment: F-UJI (74%), FAIR-Checker (70%), FAIR-Evaluator and FAIR Enough (61%). They all follow good software development practices and use state-of-the-art technologies in Software Engineering and the Semantic Web. FAIR-Evaluator is implemented in Ruby on Rails, and the others are implemented in Python. The reporting features should be improved, considering user-experience techniques and user evaluations. The storage of results and versioning are complex features to be implemented, and no tool appraised attempts to do it.

Therefore, to make a tool choice, one should consider not only the percentage of fulfillment but also understand the more critical requirements for their specific scenario, the details of how each tool was appraised, and the difficulties in improving each tool's implementations in case it becomes vital to support requirements not adequately addressed.

5 Related Work

This section presents an overview of the works found in the literature and, afterward, highlights the contribution of our work related to them.

Krans *et al.* [27] list ten tools, including manual, semi-automated, and automated resources for FAIRness assessment. They focus on each tool's ease of use and performance, aiming to give users suggestions on which to choose according to their specific needs and for developers on how to improve them.

Sun *et al.* [40] also compare three automated FAIRness evaluation tools our work appraises. Their study is more focused on comparing each application's results against one another instead of the requirements each one fulfills. They present the issues they found generally with all tools, discuss the advantages and limitations of each one, and give insights into how the disparities among them can lead to different results for evaluating the same datasets.

In turn, Peters-von Gehlen *et al.* [31] offer an analysis of five different FAIRness evaluation approaches, two fully manual, one semi-automated, and two fully automated. Their primary interest also lies in comparing each resource's results when applied to the same datasets to determine which would work best for the task at hand, concluding with a recommendation for mature hybrid approaches and the importance of community efforts.

Slamkov *et al.* [38] consider five different tools, including three automated and two requiring manual labor for arriving at a FAIRness score. While their work compares the existence of eight features in total among the tools under analysis, their focus is also on comparing the results that each one gives to a collection of datasets and the possible reasons for the discrepancies found.

Almost none of the related work supply the rationale that was followed for choosing the tools for analysis, save for Peters-von Gehlen *et al.* [31] who opted to start with a small subset derived from a collection of FAIRness evaluation tools prepared by the Research Data Alliance FAIR Data Maturity Working Group and supplement their findings with a simple Web search.

Compared to these works, our study's uniqueness derives from the fact that we ground our work in the literature since (i) we found the automated tools performing a literature review and (ii) we elicited the requirements to evaluate the tools from that literature review and the papers describing the tools. Besides, we present why the requirements matter and the rationale about how the automated tool fulfills or not each requirement.

6 Conclusion

This work analyzed automated tools found in a literature review on FAIRness assessment. We also compiled a list of 23 desirable requirements that tools for automated FAIRness evaluation could fulfill, grouping them under four categories. We offered an analysis of if and how each of the tools under appraisal meets each of the elicited requirements.

The tools are very similar regarding overall requirement fulfillment (R1, R3 to R8, R10, R13, R15, R16, R18, R19, R22, and R23) but diverge on supporting the other requirements. No tool meets all requirements and stands out as state-of-the-art. Choosing a tool is challenging, and there is room for evolving existing tools or developing a new one to overcome the existing gaps. To choose a tool, one should consider not only the percentage of fulfillment but also the following: (i) the more critical requirements for their specific scenario; (ii) the details of the appraisal presented in this work; (iii) the difficulties in customizing each tool's implementations.

The results of our work can aid other researchers and developers by providing insights into the available automated tools for FAIRness assessment. The consolidated requirements can form the basis for creating a benchmark for the appraisal of FAIRness assessment tools, including enhancing existing options or even designing new approaches.

One limitation of our work is the search scope. We considered tools cited by academic works of Scopus, IEEE, and ACM. These digital libraries include papers from the most relevant journals and conferences in Computer Science.

As a future work, we propose extending the search scope to other digital libraries and to the gray literature (which concerns, *e.g.*, blog posts, videos, and white papers), *i.e.*, works outside of the published (formal) literature (*e.g.*, journal and conference papers) [20]. One example is the FAIRassist.org [18]. It collects and describes resources aimed at helping developers and stakeholders make their digital objects FAIR. It lists manual questionnaires, checklists, and semi-automated and automated tools, which include the ones we evaluated. FAIRassist.org is provided by FAIRsharing.org.

We also plan to engage with users who intend to use automated tools to verify our requirements proposal. Users could also indicate the weights of the requirements and organize them as mandatory, recommended, and optional since the requirements may be of distinct importance for different communities.

Another future work is the development of benchmarks, considering our requirements proposal. We also intend to appraise the automated tools in practice against those benchmarks and existing ones like the "Apples-to-Apples" (A2A) [46] benchmarks, which were developed to evaluate, in a standard way, the tools compliance with (meta)data publishing based on well-established Web standards in use by communities. They were developed because each tool usually produces different results due to distinct metrics, the use of metadata publishing paradigms, and the context considered of the FAIRness evaluation.

References

1. FAIR data assessment tool. https://www.surveymonkey.com/r/fairdat
2. Amdouni, E., Jonquet, C.: FAIR or FAIRer? An integrated quantitative FAIRness assessment grid for semantic resources and ontologies. In: Garoufallou, E., Ovalle-Perandones, M.-A., Vlachidis, A. (eds.) Metadata and Semantic Research: 15th International Conference, MTSR 2021, Virtual Event, November 29 – December 3, 2021, Revised Selected Papers, pp. 67–80. Springer International Publishing, Cham (2022). https://doi.org/10.1007/978-3-030-98876-0_6
3. Aronsen, J.M., Beyan, O., Harrower, N., Holl, A., et al.: Recommendations on FAIR metrics for EOSC. Publications Office of the European Union, LU (2021). https://doi.org/10.2777/70791
4. Austin, C., Cousjin, H., Diepenbroek, M., Petters, J., Soares E Silva, M., Alliance, W.D.S.R.D.: WDS/RDA Assessment of Data Fitness for Use WG Outputs and Recommendations (2019). https://www.rd-alliance.org/group_output/wds-rda-assessment-of-data-fitness-for-use-wg-outputs-and-recommendations/
5. Australian Research Data Commons: FAIR Data Self Assessment Tool. https://ardc.edu.au/resource/fair-data-self-assessment-tool/
6. Bonaretti, S., Willighagen, E.: Two real use cases of FAIR maturity indicators in the life sciences (2019). https://doi.org/10.1101/739334
7. Bonaretti, S., Willighagen, E.: BiGCAT-UM/FAIR_metrics. Department of Bioinformatics - BiGCaT (2021)
8. Carrera-Rivera, A., Ochoa, W., Larrinaga, F., Lasa, G.: How-to conduct a systematic literature review: a quick guide for computer science research. MethodsX **9**, 101895 (2022). https://doi.org/10.1016/j.mex.2022.101895
9. CFDE-CC: FAIRshake: a System to Evaluate the FAIRness of digital objects. https://fairshake.cloud/
10. Clarke, D.J., Wang, L., Jones, A., Wojciechowicz, M.L., et al.: FAIRshake: toolkit to evaluate the FAIRness of research digital resources. Cell Syst. **9**(5), 417–421 (2019). https://doi.org/10.1016/j.cels.2019.09.011
11. Data Archiving and Networked Service (DANS): FAIR self-assessment tool. https://satifyd.dans.knaw.nl/
12. David, R., Mabile, L., Yahia, M., Cambon-Thomsen, A., et al.: Comment opérationnaliser et évaluer la prise en compte du concept "FAIR" dans le partage des données: Vers une grille simplifiée d'évaluation du respect des critères FAIR (2018). https://doi.org/10.5281/zenodo.2551500
13. Devaraju, A., Huber, R.: F-UJI - an automated FAIR data assessment tool. Zenodo (2020). https://doi.org/10.5281/zenodo.4063720
14. Devaraju, A., Huber, R.: An automated solution for measuring the progress toward FAIR research data. Patterns **2**(11), 100370 (2021). https://doi.org/10.1016/j.patter.2021.100370
15. Devaraju, A., et al.: FAIRsFAIR data object assessment metrics. Tech. rep., Zenodo (2020). https://doi.org/10.5281/zenodo.3934401
16. Ehrlinger, L., Wöß, W.: Towards a definition of knowledge graph. SEMANTiCS 2016: Posters and Demos Track **48**(1-4), 2 (2016)
17. FAIRMetrics Working Group: FAIRMetrics/Metrics. FAIR Maturity Testing and Evaluation (2024)
18. fairsharing: Fairassist.org. https://fairassist.org/. Accessed 04 Dec 2024
19. Gaignard, A., Rosnet, T., De Lamotte, F., Lefort, V., Devignes, M.D.: FAIR-Checker: supporting digital resource findability and reuse with knowledge graphs

and semantic web standards. J. Biomedical Semant. **14**(1), 7 (2023). https://doi.org/10.1186/s13326-023-00289-5
20. Garousi, V., Felderer, M., Mäntylä, M.V.: Guidelines for including grey literature and conducting multivocal literature reviews in software engineering. Inf. Softw. Technol. **106**, 101–121 (2019). https://doi.org/10.1016/j.infsof.2018.09.006
21. Institute of Data Science: FAIR Enough. https://fair-enough.semanticscience.org/
22. Institute of Data Science: FAIR Enough - Metrics. https://fair-enough.semanticscience.org/metrics
23. ISACA: CMMI Institute - CMMI. https://cmmiinstitute.com/cmmi
24. Jacobsen, A., de Miranda Azevedo, R., Juty, N., et al.: FAIR Principles: interpretations and implementation considerations. Data Intell. **2**(1-2), 10–29 (2020). https://doi.org/10.1162/dint_r_00024
25. Jones, S., Grootveld, M.: How FAIR are your data? (2017). https://doi.org/10.5281/zenodo.3405141
26. Kitchenham, B., Charters, S.: Guidelines for performing Systematic Literature Reviews in Software Engineering. Durham University Evidence-Based Software Engineering, Tech. rep. (2007)
27. Krans, N., Ammar, A., Nymark, P., Willighagen, E., Bakker, M., Quik, J.: FAIR assessment tools: evaluating use and performance. NanoImpact **27** (2022). https://doi.org/10.1016/j.impact.2022.100402
28. Machado, M.D.O.C., Bravo, N.F.S., Martins, A.F., Bernardino, H.S., Barrere, E., Souza, J.F.D.: Metaheuristic-based adaptive curriculum sequencing approaches: a systematic review and mapping of the literature. Artif. Intell. Rev. **54**(1), 711–754 (2020). https://doi.org/10.1007/s10462-020-09864-z
29. Pergl, R., Hooft, R., Suchánek, M., Knaisl, V., Slifka, J.: "Data Stewardship Wizard": a tool bringing together researchers, data stewards, and data experts around data management planning. Data Sci. J. **18**(1), 59 (2019). https://doi.org/10.5334/dsj-2019-059
30. Pergl, R., Hooft, R., Vondrášek, J., et al.: Data Stewardship Wizard. https://ds-wizard.org/
31. Peters-Von Gehlen, K., Höck, H., Fast, A., Heydebreck, D., Lammert, A., Thiemann, H.: Recommendations for Discipline-Specific FAIRness Evaluation Derived from Applying an Ensemble of Evaluation Tools. Data Sci. J. **21**(1) (2022). https://doi.org/10.5334/dsj-2022-007
32. Petticrew, M., Roberts, H.: Systematic reviews in the social sciences: a practical guide. Blackwell Publishing, Malden (2006). https://doi.org/10.1002/9780470754887
33. RDA: FAIR Data Maturity Model: specification and guidelines (2020). https://doi.org/10.15497/rda00050
34. Richardson, L., Amundsen, M., Ruby, S.: RESTful web APIs: services for a changing world. O'Reilly Media Inc. (2013)
35. Rocca-Serra, P., Gu, W., Ioannidis, V., Abbassi-Daloii, T., et al.: The FAIR Cookbook - the essential resource for and by FAIR doers. Sci. Data **10**(1), 292 (2023). https://doi.org/10.1038/s41597-023-02166-3
36. Rosnet, T., Gaignard, A., Devignes, M.D.: FAIR-checker. https://fair-checker.france-bioinformatique.fr/
37. Sansone, S.A., et al.: FAIRsharing as a community approach to standards, repositories and policies. Nat. Biotechnol. **37**(4), 358–367 (2019). https://doi.org/10.1038/s41587-019-0080-8

38. Slamkov, D., Stojanov, V., Koteska, B., Mishev, A.: A comparison of data FAIRness evaluation tools. In: CEUR Workshop Proceedings, vol. 3237. CEUR-WS (2022)
39. van Soest, J., Choudhury, A., Gaikwad, N., Sloep, M., Dekker, A.: Annotation of existing databases using semantic web technologies: making data more FAIR. In: 12th International Conference on Semantic Web Applications and Tools for Health Care and Life Sciences (2019)
40. Sun, C., Emonet, V., Dumontier, M.: A comprehensive comparison of automated FAIRness evaluation tools. In: CEUR Workshop Proceedings, vol. 3127 (2022)
41. Trojahn, C., Kamel, M., Annane, A., et al.: A FAIR core semantic metadata model for FAIR multidimensional tabular datasets. In: Knowledge Engineering and Knowledge Management, pp. 174–181. Springer International Publishing (2022). https://doi.org/10.1007/978-3-031-17105-5_13
42. Wilkinson, M., Dumontier, M., Durbin, P.: DataFairPort: The Perl libraries version 0.231 (2015). https://doi.org/10.5281/zenodo.33584
43. Wilkinson, M., et al.: The FAIR maturity evaluation service. https://fairsharing.github.io/FAIR-Evaluator-FrontEnd
44. Wilkinson, M.D., Dumontier, M., Sansone, S.A., Bonino da Silva Santos, L.O., et al.: Evaluating FAIR maturity through a scalable, automated, community- governed framework. Sci. Data **6**(1), 1–12 (2019). https://doi.org/10.1038/s41597-019-0184-5
45. Wilkinson, M.D., Dumontier, M., et al.: The FAIR guiding principles for scientific data management and stewardship. Sci. Data **3**(1), 1–9 (2016). https://doi.org/10.1038/sdata.2016.18
46. Wilkinson, M.D., Sansone, S.A., Marjan, G., Nordling, J., Dennis, R., Hecker, D.: FAIR Assessment Tools: Towards an "Apples to Apples" comparisons (2022). https://doi.org/10.5281/zenodo.7463421

An Extended Evaluation of Single-Label Multi-modal Field of Research Classification Using a Taxonomy-Based Metric

Florian Ruosch[1(✉)], Rosni Vasu[1], Ruijie Wang[1,2], Luca Rossetto[1], and Abraham Bernstein[1]

[1] Department of Informatics, University of Zurich, Zürich, Switzerland
{ruosch,rosni,ruijie,rossetto,bernstein}@ifi.uzh.ch

[2] University Research Priority Program "Dynamics of Healthy Aging", University of Zurich, Zürich, Switzerland

Abstract. This paper presents a multi-modal approach to the single-label field of research classification shared task. Our method, **SLAMFORC**, incorporates metadata, full text, and image data from scholarly articles to generate comprehensive document embeddings. We built a voting ensemble of pre-trained BERT models (SciBERT and SciNCL) and traditional classifiers and achieved competitive performance in the *Field of Research Classification of Scholarly Publications* shared task. SLAMFORC scored highest in F1 score and precision and second best in recall and accuracy. We extend our original analysis by examining misclassified samples to improve future iterations. Additionally, we apply a taxonomy-based evaluation metric to better assess our results.

Keywords: Natural Scientific Language Processing · Field of Research Classification · Multi-modality · Taxonomy-Based Evaluation

1 Introduction

Keywords and other classifications may help when searching or organizing scholarly publications [22]. They can be annotated by the authors or the publishers, with a corresponding manual effort, or may be machine-generated. The latter has been an application of natural language processing, which, with the advent of pre-trained large language models such as BERT [15], has recently gained momentum. Still, the automated classification of research papers remains challenging [31].

This paper describes an extension to our original submission [29] for the shared task *Field of Research Classification of Scholarly Publications*[1] [3] of the *1st Workshop on Natural Scientific Language Processing and Research Knowledge Graphs (NSLP 2024)* [28]. Its *Subtask I*, which our contribution addresses, is

[1] https://nfdi4ds.github.io/nslp2024/docs/forc_shared_task.

A. Meroño Peñuela et al. (Eds.): ESWC 2024, LNCS 15345, pp. 167–182, 2025.
https://doi.org/10.1007/978-3-031-78955-7_16

to develop a single-label classifier for general scholarly publications. We trained and tested it on a dataset of around 60,000 English scientific papers [1,2], each from one of 123 hierarchical classes of a subset of the Open Research Knowledge Graph taxonomy.[2]

Our approach, dubbed **SLAMFORC** (short for *Single-Label Multi-modal Field of Research Classification*), is multi-modal in that we incorporated data from three different sources: the dataset provided by the organizers of the challenge containing metadata of the articles (e.g., title, abstract), the semantic information provided by Crossref,[3] and the contents of the papers (i.e., full text and images). Using this data as features, we engineered a classifier that produces single-label predictions for a given input document. For this endeavor, we computed the embeddings with two different flavors of a pre-trained BERT [15] model and, subsequently, fed these vectors to a handful of traditional classifiers. Then, we applied a voting ensemble [23] to their output to combine them into a final classifier, incorporating all of them as well as the entirety of the available features.

The shared task was very competitive, with 13 system submissions. The margin among the top five submissions was very narrow (±0.75%), illustrating that the boundaries were pushed of what was possible with the provided data and task. In the end, our approach came in among the top results, scoring the highest values for two out of four evaluated aspects and the second-best for the others: accuracy (75.6%), precision (75.7%), recall (75.6%), and F1 (75.4%).

In addition to the original paper, we perform an extended analysis of our results to better understand the misclassified samples in the hopes of enabling future systems to avoid these fallacies in the field of research classification. We identify problematic cases and point out possible improvements for future iterations. Also, we add a taxonomy-based metric to the evaluation. Wwe use it to show that SLAMFORC classifies the majority of the samples correctly but struggles in some cases.

The remainder of this paper is structured as follows. Section 2 presents the related work, and Sect. 3 introduces our methodology. In the ensuing Sect. 4, we describe our experiments. Then, Sect. 5 analyzes the results more in-depth. Finally, we draw conclusions in Sect. 6.

2 Related Work

The classification of scholarly papers into research fields has found ample applications: for example, to ease organizing or searching the flood of new publications.

One such system [9] groups biomedical papers by applying non-negative matrix factorization [19] to the term relevance vectors of the documents. It uses bisecting k-means clustering [7], and, at the same time, assigns semantic meaning to each document and cluster inferred from the matrix decompositions.

[2] https://orkg.org/fields.

[3] https://www.crossref.org/.

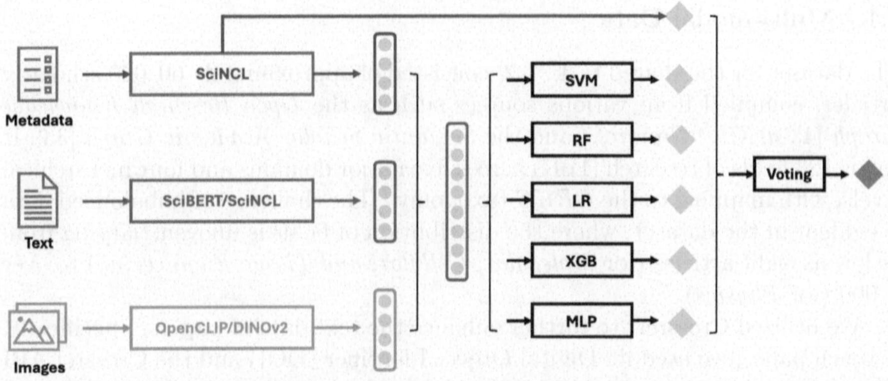

Fig. 1. Overview of the system architecture.

The work by Taheriyan [31] describes an approach to classifying papers by using relationships such as common authors and references as well as citations in a graph. This information allows new papers to be assigned topics automatically instead of requiring manual annotations.

Nguyen and Shirai [22] focus on various text features such as the segmentation of the paper and apply three different classifiers: multi-label kNN [34], binary approach [32], and their newly proposed back-off model. While the latter performs the best, another interesting insight from their results is that only using the title, abstract, and the sections *Introduction* and *Conclusions* of papers improves over using the full text as a feature.

Another approach is presented by Kim and Gil [18]: They describe a classification system based on latent Dirichlet allocation [8] and term frequency-inverse document frequency [27]. The former is employed to extract relevant keywords from the abstracts, the latter for k-means clustering [5] papers with similar topics.

More recently, SPECTER [13] uses pre-trained language models (e.g., SciBERT [6]) to generate document-level embeddings from the titles and abstracts. These can be used for downstream tasks, such as predicting the class of a document, which is demonstrated by applying SPECTER to a new dataset with papers in 19 classes. In this work, incorporating the entire text of papers remains an open issue due to limitations on memory and the availability of the paper contents.

3 The SLAMFORC System

This section describes our approach to solving the shared task. We first explain the multi-modal data of our system. Then, we detail the classifiers we used with this data.

Figure 1 shows an overview of the system. Its code is publicly available.[4]

[4] https://gitlab.ifi.uzh.ch/DDIS-Public/forc24.

3.1 Multi-modal Data

The dataset for the shared task [1,2] consisted of approximately 60,000 scholarly articles, compiled from various sources such as the *Open Research Knowledge Graph* [4], *arXiv*,[5] *Crossref*,[6] and the *Semantic Scholar Academic Graph* [33]. It spans 123 fields of research (FoR) across five major domains and four hierarchical levels, with mapping to the *ORKG* taxonomy.[7] The challenge of imbalanced data is evident in the dataset, where the distribution of fields is uneven, varying from as low as eight articles (for *Molecular, Cellular, and Tissue Engineering*) to over 6,000 (for *Physics*).

We utilized Crossref[3] to further enhance the text data of papers. Specifically, for each paper, we used its Digital Object Identifier (DOI) and the Crossref API client[8] to retrieve its annotated subjects and references from the Crossref Unified Resource API.[9] For the paper with the DOI "*10.1007/JHEP06(2012)126*," for example, we retrieved the subject "*Nuclear and High Energy Physics*" and the metadata of 37 reference papers. Despite Crossref adopting a different taxonomy, this retrieved subject remains highly useful for predicting the target label of this paper (i.e., "*Physics*"). Also, the reference papers are mostly in the Physics domain, and this information can be very useful.

We used the title, abstract, and publisher information from the provided dataset, along with the subject data, to generate the metadata embeddings for each paper. We appended all this data as input text to SciNCL [25], a pre-trained BERT model, for computing an embedding as a comprehensive representation of each paper.

In order to make use of the full text for the papers in the dataset, we first had to obtain the respective documents. This was straightforward for items that already had a download link annotated. For all other papers, we used the DOI field, where available, to find the PDFs. There were some cases where neither was available. For those, we relied on Crossref's API to resolve the paper title to its DOI, which allowed us to download the full text document, if it was available.

To extract the text from the PDFs, we employed PaperMage [21]. For each PDF, it produces a JSON file with information about its content and structure. We only relied on the extracted symbols, which we used to reconstruct the full text of the respective papers. Using this data, we computed the document-level embeddings with two pre-trained BERT models: SciBERT [6] and SciNCL [25]. Because of BERT's limitation to processing 512 tokens at a time [15] and papers exceeding this, we batched the input data accordingly. We employed a sliding window of size 512 tokens with an overlap of 128 to conserve semantics near the window borders. After computing the embeddings for each such chunk, we averaged them to obtain the final document-level embedding.

[5] https://arxiv.org.

[6] https://www.crossref.org/.

[7] https://huggingface.co/spaces/rabuahmad/forcI-taxonomy/blob/main/taxonomy.json.

[8] https://github.com/fabiobatalha/crossrefapi.

[9] https://api.staging.crossref.org/swagger-ui/index.html.

To incorporate the visual information contained in the PDFs, we extracted all their images and converted them to raster graphics. For each image, we used an OpenCLIP [12] model pre-trained on the LAION-5B dataset [30] as well as a pre-trained DINOv2 [24] model to extract image features. When PDFs contained multiple images, we used mean-pooling to aggregate the multiple feature vectors per model, resulting in two vectors per PDF; one for each applied model. For papers where the PDF did not contain any images or the PDF was not available, these vectors were set to zero.

3.2 Classifier

For the final system, we used a mixture of traditional classifiers and neural methods that we combined with an ensemble voting method [23]. Figure 1 shows an overview of the system. After computing the embeddings for the various data sources, we trained several classifiers that could handle vectors as input and predict the single-label class for each item in the dataset.

An obvious choice are Support Vector Machines [14], or SVM for short. Due to the nature of the input data, they can naturally classify them in a high-dimensional space and predict the field of research label. We employed a Random Forest (RF) [17] since it reduces overfitting to the training data, which was an overt problem to be expected because of the skew in classes in the dataset. Logistic Regression (LR) is another widely used traditional classifier to predict single labels on linearly separable data. With eXtreme Gradient Boosting (XGB) [11], we used another popular method that can achieve good performance while sacrificing interpretability. Next, we also employed a fully-connected Multilayer Perceptron (MLP) to deal with the nonlinearity of the data. Furthermore, we fine-tuned SciNCL [25] as an end-to-end solution on the metadata.

Finally, we combined the output of the classifiers described above into an ensemble method [23] with hard voting [20]. This enabled the use of all techniques and all available data at the same time while still producing a single predicted label for each item in the dataset.

4 Experiments

Table 1 shows the results of the initial experiments. We used a set of traditional classifiers as implemented by scikit-learn [26] with all of the available data for each paper consisting of the stacked embedding vectors. Since no method significantly outperformed the others, we combined all of them post hoc using a voting ensemble method, giving us our final classifier for the results of which we submitted to the shared task.

To illustrate the impact of each data source and dissect our multi-modal approach, we performed a feature ablation study, the results of which are shown in Table 2. We used our final system architecture with all classifiers combined with voting on the powerset of possible feature combinations. It is evident that the (embeddings of the) metadata have the most positive influence on the results.

Table 1. The first results on the *validation set* of the individual classifiers with all features (embeddings of metadata, full text, and images) as measured by accuracy, weighted precision, recall, and F1.

Classifier	Accuracy	Precision	Recall	F1
Support Vector Machine	0.755	0.754	0.755	0.752
Random Forest	0.755	0.754	0.755	0.753
Logistic Regression	0.750	0.755	0.750	0.750
XGBoost	0.731	0.735	0.731	0.731
Multilayer Perceptron	0.743	0.748	0.743	0.743

Table 2. Ablation study on the *validation set* by feature combination.

Meta	Text	CLIP	DINO	Accuracy	Precision	Recall	F1 score
✓				0.774	0.776	0.774	0.773
	✓			0.437	0.709	0.437	0.463
		✓		0.254	0.552	0.254	0.241
			✓	0.259	0.505	0.259	0.250
✓	✓			0.776	0.778	0.776	0.775
✓		✓		0.772	0.775	0.772	0.772
✓			✓	0.776	0.777	0.776	0.774
	✓	✓		0.438	0.700	0.438	0.463
	✓		✓	0.437	0.700	0.437	0.461
		✓	✓	0.271	0.529	0.271	0.265
✓	✓	✓		0.776	0.777	0.776	0.775
✓	✓		✓	0.779	0.781	0.779	0.778
✓		✓	✓	0.776	0.778	0.776	0.774
	✓	✓	✓	0.433	0.701	0.433	0.456
✓	✓	✓	✓	0.777	0.779	0.777	0.775

Still, adding extra information to the classifier is not detrimental but rather contributes to a higher score. This holds more for the (embeddings of the) full texts of the papers, which perform decently independently. Using the embeddings of the images in the papers alone, where applicable, achieves clearly worse results than the other two data sources. Nevertheless, the combination of all features is among the highest scoring for all four employed metrics, and there was no reason not to rely on everything available.

Finally, Table 3 shows the results of the shared task evaluation.[10] Our submission (ID 683689, top row) scored the highest for precision (75.7%) and F1 (75.4%) while achieving the second-best values for accuracy (75.6%) and recall (75.6%). This shows that our multi-modal approach worked and performed well

[10] https://codalab.lisn.upsaclay.fr/competitions/16684#results.

Table 3. The final evaluation results on the *test set* as measured by accuracy, weighted precision, recall, and F1 (best for each in **bold**, runner-up <u>underlined</u>). Our submission is the first line.

ID	Accuracy	Precision	Recall	F1 ↓
683689	<u>0.756</u>	**0.757**	<u>0.756</u>	**0.754**
688995	0.754	<u>0.755</u>	0.754	<u>0.752</u>
687946	**0.757**	0.754	**0.757**	0.750
689747	0.748	0.744	0.748	0.743
688510	0.743	0.742	0.743	0.739
651741	0.730	0.725	0.730	0.724
649383	0.726	0.719	0.726	0.720
686435	0.706	0.703	0.706	0.693
686384	0.702	0.695	0.702	0.692
689251	0.682	0.679	0.682	0.678
689454	0.658	0.659	0.658	0.653
647796	0.058	0.061	0.058	0.057
678150	0.004	0.002	0.004	0.002

in this competition. Without further knowledge of the other systems, no comparisons can be made or insights gained, and are, thus, left for future work. In conclusion, the automated field of research classification of scientific papers is still challenging, but the submissions for this shared task seemed to have pushed the boundaries of what was possible with the given tools and information, seeing how close the top results were.

5 Analysis

In this section, we perform an extended analysis of our results from the shared task *Field of Research Classification of Scholarly Publications* [3]. First, we explore which categories of misclassified samples contributed negatively to our F1 score. Then, we investigate how collapsing the field of research categories to their respective super-classes affects our results. Finally, we perform an additional evaluation using a metric with regard to taxonomy-based assignments that also takes the distances among the categories into account. Data and code of the extended analysis are available in our online repository.[4]

5.1 Impact of Misclassified Samples

To analyze the misclassification errors of SLAMFORC, we look into the categories that contributed negatively to our F1 score. That is fields of research classes for which the F1 is below our threshold of 75.4%. Additionally, to avoid overfitting, we also set the requirements that these categories need to make up

Table 4. Results for categories making up at least 1% of the test data set ($n \geq 89$) that influenced our F1 results negatively.

Category	Top-Level	Precision	Recall	F1 ↑	Support
Computer Sciences	Physical Sciences & Mathematics	0.39	0.37	0.38	112
Applied Mathematics	Physical Sciences & Mathematics	0.56	0.53	0.54	142
Mathematics	Physical Sciences & Mathematics	0.52	0.64	0.57	145
Condensed Matter Physics	Physical Sciences & Mathematics	0.58	0.59	0.59	200
Analysis	Physical Sciences & Mathematics	0.62	0.68	0.65	131
Artificial Intelligence	Physical Sciences & Mathematics	0.65	0.67	0.66	137
Cosmology	Physical Sciences & Mathematics	0.73	0.61	0.66	137
Algebra	Physical Sciences & Mathematics	0.68	0.65	0.67	92
External Galaxies	Physical Sciences & Mathematics	0.69	0.66	0.68	162
Atomic, Molecular and Optical Physics	Physical Sciences & Mathematics	0.65	0.72	0.69	197
Theory/Algorithms	Physical Sciences & Mathematics	0.78	0.62	0.69	99
Materials Science and Engineering	Engineering	0.71	0.70	0.71	239

at least 1% of the test data set; i.e., they need to have a support of at least 89. Table 4 shows the 12 categories we identified in this manner, along with their top-level class, precision, recall, F1, and number of samples (support) in the test data set.

The *Computer Sciences* category exhibits the lowest F1 score by far at 0.38. This indicates significant challenges in correctly identifying true positives, leading to a substantial number of false positives and false negatives, as evident by precision (0.39) and recall (0.37). It is important to note that this only concerns samples with the target field of research *Computer Sciences* and none of its various sub-fields. Therefore, it is understandable that misclassifications occur as they might also be rooted in the ground truth annotations, which may not be specific enough. Accordingly, we cannot necessarily fault SLAMFORC for this shortcoming but rather a closer look at this part of the data set is required.

The other two categories with striking results are *Theory/Algorithms* and *Cosmology*. Both show a distinctly higher precision (0.73 and 0.78, respectively) than recall (0.61 and 0.62, respectively). This indicates the tendency of SLAMFORC to miss many true instances but also to have few false positives. Thus, the capabilities of future iterations of SLAMFORC to capture these two specific categories should be addressed in particular.

The results for the other categories in Table 4 do not reveal any useful new insights. The balance between precision and recall numbers suggests that SLAMFORC misclassifies these categories by including incorrect and missing actual instances. This shows the need for improved model discrimination capabilities in these fields.

Finally, Fig. 2 shows the normalized confusion matrix of the top-level classes for the categories in Table 4. Notably, *Arts and Humanities* is absent from the plot since no sample was misclassified from or to it.

We can observe that SLAMFORC largely classifies the samples in (the subcategories of) *Physical Sciences & Mathematics* correctly (0.94). Only a small fraction of 0.04 is misclassified as belonging to *Engineering* or one of its sub-

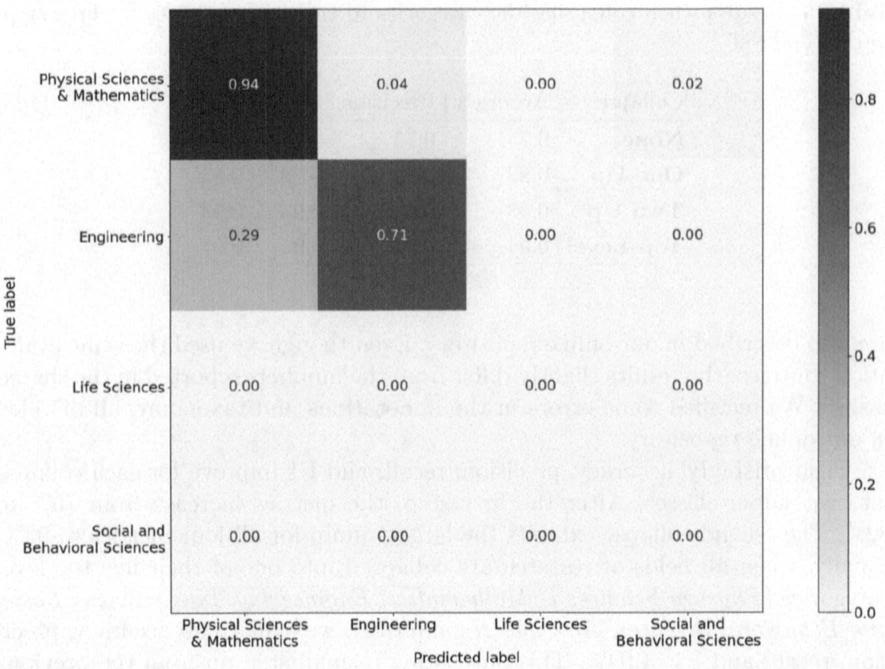

Fig. 2. Normalized confusion matrix of the top-level categories for the results negatively contributing to our F1 (see Table 4). Notice the absence of the top-level category *Arts and Humanities.*

categories. Vice versa, there is a significant amount of samples from *Engineering* that are wrongly predicted to be from *Physical Sciences & Mathematics* or one of its sub-categories (0.29). This is understandable since there is some connection between the two fields since it can be considered an application of *Physical Sciences & Mathematics.* Still, it highlights a shortcoming of SLAMFORC and its underlying classifiers. All other cells in the confusion matrix show negligible percentages of misclassification (i.e., ≤ 0.01).

5.2 Collapsing to Super-Classes

Table 5 shows accuracy, precision, recall, and F1 for the original results and their collapsing into the super-classes of the predicted research fields in three steps up to the top-level categories. For example, *Machine Learning* would be collapsed into *Artificial Intelligence* in the first step, then into *Computer Sciences* in the next, and, finally, into *Physical Sciences & Mathematics.* For taxa of lower than maximum rank in the taxonomy, they are collapsed into their parents up to the top level and then stay there for subsequent steps (e.g., *Computational Linguistics* → *Linguistics* → *Social and Behavioral Sciences* → *Social and Behavioral Sciences*). Details can be found in the ORKG taxonomy,[7] and the parent classes

Table 5. Results when collapsing the categories to their super-classes in three steps to the top-level.

Collapse	Accuracy	Precision	Recall	F1
None	0.75	0.75	0.75	0.75
One Up	0.82	0.82	0.82	0.82
Two Up	0.93	0.93	0.93	0.93
Top-Level	0.94	0.94	0.94	0.94

are also described in our online repository. Even though we used the same evaluation routines, the results slightly differ from the numbers reported in the shared task.[10] We rectified some errors in the annotations and taxonomy, all detailed in our online repository.

Unsurprisingly, accuracy, precision, recall, and F1 improve for each collapse into the super-classes. After the first step, the metrics increase from 75% to 82%. The second collapse exhibits the largest jump for all four metrics to 93%. Finally, when all fields of research are collapsed into one of their five top-level categories (*Physical Sciences & Mathematics*, *Engineering*, *Life Sciences*, *Social and Behavioral Sciences*, *Arts and Humanities*), we achieve an accuracy, precision, recall, and F1 of 94%. This only being a small step up from the previous may be owed to the fact that few categories have maximum rank in the taxonomy. Still, these can be considered impressive results given the complexity of predicting the field of research for papers.

Figure 3 shows the normalized confusion matrix of the top-level classes for all fields of research in the taxonomy. As the majority of misclassifications by SLAMFORC is to assign them to *Physical Sciences & Mathematics* or one of its sub-categories, we see a tendency. The second-most wrongly predicted subcategories are from the top-level class of *Engineering*. As mentioned earlier, there is a connection between these two fields. Still, this reveals a possible bias in SLAMFORC and its underlying classifiers.

5.3 Taxonomy-Based Evaluation

Figure 4 shows the confusion matrix as a heatmap for all categories in the taxonomy. The full list for the axis labels can be found in the online repository.[4] It illustrates that most samples are predicted correctly, indicated by the strong diagonal line. Still, the following classes do not have any correctly classified instances in the test set: *Biomedical Engineering and Bioengineering*, *Cell Behavior*, *Civil and Environmental Engineering*, *Energy Systems*, *Hardware Systems*, *Molecular, Cellular, and Tissue engineering*, *OS/Networks*, *Other Quantitative Biology*, *Physical Sciences & Mathematics*, *Popular Physics*, *Quantitative Methods*, *Space Physics*, *Tissues and Organs*. Their support ranges from one to eight, making them only very small fractions considering the size of the test set ($n = 8903$).

The application of traditional metrics, like done in the shared task, is, thus, problematic. They score everything not on the diagonal of the confusion matrix

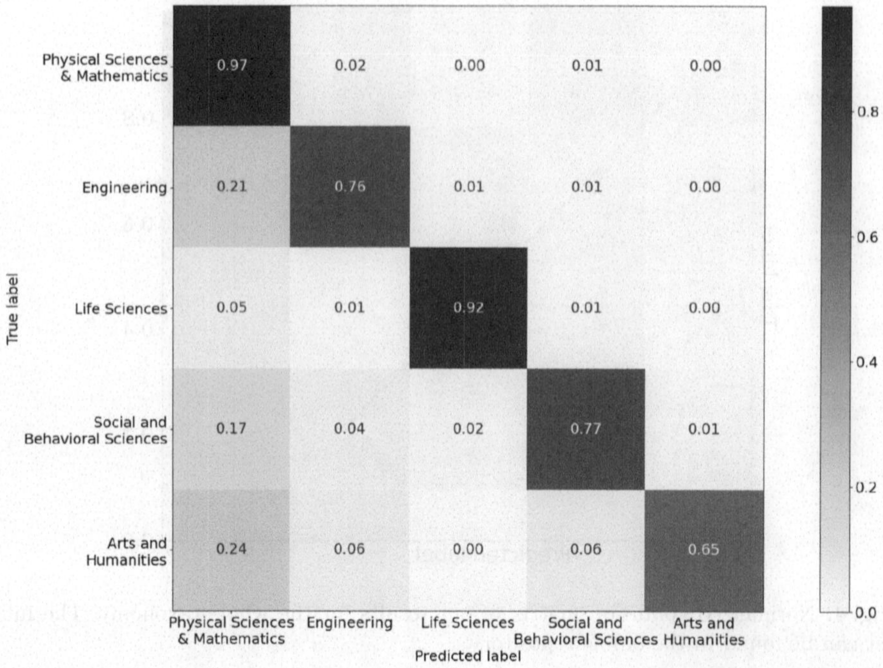

Fig. 3. Normalized confusion matrix of our results for the five top-level categories.

as zeroes by treating all the classes as independent. Still, the distribution in Fig. 4 shows there are some connections between the labels. There is a defined hierarchy in the taxonomy and, inherently, some semantics. The labels on the axis are grouped by that hierarchy. Therefore, not every distance is equal, but proximity in the confusion matrix also indicates "less of an error".

Table 6 shows the label pairs with a misclassification rate of more than 0.5. Looking at these sets, it becomes evident that the errors should not be punished by giving a score of zero instead of one (i.e., giving an error of one) since the classes in the pairs are somewhat related. Accordingly, we should evaluate considering these distances.

Hence, we applied a taxonomy-based metric [10,16] to assess the performance of SLAMFORC by considering the hierarchical structure of the labels. Inspired by the taxonomy similarity (TS) definition [16], we define the taxonomy distance $TD = 1 - TS$. For two labels a and b with the hierarchical sequences $a_1 \dots a_m$ and $b_1 \dots b_n$ respectively, the TS is the following:

$$TS = \frac{\sum_{l=1}^{\min(m,n)} 1[a_l = b_l]}{\max(m,n)}$$

Hence, we obtain $0 \leq TD = 1 - TS \leq 1$, where bigger signifies better. For the example above, the hierarchical sequence would look as follows: $a_1 =$ *Social and Behavioral Sciences*, $a_2 =$ *Linguistics*, $a_3 =$ *Computational Linguistics*.

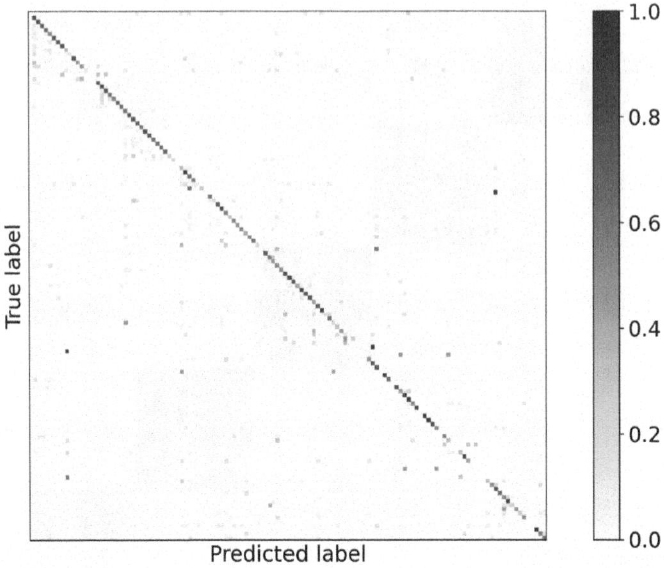

Fig. 4. Normalized confusion matrix of our results for the whole taxonomy. The full list can be found in the online repository.

Table 6. Label pairs where the misclassification rate exceeds 0.50.

True Label	Predicted Label	Miscl. Rate	Support
Audio and Speech Processing	Computational Linguistics	1.00	2
Biomedical Engineering and Bioengineering	Computer and Systems Architecture	1.00	1
Molecular, Cellular, and Tissue Engineering	Biological and Chemical Physics	1.00	1
Multiagent Systems	Artificial Intelligence	0.67	3
OS/Networks	Digital Communications and Networking	0.67	3
Cell Behavior	Biological and Chemical Physics	0.67	3
Controls and Control Theory	Mathematics	0.50	24
Energy Systems	Mechanical Engineering	0.50	4
Tissues and Organs	Life Sciences	0.50	2
Tissues and Organs	Quantitative Methods	0.50	2
Hardware Systems	Computer Sciences	0.50	2
Hardware Systems	Controls and Control Theory	0.50	2
Genomics	Bioinformatics	0.50	2
Genomics	Medicine	0.50	2
Economic Theory	Economics	0.50	2

The average taxonomy distance (ATD) is defined as the mean of the taxonomy distances between each sequence and its predicted label, calculated by the sum of these distances divided by the number of instances [10]. Figure 5 shows that the majority of the classifications are accurate, as indicated by the initial flat segment with zero taxonomy distance. However, there is a sharp increase towards the end, which reflects the misclassification in some instances. This suggests that SLAMFORC performs well overall, but it struggles with a few challenging instances that result in larger taxonomy distances.

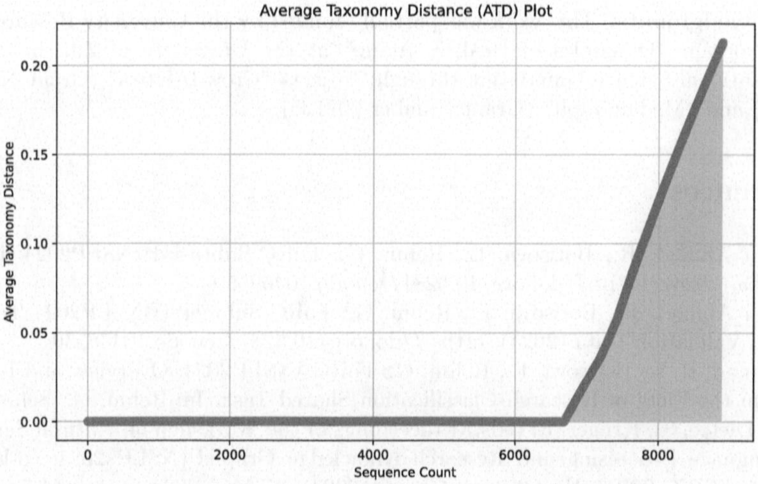

Fig. 5. Average Taxonomy Distance (ATD) plot.

6 Conclusions

In this paper, we presented an extended analysis of **SLAMFORC** [29], a system for the *Single-Label Multi-modal Field of Research Classification.* It was used to produce the results for our submission to the shared task *Field of Research Classification of Scholarly Publications* [3] of the *1st Workshop on Natural Scientific Language Processing and Research Knowledge Graphs (NSLP 2024)* [28]. Pursuing a multi-modal approach by incorporating not only the given dataset containing metadata of the papers but also the full text of publications as well as images in these documents, we built an ensemble classifier by combining a set of traditional classifiers using a voting ensemble. We computed the embeddings with pre-trained large language models, stacked these vectors, and trained the individual classifiers. Then, we used them jointly to obtain a single-label prediction for each item in the dataset.

Our system achieved the highest precision and F1 and the second-best accuracy and recall values of all submissions, demonstrating its effectiveness. Judging by the range of top submissions, the ceiling of what was possible in the shared task seems to have been reached.

This paper adds to the original publication by performing an extended analysis of the results and also incorporates a taxonomy-based metric. We investigated the classes that contributed negatively to our F1 score. Furthermore, we explore how collapsing the categories to their parents affects the results, showing an increase in each step. Finally, we use the taxonomy distance, which is based on the taxonomy similaritys [16], to show that SLAMFORC classifies the majority of the samples correctly, struggling only with a few challenging instances.

Acknowledgments. This work was partially funded by the University Research Priority Program "Dynamics of Healthy Aging" at the University of Zurich and the Swiss National Science Foundation through Projects "CrowdAlytics" (Grant Number 184994) and "MediaGraph" (Grant Number 202125).

References

1. Abu Ahmad, R., Borisova, E., Rehm, G.: FoRC-Subtask-I@NSLP2024 Testing Data (2024). https://doi.org/10.5281/zenodo.10469550
2. Abu Ahmad, R., Borisova, E., Rehm, G.: FoRC-Subtask-I@NSLP2024 Training and Validation Data (2024). https://doi.org/10.5281/zenodo.10438530
3. Ahmad, R.A., Borisova, E., Rehm, G.: FoRC@NSLP2024: Overview and Insights from the Field of Research Classification Shared Task. In: Rehm, G., Schimmler, S., Dietze, S., Krüger, F. (eds.) Proceedings of the Workshop on Natural Scientific Language Processing and Research Knowledge Graphs (NSLP 2024; co-located with ESWC 2024). Hersonissos, Greece (2024), 27 May 2024. Accepted for publication
4. Auer, S., et al.: Improving access to scientific literature with knowledge graphs. Bibliothek Forschung und Praxis **44**(3), 516–529 (2020)
5. Balabantaray, R.C., Sarma, C., Jha, M.: Document clustering using k-means and k-medoids. CoRR abs/1502.07938 (2015). http://arxiv.org/abs/1502.07938
6. Beltagy, I., Lo, K., Cohan, A.: SciBERT: a pretrained language model for scientific text. In: Inui, K., Jiang, J., Ng, V., Wan, X. (eds.) Proceedings of the 2019 Conference on Empirical Methods in Natural Language Processing and the 9th International Joint Conference on Natural Language Processing, EMNLP-IJCNLP 2019, Hong Kong, China, November 3–7, 2019, pp. 3613–3618. Association for Computational Linguistics (2019). https://doi.org/10.18653/V1/D19-1371
7. Bishop, C.M.: Pattern recognition and machine learning, 5th Edition. Information science and statistics, Springer (2007). https://www.worldcat.org/oclc/71008143
8. Blei, D.M., Ng, A.Y., Jordan, M.I.: Latent Dirichlet allocation. J. Mach. Learn. Res. **3**, 993–1022 (2003). http://jmlr.org/papers/v3/blei03a.html
9. Bravo-Alcobendas, D., Sorzano, C.: Clustering of biomedical scientific papers. In: 2009 IEEE International Symposium on Intelligent Signal Processing, pp. 205–209. IEEE (2009)
10. Chen, C.Y., Tang, S.L., Chou, S.C.T.: Taxonomy based performance metrics for evaluating taxonomic assignment methods. BMC Bioinform. **20**(1), 310 (2019). https://doi.org/10.1186/s12859-019-2896-0
11. Chen, T., Guestrin, C.: XGBoost: a scalable tree boosting system. In: Proceedings of the 22nd ACM SIGKDD International Conference on Knowledge Discovery and Data Mining, pp. 785–794. KDD '16, Association for Computing Machinery, New York, NY, USA (2016). https://doi.org/10.1145/2939672.2939785
12. Cherti, M., et al.: Reproducible scaling laws for contrastive language-image learning. In: IEEE/CVF Conference on Computer Vision and Pattern Recognition, CVPR 2023, Vancouver, BC, Canada, June 17-24, 2023, pp. 2818–2829. IEEE (2023). https://doi.org/10.1109/CVPR52729.2023.00276
13. Cohan, A., Feldman, S., Beltagy, I., Downey, D., Weld, D.S.: SPECTER: document-level representation learning using citation-informed transformers. In: Jurafsky, D., Chai, J., Schluter, N., Tetreault, J.R. (eds.) Proceedings of the 58th Annual Meeting of the Association for Computational Linguistics, ACL 2020,

Online, July 5-10, 2020, pp. 2270–2282. Association for Computational Linguistics (2020). https://doi.org/10.18653/V1/2020.ACL-MAIN.207
14. Cortes, C., Vapnik, V.: Support-vector networks. Mach. Learn. **20**(3), 273–297 (1995). https://doi.org/10.1007/BF00994018
15. Devlin, J., Chang, M.W., Lee, K., Toutanova, K.: BERT: Pre-training of deep bidirectional transformers for language understanding. In: Burstein, J., Doran, C., Solorio, T. (eds.) Proceedings of the 2019 Conference of the North American Chapter of the Association for Computational Linguistics: Human Language Technologies, Volume 1 (Long and Short Papers), pp. 4171–4186. Association for Computational Linguistics, Minneapolis, Minnesota (2019). https://doi.org/10.18653/v1/N19-1423, https://aclanthology.org/N19-1423
16. Hasson, I., Novgorodov, S., Fuchs, G., Acriche, Y.: Category recognition in e-commerce using sequence-to-sequence hierarchical classification. In: Proceedings of the 14th ACM International Conference on Web Search and Data Mining, pp. 902–905 (2021)
17. Ho, T.K.: Random decision forests. In: Third International Conference on Document Analysis and Recognition, ICDAR 1995, August 14 - 15, 1995, Montreal, Canada, vol. I, pp. 278–282. IEEE Computer Society (1995). https://doi.org/10.1109/ICDAR.1995.598994
18. Kim, S., Gil, J.: Research paper classification systems based on TF-IDF and LDA schemes. Hum. Centric Comput. Inf. Sci. **9**, 30 (2019). https://doi.org/10.1186/S13673-019-0192-7
19. Lee, D.D., Seung, H.S.: Learning the parts of objects by non-negative matrix factorization. Nature **401**(6755), 788–791 (1999)
20. Littlestone, N., Warmuth, M.K.: The weighted majority algorithm. Inf. Comput. **108**(2), 212–261 (1994)
21. Lo, K., Shen, Z., Newman, B., Chang, J., Authur, R., Bransom, E., Candra, S., Chandrasekhar, Y., Huff, R., Kuehl, B., Singh, A., Wilhelm, C., Zamarron, A., Hearst, M.A., Weld, D., Downey, D., Soldaini, L.: PaperMage: A unified toolkit for processing, representing, and manipulating visually-rich scientific documents. In: Feng, Y., Lefever, E. (eds.) Proceedings of the 2023 Conference on Empirical Methods in Natural Language Processing: System Demonstrations, pp. 495–507. Association for Computational Linguistics, Singapore (2023). https://doi.org/10.18653/v1/2023.emnlp-demo.45, https://aclanthology.org/2023.emnlp-demo.45
22. Nguyen, T.H., Shirai, K.: Text classification of technical papers based on text segmentation. In: Métais, E., Meziane, F., Saraee, M., Sugumaran, V., Vadera, S. (eds.) Natural Language Processing and Information Systems - 18th International Conference on Applications of Natural Language to Information Systems, NLDB 2013, Salford, UK, June 19-21, 2013. Proceedings. Lecture Notes in Computer Science, vol. 7934, pp. 278–284. Springer (2013). https://doi.org/10.1007/978-3-642-38824-8_25,
23. Opitz, D., Maclin, R.: Popular ensemble methods: an empirical study. J. Artif. Intell. Res. **11**, 169–198 (1999)
24. Oquab, M., et al.: DINOv2: learning robust visual features without supervision. CoRR abs/2304.07193 (2023). https://doi.org/10.48550/ARXIV.2304.07193
25. Ostendorff, M., Rethmeier, N., Augenstein, I., Gipp, B., Rehm, G.: Neighborhood contrastive learning for scientific document representations with citation embeddings. In: Goldberg, Y., Kozareva, Z., Zhang, Y. (eds.) Proceedings of the 2022 Conference on Empirical Methods in Natural Language Processing, pp. 11670–11688. Association for Computational Linguistics, Abu Dhabi,

United Arab Emirates (2022). https://doi.org/10.18653/v1/2022.emnlp-main.802, https://aclanthology.org/2022.emnlp-main.802
26. Pedregosa, F., et al.: Scikit-learn: machine learning in Python. J. Mach. Learn. Res. **12**, 2825–2830 (2011)
27. Ramos, J., et al.: Using TF-IDF to determine word relevance in document queries. In: Proceedings of the First Instructional Conference on Machine Learning, vol. 242, pp. 29–48. Citeseer (2003)
28. Rehm, G., Schimmler, S., Dietze, S., Krüger, F. (eds.): Proceedings of the Workshop on Natural Scientific Language Processing and Research Knowledge Graphs (NSLP 2024; co-located with ESWC 2024). No. 14770 in Lecture Notes in Artificial Intelligence (LNAI), Springer (2024)
29. Ruosch, F., Vasi, R., Wang, R., Rossetto, L., Bernstein, A.: Single-label multi-modal field of research classification. In: Rehm, G., Schimmler, S., Dietze, S., Krüger, F. (eds.) Proceedings of the Workshop on Natural Scientific Language Processing and Research Knowledge Graphs (NSLP 2024; co-located with ESWC 2024). Hersonissos, Greece (2024), 27 May 2024. Accepted for publication
30. Schuhmann, C., et al.: LAION-5B: an open large-scale dataset for training next generation image-text models. In: Koyejo, S., Mohamed, S., Agarwal, A., Belgrave, D., Cho, K., Oh, A. (eds.) Advances in Neural Information Processing Systems 35: Annual Conference on Neural Information Processing Systems 2022, NeurIPS 2022, New Orleans, LA, USA, November 28 - December 9, 2022 (2022). http://papers.nips.cc/paper_files/paper/2022/hash/a1859debfb3b59d094f3504d5ebb6c25-Abstract-Datasets_and_Benchmarks.html
31. Taheriyan, M.: Subject classification of research papers based on interrelationships analysis. In: Proceedings of the 2011 Workshop on Knowledge Discovery, Modeling and Simulation, pp. 39–44 (2011)
32. Tsoumakas, G., Katakis, I., Vlahavas, I.P.: Mining multi-label data. In: Maimon, O., Rokach, L. (eds.) Data Mining and Knowledge Discovery Handbook, 2nd ed, pp. 667–685. Springer (2010). https://doi.org/10.1007/978-0-387-09823-4_34
33. Wade, A.D.: The semantic scholar academic graph (S2AG). In: Companion Proceedings of the Web Conference 2022, p. 739. WWW '22, Association for Computing Machinery, New York, NY, USA (2022). https://doi.org/10.1145/3487553.3527147
34. Zhang, M., Zhou, Z.: ML-KNN: a lazy learning approach to multi-label learning. Pattern Recogn. **40**(7), 2038–2048 (2007). https://doi.org/10.1016/J.PATCOG.2006.12.019

Challenges and Opportunities of LLM-Augmented Semantic Model Creation for Dataspaces

Sayed Hoseini[1(✉)], Andreas Burgdorf[2], Alexander Paulus[2], Tobias Meisen[2], Christoph Quix[1,3], and André Pomp[2]

[1] Hochschule Niederrhein,Krefeld, Germany
{sayed.hoseini,christoph.quix}@hs-niederrhein.de
[2] Institute for Technologies and Management of Digital Transformation, University of Wuppertal,Wuppertal, Germany
{burgdorf,paulus,meisen,pomp}@uni-wuppertal.de
[3] Fraunhofer FIT,St. Augustin, Germany

Abstract. The objective of dataspaces is to facilitate seamless and reliable data exchange between different organizations. In Europe, their prominence has grown with the implementation of the European Data Governance Act. This legislation emphasizes the importance of trust, accessibility, and shared dataspaces, which necessitate semantic interoperability grounded in the FAIR principles. While semantic descriptions in the form of semantic models and ontologies are indispensable to dataspaces, their full potential remains unexploited. Meaningful metadata, including contextual information, enhances data usability, but the manual creation of semantic models can be challenging. Large Language Models (LLMs) offer a new way to utilize data in dataspaces. Their advanced natural language processing capabilities enable context-aware data processing and semantic understanding. This paper presents initial experiments on customizing and optimizing LLMs for semantic labeling and modeling tasks. The contributions of this work include research questions for future investigations, early experiments demonstrating the applicability of LLM for semantic labeling, and proposed directions to address discovered challenges.

Keywords: Dataspace · Semantic Modeling · LLMs

1 Introduction

The European Data Governance Act [5,30] outlines definitions and objectives aimed at bolstering trust, broadening data accessibility, and promoting shared dataspaces. Its impact extends across various data consumers and providers from academia as well as businesses. Efficient data sharing within dataspaces necessitates semantic interoperability as an essential design principle, grounded in the required adherence to FAIR principles [44]. Thereby, the utilization of semantic

A. Meroño Peñuela et al. (Eds.): ESWC 2024, LNCS 15345, pp. 183–200, 2025.
https://doi.org/10.1007/978-3-031-78955-7_17

descriptions and ontologies are already part of many dataspaces, but the potential is far from being fully utilized in actual implementations [40]. An example of this is semantic interoperability and integration, a key aspect of dataspaces that requires aggregating and integrating large amounts of heterogeneous data from different sources. Managing data can be challenging, not only due to the variety of data formats such as XML, CSV, JSON, relational data, and graph data. In addition, data is often distributed across different departments within an organization, under different governance regimes, and data models. It is important to have a clear and logical structure of information, which fosters a common understanding in dataspaces, i.e., *a lingua franca for data moderation* [3] based on the Linked Data principles.

Meaningful metadata is crucial for enhancing data usability, particularly for users with limited domain knowledge or those unfamiliar with a dataset. Annotating raw data from heterogeneous data sources with semantically rich models enhances data interpretability and usability [27,46]. This type of semantic data expands beyond typical extractable metadata, such as schema, data types, sizes, and formats, to include contextual information that is not inherent to the specific data source. The field of *Semantic Data Management* (SDM) [17] aims to represent the metadata about heterogeneous data sources in the form of ontologies or knowledge graphs (KG) serialized in a language of the Semantic Web. Hence, the goal is to establish an additional layer between the data and the knowledge layer [36]. This is highly relevant for dataspaces because they integrate data from various systems and platforms, which requires data to be interoperable and seamlessly exchangeable between systems. In order to implement SDM in practice, conceptualizations in the form of KGs and/or ontologies [15], and a mapping between concepts and data items are required. *Semantic models* provide these mappings from single datasets to a common data model to represent data consistently across different applications in a way that is understandable and interpretable by both humans and machines [37].

With companies increasingly acknowledging the importance of data for their business operations, semantic descriptions are often integrated into data management and governance strategies [9,41], where an ontology or KG serves as a conceptual representation of an organization's data assets. A data source that is semantically well-annotated can be identified and interpreted by leveraging conceptual representations of the data and by comprehending the provided context information stored in the model. However, a huge initial overhead, coming from the time-consuming manual process of creating meaningful semantic descriptions for data sources, hampers the widespread adoption of SDM in practise [17]. Creating semantic models entails deciphering the existing data source, consulting appropriate conceptualizations, and establishing connections between data attributes and concepts provided by the conceptualization.

Automating this task can be challenging and complex. Futia et al. [11] present a method based on graph neural networks covering the process of the process of semantic modeling. However, the model can only optimize semantic models for which historic training data exists. Xu et al. [45] train a cross-modal network to learn semantic features between data sources and semantic models. They admit that the method has shortcomings in dynamically augmenting the semantic models to cover concepts that are not part of the original training data. Moreover, challenges remain with detecting and correcting potentially incorrect attribute types if a source attribute has more than one attribute type, and distinguishing similar attributes with the same entities and semantic types.

Following the rise of Large Language Models (LLMs), one can expect to see a major impact on the landscape of data utilization and exchange within dataspaces. LLMs, such as OpenAI's GPT-3.5 and GPT-4.0, have demonstrated remarkable capabilities in understanding, generating, and processing vast amounts of textual data [8,25]. Their abilities in natural language processing enable advanced semantic understanding and context-aware data processing within dataspaces. A promising field of LLM application is the integration of heterogeneous data sources stored in a dataspace.

In this article, we highlight initial experiments in this direction to examine the question of how such general-purpose AI systems can be customized and optimized for data integration tasks in the sense of SDM. In particular, we make the following contributions:

- A set of research questions to be answered in future research endeavors
- Early experiments to illustrate the applicability of LLMs to the tasks of semantic labeling
- Potential future research directions to address the identified challenges with the applicability of LLMs to the tasks of semantic labeling and modeling.

This article is an extended version of [16], in which we evaluated the semantic labeling capabilities of GPT-4. In this paper, we include additionally experiments with GPT-4o as well as the open-source model LLaMA-3 (see Table 1). Section 5.1 now includes a discussion of KG-enhanced LLMs with some concrete examples to clarify the potential of the unification between semantic technologies and contemporary LLMs as well as challenges faced along the way. In addition, we have detailed the possibilities of integrating LLMs into semantic modeling platforms by outlining an automated approach, in which LLMs act as a recommendation engine, and an interactive approach, in which the user is actively communicating with the LLM through prompts.

2 Semantic Data Management

Fig. 1 illustrates the basic idea of semantic models. The raw datasets in the dataspace are represented at the bottom; they can be in different formats and structures, such as tabular data or hierarchical JSON data, but have partially overlapping content. The semantic model is a *projection* from a shared conceptualization onto the different datasets. It utilizes relevant entities and relationships of the conceptualization, in this case, the *schema.org* ontology (prefix *schema:*), to formalize the context information of the dataset. An essential part of each semantic model are the mappings, indicated as dotted lines, which link

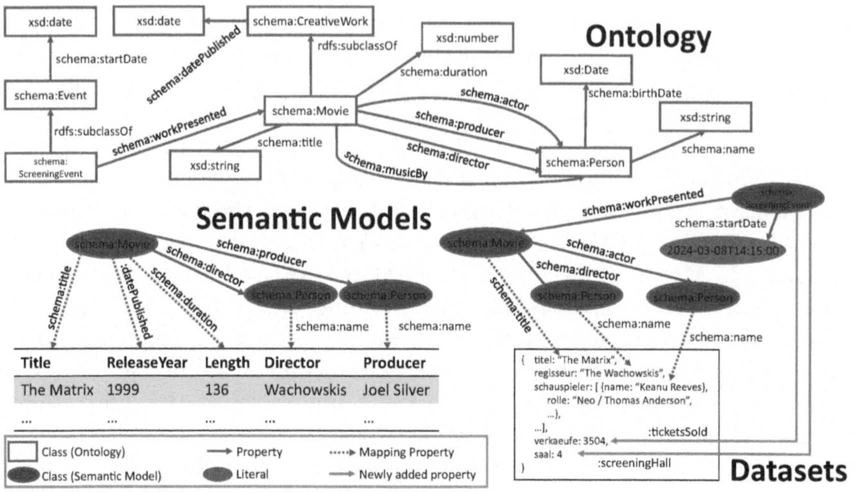

Fig. 1. Semantic models creating a unified mapping from different data sources (datasets) to an ontology.

attributes in the datasets to classes in the semantic model using properties of these classes. These elementary mappings are referred to as *semantic labels*. The semantic model captures the precise meaning of the dataset, explicitly encoding the semantic types and relationships among its attributes within the graph.

Following the definition of semantic labeling by Pham et al. [33], a semantic label is an annotation of a dataset attribute by a tuple consisting of a class (subject) and a property (predicate). In this work, a semantic label is represented as a triple: (subject, predicate, schema attribute). For example, the semantic label of the table's column 'Title' is constructed through the subject 'schema:Movie' and the predicate 'schema:title' modeling the relationship between them. This connects the table's content to the attribute 'titel' in the JSON object, indicating an entry point for data integration between the two (heterogeneous) datasets. Moreover, the semantic model doesn't merely rely on a static conceptualization; it can also introduce novel classes and properties [34]. The necessity for evolution becomes apparent when users contribute datasets containing concepts and relationships not yet included in the conceptualization. The semantic label for the JSON key 'verkaeufe' is represented as the triple: (schema:ScreeningEvent, :ticketsSold, 'verkaeufe'). Here, the predicate is a novel property for that specific domain, which is not (yet) present in this form in the general-purpose schema.org ontology. This new knowledge can be systematically integrated, thus perpetually advancing the conceptualization layer [35]. Semantic models complement extractable metadata (such as data types, sizes, formats, etc.) to convey context information that may not be inherent to the dataset at hand, for instance, a starting date of a 'schema:ScreeningEvent' as shown in Fig. 1.

The underlying process of semantic model creation has been formalized by [32] starting with the identification of the schema of the dataset, followed by a *semantic labeling* phase, in which basic concepts are assigned to the identified attributes. Automated semantic labeling, referred to as *Semantic Type Detection* [19], is the process of identifying these labels using algorithms and machine learning models. After the semantic labeling, the *semantic modeling* phase builds the remaining semantic model by formalizing the context information. During semantic modeling, *semantic relation inference* [11] refers to the process of automated identification of relationships and additional concepts, resulting in a generated semantic model. All automation is followed by the semantic refinement phase, where the modeler is involved in the modeling process to correct any errors present before the semantic model is finalized and stored for documentation purposes. In practice, semantic relation inference depends heavily on accurate semantic labels [39,42], which underscores the importance of semantic type detection in fully automated systems to induce as few errors as possible for the modeler to correct.

Research Questions. With an introduction to the field of SDM at hand, we move on to formulate the research questions that have motivated this work. The goal is to leverage LLMs to improve the automation of semantic model creation for large quantities of heterogeneous data sources that share a common domain in a dataspace.

- **RQ1:** How to utilize LLMs to perform semantic type detection with a fixed set of labels coming from a pre-selected conceptualization (such as *Wikidata*, or *schema.org*)?
- **RQ2:** How to utilize LLMs to perform semantic type detection against an arbitrary domain ontology, i.e., with no labeled dataset or zero-shot classification?
- **RQ3:** How can LLMs be utilized to identify and formalize the context of a given dataset, creating a full semantic model?

3 Related Work

First, in the scope of this contribution, we consider only works after the launch of *ChatGPT* in November 2022. While one can make a strong case that (large) language models have existed before this date, we decided to draw a line due to the massive performance increase which was quite suddenly accessible to the public. Most of the works found in this limited range are pre-prints that have not yet been peer-reviewed and published in scientific journals. To the best of our knowledge, so far, except for the below-mentioned approaches, there seems to be no further LLM-based efforts on the integration of the semantics of several heterogeneous data sources modeled directly in a language of the Semantic Web in order to generate semantic models in the sense of Fig. 1.

Korini et al. [23] are among the first to report the application of LLMs for the Column Type Annotation (CTA) task. CTA is a schema-level annotation task that represents a simplified form of our interpretation of semantic labeling (no predicate) as it aims to map the underlying table schema to a conceptualization. They view CTA as a multi-class classification problem and evaluate different prompt designs. One important artifact that is highlighted is that *ChatGPT* tends to ignore the instruction to use terms from the label space, and instead answers using different terms. This is a known drawback of contemporary LLMs known as the Hallucination problem [21]. Their proposed solutions for this challenge involve first determining a set of classes of the entities described in the table and depending on this set asking *ChatGPT* to annotate columns using only the relevant subset of the overall vocabulary. The evaluation of the approach reports competitive performance when evaluated against the more traditional models which are mostly directly fine-tuned for the CTA task and require significant amounts of task-specific training data [38].

A dataspace stores heterogeneous data of any type of which the majority may be in some form relational, but an important fraction may be more complex, e.g. nested and even unstructured (video, text, audio, ...). We found several works [14,24,49] that aim at customizing LLMs via fine-tuning for tables in particular. The goal is to solve the challenge of table understanding which is closely related to understanding the semantics of a data source as it includes the CTA task for example. Usmani et al. [41] highlight the importance of multi-modal knowledge graphs for dataspaces, present a review of the current state, and propose an ontology towards further development. Furthermore, since important use cases for datasets can be attributed to numerical data, it is important to have solid numerical reasoning skills [12]. Several works suggest that modern LLMs excel in simple problem settings, but they fall short of human expert performance in problems requiring numerical reasoning over long contexts. As the complexity of challenging mathematical problems increases, LLMs currently exhibit suboptimal performance [8,50].

There exist several works that investigate the use of LLMs for Knowledge Graph Engineering [2,10,28]. Here the goal is to utilize the LLM for common tasks related to KGs. For example, Meyer et al. [29] investigate SPARQL query generation as well as knowledge extraction from fact sheets and KG exploration among others. They present several prompts that essentially test how to pose questions in natural language executed against serialized KGs. The experiments show that LLMs can return syntactically correct SPARQL queries and even entire serialized RDF models with the desired form based on a task formulated in natural language. Further, LLMs can find relationships in KG and answer basic questions correctly, e.g., *"Are there any connections between US and UK?"*. They report major performance differences between GPT-3.5 and GPT-4 in favor of the latter. One particular prompt aims at extracting knowledge from tables and converting it into a serialized KG, which is very close to the idea of semantic modeling. The experiment illustrates several problems with the output of contemporary LLMs:

- A tendency to prioritize the usage of *schema.org* vocabulary. While this works well for well-known entities and properties, the LLMs invent reasonable, but

non-existent classes and properties (in the *schema.org* namespace) for concepts and relations that are too specific.
- Non-deterministic output: For multiple runs of the same prompt to the LLM, the output varies. For instance, while in three out of four runs a printer manufacturer was represented as a separate typed entity, in one run it was only expressed as a string literal.
- Invention of non-existent properties, prefixes, and classes: If the LLM cannot identify a fully matching class for a concept or a relation, URIs for those elements are invented for the raw RDF output. While this would be possible in its own namespace, the classes and properties are placed in existing namespaces, such as *schema.org*, resulting in the URIs not being resolvable.
- Non-functional queries: SPARQL queries generated by GPT-3 did not return the expected results when executed against a knowledge graph, albeit being syntactically correct. All queries needed slight modifications to work, such as correcting the referencing of non-existent classes.

To conclude, the results obtained by Meyer et al. show that the problems commonly observed with LLMs also limit their ability to conduct tasks in the semantic domain. It is therefore not possible to use LLMs out-of-the-box for semantic relation inference. Since semantic type detection is simpler than semantic relation inference and also relies heavily on obtaining context, this area of automation is investigated more closely.

4 Semantic Type Detection with LLMs

To assess the effectiveness of LLMs in semantic type detection, we conducted a series of four exemplary experiments. For these experiments, we employed three advanced state of the art LLMs: GPT-4, GPT-4o, and LLaMA 3-70B. For evaluation, we manually selected three datasets from the VC-SLAM corpus [7] which contains datasets created by human modelers in combination with their data description and semantic model as evaluation datasets. Dataset 1 (VC-SLAM 0001) has seven labels that are close to natural language, Dataset 2 (VC-SLAM 0018) has 21 labels that are mostly human readable, and Dataset 3 (VC-SLAM 0068) consists of 24 labels, some of which are abbreviations. The experiments are briefly described in the following and the results are given in Table 1.

4.1 Experiments

Experiment 1 - Mapping to VC-SLAM: This experiment explores the ability of LLMs to map dataset labels to the corresponding concepts within the VC-SLAM ontology, provided solely in Turtle (TTL) format, without any additional contextual information. This setup is designed to evaluate the basic capability of LLMs to leverage the ontology's structure and content for semantic type detection. The task involves providing dataset labels to the LLM and instructing it to identify the most appropriate ontology concept for each label.

Prompt Experiment 1

- You are a tool for semantic type detection. I will provide you an owl ontology that consists of all the concepts you know. This ontology is called VC-SLAM. Later I will additionally provide the labels of three data sets. For each label you return the fitting concept from the ontology.
- The first data set consists of the following labels: type, longitude, address, latitude, tvm_identifier, pay_by_credit_card, pay_by_cash
  Please return the results in the following form: label,concept

Experiment 2 - VC-SLAM with Documentation: In this experiment, the methodology is similar to the *Mapping to VC-SLAM* experiment, but it includes comprehensive documentation of the VC-SLAM ontology and datasets. This tests the hypothesis that additional contextual information enhances the accuracy of semantic type detection.

Experiment 3 - schema.org Ontology: This experiment shifts the focus to a general-purpose ontology to compare the adaptability and performance of the LLMs with a different ontology structure. It provides insights into the model's versatility and the challenges of applying a broad ontology like *schema.org* to a specific dataset, highlighting differences in specificity and applicability. Results are manually compared with the described concepts in the data documentation.

Experiment 4 - Simplified VC-SLAM: The final experiment aims to investigate the impact of ontology complexity on semantic type detection accuracy. By reducing the VC-SLAM ontology to only include concept names and their descriptions without further relations, this experiment seeks to determine whether a simplified ontology framework would enhance mapping accuracy of LLMs due to decreased complexity and ambiguity.

4.2 Results

The outcomes of the experiments are measured across the three different datasets.

Experiment 1 - Mapping to VC-SLAM: In this experiment, the models mapped the labels directly to the VC-SLAM ontology. GPT-4 achieved 57% accuracy for ds1, 33% for ds2, and a notably lower 13% for ds3, indicating its struggle without additional contextual data. GPT-4o showed improved performance with 71% for ds1, 100% for ds2, and 26% for ds3, demonstrating better handling of the VC-SLAM ontology, especially for the second dataset. Llama3 70b had 57% for ds1, 38% for ds2, and 13% for ds3, performing similarly to GPT-4, which suggests that it also struggles without additional context.

Experiment 2 - VC-SLAM with Documentation: When provided with additional documentation, the models showed improved performance. GPT-4

Table 1. The table demonstrates the results of the four experiments that we run on three datasets. The datasets refer to the following original datasets from VC-SLAM [7]: 1: 0001, 2: 0018, 3: 0068

	Nr of labels	ds1	ds2	ds3
		7	21	23
Total Hits (Accuracy) GPT-4	Mapping to VC-SLAM	4 (0.57)	7 (0.33)	3 (0.13)
	VC-SLAM with Documentation	5 (0.71)	13 (0.62)	5 (0.22)
	schema.org Ontology	7 (1.0)	16 (0.76)	11 (0.48)
	Simplified VC-SLAM	4 (0.57)	9 (0.43)	12 (0.52)
Total Hits (Accuracy) GPT-4o	Mapping to VC-SLAM	5 (0.71)	21 (1.0)	6 (0.26)
	VC-SLAM with Documentation	5 (0.71)	19 (0.9)	23 (1.0)
	schema.org Ontology	7 (1.0)	18 (0.86)	20 (0.87)
	Simplified VC-SLAM	5 (0.71)	16 (0.76)	21 (0.91)
Total Hits (Accuracy) Llama3 70b	Mapping to VC-SLAM	4 (0.57)	11 (0.52)	13 (0.57)
	VC-SLAM with Documentation	4 (0.57)	8 (0.38)	7 (0.3)
	schema.org Ontology	7 (1.0)	14 (0.67)	18 (0.78)
	Simplified VC-SLAM	2 (0.29)	6 (0.29)	1 (0.04)

achieved 71% accuracy for ds1, 61% for ds2, and 21% for ds3. GPT-4o further improved with 71% for ds1, 71% for ds2, and 43% for ds3. Llama3 70b had 57% for ds1, 38% for ds2, and 30% for ds3. These findings highlight the significant impact of extra contextual information in enhancing semantic type detection capabilities, with GPT-4o benefiting the most from the documentation.

Experiment 3 - schema.org Ontology: This experiment demonstrated the adaptability of the models with the schema.org ontology. GPT-4 showed strong performance with 100% accuracy for ds1, 76% for ds2, and 47% for ds3. GPT-4o performed exceptionally well, achieving 100% for ds1, 85% for ds2, and 87% for ds3. Llama3 70b also showed impressive results with 100% for ds1, 67% for ds2, and 78% for ds3. These results suggest that all models, particularly GPT-4o, handle general-purpose ontologies like schema.org effectively, possibly due to their inclusion in the training data or the meaningfulness of the descriptions.

Experiment 4 - Simplified VC-SLAM: In this experiment, the models mapped labels to a simplified version of the VC-SLAM ontology. In comparison to experiment 1 we achieved the following results: GPT-4 achieved same results for ds1, improvements of 10% ds2, and 39% for ds3, indicating that simplification partly improves performance. GPT-4o showed same results for ds1, a performance decrease of 24% for ds2 and an improvement of 65%. In contrast, Llama3-70b had performance losses of 28% for ds1, 23% for ds2, and 53% for ds3, indicating a significant struggle with the simplified ontology compared to the other models.

During these experiments, several key findings emerged. First, the availability of additional contexts, such as ontology documentation, significantly improves the models' ability to accurately map dataset labels to ontology concepts, underscoring the importance of rich contextual information for semantic type detection. Second, the experiments revealed the models' adaptability to different ontologies, with performance variations highlighting their capability to handle both specialized and general-purpose ontologies. Notably, the schema.org ontology showed high accuracy, particularly for GPT-4o. Lastly, the simplification of the ontology structure was shown to potentially enhance semantic type detection accuracy, particularly benefiting GPT-4o, although this was not a universal trend. These findings contribute valuable insights into the potential of leveraging LLMs for semantic type detection, indicating promising pathways for automating and refining the data categorization process. The experiments underscore the significance of ontology design and contextual information in optimizing the performance of semantic type detection tasks using AI models like GPT-4 and GPT-4o.

5 Semantic Model Creation with LLMs

Adding LLMs into the process of semantic model creation provides automation algorithms with the ability to profit from the advantages that these pre-trained models provide. Taking the findings from both related work and our experiments into account, it can be deduced that results obtained from LLMs need to be verified and checked before being applied in a semantic model creation scenario within dataspaces. In the following, two approaches on how to utilize LLM-generated output in automated semantic model creation are conceptualized.

Table 2. The pros and cons of LLMs vs KGs as described by [31]

LLM		**KG**	
Pros +	Cons -	Pros +	Cons -
General knowledge	Implicit knowledge	Structural knowledge	Incompleteness
Language processing	Hallucinations	Accuracy	Lacking language understanding
Generalizability	Indecisiveness	Decisiveness	
	Black-Box	Interpretability	Unseen facts
	Lacking domain-specific/new knowledge	Domain-specific knowledge	
		Evolving knowledge	

5.1 Unifying KGs with LLMs for Semantic Modeling

Although the technologies for linked data and the Semantic Web have become more mature in recent years, the amount of data considered in Semantic Web applications is far less than in Big Data applications [13]. Thus, scalability to large, heterogeneous data sets is a major challenge for applying Semantic Web technologies in dataspaces for which LLMs can be a great help. However, even though LLMs can effectively possess rich knowledge learned from massive amounts of training data and benefit downstream tasks at the fine-tuning stage, as previously described, they still have significant limitations due to the lack of external knowledge [8]. In contrast, KGs are structured knowledge models that explicitly store rich factual knowledge, but they are difficult to construct and evolve by nature, making it challenging to generate new facts and represent unseen knowledge [20]. Therefore, it is reasonable to view KGs and LLMs as two complementary technologies whose integration has the potential to produce synergy, capitalizing on the strengths of each while mitigating their respective weaknesses. Their integration may address some of the contemporary challenges discussed in Sect. 3 and represent one answer to the third research question **(RQ3)** on how LLMs can enhance the semantic model creation process.

Pan et al. [31] present a detailed discussion on research towards the unification of language models and KGs, where they contrast the pros and cons of (large) language models vs KGs. Table 2 confirms the previous findings about the drawbacks of LLMs, namely hallucination, a lack of domain-specific knowledge, indecisiveness, and a lack of interpretability. As the most basic semantic unit, entities play a crucial role, and incorporating their knowledge into LLMs helps to improve semantic understanding. In addition, there are also a large number of relational triples in the KG, which can provide sufficient structured information to improve the semantic understanding further. Since conventional LLMs trained on plain text data are not designed to understand (graph-)structured data such as knowledge graphs, they might not fully grasp or understand the information conveyed by the KG structure. This assumption is confirmed by our experiments (see Sect. 4), since reducing the representation of ontologies to plain text significantly improves the performance. This indicates that GPT does not handle the graph structure well. Conversely, the automated construction of KGs is equally challenging, and current approaches to KGs are inadequate in handling the incomplete and dynamically changing nature of real-world KGs. Additionally, many of the current techniques for KGs are tailored to particular tasks and, therefore not easy to generalize to broader applications. This suggests that KGs and LLMs indeed complement and may synergize.

So-called *KG-enhanced LLMs* integrate KGs with LLMs to address their difficulty in recalling factual knowledge while generating knowledge-grounded contents [18]. Yang et al. [47] review recent developments in this area and categorize them into before-, during-, and post-training enhancement according to the stage at which KGs participate in training.

An example of training enhancement before and during training is *K-BERT* [26]. Before training the input text is expanded into graph structure to merge the structured knowledge of KGs and then converts the merged graph back into text for training. It converts input texts to knowledge-rich sentence trees by injecting related triples and fusing them with relevant subgraphs of the KG. For example, an original input sentence such as *"Tim Cook is currently visiting Beijing now"* is expanded by further sentences such as *"Tim Cook is the CEO of Apple"*, *"Bejing is the capital of China"* and "*Bejing is a City*" through factual knowledge coming from a KG. The resulting sentence tree reads, *"Tim Cook CEO Apple is visiting Beijing capital China is a City now"*. Because this procedure makes the sentence unreadable due to incorrect structural information, during training techniques to overcome this problem of knowledge noise are introduced.

An example of post-training enhancement is *KG-Rank* [48], where the authors leverage a medical KG with ranking techniques, aiming to improve free-text question-answering in the medical domain. Upon receiving a question, they initially retrieve factual information from a medical KG and then apply a ranking to obtain the most relevant triplets which then, combined with the task prompt, are input into LLMs for answer generation. To illustrate the potential benefits the authors consider an example to address hallucinations by *LLaMa2-13b*:

Question

"What would be the ideal diet recommendations for a 53-year-old male with acute renal failure and hepatic failure?"

LLaMa2-13b answer

"... Protein intake: Provide adequate protein to support liver function and wound healing. The recommended daily intake of protein for a 53-year-old male is approximately 1.6-2.2 grams per kilogram of body weight..."

KG-enhanced LLaMa2-13b answer

"Low protein intake: Protein intake should be limited to about 0.8-1.0 gram per kilogram of body weight per day, as excessive protein intake can exacerbate renal failure and liver disease..."

These examples highlight the potential of combining LLMs' language understanding capabilities with the rich, structured knowledge in KGs to produce more reliable and contextually relevant responses, thereby addressing the limitations of each technology when used independently.

5.2 LLM-Supported Interactive Semantic Model Design

Since semantic model creation is usually performed inside a semantic modeling platform, integrating LLMs into the semantic model creation following an interactive pattern requires the surrounding platforms to offer additional functions. None of the existing semantic modeling platforms, such as *SAND* [43],

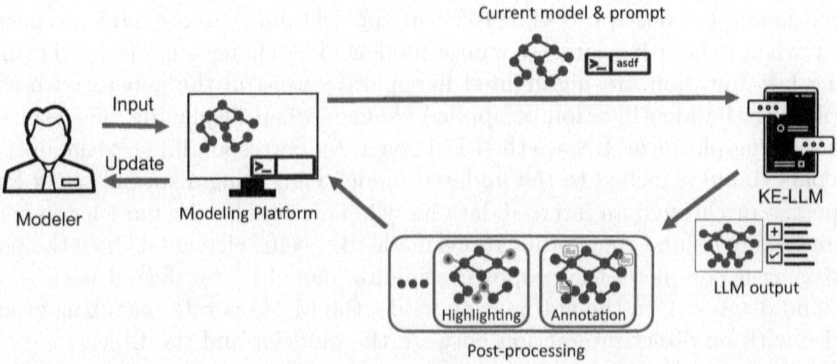

Fig. 2. LLM-based semantic model modification process

MantisTable [4] or *PLASMA* [1], offer the ability to communicate with a generative AI to refine semantic models. Future platforms to support manual semantic model creation will likely integrate the interaction with an LLM as a central component of their design. For example, a semantic model creation could be fitted into a session with an interactive LLM. Any type of generative LLM can be used, however, using knowledge-enhanced LLMs helps to reduce the effects of unwanted phenomena, such as hallucinations.

Two modes of including an LLM into the semantic model creation process are discussed in this contribution. The automation mode utilizes the LLM as a background operation, replacing or supporting existing automated semantic modeling approaches in order to automatically generate recommendations. The interactive mode exploits the LLM's capabilities of natural language processing to offer a simplified interface for non-expert users, i.e., users with little or no previous knowledge of semantic technologies, to create or modify (refine) semantic models.

Figure 2 visualizes the general process in which the modeler and the LLM serve as the participants of a communication. All interactions between both parties are conducted through various services, such as the modeling platform and the LLM's API. These services apply modifications and transform the contained data to match the other side's data model. In case the LLM used provides a session-based communication, this feature can be exploited to maintain context between different requests, for instance to prevent the LLM to propose changes that have been rejected by the user in previous exchanges.

In automation mode, whenever recommendations or a full semantic model generation is requested, the current semantic model is provided to the LLM, preferably using a pre-configured GPT specialized in semantic model creation. The used prompt is generated by the modeling platform based on predefined parameters such as expected output format or choices made by the modeler, such as a selection of the ontologies to use. However, the modeler cannot directly edit the prompt. Once the LLM generated output based on the provided prompt, this output undergoes post-processing to ensure presentability to the modeler, particularly when generating large semantic models. The changes made by the LLM in the last iteration are highlighted in separate steps in the generated model, simplifying the identification of applied changes when displaying the results in the modeling platform. In case the LLM generates corresponding textual output, it is parsed and attached to the updated model, e.g., using a special set of RDF properties or through an internal data model. This enables the modeler to verify the reasoning behind the modifications made to specific elements. Once the post-processing is complete, the proposed semantic model is transferred back to the user and displayed. In the automation mode, the LLM operates as a background service with no direct interaction between the modeler and the LLM.

While fully automated approaches provide advantages regarding the time consumption of creating semantic models, the modeler often has to be included in the process. This integration happens through the modeling platform. One of the main challenges of semantic modeling platforms is usability. Interfaces and interaction patterns needed to operate a modeling platform can be challenging for non-expert users. Furthermore, (manually) modifying complex semantic models requires modelers to mindfully select matching properties and classes to express desired changes in a formal way. At the same time, there may be many restrictions and guidelines a modeler has to regard, for instance regulations imposed by the ontology, such as *rdfs:domain* and *rdfs:range*, or existing validations and shapes, such as SHACL or ShEx [6].

With an LLM providing assistance, in the interactive mode, users input their desired changes using natural language. The input is included into a prompt and interpreted by the LLM which identifies suitable semantic elements in the process while also regarding the imposed constraints. The LLM's extensive knowledge

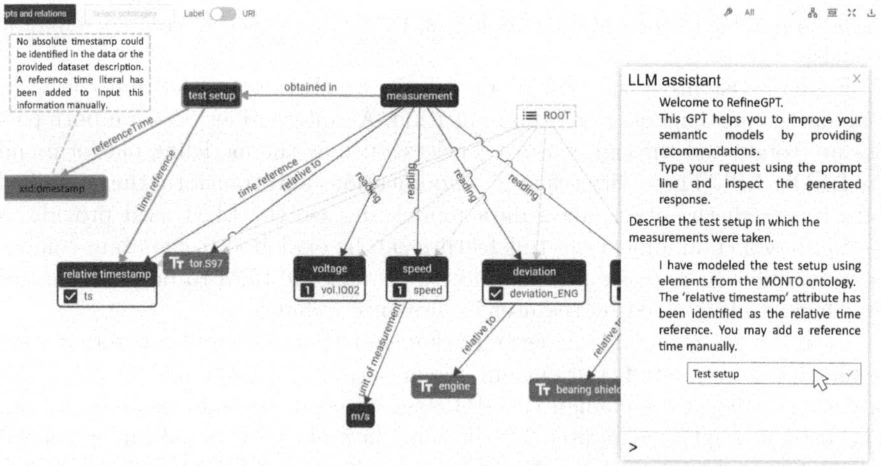

Fig. 3. Conceptual visualization of an LLM assistant in PLASMA featuring a prompt-based interaction to formulate desired changes to a semantic model.

and advanced capability to process natural language input allows it to modify the semantic model based on the perceived modeler's intentions, proposing a formalized solution to shortcomings such as syntactical errors. The resulting changes are then applied to the model. To enable this mode, users must be able to formulate their changes using a prompt-like interface in the modeling platform. Fig. 3 shows a conceptual design of providing users with a prompt input. The adjustments proposed by the LLM are then highlighted and extra information is provided through the modeling UI in case the LLM identified a problem for one or more elements.

6 Conclusion

This article explores the applicability of modern LLMs for semantic data management in dataspaces, in particular to the tasks of semantic model creation. Our objective is to address the provided research questions to offer directions of future research for preparing LLMs for the complex task of creating semantic models for vast amounts of heterogeneous data sources in dataspaces.

Regarding **RQ1** and **RQ2**, the experiments in Sect. 4 demonstrate the feasibility of utilizing LLMs for semantic type detection with a fixed or limited set of labels derived from legacy knowledge graphs. LLMs show promise in achieving significant accuracy in semantic type detection tasks, especially when additional contextual information or documentation is provided alongside the ontology. In particular, Experiment 3, which used the *schema.org* ontology, showcases the high adaptability and potential of LLMs to accurately map dataset labels to ontology concepts with an accuracy reaching up to 100% for certain datasets. This indicates that LLMs can serve as a powerful tool for semantic type detection. Experiment 4's approach, using a simplified version of the VC-SLAM ontology, offers insight into how LLMs might tackle semantic type detection tasks when the ontology is minimized to basic concept names and descriptions, achieving up to 57.1% accuracy in some cases. The findings suggest that LLMs, including *ChatGPT*, can effectively engage in semantic type detection tasks even when presented with new, unfamiliar, or arbitrary domain ontologies, by leveraging their inherent understanding of language and context.

Regarding **RQ3**, exploiting the vast knowledge and reasoning capabilities of LLMs to automate semantic modeling is an attractive idea. However, significant research is still necessary to integrate KGs with LLMs to produce synergy between these two complementary technologies. LLMs do not navigate on graphs or handle numerical data sets well. They may suffer from hallucinations and cannot acquire domain-specific knowledge [22] easily.

The LLM-supported automation and interactive modes for semantic model refinement (see Sect. 5) establish a new way of generating semantic models, providing another possible answers to **RQ3** on how LLMs can enhance the semantic model creation process. However, the advantages requires several additions to today's semantic modeling platforms. For both automation and interactive approaches, prompts are generated, interpreted by the natural language processing capabilities of LLMs and the proposed changes to a model displayed as a recommendation or applied directly. While the presented results and concepts represent a first approach to the topic, the stated research questions remain open to inspire future research in this area.

Acknowledgments. This work has been sponsored by the German Federal Ministry of Education and Research in the funding program "Forschung an Fachhochschulen" (grant no. 13FH557KX0) and funding program "Datenkompetenzzentren für die Wissenschaft" (grant no. 16DKZ2056B).

Disclosure of Interests. The authors have no competing interests to declare that are relevant to the content of this article.

References

1. Paulus, A., Burgdorf, A., Puleikis, L., Langer, T., Pomp, A., Meisen, T.: PLASMA: platform for auxiliary semantic modeling approaches. In: International Conference on Enterprise Information Systems (2021)
2. Allen, B.P., Stork, L., Groth, P.: Knowledge engineering using large language models. Trans. Graph Data Knowl. **1**(1), 3:1–3:19 (2023)
3. Auer, S.: Semantic integration and interoperability. In: Otto, B., ten Hompel, M., Wrobel, S. (eds.) Designing Data Spaces. Springer, Cham (2022). https://doi.org/10.1007/978-3-030-93975-5_12
4. Avogadro, R., Cremaschi, M.: Mantistable v: a novel and efficient approach to semantic table interpretation. In: SemTab@ ISWC (2021)
5. Baloup, J., e tla.: White paper on the data governance act. In: CiTiP Working Paper 2021 (2021)
6. Boneva, I., Labra Gayo, J.E., Prud'hommeaux, E.G.: Semantics and validation of shapes schemas for RDF. In: d'Amato, C., et al. (eds.) ISWC 2017. LNCS, vol. 10587, pp. 104–120. Springer, Cham (2017). https://doi.org/10.1007/978-3-319-68288-4_7
7. Burgdorf, A., Paulus, A., Pomp, A., Meisen, T.: VC-SLAM - a handcrafted data corpus for the construction of semantic models. Data **7**(2) (2022)
8. Chang, Y., et al.: A survey on evaluation of large language models. ACM Trans. Intell. Syst. Technol. **15**(3) (2024)
9. Dibowski, H., Schmid, S., Svetashova, Y., Henson, C., Tran, T.: Using semantic technologies to manage a data lake: Data catalog, provenance and access control. In: Proceedings of Scalable Semantic Web Knowledge Base Systems Workshop, vol. 2757. CEUR WS (2020)
10. Frey, J., Meyer, L.P., Arndt, N., Brei, F., Bulert, K.: Benchmarking the abilities of large language models for RDF knowledge graph creation and comprehension: how well do LLMS speak turtle? (2023). arXiv:2309.17122
11. Futia, G., Vetrò, A., De Martin, J.C.: Semi: a semantic modeling machine to build knowledge graphs with graph neural networks. SoftwareX **12** (2020)
12. Gottschalk, S., Demidova, E.: Tab2kg: semantic table interpretation with lightweight semantic profiles. Semant. Web **13**(3) (2022)
13. Haller, A., Polleres, A., Dobriy, D., Ferranti, N., Rodríguez Méndez, S.J.: An analysis of links in Wikidata. In: Groth, P., et al. (eds.) ESWC 2022. LNCS, vol. 13261, pp. 21–38. Springer, Cham (2022). https://doi.org/10.1007/978-3-031-06981-9_2

14. Hegselmann, S., Buendia, A., Lang, H., Agrawal, M., Jiang, X., Sontag, D.: TabLLM: few-shot classification of tabular data with large language models. In: International Conference on Artificial Intelligence and Statistics. PMLR (2023)
15. Hogan, A., et al.: Knowledge graphs. ACM Comput. Surv. **54**(4) (2022)
16. Hoseini, S., Burgdorf, A., Paulus, A., Meisen, T., Quix, C., Pomp, A.: Towards LLM-augmented creation of semantic models for dataspaces. In: The Second International Workshop on Semantics in Dataspaces, co-located with the Extended Semantic Web Conference (2024)
17. Hoseini, S., Theissen-Lipp, J., Quix, C.: A survey on semantic data management as intersection of ontology-based data access, semantic modeling and data lakes. J. Web Semant. **81**, 100819 (2024)
18. Hu, L., Liu, Z., Zhao, Z., Hou, L., Nie, L., Li, J.: A survey of knowledge enhanced pre-trained language models. IEEE Trans. Knowl. Data Eng. (2023)
19. Hulsebos, M., Hu, K., Bakker, M., et al.: Sherlock: a deep learning approach to semantic data type detection. In: Proceedings of the 25th ACM SIGKDD. ACM (2019)
20. Iglesias, E., Jozashoori, S., Vidal, M.E.: Scaling up knowledge graph creation to large and heterogeneous data sources. J. Web Semant. **75** (2023)
21. Ji, Z., et al.: Survey of hallucination in natural language generation. ACM Comput. Surv. **55**(12) (2023)
22. Kandpal, N., Deng, H., Roberts, A., Wallace, E., Raffel, C.: Large Language Models Struggle to Learn Long-Tail Knowledge (2022)
23. Korini, K., Bizer, C.: Column type annotation using ChatGPT (2023). arXiv:2306.00745
24. Li, P., et al.: Table-GPT: table fine-tuned GPT for diverse table tasks. Proc. ACM Manag. Data **2**(3), 1–28 (2024)
25. Liu, H., Ning, R., Teng, Z., Liu, J., Zhou, Q., Zhang, Y.: Evaluating the logical reasoning ability of ChatGPT and GPT-4 (2023). arXiv:2304.03439
26. Liu, W., et al.: K-BERT: enabling language representation with knowledge graph. In: Proceedings of the AAAI Conference on Artificial Intelligence, vol. 34, pp. 2901–2908 (2020)
27. Meckler, S., Dorsch, R., Henselmann, D., Harth, A.: The web and linked data as a solid foundation for dataspaces. In: Companion Proceedings of the ACM Web Conference (2023)
28. Meyer, L.P., et al.: Developing a scalable benchmark for assessing large language models in knowledge graph engineering (2023). arXiv:2308.16622
29. Meyer, L.P., Stadler, C., Frey, J., et al.: LLM-assisted knowledge graph engineering: experiments with ChatGPT (2023). arXiv:2307.06917
30. Nagel, L., et al.: Design principles for data spaces: position paper. Technical report, E. ON Energy Research Center (2021)
31. Pan, S., Luo, L., Wang, Y., et al.: Unifying large language models and knowledge graphs: a roadmap. IEEE Trans. Knowl. Data Eng. (2024)
32. Paulus, A., Burgdorf, A., Pomp, A., Meisen, T.: Recent advances and future challenges of semantic modeling. In: Proceedings of 15th IEEE ICSC. IEEE (2021)
33. Pham, M., Alse, S., Knoblock, C.A., Szekely, P.: Semantic labeling: a domain-independent approach. In: Groth, P., et al. (eds.) ISWC 2016. LNCS, vol. 9981, pp. 446–462. Springer, Cham (2016). https://doi.org/10.1007/978-3-319-46523-4_27
34. Pomp, A.: Bottom-up Knowledge Graph-Based Data Management. Berichte aus dem Maschinenbau, Shaker (2020)
35. Pomp, A., Lipp, J., Meisen, T.: You are missing a concept! enhancing ontology-based data access with evolving ontologies. In: Proceedings of ICSC. IEEE (2019)

36. Pomp, A., Paulus, A., Kirmse, A., Kraus, V., Meisen, T.: Applying semantics to reduce the time to analytics within complex heterogeneous infrastructures. Technologies **6**(3) (2018)
37. Solmaz, G., et al.: Enabling data spaces: existing developments and challenges. In: Proceedings of the 1st International Workshop on Data Economy. DE '22. ACM (2022)
38. Suhara, Y., et al.: Annotating columns with pre-trained language models. In: Proceedings of the 2022 International Conference on Management of Data. SIGMOD '22. ACM (2022)
39. Taheriyan, M., Knoblock, C.A., Szekely, P., Ambite, J.L., Chen, Y.: Leveraging linked data to infer semantic relations within structured sources. In: Proceedings of the 6th International Workshop on Consuming Linked Data (COLD 2015) (2015)
40. Theissen-Lipp, J., et al.: Semantics in dataspaces: Origin and future directions. In: Companion Proceedings of the ACM Web Conference 2023. WWW '23 Companion. ACM (2023)
41. Usmani, A., Khan, M.J., Breslin, J.G., Curry, E.: Towards multimodal knowledge graphs for data spaces. In: Companion Proceedings of the ACM Web Conference 2023. WWW '23 Companion. ACM (2023)
42. Vu, B., Knoblock, C., Pujara, J.: Learning semantic models of data sources using probabilistic graphical models. In: The World Wide Web Conference. WWW '19. ACM (2019)
43. Vu, B., Knoblock, C.A.: SAND: a tool for creating semantic descriptions of tabular sources. In: Groth, P., et al. (eds.) ESWC 2022. LNCS, vol. 13384, pp. 63–67. Springer, Cham (2022). https://doi.org/10.1007/978-3-031-11609-4_12
44. Wilkinson, M.D., et al.: The fair guiding principles for scientific data management and stewardship. Sci. Data **3**(1) (2016)
45. Xu, R., et al.: Automatic semantic modeling of structured data sources with cross-modal retrieval. Pattern Recogn. Lett. **177** (2024)
46. Yahya, M., Breslin, J.G., Ali, M.I.: Semantic web and knowledge graphs for industry 4.0. Appl. Sci. **11**(11) (2021)
47. Yang, L., Chen, H., Li, Z., Ding, X., Wu, X.: Give us the facts: enhancing large language models with knowledge graphs for fact-aware language modeling. IEEE Trans. Knowledge Data Eng. (2024)
48. Yang, R., et al.: Kg-rank: enhancing large language models for medical QA with knowledge graphs and ranking techniques. arXiv preprint arXiv:2403.05881 (2024)
49. Zhang, T., Yue, X., Li, Y., Sun, H.: TableLLAMa: towards open large generalist models for tables (2023). arXiv:2311.09206
50. Zhao, Y., Long, Y., Liu, H., et al.: Docmath-eval: evaluating numerical reasoning capabilities of LLMs in understanding long documents with tabular data (2023). arXiv:2311.09805

Versioning Virtual Reconstruction Hypotheses: Revealing Counterfactual Trajectories of the Fallen Voussoirs of Notre-Dame de Paris Using Reasoning and 2D/3D Visualization

Anaïs Guillem[1,5(✉)], John Samuel[2,4], Gilles Gesquière[3,4], Livio De Luca[1], and Violette Abergel[1,4]

[1] MAP UPR-CNRS 2002, Marseille, France
anais.guillem@map.cnrs.fr
[2] CPE Lyon, LIRIS, UMR5205, 69621 Villeurbanne, France
john.samuel@cpe.fr
[3] Université Lumière Lyon 2, LIRIS, UMR5205, 69007 Lyon, France
[4] CNRS, INSA Lyon, Universite Claude Bernard Lyon 1, Villeurbanne, France
[5] Ludwig Maximilian University of Munich (LMU), Munich, Germany
https://hal.science/hal-04625698

Abstract. Virtual reconstruction should move beyond merely presenting 3D models by documenting the scientific context and reasoning underlying the reconstruction process. For instance, the collapsed arch in the nave of Notre-Dame de Paris serves as a case study to make explicit the reconstruction argumentation encapsulated in relation to the spatial configuration of the arch and the voussoirs. The experiment is twofold: (1) setting up of the 3D dataset where the hypotheses are modeled as versions using logic programming, and (2) evaluating the scientific narrative of reconstruction through both a custom 2D-3D visualization and competency questions on the enriched 3D data. Formalization, reasoning, and visualization are combined to explore the nonlinear scientific hypotheses and narrative of the reconstruction. The results explicitly show both the factual information on the physical and digital objects, as well as the counterfactual propositions allowing the reasoning at play in the reconstruction. The hypotheses are visualized as counterfactual trajectories creating an open dynamic visualization that makes possible the spatialized querying of conflicting interpretations and embedded memory in place.

Keywords: Virtual reconstruction · Notre-Dame de Paris · argumentation · scientific narrative · 3D visualization · logic programming · counterfactual reasoning · scientific hypothesis

---

This is an extended version of the article [20]: *Let the fallen Voussoirs of Notre-Dame de Paris Speak: Scientific Narration and 3D Visualization of Virtual Reconstruction Hypotheses and Reasoning* by A. Guillem, J. Samuel, G. Gesquière, L. De Luca, and V. Abergel, presented at the SEMMES Workshop 2024, ESWC 2024.

A. Meroño Peñuela et al. (Eds.): ESWC 2024, LNCS 15345, pp. 201–219, 2025.
https://doi.org/10.1007/978-3-031-78955-7_18

1 Introduction

A virtual reconstruction has the amazing power to bring a past to life and it is a common exercise for the disciplines interested in cultural history to represent some aspect of a past reality. The resulting images and 3D visualizations conceal the underlying scientific process and hypothetical reasoning that contributed to their production. In this article, we tackle the gap between the knowledge that is produced in a reconstruction study and actual reconstruction data that one can either query or visualize. Following the 2019-fire of Notre-Dame de Paris, the fallen transverse arch in the nave provides a case study (Fig. 1), where the challenge is to determine the positioning of its voussoirs before its destruction. The presentation of the current reconstruction hypothesis [1] is visible and accessible in the nDame_3Dviewer [2]. Given the fragmentary documentation available, there are several plausible solutions to reconstruct this arch, some more valid than others. It requires to represent alternative reconstruction solutions and the reasoning behind these. Such a case study allows for testing a data workflow on the reconstruction argumentation reasoning.

The question of virtual reconstruction can be defined as a scientific study that aims at formulating an argumentation linking three elements: (1) the material objects (voussoirs, arch), (2) the digital objects (pointclouds, digital photographs, datasets), and (3) expert knowledge (archaeology, art history, architecture, computer science, etc.) and hypothetical scientific reasoning (reconstruction question). In this work, we posit that the 2D/3D-visualization and querying are constitutive research tools for the virtual reconstruction research, rather than an end result medium for dissemination. The materiality of the voussoirs and immateriality of digital surrogates are the support to make explicit the argumentation of the reconstruction. The virtual reconstruction research is rooted both in the real (material and immaterial object) and the unreal (hypotheses formulation), where the scientific inquiry about the past can be developed. The challenge is about reasoning both about factual knowledge and counterfactual propositions: a reconstruction formulates a hypothesis about something that might have existed based on the existing presence of objects that are surviving witnesses of this lost past.

This contribution proposes a twofold experiment. Firstly, it sets up the 3D dataset of Notre-Dame's de Paris' transverse arch reconstruction, including the data enrichment with archaeological knowledge proposed by archaeologists and subject experts. These requirements were detailed in previous studies [5,16–19,27]. Far from being straightforward, this step introduces the innovative elements of linking counterfactual reasoning to real things (physical or digital) and unreal things (competitive reconstruction hypotheses) at the dataset level. The scientific narrative of the reconstruction study is tested using Prolog programming, where the formal expressions of relations between hypotheses, arguments, and objects are modeled. Secondly, after the transformation to Prolog facts and rules of the initial reconstruction dataset, the evaluation of the scientific narrative of reconstruction argumentation is tested through the 2D-, 3D-visualization and query of the 3D enriched data. The humanistic question of reconstruction is

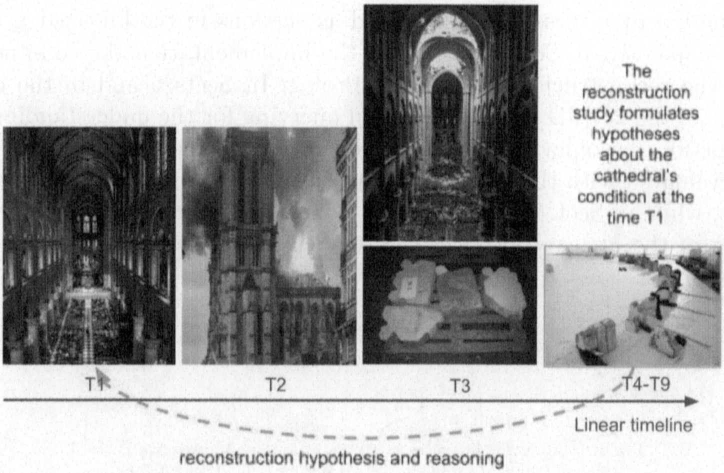

Fig. 1. the Notre-Dame de Paris arch reconstruction study (T4–T9) aims at formulating knowledge about a disappeared past (T1), the arch before its destruction (T2). T[4–9] corresponds to the time of the reconstruction study activities. (©Images: T1/T3a/T3b: LRMH/Thierry Zimmer; T2: Wikipedia/LeLaisserPasserA38; T4–T9: DRAC/RNDP/David Bordes).

the starting point for the nonlinear scientific narrative composed of hypotheses and argument loops that we want to query and visualize. 2D/3D visualization prototyping and querying bring to the foreground the hypotheses and argumentation of the reconstruction question.

Do the 2D/3D visualization and querying have this ability to explicitly convey the reconstruction study process and arguments? To answer positively, the visualization needs to move away from a static and finalized illustrative output of the reconstruction study toward an open, dynamic visualization of reconstruction data. Following the principles of open science, the proposed data practice (i.e., enrichment, transformation, inference etc.) can serve as a lever for the scientific narrative and the argumentation. Beyond the factual level, we consider the interpretation of results and the counterfactual knowledge encapsulated in relation to its spatial configuration. The interpretation of results and 3D visualization become interdependent and complementary. Whereas 3D visualization tools typically represent 3 dimensional objects + 1 dimension for time, this experiment aims to encompass counterfactual information (hypothetical reasoning of the reconstruction) in relation to spatial (3D) and temporal information.

In Sect. 2, we present the existing gap in documenting counterfactual reasoning of virtual reconstruction. The scientific inquiry over reconstruction leads to formalizing concurrent points of view about space, place, and memory, that bring the theoretical concept of place making. Querying and visualizing reconstruction data opens the problem of representing factual/counterfactual and spatio-temporal data. In Sect. 3, we develop the methodology of the experiment: the reconstruction hypotheses are considered as versions in the knowledge production. Subsequently, in Sect. 4, we detail the implementation the counterfactual layer in the reconstruction data using Prolog. In Sects. 5 and 6, the complementarity of the 2D/3D visualization and querying for the understanding of the reconstruction reasoning is demonstrated: in Sect. 5, the resulting transformed data is evaluated with the competency questions focusing on the counterfactual elements, while in Sect. 6, the 2D/3D visualization shows how the hypothetical reasoning of the arch reconstruction is embedded in the spacetime volumes of the voussoirs.

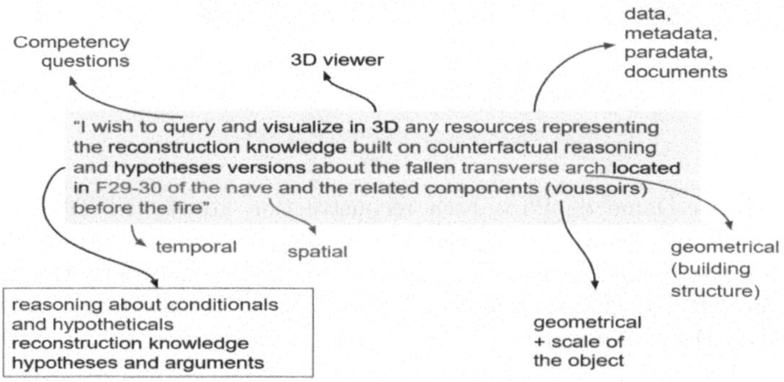

Fig. 2. Formulation of research question posed by virtual reconstruction in archaeology, highlighting the different components using the Notre-Dame's example. The root of the problem dwells in the formalization, reasoning, and visualization of hypotheticals and conditionals, where one usually considers factual information and datum.

2 State of the Art

2.1 Reconstruction in Archaeology: the Problem of Documenting Counterfactual Reasoning

In this part, we present the gap in the literature between the knowledge about the past in a reconstruction study and the actual reconstruction data. The problem of documenting virtual reconstruction has roots in philosophy of language, semantics, and logic. For Clark [10], the reconstruction of the past in archaeology is a misnomer since virtual reconstruction is rather the construction of a model for the study of the past as "tools for understanding, not statements of reality". This debate is exacerbated with the development of virtual archaeology and the democratization of digital documentation [7,12,21,32,34]. A reconstruction study is "based on complex chains of reasoning grounded in primary and secondary evidence that enable a historically probable whole to be reconstructed from the partial remains left in the archaeological record" [7]. In a previous work [18], we demonstrated that these complex chains of reasoning in virtual reconstructions experience a phenomenon of compression both at a level of representation and reconstruction. The reconstruction study builds on knowledge of real/"actual" things (artifacts, remains etc.), as well as unreal or "intricate counterfactual blends" [15].

For memorizing the reconstruction reasoning, the problem can be formulated as follows (Fig. 2): the reconstruction study (or model) formulates implicitly a knowledge object that is in-between real objects and counterfactual propositions. We aim at unfolding and explicitly formulating these intricate counterfactual blends. The goal is the explanation of the proposition sets, arguments, and inference logic that are used in the argumentation of the reconstruction [18]. From the perspective of data science, Pearl [30] posits interpretation as how to connect the reality and the data, as a way to encode causal assumptions. Transparency and testability are proposed as requirements for data transformation: "Transparency enables analysts to discern whether the assumptions encoded are plausible (on scientific grounds) or whether additional assumptions are warranted. Testability permits us (whether analyst or machine) to determine whether the assumptions encoded are compatible with the available data [...]" ([30], p. 58). Our proposed experiment enriches the reconstruction data and encodes the reconstruction arguments as the causal assumptions used in the virtual reconstruction, applying the transparency and testability criteria.

2.2 Formalizing the Concurrent Points of View About Space, Place, Memory, and Placemaking

We explore the problem of the reconstruction of historical buildings and their restoration, considering a series of competing interpretations. This leads us to look at space as meaning-laden, that is a place. Nora introduced the notion of *lieu de mémoire* (place of memory) [29], which can help in formalizing our understanding of the interrelations between space and memory. *Lieu de mémoire*, as defined by Nora, is not just a physical location, it embraces the "embodiment of memory in certain sites where a sense of historical continuity persists" [29]. The *lieux de mémoire* exist because of the disappearance of *milieux de mémoire* (cultural material environment). The virtual reconstruction of the transverse arch is consecutive to its destruction. The voussoirs have survived and became the material witnesses of the destroyed arch. *Lieux de mémoire* are the surviving, remaining material elements of embedded memory. Memory, either social, collective or individual, is affected by its relation to space and materiality: its meaning attachment to a space creates a place. Stories and events play an important role in making a space a place. For every place, different people have different associated memories [24,45], often providing a subjective version of the same place and the events that occurred. Multiple research works records and documents oral, sensorial, and written histories associated with places. Place encompasses materiality that ranges from the scale of objects, buildings to urban fabric or landscapes. That explains why urban planners, historians, architects, and anthropologists give a significant importance to the concept of placemaking since memories give meaning to the surrounding materiality.

At the urban scale, memories may be available in several forms [36], media documents forming a key form of recording. The documents narrating the historical events and their chronology frequently serve as evidence for understanding the incremental changes that happened to urban and architectural objects. Historical documents and archives have been used with their 2D/3D representations [9,39] to represent concurrent points of view of urban evolution capable of narrating numerous possible scenarii of city changes at different levels of detail. Numerous ontologies and documentation standards have been proposed to represent (historical) episodes, events (CIDOC CRM as event-centric ontology), stories, historical narratives [24], and argumentation using CIDOC CRMinf [13,43] or other argumentation models [3].

With the models and ontologies in place, a methodological approach based on versioning is used to store and visualize historical narratives about cultural heritage artifacts at different scales. Extending the use of version control systems like Git, Samuel et al. [38] proposes to store multiple scenarios of urban evolution as city versions. Another research direction is to use hypermedia stories [6,24] - graph-structured stories with navigation links -, where media elements help explain these narratives about the urban fabric and heritage assets. At the architectural scale, the evolution of objects is apprehended through diagrammatic visualizations called diachrogram to capture the changes and periods of stability in building lives [14]. [7,26] show the compatibility and applicability of knowledge representation and ontology design approach respectively to the urban and built heritage domain.

In this article, we want to go beyond the use case of representing and visualizing urban evolution, as well as the linear [23,48] or the graph-structured stories [24,37] of a series of events [33]. We propose the extension of some of the above works to represent the hypotheses evolution during the reconstruction process as versions. We build upon the studies on historical changes to model virtual reconstruction knowledge based on hypothetical propositions, since the goal is to ultimately bring back a damaged object to its hypothetical lost state.

2.3 Visualization

For the visualization in heritage field, one observes a duality between semantic-oriented approaches and 3D visualization-oriented approaches. On one hand, the approaches centered on knowledge modeling mainly present information systems designed to manage documentation activities, without directly exploiting the full wealth of heterogeneous data mobilized in heritage contexts, in particular 3D data [8,25,28]. On the other hand, approaches based on the exploitation of 3D digital data, focus mostly on their description, omitting any reference to the complex relationships specific to the observation, interpretation, or documentation processes [41,49]. Some works [4,42] clearly demonstrate the strong interest in bringing these two approaches together, making it possible to spatialize and query heterogeneous information in the context of restoration operations. However, these initiatives are generally built around isolated 3D models, excluding the possibility of handling and confronting the diversity of resources involved in heritage studies, like Notre-Dame scientific action.

From a software point of view, there are a number of very effective libraries dedicated to the manipulation of 3D data, which can be used for reconstruction studies [31,35,40]. But these tools focus on visualization and interaction modalities, allowing only in the best cases to display provenance metadata, and in most cases ignoring the full potential of an upstream work on data curation and conceptual modeling. In [44], spatio-temporal information of 3D data is characterized by describing the transformations affecting buildings over time and considering their changes (demolition, amplification, division, or change of function). It is based on the addition of a semantic layer to the geometric restitution through description graphs, enabling information on buildings to be enriched according to existing documentary sources. While this approach is of considerable interest, it remains ill-suited to virtual reconstruction data documenting the scientific context and reasoning about the reconstruction process. The temporal dimension addressed in [44] is linear, making it difficult to semantically and geometrically characterize competing hypotheses and their underlying arguments. Samuel et al. [39] and Jaillot et al. [22] propose knowledge versioning in 3D urban contexts. While this approach is interesting in terms of data structuring, all the narrative potential remains to be explored. Beyond the 3D/semantic duality, Windhager et al. [47] proposes a broad comprehensive survey about the uses of visualization for cultural heritage data. They identify transversal key elements: serendipity, generosity, criticality, user guidance and narration, remote access versus being there, facets of uncertainty, and contextualization.

3 Methodology

In this section, we consider the example of the arch of Notre-Dame de Paris that was damaged during the 2019-fire. The voussoirs that together formed the arch fell on the nave's floor and were displaced. The scientific research and restoration activities have divergent objectives and interpretations, while working on the same object. The virtual reconstruction study aims at gathering knowledge about the destroyed arch and understanding which original place or slot was for each authentic voussoir in the arch before the fire [16,17,19]. This process is extremely difficult and several sessions were held [5,27], where historians discussed and proposed reconstruction hypotheses. Figure 3 shows multiple rounds of discussion for placing a voussoir in specific slots. Six overall hypotheses were formulated at different times for identifying the position of voussoirs. It is important to note that a given voussoir may have changed their slots during the different hypotheses based on additional collected evidence. The ultimate goal is to possibly relocate the voussoirs and the arch to their hypothetical original positions on time T1 (i.e., before the fire). Unlike [9] or [39] that look at the evolution of historical artifacts or city objects (T1, T2, T3) as recorded in time, the reconstruction uses a fiction as if we were looking backward in time. In fact, the past object of study (T1) is a hypothetical model for knowledge, where the reconstruction hypotheses can be seen as versions. At the time T1, there are several hypothetical versions that were proposed with the end goal of creating a reconstructed arch that gets as close as the arch before the fire (i.e. the hypothetical original version V0 at T1). It must be pointed out that we may never arrive at the ultimate version of the reconstruction V?? (shown in Fig. 3) that approximates V0 at best.

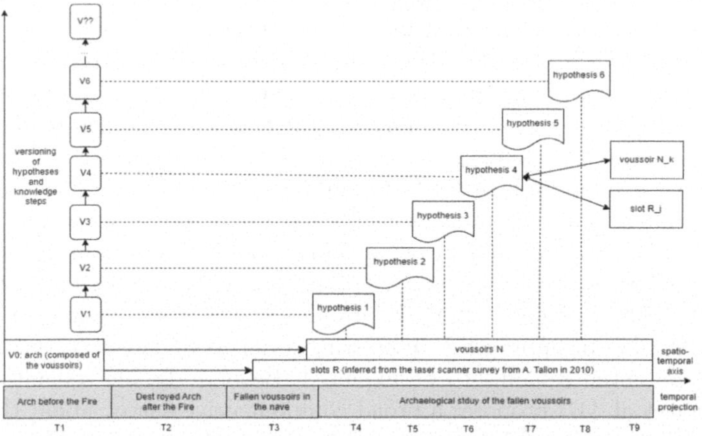

Fig. 3. Diagram representing the different hypotheses of reconstruction, as versions of knowledge about the arch.

In order to restore the arch to its hypothetical original state, it is critical to understand that the arch has two sides, the northern and southern sides. A number of 122 voussoirs together form the whole arch with 40 voussoirs still in place and 77 recovered voussoirs. The (possible) slots for the fallen voussoirs have been identified and numbered, using survey documentation prior to the fire. The slots on the south side are numbered with even numbers, while those on the north are numbered with odd numbers, starting with R0 for the keystone. Thus, it is easy to understand that R12 is the 6th slot on the north side of the arch. The fallen voussoirs have also been identified and inventoried N1,..., etc. The goal of reconstruction is to assign a slot R_n (values of n are between 0 and 121) to every voussoir N_k (values of k are between 0 and 121). There are multiple collaborative work sessions between researchers (archaeologists, architects, art historians, etc.) to produce such possible reconstruction hypotheses. Each hypothesis has its associated arguments.

In Fig. 3, the arrows between the two versions may have different significance for the reconstruction reasoning. A decision about a voussoir based on a particular argument may remain valid across different versions. However, this also means that any initial hypotheses, if proven false at a later date may lead to the falsification of some pairs of slot-voussoirs from another hypothesis. Take, for example, the evolution of the argumentation process related to cross-shaped marks on the joint sides of the voussoirs. These lapidary marks constitute an archaeological predicate for the arch reconstruction. The marks were believed to possibly serve as guide the masons to orient the positioning of the voussoir during the construction. The mark could indicate either the downward or upward side. In a first hypothesis the voussoirs were oriented with their lapidary mark facing downward. This was later revised. This meant that we need to be able to go back to all the previous arguments, track changes, and make corrections to the assigned facts: slot-voussoir pairs, voussoirs, if necessary. This makes the problem particularly challenging since we need to record this aspect for every voussoir and the assigned slot along with the associated arguments in the different hypotheses. In the reconstruction data, we have a selection of relevant information about the physical objects (voussoirs) and possible locations (slots) in the state of the arch before destruction. The difficulty lies in the reasoning about the characteristics about the real objects in relation to the argumentation hypothesis of the reconstruction, i.e., counterfactual reasoning. The reconstruction data is an open-ended hypothesis, as shown in Fig. 3.

4 Implementation

After exploring the initial reconstruction dataset available in [16], the experiment proposes to encode the reconstruction arguments as the causal assumptions used in the virtual reconstruction. It was important to represent them in a format so that we could easily perform analyses, querying and reasoning, applying the transparency and testability criteria [30]. The first step consists of the representation of reconstruction hypotheses and the associated metadata as RDF. The full list of information of voussoirs and slots is available in textual format [5,16,27]. We represent essential information about the proposed locations of the voussoirs along with the arguments for this hypothesis (Tables 1 and 2).

Prolog is a versatile declarative programming language that allows a set of facts and rules (e.g., the details of a voussoir or the details of a hypothesis) and rules (e.g., linking hypotheses to voussoirs and proposed slots), which define relations [11]. Prolog has been chosen, considering its declarative nature and as a useful language for quick prototyping and short iterative tests on the data. It allows inference and reasoning, data validation and verification. The dataset has been transformed as facts and rules in Prolog (Table 1) to explicitly express the argumentative relations between slots, hypotheses, and archaeological predicates (Fig. 4) [13]. We apply the testability criteria on the counterfactual reasoning of the reconstruction to verify whether there are incoherent elements in the data. Additional information is inferred about the reconstruction reasoning from the existing data: for any voussoir, we know the sequence of hypotheses that a voussoir went through. Instead of tracking events (temporal data) of the reconstruction work sessions, we are more interested in modeling the hypotheses (Hypothesis [N:1-6] in Fig. 3). To say it differently, each voussoir can tell its own story in the reconstruction. As in [39], another facet of the reconstruction reasoning is inferred: the transition (as event) between two versions (as stabilized state of an hypothesis) are made explicit, e.g., when a voussoir was replaced in a given slot. A sequence of hypotheses and hypothesis transitions can be considered as an overall story, i.e., one possible narration of the reconstruction. We move from the known documented state to the implied events that lead to it.

Table 1. Some key reconstruction predicates that were used for querying and inference.

No.	Predicates in Prolog	Description
F1.	$voussoir(N, W, X, Y, Z, F)$	information related to a voussoir: N, its identifier, W, the width, F, the face where the crossmark is present (up or down), the center of gravity given by X,Y,Z.
F2.	$slot(R, X, Y, Z)$	location of the slot with R its identifier and X,Y,Z the center of gravity (useful for visualization).
F3.	$hypothesis(H, R, N, C)$	details of a hypothesis H linking the voussoir N to the slot R, with the comment C.
F4.	$hypothesispredicate(H, P)$.	details of a hypothesis predicate linking hypothesis H with predicate P.

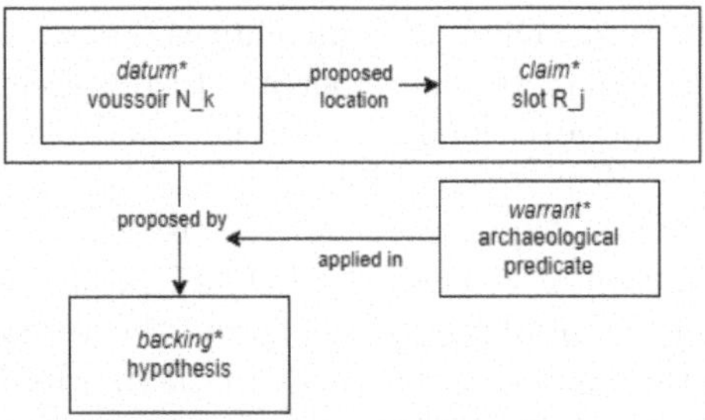

Fig. 4. Links between voussoir, slot, hypothesis, and archaeological predicate as modeled in the experiment. The terms in *italic** come from the argument model of Toulmin [13,46].

5 Evaluation Using Competency Questions and Prolog Queries

The objective here is to go beyond commonly found linear temporal visualization, where a temporal bar shows the state of an object at different time spans. Instead, archaeologists and subject experts need a more granular hypothesis versioning level. Their focus ranges from individual objects (voussoirs) or the overall main structure (arch) or a combination of both. It opens up parallel narratives about the arch, representing the virtual reconstruction hypotheses with the argumentation about the authentic voussoirs as archaeological artifacts.

Table 2. Some competency questions to query the reconstruction data using Prolog fact and rules in regards to the reconstruction question.

No.	Competency questions	Query (Prolog)
CQ1.	What do we know about all the voussoirs and their associated information (N as the identifier, W as the width, X as ...)?	$voussoir(N, W, X, Y, Z, F).$
CQ2.	What do we know about all the reconstruction locations for the voussoirs, i.e. the slots and their related information (R as the slot identifier, W as the slot width, ...)?	$slot(R, W, X, Y, Z).$
CQ3.	What are all the hypotheses?	$hypothesis(H, N, R, C).$
CQ4.	What are the pairs of voussoirs and the associated hypotheses?	$hyppair(H, N, R) : -hypothesis(H, R, N, \_), voussoir(N, \_, \_, \_, \_, \_), slot(R, \_, \_, \_, \_).$
CQ5.	What are the pairs of voussoirs and the associated hypotheses and their widths (for verification)	$hyppair(H, N, R, W1, W2) : -hypothesis(H, R, N, \_), voussoir(N, W1, \_, \_, \_, \_), slot(R, W2, \_, \_, \_).$
CQ6.	Compare the slot position and the voussoir position in a specific hypothesis.	$verifyxposhyppair(H, N, R, X1, X2, L) : - hypothesis(H, R, N, \_), voussoir(N, \_, X1, \_, \_, \_), slot(R, \_, X2, \_, \_), X1 \backslash ==' unk', L \;\; is \;\; float(X1) - float(X2).$
CQ7.	In regards to the reconstruction question, what do we know about all the hypothesis predicates and their associated information?	$hypothesispredicate(H, P).$
CQ8.	In regards to the reconstruction question, what do we know about all the hypothesis predicates related to the voussoir and their slot attribution in the different hypotheses.	$hyppredpair(H, N, R, W1, W2, P) : - hypothesis(H, R, N,) , voussoir(N, W1,,,,), slot(R, W2,,,), hypothesispredicate(H, P).$
CQ9.	In regards to the reconstruction question, what do we know about all the hypothesis predicates related to the slots and their voussoirs in the different hypotheses?	$hyppredpair(H, N, R, W1, W2, P) : - hypothesis(H, R, N,) , voussoir(N, W1,,,,), slot(R, W2,,,), hypothesispredicate(H, P).$

The virtual reconstruction process is not just about the story before and after the reconstruction, but the narrative in-between. The study of different possible arguments used in this process serve as lessons for future research. To evaluate the experiment, a list of queries are formulated as competency questions (Table 2). For example, the analysis (based on semantic, temporal, spatial elements) helps in understanding the case of a voussoir staying at the same place across certain hypotheses or all hypotheses. A subset of the research questions have been formalized as competency questions and translated using Prolog queries. The Table 2 shows how to use the predicates formatted in Prolog to answer competency questions for reconstruction. Finally, the validated data is visualized for evaluation, as shown in the next section.

The Prolog CQ4 query (Table 2) gives us all the voussoir-slot pairs relating to the different hypotheses. Visualizing these results in 2D and 3D provides a new understanding of these datasets, highlighting the knowledge paths that guided the passage between the different versions of the arch reconstruction. A 2D visualization (Figs. 5, 6) was built using a slope graph, which is particularly effective for showing the trend of a variation between several states - either temporal or hypothetical - of a given dataset. Slope graphs are often used to

Table 3. Prolog query "Give me all the hypotheses (H) and the associated slots (R) for the voussoirs N236 (left) and N281 (right)" based on CQ#4 (see Table 2). This is the output obtained and visualized in Sect. 6. The columns 2 and 4 are obtained while interrogating Prolog sequentially on prompted by a ";".

?- hyppair(H,n236,R).		?- hyppair(H,n281,R).	
H = sol_pa_201218	R = r13 ? ;	H = sol_pa_201218	R = r15 ? ;
H = sol_glecr_0x4fbefadd	R = r64 ? ;	H = sol_glecr_0x4fbefadd	R = r12 ? ;
H = sol_hh_glecr_0xab2f966e_pa_201218	R = r13 ? ;	H = sol_hh_glecr_0xab2f966e_pa_201218	R = r23 ? ;
H = sol_glecr_0xol68svdj	R = r64 ? ;	H = sol_glecr_0xol68svdj	R = r18 ? ;
H = sol_glecr_0xyh10l69o_pa_211214	R = r55 ? ;	H = sol_glecr_0xyh10l69o_pa_211214	R = r57 ? ;
H = sol_glecrt_0x76e988bf_pa_211214	R = r31 ? ;	H = sol_glecrt_0x76e988bf_pa_211214	R = r33 ? ;

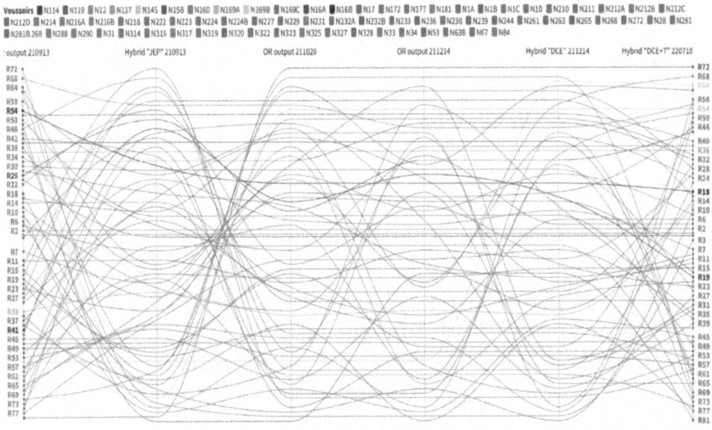

Fig. 5. Results of the query CQ4 query as visualized in 2D.

show changes over a period by presenting a "before/after" view of several values, compared at different times. Related values are linked by slope lines. This type of graph is often used to compare two groups or to show relationships between two categories of unrelated values. In our case, the vertical axes represent the arch slots R, ordered according to parity (odd slots to the north, even slots to the south). Each curve represents a voussoir N, passing, for each hypothesis H, through its assigned slot.

6 Results: 2D and 3D Visualization of the Reconstruction Narrative and Hypotheses

This representation is particularly useful for revealing the variability of these interpretive trajectories: a flat curve demonstrates a stable (N, R) association over the course of the different hypotheses, while a curve with multiple inflections shows that the voussoir-slot association has often been reconsidered. In Fig. 6, the knowledge paths of the N236 and N281 voussoirs are compared (Table 3). Both voussoirs show a high level of variability in the reconstruction hypotheses.

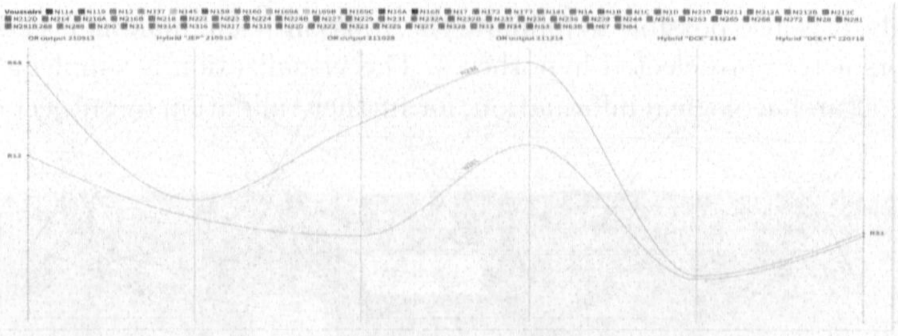

Fig. 6. Results of the query CQ4 query as visualized in 2D with focus on the voussoirs N236 and N281.

However, the graph reveals that these two voussoirs have been placed side by side in the last two hypotheses, suggesting that a series may have been identified. Once validated, this information can be integrated as a new argument in the formalization, strengthening the plausibility of any related subsequent hypotheses.

The reconstruction hypothesis is projected in the real existing space of Notre-Dame de Paris cathedral. This is the reason why it is equally essential to verify the reconstruction reasoning using visualization and query-based data validation approaches. Once the required responses are obtained using Prolog, these are visualized in the 3D nd-Viewer [2] allowing the use of multi-faceted variables in their spatial context. The objective is to project these results in the 3D digital space to visually assess them. The 3D visualization is a complementary approach to querying. Whereas Prolog gives information concerning the way that data and causal assumptions are encoded and described, the 3D visualization investigates the relation of digital place making as the relation between space, time, semantics, and memory. It is one thing to note that the position of the keystone is never called into question and remains stable between all hypotheses, and another to see it in context and understand that this stability can be explained by the spatial or geometric relations linking this keystone to its direct environment. The concurrent states of the same voussoir in different hypotheses can be highlighted and compared (Fig. 7), since the reconstruction reasoning is made visible in the 3D viewer. Thanks to inferred data about reconstruction reasoning (state of hypotheses + events of change), the 3D viewer can animate the voussoirs in regards to the reconstruction reasoning as trajectory. Unlike 3D visualization with temporal bars, where the different states are successively visualized, the goal here is also to obtain a smooth animation of transition of these hypotheses for one voussoir. Several problems arise: the smoothing of orientation changes between two successive states, the construction of an intelligible trajectory from the interpolation of the voussoir positions, or even the collision detection of the different voussoirs in the case of multi-objects animation. In Fig. 7, the voussoir position is fixed in one slot and we show its possible trajectory across different hypotheses, positioned successively to the slots R63, R17, R58, R16. Here, we can see that each green point corresponds to the slots in different hypotheses.

Conversely, it is also possible to animate the voussoir itself, making it glide in different slots across preselected hypotheses. The visualization is supplemented by the voussoir archaeological information, for further validation by subject experts.

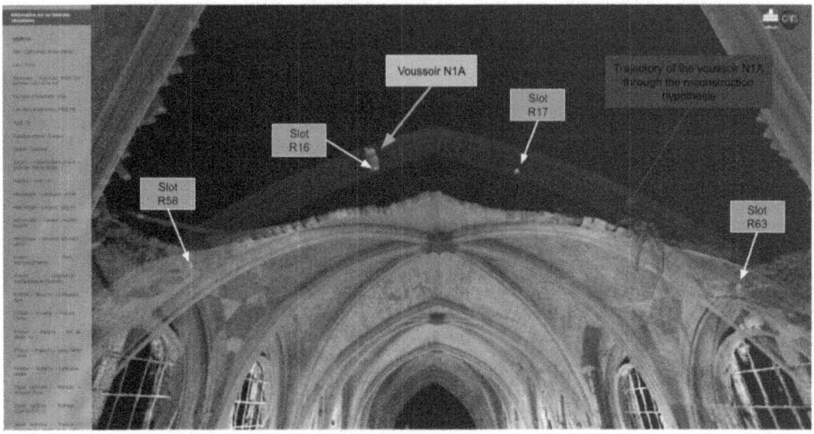

Fig. 7. Visualization of the voussoir N1A trajectory through the different reconstruction hypotheses (slots successively R63, R17, R58, R16) associated with its archaeological information. (©nd_viewer3D: V. Abergel, [2]).

7 Discussion

Virtual reconstruction of Notre-Dame's arch is a complex question, several rounds of hypothesis sessions have been conducted since 2020. The data does not represent a finished process: the ongoing input of new data leads to new arguments that will themselves enrich further the argumentation of future hypotheses, as shown in Fig. 3. Because it is an interdisciplinary research, it ensues that communication is a crucial aspect. We require different ways to communicate, document, and visualize the evolution of these hypotheses about the reconstruction. Neither 3D visualization nor formalizing/querying may be enough separately. A data spreadsheet, obtained from inference tools, like Prolog, lacks readability without visualization. 3D visualization, on the contrary, without data formalization and inference, is missing the depth of reconstruction knowledge. The combination - formalization, reasoning, 3D visualization - helps to demonstrate the hypotheses and can also be used to explore new questions that were inaccessible previously. For example, we can assess whether a high degree of variability between different hypotheses can still exhibit some form of local stability (e.g., voussoirs whose position have been much questioned but which are still stuck together as clusters).

The questions on semiotic visualization still remain open: the semiology about 2D graphics is part of the general culture due to geography and architecture, while the 3D graphics mostly represent a mimetic relation with the reality.

The codes and symbols for representation in 3D are not yet conveying interpretation and narration, which impacts the cognitive engagement and interactions from the users. They are yet to be invented and explored as spatial patterns.

8 Conclusion and Future Works

This article presented an experiment on virtual reconstruction data, focusing on the multiple hypotheses made for the destroyed arch in Notre-Dame de Paris. A number of past research works on cultural heritage, storytelling, and urban evolution have previously explored models, methodologies, or ontologies for narrating linear or concurrent scenarii of evolution. In this article, we presented a different case, where the goal is not to obtain the past evolution of objects, but to build knowledge about objects in a hypothetical state. The granularity of argumentation is still to be explored, i.e., the possibility to find the most granular arguments (or atomic arguments) upon which further arguments can be built.

We proposed a quick prototyping and short iterative tests on the data for exploration. Making use of the hypotheses' data, both logic and visualization tools were tested. It allowed us to track competitive hypotheses, and rediscover the reconstruction problem under a new light. The combination of enrichment, formalization, and visualization changes the paradigm for reconstruction scholarship. The need goes beyond data provenance and reusability. It opens avenues for exploring data intensive collaborative environments. The experiment nourished our initial intuition that serendipity is a key component for data visualization. It allows the users to navigate and interact with objects and discover some additional characteristics that are inferred via reasoning over the data. The experiment shows that 3D visualization setup opens the possibility for spatial serendipity as spatialized query of embedded memory in place.

Acknowledgments. This work was supported by: the projects TEATIME funded by the Mission pour les Initiatives Transverses et Interdisciplinaires (MITI) of the Centre National de la Recherche Scientifique (CNRS, France), the ERC nDame_Heritage (Grant agreement ID: 101055423) funded by ERC-2021-ADG, and the project REPERAGE funded by the Fondation des Sciences du Patrimoine (ANR-17-EURE-0021). The authors wish to acknowledge the help and collaborative support from: the chief architects of historical monuments in charge, Philippe Villeneuve, Pascal Prunet and Rémi Fromont, the Etablissement public chargé de la conservation et de la restauration de la cathédrale Notre-Dame de Paris (RNDP), and the heritage conservators. The authors thank the numerous scientific partners and collaborators from the research groups working on Notre-Dame de Paris cathedral, with special recognition for the Digital Data, the Stone working groups.

References

1. Public viewer - reconstruction f29-30. https://public.aioli.map.cnrs.fr/reperage/index.html?projectId=645389afd3da2
2. Abergel, V.: 3D Environment for Interactive Visualization for Notre-Dame de Paris' Scientific Research (2024). https://nd.aioli.map.cnrs.fr/
3. Al-Khatib, K., de Waard, A., Freitag, D., Gurevych, I., Hou, Y., Scells, H.: Towards a unified model of scholarly argumentation (Dagstuhl Seminar 22432). Technical report, [object Object] (2023). https://doi.org/10.4230/DAGREP.12.10.175, https://drops.dagstuhl.de/entities/document/10.4230/DagRep.12.10.175
4. Apollonio, F.I., et al.: A 3D-centered information system for the documentation of a complex restoration intervention. J. Cult. Herit. **29**, 89–99 (2018). https://doi.org/10.1016/j.culher.2017.07.010, https://linkinghub.elsevier.com/retrieve/pii/S1296207417301905
5. Baillieul, E., Leroux, L., Chaoui-Derieux, D.: Reconstructing the fallen arch of notre-dame. new insights into gothic vault-building. J. Cult. Herit. **65**, 68–73 (2024). https://doi.org/10.1016/j.culher.2023.05.010, https://www.sciencedirect.com/science/article/pii/S1296207423000638, Notre-Dame de Paris : a multidisciplinary scientific site
6. Baloian, N., Zurita, G., Pino, J.A., Peñafiel, S., Luther, W.: Developing hyperstories in the context of cultural heritage appreciation. In: Nakanishi, H., Egi, H., Chounta, I.-A., Takada, H., Ichimura, S., Hoppe, U. (eds.) CRIWG+CollabTech 2019. LNCS, vol. 11677, pp. 110–128. Springer, Cham (2019). https://doi.org/10.1007/978-3-030-28011-6_8
7. Bruseker, G., Guillem, A., Carboni, N.: Semantically documenting virtual reconstruction: building a path to knowledge provenance. In: ISPRS Ann. Photogram. Remote Sens. Spat. Inf. Sci. **II-5/W3**, 33–40 (2015). https://doi.org/10.5194/isprsannals-II-5-W3-33-2015, https://isprs-annals.copernicus.org/articles/II-5-W3/33/2015/
8. Calvanese, D., Liuzzo, P., Mosca, A., Remesal, J., Rezk, M., Rull, G.: Ontology-based data integration in EPNet: production and distribution of food during the Roman Empire. Eng. Appl. Artif. Intell. **51**, 212–229 (2016)
9. Chaturvedi, K., Smyth, C.S., Gesquière, G., Kutzner, T., Kolbe, T.H.: Managing versions and history within semantic 3D city models for the next generation of CityGML. In: Abdul-Rahman, A. (ed.) Advances in 3D Geoinformation. LNGC, pp. 191–206. Springer, Cham (2017). https://doi.org/10.1007/978-3-319-25691-7_11
10. Clark, J.T.: The fallacy of reconstruction. Cyber-Archaeol. **2177**, 63–73 (2010)
11. Colmerauer, A.: An introduction to Prolog III. Commun. ACM **33**(7), 69–90 (1990)
12. Demetrescu, E., Ferdani, D.: From field archaeology to virtual reconstruction: a five steps method using the extended matrix. Appl. Sci. **11**(11), 5206 (2021)
13. Doerr, M., Kritsotaki, A., Boutsika, K.: Factual argumentation-a core model for assertions making. J. Comput. Cult. Herit. **3**(3) (2011). https://doi.org/10.1145/1921614.1921615
14. Dudek, I., Blaise, J.Y.: Diachrograms - a theoretical framework for the modelling and analysis of a heritage artefact's diachronic evolution (2020). https://shs.hal.science/halshs-03070375
15. Fauconnier, G., Turner, M.: The Way We Think: Conceptual Blending and the Mind's Hidden Complexities. Basic Books (2008)

16. Gros, A., et al.: Faceting the post-disaster built heritage reconstruction process within the digital twin framework for Notre-Dame de Paris. Sci. Rep. **13**(1), 5981 (2023)
17. Guillem, A., Gros, A.: La restitution hybride de l'arc doubleau effondré dans la nef de la cathédrale Notre-Dame de Paris. In: Monumental (2023)
18. Guillem, A., Gros, A., Abergel, V., De Luca, L.: Reconstruction beyond representation in Notre-Dame de Paris. In: 2023 IMEKO TC-4 International Conference on Metrology for Archaeology and Cultural Heritage (2023)
19. Guillem, A., Gros, A., Deluca, L.: Faire parler les claveaux effondrés de la cathédrale Notre-Dame de Paris. In: Humanistica 2023. Données et patrimoine, Association francophone des humanités numériques, Genève, Switzerland (2023). https://hal.science/hal-04106101
20. Guillem, A., Samuel, J., Gesquière, G., De Luca, L., Abergel, V.: Let the Fallen Voussoirs of Notre-dame de Paris speak: scientific narration and 3D visualization of virtual reconstruction hypotheses and reasoning. In: Semantic Methods for Events and Stories (SEMMES) Workshop at ESWC 2024. https://hal.science/hal-04614354
21. Guillem, A., Zarnic, R., Bruseker, G.: Building an argumentation platform for 3D reconstruction using CIDOC-CRM and Drupal. In: 2015 Digital Heritage, vol. 2, pp. 383–386 (2015). https://doi.org/10.1109/DigitalHeritage.2015.7419529, https://ieeexplore.ieee.org/abstract/document/7419529/
22. Jaillot, V., Rigolle, V., Servigne, S., Samuel, J., Gesquière, G.: Integrating multimedia documents and time-evolving 3D city models for web visualization and navigation. Trans. GIS **25**(3), 1419–1438 (2021)
23. Khan, A.F., Bellandi, A., Benotto, G., Frontini, F., Giovannetti, E., Reboul, M.: Leveraging a Narrative Ontology to Query a Literary Text, 10 p. 1548145 bytes (2016). https://doi.org/10.4230/OASICS.CMN.2016.10, https://drops.dagstuhl.de/entities/document/10.4230/OASIcs.CMN.2016.10
24. Lisena, P., et al.: An ontology for creating hypermedia stories over knowledge graphs. In: Bikakis, A., Ferrario, R., Jean, S., Markhoff, B., Mosca, A., Asmundo, M.N. (eds.) Proceedings of the International Workshop on Semantic Web and Ontology Design for Cultural Heritage Co-located with the International Semantic Web Conference 2023 (ISWC 2023), Athens, Greece, 7 November 2023. CEUR Workshop Proceedings, vol. 3540. CEUR-WS.org (2023). https://ceur-ws.org/Vol-3540/paper5.pdf
25. Meghini, C., et al.: ARIADNE: a research infrastructure for archaeology. J. Comput. Cult. Herit. **10**(3), 1–27 (2017)
26. Metral, C., Billen, R., Cutting-Decelle, A.F., Van Ruymbeke, M.: Ontology-based approaches for improving the interoperability between 3D urban models. J. Inf. Technol. Constr. **15** (2010). https://orbi.uliege.be/handle/2268/26716
27. Moulis, C., Phalip, B., Baillieul, E.: Les claveaux de l'arc doubleau effondre de la nef de Notre-Dame de Paris, rapport intermediaire (2020)
28. Niang, C., et al.: Supporting semantic interoperability in conservation-restoration domain: the PARCOURS project. J. Comput. Cult. Herit. **10**(3), 1–20 (2017)
29. Nora, P.: Between memory and history: Les Lieux de Mémoire. Representations **26**, 7–24 (1989)
30. Pearl, J.: The seven tools of causal inference, with reflections on machine learning. Commun. ACM **62**(3), 54–60 (2019)
31. Picavet, V., Brédif, M., Konini, M., Devaux, A.: iTowns, framework web pour la donnée géographique 3D. Revue XYZ **147**, 49–52 (2016). https://hal.science/hal-02551483

32. Pietroni, E., Ferdani, D.: Virtual restoration and virtual reconstruction in cultural heritage: terminology, methodologies, visual representation techniques and cognitive models. Information **12**(4) (2021). https://doi.org/10.3390/info12040167, https://www.mdpi.com/2078-2489/12/4/167
33. Piryani, R., Aussenac-Gilles, N., Hernandez, N.J.: Comprehensive survey on ontologies about event. In: ESWC Workshops on Semantic Methods for Events and Stories (SEMMES @ ESWC 2023), vol. 3443, pp. 1–15. Pasquale Lisena and Ilaria Tiddi and Simon Gottschalk and Luc Steels, ceur-ws.org, Hersonissos, Greece (2023). https://hal.science/hal-04283673
34. Pletinckx, D.: An epoch common infrastructure tool for interpretation management. Paradata and Transparency in Virtual Heritage (2008)
35. Potenziani, M., Callieri, M., Dellepiane, M., Corsini, M., Ponchio, F., Scopigno, R.: 3DHOP: 3D heritage online presenter. Comput. Graph. **52**, 129–141 (2015). https://doi.org/10.1016/j.cag.2015.07.001, https://linkinghub.elsevier.com/retrieve/pii/S0097849315001041
36. Ringas, D., Christopoulou, E., Stefanidakis, M.: Urban memory in space and time. In: Handbook of Research on Technologies and Cultural Heritage: Applications and Environments, pp. 325–340. IGI Global (2011)
37. Rissen, P., et al.: Storyline Ontology (2013). https://www.bbc.co.uk/ontologies/storyline-ontology/bbc.com/ontologies/storyline-ontology/
38. Samuel, J., Servigne, S., Gesquière, G.: UrbanCo2Fab: comprehension of concurrent viewpoints of urban fabric based on GIT. ISPRS Ann. Photogram. Remote Sens. Spat. Inf. Sci. **IV-4/W6**, 65–72 (2018). https://doi.org/10.5194/isprs-annals-IV-4-W6-65-2018, https://isprs-annals.copernicus.org/articles/IV-4-W6/65/2018/
39. Samuel, J., Servigne, S., Gesquière, G.: Representation of concurrent points of view of urban changes for city models. J. Geogr. Syst. (2020)
40. Schütz, M., Ohrhallinger, S., Wimmer, M.: Fast Out-of-core octree generation for massive point clouds. Comput. Graph. Forum **39**(7), 155–167 (2020)
41. Shi, W., Kotoula, E., Akoglu, K., Yang, Y., Rushmeier, H.: CHER-Ob: a tool for shared analysis in cultural heritage. In: Eurographics Workshop on Graphics and Cultural Heritage, 4 p. (2016). https://doi.org/10.2312/GCH.20161404, https://diglib.eg.org/handle/10.2312/gch20161404
42. Soler, F., Melero, F.J., Luzón, M.V.: A complete 3D information system for cultural heritage documentation. J. Cult. Herit. **23**, 49–57 (2017). https://doi.org/10.1016/j.culher.2016.09.008, https://linkinghub.elsevier.com/retrieve/pii/S1296207416302576
43. Stead, S.: A new approach to interoperable argumentation documentation. In: Gonzalez-Perez, C., Martin-Rodilla, P., Pereira-Fariña, M. (eds.) Discourse and Argumentation in Archaeology: Conceptual and Computational Approaches. QAAM, pp. 29–36. Springer, Cham (2023). https://doi.org/10.1007/978-3-031-37156-1_2
44. Stefani, C., De Luca, L., Véron, P., Florenzano, M.: Time indeterminacy and spatio-temporal building transformations: an approach for architectural heritage understanding. Int. J. Interact. Des. Manuf. (IJIDeM) **4**(1), 61–74 (2010)
45. Styliaras, G., Koukopoulos, D., Lazarinis, F. (eds.): Handbook of Research on Technologies and Cultural Heritage: Applications and Environments. IGI Global (2011). https://doi.org/10.4018/978-1-60960-044-0, http://services.igi-global.com/resolvedoi/resolve.aspx?doi=10.4018/978-1-60960-044-0
46. Toulmin, S.E.: The Uses of Argument. Cambridge University Press, Cambridge (2003)

47. Windhager, F., et al.: Visualization of cultural heritage collection data: state of the art and future challenges. IEEE Trans. Vis. Comput. Graph. **25**(6), 2311–2330 (2019)
48. Yeh, J.: StoryTeller: an event-based story ontology composition system for biographical history. In: 2017 International Conference on Applied System Innovation (ICASI), pp. 1934–1937. IEEE, Sapporo, Japan (2017). https://doi.org/10.1109/ICASI.2017.7988448, http://ieeexplore.ieee.org/document/7988448/
49. Yu, C.H., Hunter, J.: Documenting and sharing comparative analyses of 3D digital museum artifacts through semantic web annotations. J. Comput. Cult. Herit. **6**(4), 1–20 (2013)

Designing an Ontology Network for Digital Product Passports

Maike Jansen[1(✉)], Eva Blomqvist[2(✉)], Robin Keskisärkkä[2], Huanyu Li[2], Mikael Lindecrantz[3], Karin Wannerberg[3], André Pomp[4], Tobias Meisen[4], and Holger Berg[1]

[1] Wuppertal Institute for Climate, Environment and Energy, 42103 Wuppertal, Germany
maike.jansen@uni-wuppertal.de, holger.berg@wupperinst.org
[2] Linköping University, Linköping, Sweden
{eva.blomqvist,robin.keskisarkka,huanyu.li}@liu.se
[3] Ragn-Sells AB, Stockholm, Sweden
{mikael.lindecrantz,karin.wannerberg}@ragnsells.com
[4] Chair for Technologies and Management of Digital Transformation, University of Wuppertal, 42119 Wuppertal, Germany
{pomp,meisen}@uni-wuppertal.de

Abstract. The transition from a linear economic model to a circular model is crucial, due to the limited resources of our planet. The Circular Economy (CE) aims to maintain material continuity through the cycle of production, consumption and recycling. The Digital Product Passport (DPP) is recognised as a critical instrument for advancing CE, serving as a comprehensive digital repository for product lifecycle information. The DPP paradigm fosters transparency and traceability. However, so far there is no agreed-upon standard for technically representing and expressing DPPs. This paper aims to provide a comprehensive analysis of the requirements of a general (cross-sectoral) DPP, and to discuss a core DPP model. We propose to express this in the form of an ontology network, i.e., a formal model serving as a "translation layer" from raw data to interpreted information, along with SHACL shapes for ensuring increased data quality. Despite existing research on DPPs, a comprehensive tool for technically representing DPPs is missing, making this paper a pioneering exploration into the modelling of a DPP core ontology.

Keywords: Digital Product Passport · Ontology · Circular Economy

1 Introduction

Transitioning to a Circular Economy (CE) paradigm is crucial in a world with limited resources, emphasising the continuity of materials through the

This paper is an extended version of the workshop paper "Modelling Digital Product Passports for the Circular Economy" presented in the KG4S 2024 workshop.

A. Meroño Peñuela et al. (Eds.): ESWC 2024, LNCS 15345, pp. 220–237, 2025.
https://doi.org/10.1007/978-3-031-78955-7_19

production-consumption-recycling loop. This implies implementing the "10 R strategies" [25], such as refusal, reduction, re-use, refurbishment, and recycling, where strategy effectiveness correlates with material circularity [25]. The CE concept is integral to initiatives like the European Green Deal, the CE Action Plan, and the Ecodesign for Sustainable Products Regulation (ESPR) [1], with the Digital Product Passport (DPP) serving as a digital repository, capturing comprehensive product information throughout its lifecycle, from creation to end-of-life [10,11,22].

Information about a product's components, origin, and environmental and social impacts throughout its lifecycle should be contained in a DPP [1]. Such foundational data enables the development of CE business models, as discussed in [22]. Primary objectives of a DPP include enhancing the circularity of products through the 10 R strategies and promoting transparency and traceability of products, materials, and components [22]. Therefore, a DPP is designed to encompass various data, including manufacturing details (composition, materials, process data), usage documentation for replaced or repaired parts, end-of-life information (collection, sorting, treatment), and life-cycle data like sales volume for waste anticipation and resource assessment [22].

A distinction is often made between the DPPs themselves and DPP systems [11,13]. A DPP is the resulting artifact, or document, containing the life-cycle data of a specific product, while a DPP system is responsible for consolidating and enabling the sharing of all the required data for the various DPPs [11]. Managing the life-cycle information of DPPs and ensuring interoperability among participating actors are crucial steps towards a CE. However, there is currently no tool for this purpose. This paper advocates building an infrastructure for DPP systems based on Web standards, using the Web itself as a data sharing platform, and discusses a DPP ontology as a "translation layer" to enable semantic interoperability, aligned with ongoing DPP projects like CIRPASS[1]. The analysis and ontology in this paper focus on CE information (i.e., information directly supporting the 10 R strategies), with potential expansion in the future, complemented by SHACL shapes for DPP validation.

Our overarching research question is *how semantic interoperability and data sharing for DPP systems can be achieved, by means of ontologies and existing Web standards.* However, this paper targets the analysis of the potential, feasibility and requirements of a core DPP ontology, as a vocabulary for DPP systems, while the actual data sharing is still future work. The ontology is a proof-of-concept that shows the feasibility of the approach, but is still work in progress. Section 2, reviews work on DPP systems and ontologies. Section 3 outlines the methodology, while the ontology requirements and the proposed ontology network are detailed in Sect. 4. Section 5 outlines a use case application. Section 6 deliberates on the results, while Sect. 7 summarises findings and future work.

2 Related Work

This section presents work related to the methods and results in the paper, first recent work on DPP systems and then specific work on ontologies.

[1] https://cirpassproject.eu/ (accessed on December 7, 2023).

2.1 Digital Product Passport Systems

Within the scientific community, ongoing research in the CE domain focuses primarily on the conceptual design and sector-specific content of DPPs rather than the underlying technical IT infrastructures, i.e., the DPP systems. A comprehensive overview of existing DPP concepts is, for instance, provided in [22]. One exception, that considers DPP systems specifically, is [11], in which several overarching and general DPP system requirements are identified within 8 requirement categories. Another paper that deals with the definition of a DPP ecosystem (DPPE), which can be compared to a DPP system, is [13]. They state that "*a DPPE is a socio-technical system of systems, which is collaboratively owned by the producers, users, and disposers of products*" and they describe further, more detailed aspects of their proposed definition in a structured way [13]. Also relevant is [24], in which authors introduce their vision of SPACE_DS, a data space tailored to CE data. The concept emphasises the challenges of creating DPPs, particularly due to privacy and security concerns of data providers, and provides valuable insights for the development of an effective DPP system [24]. While we base our analysis on the results in [11], neither of the mentioned works detail DPP systems, nor address semantic interoperability specifically.

We conclude that most research on DPPs focus on conceptually framing and defining them, as well their role in the regulatory and business context of CE. Very little attention has been given to DPP systems, and no work so far has addressed the semantic interoperability technically in DPP system implementation. We address this research gap through exploring DPP ontologies.

2.2 Ontology Related Work

To ground our work in related ontologies, we conducted a review of existing work on ontologies for the CE and product domains. We draw on an ontology study conducted in [15], which identified four CE ontologies and ten product ontologies. Additionally, the Onto-DESIDE[2] project, including the Circular Economy Ontology Network (CEON)[3] [4], is relevant related work. However, CEON focuses on value networks and CE itself, not on DPPs. Therefore, there is a certain overlap with our objectives, but it is not congruent. Hence, we use CEON as an alignment opportunity[4] rather than a starting point.

Reviewing the four CE ontologies, the Building Circularity Assessment Ontology (BCAO) [21] was considered. However, our analysis revealed misalignments in conceptualisation and scope, particularly in its emphasis on the construction industry. The Circular Materials and Activities Ontology (CAMO) [28] partially addressed DPP needs but was also confined to the construction industry. The BiOnto ontology [2], designed for sustainable bioeconomy and bioproducts, was found unsuitable for DPP purposes due to misalignment with the multifaceted

[2] https://ontodeside.eu/ (accessed on December 7, 2023).
[3] http://w3id.org/CEON (accessed on December 7, 2023).
[4] The initial alignment result between CEON and DPPO is presented in [16].

DPP requirements. Finally, the Circular Exchange Ontology (CEO) [28] exhibited partial suitability for DPP integration, focusing on elements crucial for material exchange within the CE. However, CEO is no longer publicly available, whereas we can only use it as inspiration.

Subsequently, our evaluation extended to the ten product ontologies identified in [15]. The examination of the Product Life Cycle Ontology for Additive Manufacturing (AMO) [20] concluded that its specialised focus on additive manufacturing processes made it unsuitable for general DPPs. The Building Product Ontology (BPO) [32] was considered potentially and partly relevant for DPPs, particularly in the context of describing building products. However, further investigation is needed to assess its applicability outside its sub-domains. Other product ontologies, including CHAMP [29], GRACE [14], ManuService [18], and VERONTO [30], displayed potential for describing manufacturing processes, quality control, and product version management if needed as extensions, but not for the core product focus of a DPP. Overall, while these ontologies show some overlap with our work on core DPP concepts, they are all targeted at specific domains, or focus on more detailed information than a general DPP model.

BONSAI-core [6] emerged as a promising candidate for DPP modelling, with its core ontology structure aligned, at least partly, with DPP requirements. More precisely, the DPP core ontology can draw inspiration and align with the BONSAI-core ontology, which captures data specifically for life cycle assessment. Additionally, the PRONTO ontology [31], tailored for the comprehensive representation of product information, has been shown to handle diverse product structures within the food industry. However, challenges arise concerning its broader reusability beyond this specific domain, posing a noteworthy obstacle for modelling DPPs spanning diverse industries and product types. For instance, while PRONTO goes into great detail on product families and variants, it does not focus on product information and composition to the extent necessary for DPPs. The PSS ontology [19], designed for Product-Service Systems (PSS), focuses on facilitating communication and integration of heterogeneous data during the PSS lifecycle in the manufacturing domain. However, it is unsuitable for DPP purposes because the DPP paradigm encompasses broader aspects related to the product lifecycle, e.g., transparency and traceability, requiring specific considerations that go beyond the scope of the PSS ontology.

Lastly, the United Nations Standard Products and Services Code (UNSPSC)[5], while robust in product and service classification, only partially serves DPP needs, emphasising the classification of products rather than addressing DPP data. For instance, product composition and characteristics are not covered.

In summary, analysing CE and product ontologies offers insights into their suitability for DPP frameworks, yet none fully meet the DPP scope and requirements, in particular in terms of generality and flexibility. Therefore, we develop a proposed DPP core ontology, leveraging strengths and addressing limitations of the 14 reviewed ontologies, but without direct reuse.

[5] https://www.unspsc.org (accessed on December 7, 2023).

3 Methodology

To fill the research gaps we (1) analyse DPP system requirements and use cases, deriving specific ontological requirements, (2) discuss the modelling of a core DPP ontology network.

3.1 Requirements Analysis Methodology

We distinguish between functional and non-functional ontological requirements, where functional requirements specify tasks of the ontology, e.g., support for answering queries or producing inferences. Similar to [3] we distinguish three types of functional requirements, Competency Questions (CQ) [7], Contextual Statements (CS), and Reasoning Requirements (RR), where the two latter complement CQs in terms of further specifying the axioms needed. Non-functional requirements cover cross-cutting aspects, e.g., usability, accessibility, provenance.

Initially, a top-down approach was adopted for defining functional and non-functional ontological requirements, drawn from the DPP system requirements in [11]. First, the requirements with implications on the DPP representation and contained information were identified. For instance, one such requirement is that the DPP needs to contain information allowing to assess compliance with the ESPR [1], which in turn includes concrete requirements of identifying product compositions and in particular regarding substances of concern (i.e., hindering recycling). Next, ontology stories were created based on those requirements, inspired by the eXtreme Design (XD) methodology [26]. Three types of actors were identified; authorities, consumers, and value chain actors. Each with their own perspective on the stories. CQs and other requirements, were then derived from the actor-related stories. For instance, regarding the example on substances of concern, all actors need to be able to retrieve data on product content. The resulting CQs are discussed further in Sect. 4.1.

To cover more specific product details, subsequently a bottom-up approach was used to elicit additional functional requirements. This involved examining the 10 R strategies in two distinct use cases (loosely based on the use cases in Onto-DESIDE (see footnote 2)): one from the textile industry, i.e., shoes' reuse, repair, and recycling, and the other from the electronics industry, i.e., smartphones' reuse, repair, refurbishment, and recycling. The required DPP information was systematically identified for each R strategy and assigned to the corresponding value chain actors. Next, also in this case a set of CQs, CSs and RRs were derived.

Results for both approaches have been discussed with experts from different domains, e.g., recycling industry and materials design[6]. The evaluated set of DPP core ontology requirements are briefly presented in Sect. 4.1, and available as supplementary material.

[6] More specifically, for this initial version one domain expert from Ragn-Sells, and one materials modelling expert, neither which where involved in writing the initial CQs.

3.2 Ontology Design

In order to design an ontology based on these requirements, we first considered the non-functional requirements, which clearly specify the need for modularity, extensibility, and flexibility. Consequently, it is essential not to develop a large monolithic ontology, but rather a set of core modules, together with their underlying Ontology Design Patterns (ODP) [5], where modules can be flexibly used, extended, and modified in response to changing legislation and standards in the area. Such an ontology is commonly referred to as an ontology network. Given these observations, we decided to apply an agile and modular ontology engineering methodology, inspired by eXtreme Design (XD) [26], but adapted for the case at hand. More specifically, we started by identifying the core notions to be covered by a DPP ontology, from the set of requirements, e.g., core concepts, such as the DPP itself, the product it describes, product compositions, and categories of information to be contained in a DPP. We then developed a core ODP describing the most central concepts, and subsequently additional modules.

4 DPP Ontology Network

In this section we describe the elicited requirements and the resulting DPP ontology network[7]. Including a brief mention of the additional SHACL validation for data quality assurance.

4.1 DPP Core Ontology Requirements

Results of the Top-Down Approach: As described in Sect. 3.1, for the requirements analysis of the DPP core ontology, we first took a top-down approach by deriving functional and non-functional requirements from the DPP system requirements in [11]. Our results consist of 37 ontology stories including 67 CQs, 3 CSs (duplicates filtered), and 5 RRs (duplicates filtered), constituting the functional requirements. It is important to state, that the ontology stories including their derived CQs (i.e., functional ontology requirements) are role-based, including the perspective of three actor categories: authorities, value chain actors, and consumers. For the non-functional requirements, we identified 13 categories (duplicates filtered), which are not role-based, where examples include *compliance with standards*, *modularity*, and *localisation*. Some examples of the functional requirements identified, derived through the top-down approach, are provided in Table 1, and the non-functional requirements in Table 2.

[7] The full list of requirements, and the ontology network itself, can be accessed via the DPP ontology landing page https://w3id.org/dppo/ and our public GitHub repository https://github.com/LiUSemWeb/DPPO.

Table 1. Examples of identified functional DPP core ontology requirements from the top-down approach.

Actor Perspective	Ontology Story	Competency Questions (CQs)	Contextual Statement (CS)	Reasoning Requirement (RR)
Authority	A product contains a substance of concern, that hinders its recycling, and does not comply with the ESPR regulation. An authority that should decide on the product's compliance with respect to regulations needs to know the details of the product composition, materials and substances to determine its compliance.	(1) Does the product contain substances of concern? (2) If the product contains at least one substance of concern, how many and what kind of substances of concern?	-	-
Value Chain Actor	A producer wants to view the DPP information of a specific product component (provided by a supplier). Also, the producer wants to change/edit/add the DPP information of this product component because it will be somehow changed.	(1) Which and what kind of information can the producer see? (2) Can the producer only view the information, or can he also change/edit/add the information for the component provided by the supplier?	Every piece of information contained in a DPP has to have an access rule.	Access rules for specific statements can be derived from rules for the DPP as a whole or parts of it.
Consumer	A new product has been released to the market. The product contains several components, where the DPP information is provided by several actors. A consumer wants to check its publicly available information which is accessible via its DPP.	(1) What is the complete public content of the DPP?	-	The DPP information is composed of the main DPP model and all its sub-models that are retrieved from other actors.

Table 2. Non-functional ontological requirements.

#	Req.	#	Req.
1.	Compliance with regulations	8.	Modular
2.	Compliance with standards	9.	Extensible/Evolvable
3.	Follow best practices	10.	Localisation (languages)
4.	Usability (humans & machines)	11.	DPP metadata
5.	FAIR publishing	12.	Verification of metadata
6.	Dereferencable identifiers	13.	Immutable statements
7.	Flexible data model		

Results of the Bottom-Up Approach: For the bottom-up approach (described in Sect. 3.1), we analysed the "10 R strategies" of the two application domains (textile and electronics, using shoes and smartphones as the example products respectively). This resulted in 7 use case scenarios, and a total set of 32 CQs. The full list of the use case specific functional ontology requirements, derived through the bottom-up approach, is available in the supplementary material (see footnote 7). In Table 3, an example is provided, consisting of the CQs and information per value chain actor for the case "repairing of a shoe". The value chain actors in this case are: material supplier, manufacturer, and repairer. As seen in Table 3, the repairer asks for specific DPP information (c.f. the CQs, which represent functional requirements of DPP ontology) in order to repair a shoe. This required information is provided by previous actors of the shoe's value chain, i.e., in this case by the material supplier and the manufacturer. Once the shoe has been repaired, the repairer in turn adds information on the repair to the DPP.

4.2 Modelling Challenges

While assessing these requirements, a number of modelling challenges were also identified, where we exemplify a few of them here:

Modelling DPP Content Provenance: The main role of a DPP is to collect information about a product in order to enable its proper treatment, and support claims. However, this information also needs to be contextualised, e.g., stating when it is valid, or in what context. As an alternative, we may consider to use the RDF-star approach for some of this information. RDF-star[8] is an extension to RDF, allowing for nested triples, to be able to state facts about triples. The intention is to allow statements about triples, rather than replacing reification in general, hence, this approach is not suitable for replacing all the reified relations needed according to our requirements analysis. However, for the provenance of DPP information, this is an option that can be explored, and which the ontology should also cater for.

Views over Data: A related modelling issue involves the different needs of different actors, in terms of the level of detail and granularity of the information needed. In order to cater for the cases where there is no need for detailed information, i.e., to avoid too detailed and complex data which may hamper its usability, there is a need to summarise detailed information into a less complex structure. One such option is to allow for different views. This can be done in different ways, e.g., with alternative ontology modules of varying complexity, or by including several layers of relations into existing modules.

Perspectives on Products: In the context of our DPP ontology network and its "Product" class, the modular structure enables substitution or addition of sub-classes without disrupting the overall ontology. For instance, if new aspects or types of product compositions emerge, they can be integrated or replaced within the ontology without affecting other components.

Table 3. Shoe repair use case: CQs and provided information per value chain actor.

Actor	Competency Questions (CQs)	Provided Information
Repairer	(1) Are there any instructions on how to repair the product? (2) What are the single components of this product? (3) What are the charecteristics of the components? (4) How can the product be disassembled (if needed)? (5) Which spare parts fit the repairing of the product? (6) What is the material composition of the spare parts?	Provides information on: what was broken, what part/component of the product was repaired or replaced, what new components were inserted (if any) and their composition, how was it repaired, by whom, and when
Manufacturer	-	Manufacturer of product: Repair instructions (1,5), list of components and their characteristics (2,3), information on the assembly of the components (4). Manufacturer of the spare parts: DPP of spare parts, with their components and material composition (6)
Material Supplier	-	Compostition of materials for original components (3) and spare parts (6)

[8] https://w3c.github.io/rdf-star/cg-spec/editors_draft.html.

4.3 Description of the DPP Ontology Network

Based on the requirements, a first version of a DPP ontology network has been developed. The resulting ontology network contains 5 main modules, where one is a basic ODP. Below, we describe each module. All the modules and supporting information, including documentation and visualisations, are available online (see footnote 7). An overview of the ontology network is presented in Fig. 1.

DPP ODP – The most foundational module is the DPP ODP, merely defining the two main concepts involved and their relation(s), i.e., the `Product` and `DPP`. The ODP states that a `DPP describes` a `Product`, and that each `DPP` and `Product` may have parts that are other `DPP`s or `Product`s respectively.

DPP Core – The DPP ODP is then detailed by the DPP core module, where different kinds of products are considered, as subclasses of `Product`, i.e., including components, materials, and substances. This conforms to the definitions listed in the ESPR [1] proposal, stating for instance that a product is "any physical good that is placed on the market or put into service", and a component is "a product intended to be incorporated into another product". Materials and

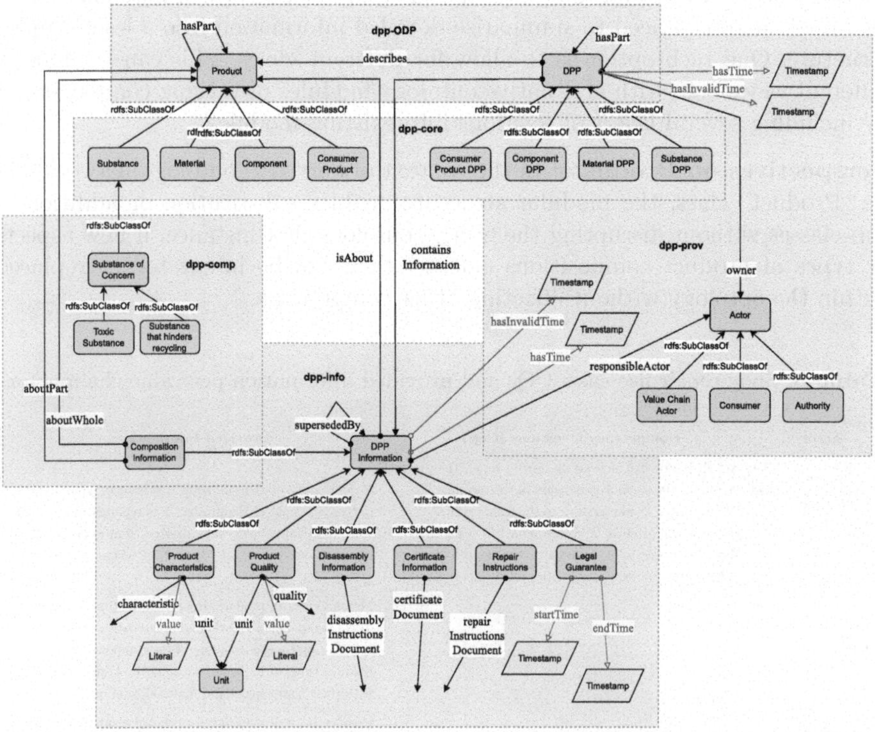

Fig. 1. An illustration of the overall DPP ontology network (where in addition, modules are represented through grey boxes).

substances are merely mentioned in the ESPR [1], but not defined. However, from the description it is clear that a material can be built up of substances, and materials make up components. Still, since a material is also a physical good that can be sold, depending on the context the material itself may also be considered a product. In the interest of reusability and flexibility, these classes are therefore not mutually disjoint. For instance, a certain `Product` may be both a `ConsumerProduct`, i.e., sold separately, as well as a `Component` in a larger complex `Product`. For instance, something that is considered a `Component` from the perspective of one actor may be considered a `Material` by another. Conversely, DPPs can be of different kinds, corresponding to these categories of products, i.e., a `ComponentDPP` is a `DPP` that describes something considered as a `Component`. In essence, this core DPP module is not intended to be a prescriptive definition, but rather reflect how the current directives talk about products and DPPs, i.e., a descriptive model. Whereas this may also change in the future. And since this is modelled in a separate module, with minimal dependencies on the other modules, it can easily be extended, updated or exchanged in the future.

DPP Information – A key component of the DPP is the information contained inside it. For describing this information, we utilise reification, i.e., expressing the relation between the `DPP`, and a piece of information about a `Product`, as a class, i.e., `DPPInformation`. In this way we are able to describe this relation further. In this module we define 7 subclasses of `DPPInformation`, c.f. Figure 1. Products may be linked to a characteristic or quality, a concrete value of the characteristic of quality, and potentially a unit of measure. An example could be that a product has a width (characteristic) of 55 (value) mm (unit), which can then be further annotated with the confidence, measurement method etc. `DisassemblyInformation`, `RepairInstructions`, and `CertificateInformation` most likely represent links to external information, such as documents, or data at a certification authority, for instance. Hence in these cases only generic properties have been included, as "stubs" for further extension. The `LegalGuarantee` is additionally modelled as a time period, with a start and an end date, which is relevant to the right to repair a product.

Product Composition – A special case of `DPPInformation` is the `Composition Information`, which is detailed in its own module. This information differs from the other types, since it relates two products to each other (e.g., the `Product` to the `Component`), i.e., the partonomy of products, also expressed through a property chain axiom on the `hasPart` relation. In this way, the direct partonomy of the `Products` can be inferred from the reified relations, represented as `CompositionInformation`. However, this also adds reasoning complexity, whereby the module may be optionally excluded in case reasoning performance is of essence. In addition, this is where one can extend the ontology network with more detailed compositions, such as chemical compositions of materials and substances. However, for now the focus is on CE-related concepts, such as `SubstanceOfConcern`, as specified by the ESPR [1]. At the moment the directives specify two kinds of substances of concern, i.e., toxic ones, and substances that hinders recycling, which are the two categories we have therefore included in the ontology module.

DPP Provenance – A module for tracking provenance of DPPs and DPP information, has been included, relating to requirements on being able to track the actors responsible for certain data, as well as timestamps for information validity (immutable statements).

4.4 SHACL Validation

While the ontology modules describe the domain, and can be used to set the general structure of DPPs, they are less suitable for data validation. Acknowledging the need for high quality data, we define a set of SHACL shapes to verify the (structural) validity of DPP information, applicable without employing OWL reasoning. This is similar to [27], where SHACL shapes were proposed as a way

Listing 1.1. The SHACL shape used to validate the main part of a DPP, i.e., an instance of the DPP class, and the DPP info class (excerpt).

```
@prefix sh: <http://www.w3.org/ns/shacl#> .
@prefix dpp-odp: <http://w3id.org/dppo/ontology/dpp-odp/> .
@prefix dpp-info: <http://w3id.org/dppo/ontology/dpp-info/> .

<DPP-Shape>
    a sh:NodeShape ;
    sh:targetClass dpp-odp:DPP ;
    sh:property [ sh:path dpp-info:containsInformation ;
                  sh:minCount 1;
                  sh:class dpp-info:DPPInformation ] ;
    sh:property [ sh:path dpp-odp:describes ;
                  sh:minCount 1;
                  sh:maxCount 1;
                  sh:class dpp-odp:Product ] ;
    sh:property [ sh:path dpp-odp:hasPart ;
                  sh:class dpp-odp:DPP ] .

<DPPInformation-Shape>
    a sh:NodeShape ;
    sh:targetClass dpp-info:DPPInformation ;
    sh:property [ sh:path dpp-info:startTime ;
                  sh:minCount 1;
                  sh:maxCount 1;
                  sh:datatype xsd:dateTime ] ;
    sh:property [ sh:path dpp-info:endTime ;
                  sh:maxCount 1;
                  sh:datatype xsd:dateTime ] ;
    ...
    sh:property [ sh:path dpp-info:supersededBy ;
                  sh:maxCount 1;
                  sh:class dpp-info:DPPInformation ] ;
    ...
    sh:or(
        [ sh:path dpp-info:supersededBy ;
          sh:maxCount 0 ]
        [ sh:path dpp-info:endTime ;
          sh:minCount 1 ]
    ).
```

of ensuring the consistency of form-based data input for Asset Administration Shell (AAS) [23] submodel templates. The shapes are defined based on a set of assumptions, such as: (1) a DPP must be defined for exactly one product, (2) a DPP must refer to at least one piece of information, (3) a DPP can have multiple DPPs as parts, etc. The full set of shapes resides in the project repository (see footnote 7), but an example is presented in Listing 1.1.

5 Validation and Use Case Evaluation

In this section we first validate the requirements, derived from DPP system requirements and the two use cases. Then we apply the DPP ontology network for annotating data in the context of flat-glass recycling at Ragn-Sells AB[9].

5.1 Requirements Verification

Non-Functional Requirements – Assessing the fulfilment of non-functional requirements is not straight-forward, but here we discuss each of the 13 non-functional requirements. A number of the requirements are covered through the choice of technology, i.e., ontologies expressed using Web standards, e.g., req. #2 (web-standards), #7 (flexible data model), #6 (dereferencable identifiers), and #9 (in the case of machine usability). Additionally, the requirement #10 (localisation) is enabled by RDF(S), which allows annotations using a language tag, enabling querying based on the language of the information. Further, also the FAIR (Findable, Accessible, Interoperable and Reusable) [33] publishing (#5) is supported by Web standards, together with publishing best practices.

Requirements related to usability and best practices (#3, #4), are covered through careful documentation of the ontologies, as well as the use of ODPs. Each documentation page contains both written documentation (generated through PyLODE[10]), and a visualisation of the ontology module generated by using WebVOWL [17]. For human usability, it is also important to keep the ontology modules small and without excessive complexity. Regarding the ontology best practices (#3), in addition we have used naming conventions, versioning schemes, and permanent dereferencable URIs, etc., all part of best practices.

Regarding the structure and content of the ontology network, choosing an ontology network and not a monolithic ontology is related both to requirements #8 (modularity) and #9 (extensibility and evolvability). By using a modular structure, and decoupling the modules as much as possible, we are preparing for future changes, without impacting the whole network if changes occur in a single module. Additionally, it is easy to add more specific modules to the network, without necessarily importing the whole network, increasing (re)usability. Concerning the content of the modules, we have added a specific module on metadata (e.g., provenance) covering #11. Also the requirement of immutable

[9] https://www.ragnsells.com/ (accessed on December 7, 2023).
[10] https://github.com/rdflib/pyLODE.

statements (#5) is covered by the provenance module, since it enables stating valid time periods of statements, allowing to keep information even when invalidated. Further, #1 (compliance with regulations) is ensured by the functional requirements being derived from regulations themselves.

The only requirement remaining is the verifiable metadata (#12), where metadata is made available, but where the verification is considered out of scope, but could be represented as annotations. Additionally, the use and compliance with CE standards (part of #2), needs to be continuously verified, since these standards are still emerging. However, we have taken into account current standards that we are so far aware of, in the ontology design and documentation.

Functional Requirements – As verification of the functional requirements, we mapped each CQ to one (or more) SPARQL queries defined using the ontology vocabulary. In total, we document a set of 29 SPARQL queries covering 78 of the CQs defined. 21 CQs were left for future work due to lack of coverage (or only partial coverage) in the ontology. The full set of SPARQL queries is available in the project GitHub repository (see footnote 7).

5.2 Use Case Validation

While the verification that the ontology network fulfills its requirements provides important evidence regarding its applicability to support the implementation of DPP systems, it still remains to apply the ontology network at scale and across industry sectors. In this paper we illustrate the applicability by means of a specific use case from the construction domain. We use the case of flat glass recycling, which is currently a process being implemented by the recycling company Ragn-Sells AB (see footnote 9) in Sweden. The process enables high quality flat glass to be recycled with maintained quality instead of ending up in landfill. In this case a window constitutes the product in focus, and the intended R-strategy is the recycling of the glass pane of the window. From the perspective of the recycler, e.g., Ragn-Sells, there are several questions that the window DPP needs to answer. Some examples are[11]: (1) What is the type of glass? (2) What is the frame material? (3) Does the window contain any substances of concern - which? (4) Is there a film mounted on the glass? (5) What are the dimensions of the window? (6) Who is the manufacturer responsible for the data?

While the first four questions are intended to assess the recyclability of the window, the fifth provides important information for the collection and transport to the recycling facility. The last question is about the provenance of the data, e.g., both for establishing trust, and to be able to contact the organisation in case of missing data. In Fig. 2, an example DPP of a window, answering the first three questions is illustrated. The DPP of a window consists of two sub-DPPs, where the glass DPP is published by the flat glass manufacturer, the frame DPP is published by the window manufacturer, and so is the overall window DPP. Hence, in the decentralised DPP system scenario, the window and frame DPPs

[11] This is a small excerpt of the actual set of questions, which are being explored in a related project, c.f. Trace4Value: https://trace4value.se/.

might reside in the data storage of the window manufacturer, while the glass DPP might be stored with the glass manufacturer and merely retrieved on-demand using a query. All annotations, such as labels and timestamps, are omitted for readability. It was concluded that the ontology can successfully describe all the necessary data, answering the formulated CQs, and the ontology was therefore well-received by Ragn-Sells in management of their flat-glass recycling data.

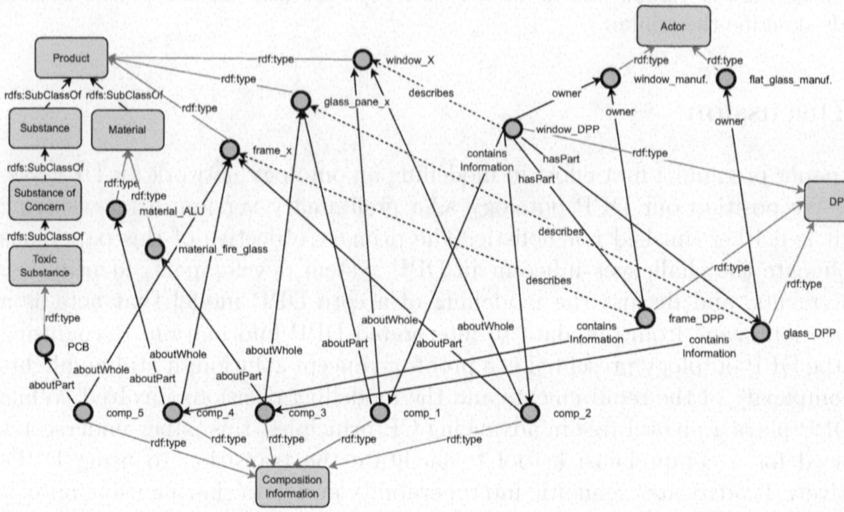

Fig. 2. Image illustrating typical DPP data used for recyclability assessments of windows, by Ragn-Sells AB.

In addition, to verify the flexibility and ability to appropriately capture data provenance of the DPP information, we illustrate how the ontology network may both describe data represented as plain RDF as well as of RDF-star statements. The main feature of RDF-star is the nesting of triples, i.e., statements about statements, similar to the way data is modeled in property graphs. In Fig. 3 we illustrate the case where a window frame has been replaced, and a new frame is now part of the window described by a DPP. This is indicated by an invalidation date on the information about frame x being a part of the window, while adding the new information about frame y, from a certain time point. In part a) of the figure, the data is represented using standard RDF, as in the previous illustration, while in part b) of the figure we show how the same information could be conveyed by using the `hasPart` property and time annotations on those triples directly (slightly modifying the Grafoo notation), using the RDF-star approach. The full timestamp format, ownership etc., have been omitted for readability. While the use of RDF-star may depend on practical choices, such as support for the data model in triple stores used for the resulting knowledge graph, its usage has the potential to create more compact RDF graphs and even potentially more understandable and more easily queryable data (c.f. the experiments in [8]).

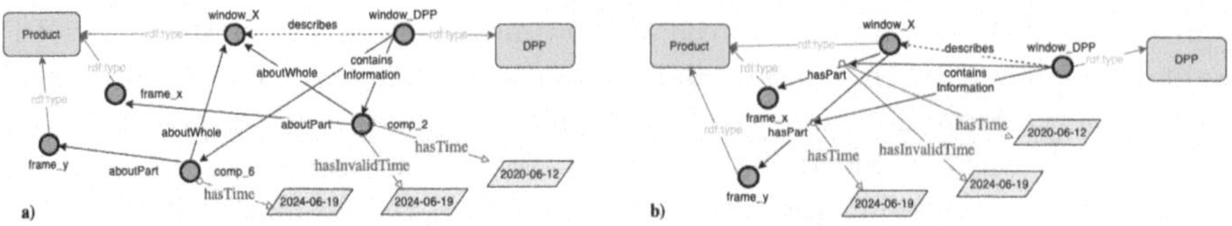

Fig. 3. Image illustrating two different ways to represent provenance of the part-whole relation between a window and its frame, where b) illustrates the use of RDF-star to directly describe the triples.

6 Discussion

This paper presents a first effort in modelling an ontology network for DPP systems. We position our DPP ontology as a preliminary version, acknowledging that it is neither finished nor holistic. The primary objective of this paper was to delineate the challenges inherent in DPP system development, identify key requirements, and discuss the modelling of a core DPP model that acts as a "translation layer" from raw data to interpreted DPP information. Recognising that the DPP ontology presented is a proof-of-concept solution, it still highlights the complexity of the requirements and the modelling decisions involved. While the DPP plays a pivotal role in advancing CE principles, this paper underscores the need for a comprehensive tool to facilitate the transition to using DPPs effectively. It advocates semantic interoperability and data sharing using ontologies and existing Web standards, aligning with ongoing DPP projects such as CIRPASS (see footnote 1) and Onto-DESIDE (see footnote 2). The analysis prioritises the contribution of the ontology to the broader discussion on DPP system development rather than its standalone existence. Overall, we believe that ontologies will play a crucial role in realising the vision of general cross-domain DPPs, and the CE as a whole. With our work as the starting point, we can thereby accelerate the transition towards a scalable CE. In summary, our DPP ontology represents a significant first step towards large-scale DPP system implementation, endorsed by positive feedback from recycling industry experts confirming its practical utility.

7 Conclusions and Future Work

Our exploration into the modelling of a DPP core ontology addresses the question of whether ontologies present a feasible approach for DPP system development, in particular for the challenge of semantic interoperability of DPP data. Our proposed DPP ontology network serves as a proof-of-concept, demonstrating the feasibility and potential for ontologies and existing Web standards to enhance semantic interoperability, a crucial component of successful DPP system implementation. While acknowledging the preliminary nature of the artefact itself, our thorough requirements analysis, as well as feedback from industry experts in the recycling sector underscores the promising practical utility of the proposed approach. We therefore conclude that relying on existing Web standards and best practices is essential.

In the future, refinement of the DPP ontology to encompass further DPP requirements is planned (c.f. Sect. 5.1), as well as alignments to other existing ontologies. Very recently, after the completion of this work, alternative conceptualisations of a DPP have also emerged [12], which will have to be taken into account in future version of the ontologies. Additionally, covering evolving standards will be critical to provide a solid foundation for the development of DPP systems in the pursuit of a sustainable and resource-efficient CE. Further, the ISO59004 [9], defining several core CE concepts, was released in May 2024, and has to be carefully considered as a source of concept definitions in future work.

Acknowledgments. This research was supported by the Vinnova-funded project Trace4Value (Dnr. 2021-04323) and the Digital Europe Program project CIRPASS, as well as the Onto-DESIDE project (grant agreement no. 101058682) from the European Union's Horizon Europe research and innovation programme.

Disclosure of Interests. The authors have no competing interests to declare that are relevant to the content of this article.

References

1. Proposal for a REGULATION OF THE EUROPEAN PARLIAMENT AND OF THE COUNCIL establishing a framework for setting ecodesign requirements for sustainable products and repealing Directive 2009/125/EC (2022). https://eur-lex.europa.eu/legal-content/EN/TXT/?uri=CELEX:52022PC0142
2. Bicchielli, C., Biancone, N., Ferri, F., Grifoni, P.: BiOnto: an ontology for sustainable bioeconomy and bioproducts. Sustainability **13**(8), 4265 (2021). https://doi.org/10.3390/su13084265
3. Blomqvist, E., Hammar, K., Presutti, V.: Engineering ontologies with patterns - the eXtreme design methodology. Ontol. Eng. Ontol. Des. Patterns **25**, 23–50 (2016)
4. Blomqvist, E., et al.: Cross-domain modelling–a network of core ontologies for the circular economy. In: Proceedings of the 14th Workshop on Ontology Design and Patterns (WOP 2023) (2023)
5. Blomqvist, E., Sandkuhl, K.: Patterns in ontology engineering: classification of ontology patterns. In: Proceedings of the Seventh International Conference on Enterprise Information Systems, pp. 413–416. SciTePress (2005). https://doi.org/10.5220/0002518804130416
6. Ghose, A., Lissandrini, M., Hansen, E.R., Weidema, B.P.: A core ontology for modeling life cycle sustainability assessment on the Semantic Web. J. Ind. Ecol. **26**(3), 731–747 (2022). https://doi.org/10.1111/jiec.13220
7. Grüninger, M., Fox, M.S.: The role of competency questions in enterprise engineering. In: Rolstadås, A. (ed.) Benchmarking—Theory and Practice. IAICT, pp. 22–31. Springer, Boston, MA (1995). https://doi.org/10.1007/978-0-387-34847-6_3
8. Iglesias-Molina, A., Ahrabian, K., Ilievski, F., Pujara, J., Corcho, O.: Comparison of knowledge graph representations for consumer scenarios. In: Payne, T.R., et al. (eds.) ISWC 2023. LNCS, vol. 14265, pp. 271–289. Springer, Cham (2023)

9. ISO/TC 323: Circular economy - Vocabulary, principles and guidance for implementation. International Organization for Standardization, Switzerland, ISO 59004:2024 edn. (2024). https://www.iso.org/standard/80648.html
10. Jansen, M., Gerstenberger, B., Bitter-Krahe, J., Berg, H., Sebestyén, J., Schneider, J.: Current approaches to the digital product passport for a circular economy: an overview of projects and initiatives. Technical report, Wuppertal Institut für Klima, Umwelt, Energie (2022). https://doi.org/10.48506/opus-8042
11. Jansen, M., Meisen, T., Plociennik, C., Berg, H., Pomp, A., Windholz, W.: Stop guessing in the dark: identified requirements for digital product passport systems. Systems **11**(3), 123 (2023). https://doi.org/10.3390/systems11030123
12. Kebede, R., Moscati, A., Tan, H., Johansson, P.: A modular ontology modeling approach to developing digital product passports to promote circular economy in the built environment. Sustain. Product. Consump. **48**, 248–268 (2024)
13. King, M.R.N., Timms, P.D., Mountney, S.: A proposed universal definition of a Digital Product Passport Ecosystem (DPPE): worldviews, discrete capabilities, stakeholder requirements and concerns. J. Clean. Product. **384**, 135538 (2023). https://doi.org/10.1016/j.jclepro.2022.135538
14. Leitão, P., Rodrigues, N., Turrin, C., Pagani, A., Petrali, P.: GRACE ontology inteGrating pRocess and quAlity Control. In: IECON 2012 - 38th Annual Conference on IEEE Industrial Electronics Society, pp. 4348–4353 (2012). https://doi.org/10.1109/IECON.2012.6389189
15. Li, H., Abd Nikooie Pour, M., Li, Y., Lindecrantz, M., Blomqvist, E., Lambrix, P.: A survey of general ontologies for the cross-industry domain of circular economy. In: Companion Proceedings of the ACM Web Conference 2023. WWW '23 Companion, pp. 731–741. Association for Computing Machinery (2023). https://doi.org/10.1145/3543873.3587613
16. Li, H., Blomqvist, E., Lambrix, P.: Initial and experimental ontology alignment results in the circular economy domain. In: Proceedings of the 2nd International Workshop on Knowledge Graphs for Sustainability (KG4S2024). CEUR-WS.org (2024)
17. Lohmann, S., Negru, S., Haag, F., Ertl, T.: Visualizing ontologies with VOWL. Semant. Web **7**(4), 399–419 (2016). https://doi.org/10.3233/SW-150200
18. Lu, Y., Wang, H., Xu, X.: ManuService ontology: a product data model for service-oriented business interactions in a cloud manufacturing environment. J. Intell. Manuf. **30**(1), 317–334 (2019). https://doi.org/10.1007/s10845-016-1250-x
19. May, G., Cho, S., Correia, A.T., Siafaka, R., Stokic, D., Kiritsis, D.: Toward a reference terminology for product-service systems in the manufacturing domain. Comput. Ind. **142**, 103729 (2022). https://doi.org/10.1016/j.compind.2022.103729
20. Mohd Ali, M., Rai, R., Otte, J.N., Smith, B.: A product life cycle ontology for additive manufacturing. Comput. Ind. **105**, 191–203 (2019)
21. Morkunaite, L., Al-Naber, F.H., Petrova, E., Svidt, K.: An open data platform for early-stage building circularity assessment: the joint conference CIBW 78 - LDAC 2021. In: Proceedings of the 38th International Conference of CIB W78, pp. 813–822 (2021)
22. Plociennik, C., Pourjafarian, M., et al.: Requirements for a digital product passport to boost the circular economy. In: Demmler, D., Krupka, D., Federrath, H. (eds.) INFORMATIK 2022, pp. 1485–1494. Gesellschaft für Informatik, Bonn (2022). https://doi.org/10.18420/inf2022_127

23. Plociennik, C., Pourjafarian, M., Nazeri, A., et al.: Towards a digital lifecycle passport for the circular economy. In: Proceedings of the 29th CIRP Conference on Life Cycle Engineering. Procedia CIRP, vol. 105, pp. 122–127 (2022). https://doi.org/10.1016/j.procir.2022.02.021
24. Pomp, A., Jansen, M., Berg, H., Meisen, T.: SPACE_DS: towards a circular economy data space. In: Companion Proceedings of the ACM Web Conference 2023, pp. 1500–1501. Association for Computing Machinery (2023). https://doi.org/10.1145/3543873.3587685
25. Pourjafarian, M., Plociennik, C., Rimaz, M.H., et al.: A multi-stakeholder digital product passport based on the asset administration shell. In: 2023 IEEE 28th International Conferece on Emerging Technologies and Factory Automation (ETFA), pp. 1–8 (2023). https://doi.org/10.1109/ETFA54631.2023.10275715
26. Presutti, V., Daga, E., Gangemi, A., Blomqvist, E.: eXtreme design with content ontology design patterns. In: Proceedings of the 2009 International Conference on Ontology Patterns. WOP'09, vol. 516, pp. 83–97. CEUR-WS.org (2009)
27. Rimaz, M.H., Plociennik, C., Kunz, L., Ruskowski, M.: Am I in good shape? Flexible way to validate asset administration shell data entry via shapes constraint language. In: 2023 IEEE 28th International Conference on Emerging Technologies and Factory Automation (ETFA), pp. 1–6. IEEE (2023). https://doi.org/10.1109/ETFA54631.2023.10275629
28. Sauter, E., Lemmens, R., Pauwels, P.: CEO and CAMO ontologies: a circulation medium for materials in the construction industry. In: 6th International Symposium on Life-Cycle Civil Engineering (IALCCE), pp. 1645–1652. CRC Press (2018)
29. Smith, B.: Coordinated holistic alignment of manufacturing processes (CHAMP). Techncial report (2018). https://apps.dtic.mil/sti/citations/AD1078282
30. Sonzini, M.S., Vegetti, M., Leone, H.: Towards an ontology for product version management. Int. J. Product Lifecycle Manag. **8**(1), 80–97 (2015)
31. Vegetti, M., Leone, H., Henning, G.: PRONTO: an ontology for comprehensive and consistent representation of product information. Eng. Appl. Artif. Intell. **24**(8), 1305–1327 (2011). https://doi.org/10.1016/j.engappai.2011.02.014
32. Wagner, A., Rüppel, U.: BPO: the building product ontology for assembled products. In: Proceedings of the 7th Linked Data in Architecture and Construction Workshop. CEUR Workshop Proceedings, vol. 2389, pp. 106–119. CEUR-WS.org (2019)
33. Wilkinson, M.D., Dumontier, M., Aalbersberg, I.J., et al.: The FAIR guiding principles for scientific data management and stewardship. Sci. Data **3**(160018), 1–9 (2016)

Explainable Moral Values: A Neuro-Symbolic Approach to Value Classification

Nicolas Lazzari[1(✉)], Stefano De Giorgis[2(✉)], Aldo Gangemi[2,3], and Valentina Presutti[4]

[1] Department of Computer Science, University of Pisa, Pisa, Italy
nicolas.lazzar3@unibo.it
[2] Institute of Cognitive Sciences and Technologies, National Research Council, Rome, Italy
{stefano.degiorgis2,aldo.gangemi}@unibo.it
[3] Department of Philosophy, University of Bologna, Bologna, Italy
[4] Department of Modern Languages, Literature, and Cultures, University of Bologna, Bologna, Italy
valentina.presutti@unibo.it

Abstract. This work explores the integration of ontology-based reasoning and Machine Learning techniques for explainable value classification. By relying on an ontological formalization of moral values as in the Moral Foundations Theory, relying on the DnS Ontology Design Pattern, the *sandra* neuro-symbolic reasoner is used to infer values (fomalized as descriptions) that are *satisfied by* a certain sentence. Sentences, alongside their structured representation, are automatically generated using an open-source Large Language Model. The inferred descriptions are used to automatically detect the value associated with a sentence. We show that only relying on the reasoner's inference results in explainable classification comparable to other more complex approaches. We show that combining the reasoner's inferences with distributional semantics methods largely outperforms all the baselines, including complex models based on neural network architectures. Finally, we build a visualization tool to explore the potential of theory-based values classification, which is publicly available at http://xmv.geomeaning.com/.

Keywords: Moral Value Detection · Neuro-symbolic Reasoning · Knowledge Representation · Explainable Classification · Synthetic Data

1 Introduction

The recent advent of AI models showing impressive performance in generative tasks, especially related to linguistic and visual production, have made the Value

WISDOMS 2024—First International Workshop on Integrating the Semantics of Data, Ontologies, Moral and cultural values and their Societal impact. Co-located with ESWC 2024.

A. Meroño Peñuela et al. (Eds.): ESWC 2024, LNCS 15345, pp. 238–255, 2025.
https://doi.org/10.1007/978-3-031-78955-7_20

Alignment [1,2] problem even more relevant for the close future. Detecting and classifying human values in multimodal data has emerged as a crucial task in various domains, especially with the proven capabilities by Large Language Models (LLMs) where aligning them with human beliefs is gaining mainstream attention [3]. The ability to automatically discern values from text holds significance for understanding human behavior, decision-making processes, and societal trends . However, achieving this classification presents several challenges.

Firstly, value classification is inherently subjective and context-dependent, making it difficult to objectively identify a unique value associated with a given sentence. Additionally, it's imperative to consider diverse perspectives when undertaking this task to ensure a comprehensive understanding of the underlying values.

Current approaches predominantly rely on Machine Learning (ML) techniques, particularly pre-trained LLMs, for value classification. While these methods demonstrate effectiveness, the opacity of their decision-making processes raises concerns regarding the semantic understanding of sentences versus mere pattern matching. As such, there is a pressing need for an approach that not only provides accurate predictions but also offers interpretability, allowing stakeholders to assess the alignment of predictions with established knowledge of values.

To address these challenges, we propose a novel framework that integrates ontology-based reasoning with ML techniques. Specifically, we leverage the *sandra* neuro-symbolic reasoner, which utilizes the DnS Ontology Design Pattern, to infer the various perspectives from which a given situation, represented as a sentence, can be interpreted. In our framework, we focus on Moral Foundations Theory by Graham and Haidt [4] as the theoretical framework guiding our ontology formalization.

A critical aspect of our approach is the structured representation of sentences, which we obtain using an open-source LLM. Through empirical evaluation, we demonstrate the feasibility and efficacy of this approach, showing desirable properties such as the correlation between detected emotion polarity in sentences and the polarity of associated values.

We establish a robust baseline for value classification by solely relying on the reasoner's inferences, demonstrating comparable performance to more complex approaches involving pre-trained LLMs. Importantly, our method ensures explainability, enabling us to provide justifications for classification decisions.

Furthermore, we showcase the synergistic benefits of combining our approach with other NLP techniques, resulting in significant performance improvements over all baselines, including LLM-based methods, without sacrificing interpretability. Through this introduction, we set the stage for the subsequent sections, where we delve deeper into the methodology, experiments, and results of our proposed framework for explainable value classification.

The paper is organized as follows: Sect. 2 presents the related works in the human value fields. Section 3 describes the approach used to produce the dataset. Section 4 provides an overview of the neuro-symbolic techniques used to perform inferences over the dataset while Sect. 5 presents the experiments performed and discuss its results, showcasing the interpretability of some methods. Finally, Sect. 7 provides an overview of the contribution and identify limitations that will be explored in future works.

2 Related Works

In this section, we review existing literature relevant to the integration of ontology-based reasoning and Machine Learning (ML) techniques for value formalization and classification, focusing on the Moral Foundations Theory, detailing our formalization via reusing the DnS Ontology Design Pattern.

Values Theoretical Frameworks. Value formalization, intended as the construction of a theoretical structure encompassing a set of entities, and consequent elicitation of semantic relation intertwining moral and cultural values has a long and cross disciplinary background. Here we focus on the Moral Foundations Theory (MFT), as detailed in the following, but other existing theoretical frameworks are Basic Human Values, by Scwhartz [5,6], and Morality as Cooperation [7,8].

From an knowledge representation perspective there have been a previous attempt to represent the notion of value: the Ethics Ontology [9], which explore the commonsense notion of "value" to a certain extent, but lacks the grounding to a specific theory. Another relevant work is the Value Awareness Ontology [10], focused on agent-based value-aware and normative systems. In this paper we extended previous existing work, focused on the above mentioned theories as ontological modules: the ValueNet ontology [11]. ValueNet is an ontology network formalising several theories, and modeling moral and cultural values as semantic frames [12,13]. The frame-based modeling commits to two main assumptions: (i) Values are modeled as n-ary relations, having roles playing a specific semantic function (e.g. Agent, Undergoer, Victim, Beneficiary, etc.) and (ii) values can be "evoked" by a set of lexical units, which could not be understood without the whole frame structure (e.g. the notion of "Victim" makes sense only if there is some form of Harm perpetrated to the victim, and therefore the lexical unit "victim", finds its meaning in this implicit semantic load.

Values Detection and Classification. In the realm of value classification, current approaches predominantly rely on ML techniques, with BERT-based models often considered state-of-the-art [14]. However, these methods typically lack transparency in their decision-making process, posing challenges for explainability. Furthermore, datasets for training such models are often constructed through manual annotation or extraction from existing sources, which may introduce biases. Previous works like [15,16] focus on more explainable methodologies, reusing semantic frames activation to detect values from MFT.

Notably, our approach differs by utilizing a generative method to automatically create structured representations of sentences. Importantly, our approach serves as a benchmark for evaluating the quality of classification methods, given the absence of human evaluation. While attempts at explainable value classification are emerging, they often lack a robust theoretical foundation. Our approach combines ML techniques with ontology-based reasoning, leveraging Moral Foundations Theory formalization, to provide both performance and interpretability. This integration allows us to anchor our classification framework in established and well-understood theories, setting our approach apart from previous methods.

Moral Foundations Theory. MFT is a proposal for a theory of social, cultural and moral behaviours. It aims at being universal and not depending on culture - at least in its dyadic oppositional structure of value vs violation. It considers values, intended as "foundations", as universal, while their real world occurrence is cultural and context-specific, namely e.g. the concept of "Care" is pan-cultural, while its actual real world realization (or its violation) is cultural dependent. MFT organises values and violations in terms of dyadic oppositions, and it explains each dyad in terms of behavioural cognitivism, namely, e.g. *Care vs Harm* is grounded in the attachment systems and some form of empathy, intended as the ability to not only understand, but also feel the same feelings as others, being able to imagine hypothetical scenarios, in which we are living some positive or negative mental or physical state, which we actually don't live. The other dyads are Fairness/Cheating, Loyalty/Betrayal, Authority/Subversion, Sanctity/Degradation, Liberty/Oppression. Original ValueNet MFT ontological module includes one class per each of these value-violations, and aligns it, following frame semantics principles, to entities from FrameNet [17], WordNet [18], VerbNet [19], PropBank [20] and several others in the Framester hub [21]. However, in this work, we use only those value-frames which are evoked by some existing frame in the Framester hub, and for which we can reuse the semantic roles, resulting in a final set of 10 value-frames out of the original 12.

3 Synthetic Data Generation

In this section, we discuss the methodology used to generate the synthetic dataset of sentences and their structured representation, and provide some insights on its quality. For the generation of the dataset, we rely on prompting a Large Language Model (LLM). In particular, we rely on Mistral-7B [22], a 7 billion parameters open-source language model. We do make use of three main techniques: *cloze*, role-playnig, and few-shot prompting [23]. Few-shot prompting refers to the technique where examples of desirable outputs are provided to the LLM. They have been shown to be particularly effective in classification tasks (to obtain *in context* learning). Cloze prompting, on the other hand, refers to the technique in which the above mentioned desired output, are presented in a specific structure. In our case Fig. 1 shows an example, as detailed in the followings. Finally, role-playing is a technique where the LLM is instructed to act as a specific agent. It has been observed that this kind of technique increases the quality of the generated responses. In our setting, we rely on it to indicate the output structure, which allows us to easily parse the sentence and its structured representation, as well as provide examples of sentences that are manually curated to express some specific value.

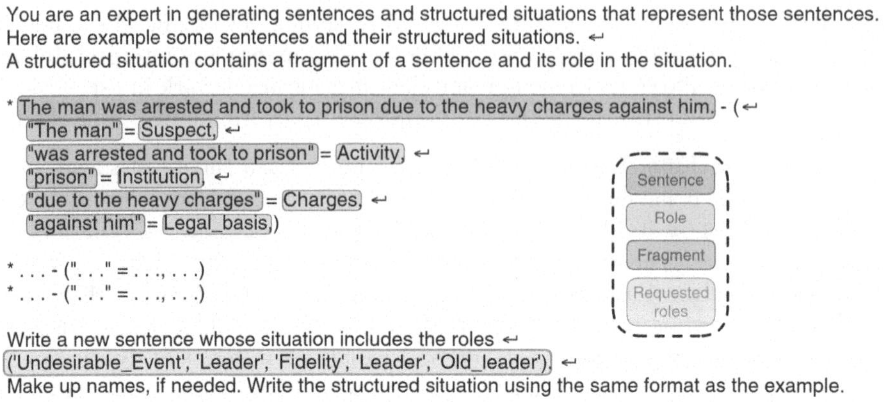

Fig. 1. Annotated prompt example.

Figure 1 shows an example of a prompt. In the first part, we implement cloze prompting and instruct the LLM on its role as a structured sentence generator. Afterwards, we present 3 example outputs structured as a tuple composed of a sentence and its representation as a structured situation. The structured representation is composed of a fragment of the sentence and its annotated role. Finally, we ask the LLM to provide a new sentence that includes some specific roles and we instruct it to provide the results compliant to the examples we gave. The requested roles are randomly sampled in the range [2, 15] from the ones in ValueNet [11]. We extract all the roles used in every description. This allows the LLM to generate sentences whose roles are not confined to a specific value. Notice that in the prompt of Fig. 1 we never explicitly mention to the LLM that the sentences to be generated have to evoke some values nor we ever mention the concept of values. This is done to avoid any bias in the generative process. The model should autonomously extrapolate the aspects that are in common between all the example sentences and generate a novel one that displays those aspects. This results in a more challenging dataset where different perspectives must be considered. It is not possible to assume that a sentence *prototypically* expresses a particular value, but rather that among all the perspectives that explain it, there exists one in which the sentence can be classified with that particular value.

In total we generate 10,000 structured sentences, 1,000 sentence for value. The values considered are *authority*, *care*, *cheating*, *degradation*, *fairness*, *harm*, *loyalty*, *oppression*, *sanctity*, *subversion*. Each value is represented as a description. On average, each description is composed of 51 roles out of a total of 513 unique roles.

The distribution of the roles within ValueNet follows the well-known Zipf distribution (see Fig. 2). Indeed, the most common roles (e.g. *Time*) are very common concepts that characterize every possible value. To guarantee variability

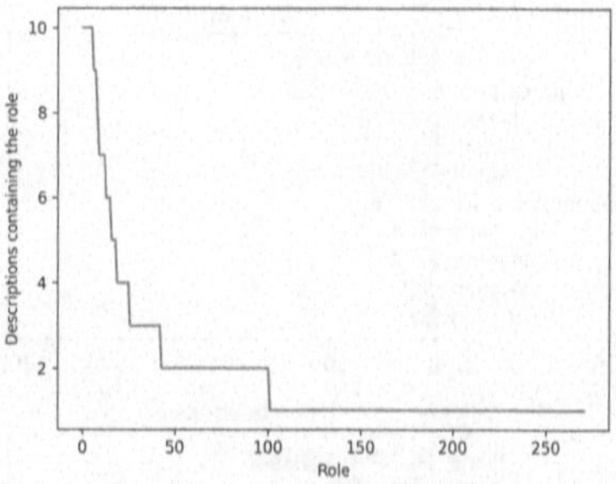

(a) Distribution of the roles within ValueNet.

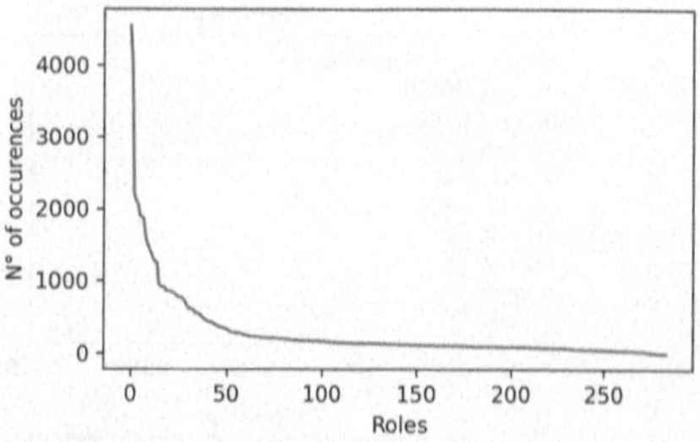

(b) Distribution of the roles within the generated dataset.

Fig. 2. Distribution of the roles within the ValueNet ontology and in the generated dataset.

within the dataset, we randomly sample the *temperature* parameter of the LLM in the range $t \in [0.01, 1]$.

Given the prompt as in Fig. 1, the extraction of the generated sentence and of its respective situation is straightforward. Nonetheless, we note that the output produced by the LLM, despite the clear indications, is not always consistent. From the total of 10,000 sentence, 1,166 sentences (more than 10%) contains hallucinated roles. We discard those sentence. Moreover, after some manual inspection we found that the LLM does not always faithfully comply with the proposed structure. We implement a straightforward parser, based on regex patterns, and find that only 77% of the sentences have been correctly extracted (we consider a sentence correctly extracted when it is terminated by a full-stop). A more carefully implemented parser might help in reducing the amount of noise within the dataset. A total of 6844 structured sentences is extracted after removing the ones that are wrongfully parsed. The distribution of roles within the dataset (Fig. 2b) is similar to the one in the ValueNet (Fig. 2a). Indeed, even though we provide a set of roles that the LLM must consider during the generation phase, it will also autonomously generate sentences that include other existing roles. The choice of those is biased towards roles that are more common within the pre-training corpus. In Fig. 3 the top 10 roles for each value used in the few-shot template are shown. Indeed, we can see that some roles, such as *Action* or *Agent*, are shared among different values. Those roles represent very general concepts that are very likely to occur in a sentence, regardless of its intended meaning. On the other hand, some roles are particularly prominent on some values rather than others, such as *Perpetrator* for the *Cheating* value. This supports the idea that specific roles have different relevance and salience among different frames.

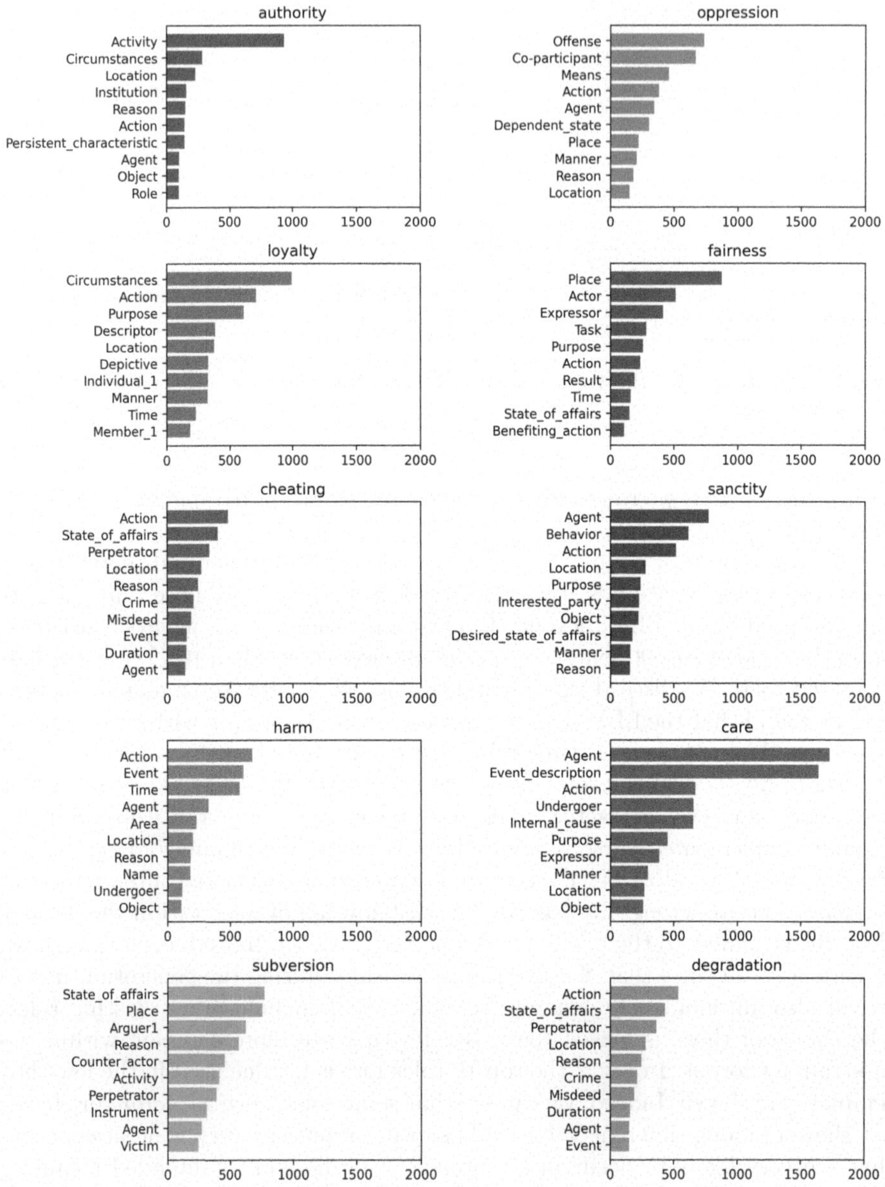

Fig. 3. Top 10 roles for each value used in few shot prompting.

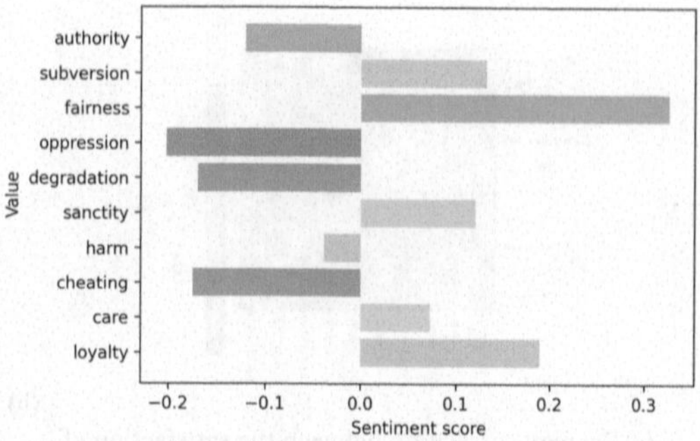

Fig. 4. Average emotion polarity detected on the generated sentences for each value used in the few-shot example.

As addressed previously, it is not possible to assume that the sentence generated by the LLM when provided with few-shots for a specific values are guaranteed to evoke that specific value. Meticulous Prompt Engineering is usually involved in order to produce reliable results [24,25]. One possible form of validation is to check whether the emotion polarity extracted from the sentences correlates with the value they are tagged as.

Figure 4 describes the emotion polarity, computed with NLTK [26], for all the sentences in the dataset grouped by the value used in the few-shot examples. It can be observed that values' polarity is coherent with those values that are *prototipically* recognised as associated with "moral emotions", such as in the CAD (Contempt-Anger-Disgust) theory [27]. E.g. values associated to positive emotions, such as *fairness* and *loyalty*, have a positive emotion polarity on average while values such as *oppression* and *cheating* have a lower polarity on average.

4 Reasoning on Descriptions and Situations

ValueNet is developed [11] by re-using the Description and Situation (DnS) ontology design pattern (ODP) [28], where knowledge is represented using a frame-based representation. DnS introduces the concepts of *description* and *situation*. Both descriptions and situations are n-ary relations over a set elements. A description is a perspective (a theory, a schema) defining concepts that can classify, hence interpret, a situation. The elements that are part of a description are called *roles*. In ValueNet, one description is created for each value/violation. Examples of roles include `Activity` or `Circumstances`, as can be seen in Fig. 3. A situation is an n-ary relation involving a set of individuals that are classified with one role. For instance, in Fig. 1, the sentence represented in blue is a situation in which a man is taken to prison due to some charges. The individuals that partake on that situation are its fragments, annotated in red. Each of those individuals are classified as a role (e.g. "The Man" is classified as the role `Suspect`).

A situation s *satisfies* a description d when d is a plausible or correct interpretation of s. This means that for every role r in d, then there exists an individual in s that has been classified by that role. For example, if we assume that the `Fairness` value is formalized as a description that only involves the roles `Suspect` and `Charges`, then the sentence of Fig. 1 satisfies the description of `Fairness`.

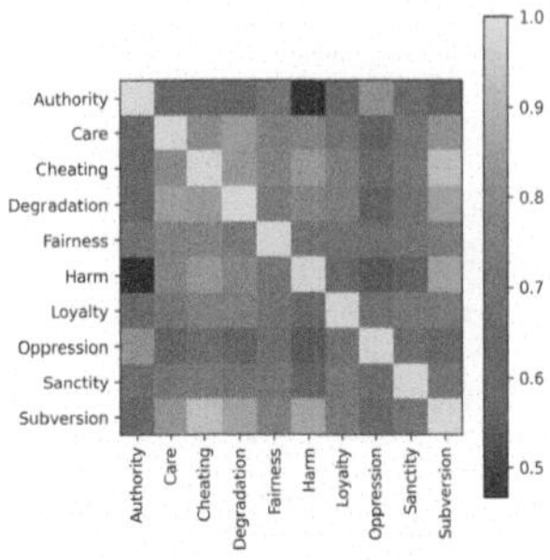

(a) Pearson correlation between the satisfaction of different description by a situation.

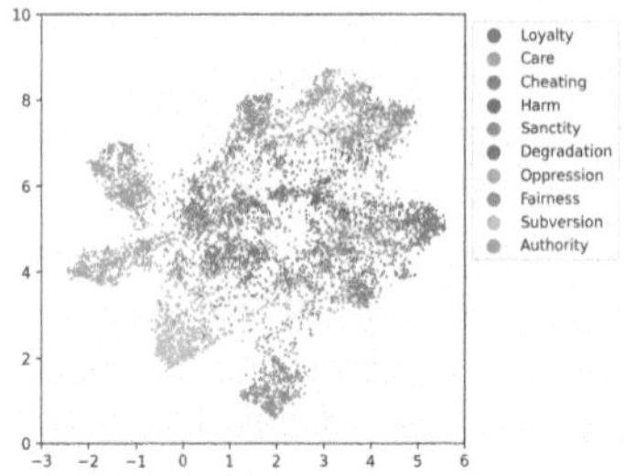

(b) Two dimensional plot of the situations where the probabilities of satisfying each description is used to compute the position in the plane.

Fig. 5. Analysis of the description satisfied by each situation.

Reasoning over DnS is performed by relying on the neuro-symbolic reasoner sandra [29]. Sandra builds a geometrical space based on descriptions and roles defined in a DnS ontology and reason over it to compute the probability of each description satifying a situation.

Given the dataset produced in Sect. 3, where each sentence's fragments are classified by one role compatible with ValueNet, is possible to infer which descriptions are satisfied by a sentence (represented as a situation). Note that inferring which description is satisfied by a situation is a different classification problem than the value detection methods described in Sect. 2. In particular, if a situation satisfies a description, then it means that the situation can be interpreted through the perspective formalized by that description. Different (contrasting) perspectives can be valid at the same time. For example, when classifying the dataset produced in Sect. 3, we find that only 30% of the sentences are predominantly satisfied by the description associated with the value used in the few-shot example. This is a consequence of the formalization in ValueNet. Different values, represented as descriptions, share many roles. As a result, it is easy to see that if a situation involves individuals that are classified by those shared roles, it will be classified by different (incompatible) descriptions with a similar probability.

Figure 5 provides additional insights that can be obtained by classifying the situations using descriptions. In particular, in Fig. 5a the Pearson correlation between the different descriptions is shown. A description is highly correlated with another description if, when considering multiple situations, it is often the case that both descriptions have *similar* probabilities. It can be seen that the positive correlations (an increase in probability on one description results in an increase on the other as well) between some descriptions has an intuitive explanation. For instance, `Sanctity` correlates with `Loyalty`, but not with `Harm`. On the other hand, some cases are surprisingly interesting. For example, `Care` is correlated with `Degradation` and `Subversion`. From a technical point of view this might be because the roles that can be found in `Care` are also in common with `Degradation` and `Subversion`. From a conceptual point of view, it could point in the direction that `Degradation` and `Subversion` could be often expressed via a negation or lack of `Care`. Another interesting case is `Oppression`, highly correlating with `Authority`, coherently with the idea that restrictions of individual freedom are usually felt as a general sense of oppression, when backed by some form of institution or systemic provenance. These unexpected correlations provide an indication that either ValueNet lacks of granularity, or rather that the formalization of values such as `Degradation` and `Subversion` could be implicitly related to presence or absence of other values in the sentence. In Fig. 5a, the probabilities of satisfying a description is used as a feature vector and plotted in two dimensions through the UMAP dimensionality reduction method [30]. Notably, situations that are generated using examples from a specific values are closely positioned in the low-dimensional space for most of the values. Some values, such as `Harm`, `Cheating` and `Degradation`, are not neatly separated. This further support the arguments described for Fig. 5b related to ValueNet's definitions.

5 Value Detection Experiments and Discussion

As anticipated in Sect. 4, the ability to infer which descriptions are satisfied by a situation should not be framed as the same classification task that traditional value detectors perform (cf. Sect. 2). The ability to infer which descriptions are valid perspectives for a situation shall be interpreted as an information upon which the final classification must be performed. In this section, we obtain a feature vector by concatenating the probability that a given situation is satisfied by every description in ValueNet.

There are two possible ways of exploiting this feature vector:

- classify a sentence only based on the descriptions it satisfies;
- rely on the feature vector to complement other features extracted from the text.

We asses both methods by training several popular ML classification methods to classify the value of a sentence. To do so, we randomly split the sentences in training and testing sets, keeping two thirds of the situations to train the models and one third to test it. To assess the influence of using sandra as complementing features, we follow two different feature extraction methods from text: TF-IDF and sentence-embeddings (sBERT) [31][1].

Table 1 describes the results obtained on the dataset presented in Sect. 3. Notably, those relying on sandra outperforms all the other methods. In particular, complementing a word-based representation, TF-IDF, with inference supported by a formal representation yields the best results with 5 out of 8 completely different methods. Interestingly sBERT, which relies on dense representation that benefits from a large pre-training phase, does almost never outperform the other models with the exeception of when being used in conjuction

[1] We use the model available at https://huggingface.co/sentence-transformers/all-mpnet-base-v2.

Table 1. Accuracy results obtained with different methods and different feature extraction algorithms. Best results for each method are underlined while the best result overall is represented in bold.

Model	sandra	TF-IDF	TF-IDF + sandra	sBERT	sBERT + sandra
Logistic regression	0.38	0.49	<u>0.53</u>	0.45	0.49
SVM	0.48	0.48	<u>0.56</u>	0.45	0.52
Random forest	0.48	0.44	<u>0.57</u>	0.34	0.45
Decision Tree	0.39	0.29	<u>0.42</u>	0.20	0.32
LightGBM	0.50	0.45	<u>**0.62**</u>	0.42	0.57
MLP	0.49	0.45	0.47	0.44	<u>0.52</u>
Naive Bayes	0.29	<u>0.43</u>	0.42	0.32	0.32
KNN	<u>0.45</u>	0.33	0.33	0.32	0.32

with sandra and an MLP classification layer. This further provides evidences that complex tasks that require a higher semantic understanding of a sentence are better solved by integrating representations that rely on the distribution of data (TF-IDF and sBERT) with representations that rely on a formal theory. We remark that out of the model used in Table 1, some are explainable models, i.e. a human-understandable explanation can be obtained from the decision process used to classify a sentence. In the following, we will provide some examples of the type of explanations that can be obtained from some of the models presented.

5.1 Logistic Regression

The logistic regression classification method is a linear model that seeks to classify a feature vector by computing a weighted sum of the features and using a logistic function (i.e. a function that squashes values between 0 and 1) to produce a probability over each class. Hence, given the set of values we are interested in, the model learns the right weight for each feature in order to produce a correct probability score. The weights can be manually inspected to understand which features are the most important to predict one label instead of another.

In Fig. 6 the importance of each feature for the logistic regression model using TF-IDF and sandra is reported. It can be seen how, as also discussed previously, the fact that a situation satisfies a description directly modeled after a value does not entail a classification result. Indeed, only for the `Authority` value the respective description is among the top 10 most important features. In general, we can see that words are not always informative. For example, the word `john` is an important feature for many values. However, this is not correlated with a value, but is rather a result of the generation method used in Sect. 3. Excluding words that should not be taken into consideration for this task (e.g. proper nouns) and only mantaining verbs and concepts could greatly enhance the explainability of the model and its performances. Interestingly, for values in which satisfying another value is important in the decision process (e.g. `Loyalty`), the emotion

Fig. 6. Feature importance for each value in the dataset. For each value, the top 10 features by weight are reported. The descriptions from ValueNet and their score are represented in red. (Color figure online)

polarity of both values is the same, in this case `Loyalty` and `Fairness` are both generally considered positive values. On the other hand it can be seen that for `Care` the `Subversion` and `Harm` descriptions are particularly important. There might be multiple reasons that explain this results, one of which includes the fact that there exist a possible perspective from which a situation satisfying a `Harm` description might actually satisfy a `NotCare` description, where `NotCare` is a possible perspective from which *harm* as a value can be interpreted. This further supports the claim that the ValueNet ontology might benefit from further refinement in terms of granularity. For example, identifying possibly conflicting perspectives from which the same value can be seen.

5.2 LightGBM

The LightGBM method [32], a gradient boosting classification technique, is currently the state-of-the-art method in classification of tabular data. It is widely used in industrial Machine Learning applications, due to its robustness and accuracy in achieving good results. Being a gradient boosting method, LightGBM is based on the use of multiple decision trees. A decision tree is a method that construct a binary tree based on the input feature. By taking into account one

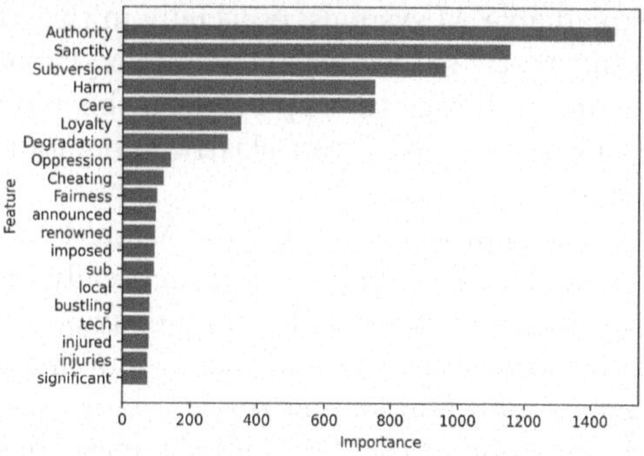

Fig. 7. Importance of the top 20 features in the LightGBM model.

feature at the time, decision trees seek to find the threshold such that a feature can be used to make a binary decision. For instance, a binary decision might be to check for the presence of a word given its TF-IDF score, or checking if the probability of satisfying a description is higher (or lower) than a specified threshold. During this procedure, the most important features are identified. These are the features that mostly help in reducing the set of choices for the final classification.

In Fig. 7 the importance of each feature is plotted. It can be seen that, similarly for the logistic regression model, the importance of each situation satisfying (or not) a description is fundamental to make an accurate prediction. It can also be seen that some descriptions are much more important than others, for instance `Authority` is one order of magnitude more important than `Oppression` or `Fairness`. This is still to be reconducted to the ValueNet formalization, as the same value as been proven to be very important also in the logistic regression model. Note that in the case of LightGBM, it is possible to obtain accurate performances through the use of multiple (usually in the order of tens of thousands) decision trees. However, it is not possible to directly understand the decision process of each tree, as it would be hard to evaluate each of them singlehandedly. From Table 1, it can be seen that a single Decision Tree model does not perform well compared to the gradient boosting technique. Nonetheless, by focusing on improving the ontology to optimize the classification performances while retaining a well-formalized theory, it might be possible to obtain a fully-explainable model which is easy to understand by humans and obtains accurate performances, comparable to more complex methods.

6 Implementation

In order to provide a comprehensive and accessible demonstration of our approach, we have developed an online service that visualizes and generalizes our methodology, shown in Fig. 8. This web-based platform is designed to make the detection of moral values from natural language both transparent and interactive. The motivation behind this implementation is rooted in the need for explainable AI systems, especially in the context of moral value detection, which is inherently subjective and complex. By providing a visual and interactive tool, we aim to bridge the gap between theoretical models and practical applications, ensuring that users can clearly understand and trust the results generated by our system.

Our approach leverages the Moral Foundations Theory (MFT) to detect values in text. The ability to automatically discern MFT values from text is significant for understanding human behavior, decision-making processes, and societal trends. However, the challenge lies in making these detections interpretable and explainable. Our online service addresses this challenge by providing a clear visualization of the data and the methodology described in previous sections.

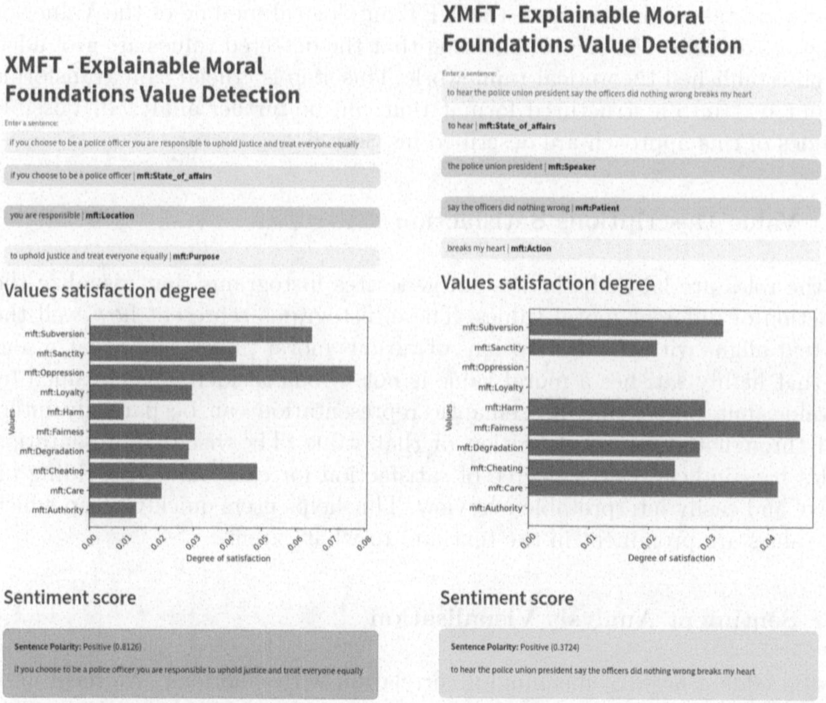

(a) Visualization of the sentence *If you choose to be a police officer your are responsible to uphold justice and treat everyone equally.*

(b) Visualization of the sentence *To hear the police union president say the officers did nothing wrong breaks my heart.*

Fig. 8. Example of visualizations from sentences extrapolated from the Moral Foundation Reddit Corpus [33].

6.1 Technical Framework

The interface of our online service, available at http://xmv.geomeaning.com, as depicted in Fig. 8, is designed with usability and clarity in mind, as well as explainability of the value detection process. Users are prompted to input a string in natural language, which initiates the processing sequence. At the core of our system is a BART-based semantic role labeling model. BART [34] is a model known for its high performance in generating contextually accurate and coherent labels on machine translation tasks. We chose BART due to its effectiveness in handling complex NLP tasks and its ability to produce reliable role annotations critical for our value detection process.

6.1.1 BART Role Labeling

The role labeling process involves assigning specific roles to segments of the input text, which are then used to determine the satisfaction of various moral values.

The roles are taken directly from the MFT ontological module of the ValueNet ontology, as described in Sect. 5, ensuring that the detected values are grounded in a well-established theoretical framework. This step is crucial as it transforms the input text into a structured format that can be further analyzed. Possible downsides of this approach are described ins Sect. 6.2.

6.1.2 Value Descriptions Satisfaction

Once the roles are labeled, the system generates histograms that visualize the satisfaction of different moral values. These histograms represent how well the input text aligns with the descriptions of various moral values. Note that a sentence that highly satisfies a moral value is not to be considered as classified by that value, but rather that its semantic representation can be partially interpreted through the formal definition of that value. The visual representation includes bars indicating the degree of satisfaction for each value, providing an intuitive and easily interpretable overview. This helps users quickly grasp which moral values are prominent in the text and to what extent.

6.1.3 Sentiment Analysis Visualisation

This step adds a layer of meaningful correlation with emotions. We have integrated a sentiment analysis component using the sentiment.Vader package. This step analyzes the emotional tone of the text and visualizes the results on a color scale ranging from red (positive sentiment) to blue (negative sentiment). By combining sentiment analysis with moral value detection, users gain a glimpse of an interconnected view of the text's moral and emotional landscape. This dual analysis enhances the interpretability of the results, showing not only which values are present but also the sentiment associated with them.

6.2 Final Remarks

The primary advantage of our implementation is its focus on explainability. By visualizing the data and providing interactive features, users can explore the results in depth. The system allows users to understand how different parts of the text contribute to the overall moral value detection, making the process transparent and understandable. One notable consequence of this approach, is that the "Non-moral" label, often included in value-annotated datasets such as MFRC [33] is by design not included in this approach, due to the structure of *quasi-satisfaction* based on presence or absence of certain general roles such as *Agent*, *Patient*, etc. Future enhancements include the integration of the classification pipeline, devised in Sect. 5, within the visualization dashboard. Additionally, incorporating user feedback mechanisms could help in continuously improving the system's accuracy and usability. One possible application of these kind of visualization systems is in the annotation process performed by human subject.

Since the tool automatically proposes an interpretation of the sentence by identifying semantic roles within a sentence, it is possible for the user to refine the element identified, effectively relying on the system as a support to the semantic annotation of sentences. Moreover, by exploiting the inferences performed by sandra, it is possible to understand how the semantic annotation influences the possible perspectives that can be applied to that sentence. The user can hence classify the sentence by taking into account those perspectives, or improve over the semantic annotations to obtain the desired inferences. This approach paves a new way of data curation and annotation for moral values. The cognitive load over the user is reduced thanks to the support of the AI model. This allows the annotator to focus on the core of the annotation task.

7 Conclusion

In this work we reused an ontological formalization of the domain of values, in particular the Moral Foundations Theory, modeled as value frames in ValueNet. We produced a synthetic dataset of 10.000 sentences, 1k for each value considered, and reused *sandra*'s reasoning approach to extract semantic roles salience and roles overlaps for each considered value. We furthermore performed preliminary value detection experiments with classic ML methods to classify the degree of satisfaction for each sentence per each value, demonstrating an improvement in performance when adopting *sandra*'s method. We show that relying on a neuro-symbolic approach allows the classification process to be explainable and understandable, since the injection of satisfied description greatly improves the performances of interpretable and explainable models. Moreover, we found that by relying on ValueNet for the classification process, it is possible to identify its gaps and limitations that can be operatively addressed by an expert to produce a better formalization. Nonetheless, by relying on a synthetic dataset, our approach suffers from the bias of the LLM used to generate sentences. As described in the previous section, it is not possible to assume that the dataset is representative of real-world sentences expressing human values. Future works include, on one side, testing our methods on well established datasets, that have been validated by humans. Similarly, the proposed approach can be used to inform the refinement of the knowledge in ValueNet, particularly in enriching semantic relations among values, to further improve performance and explainability with *sandra*'s approach.

Acknowledgments. This project has received funding from the FAIR - Future Artificial Intelligence Research foundation as part of the grant agreement MUR n. 341, code PE00000013 CUP 53C22003630006.

References

1. Sierra, C., Osman, N., Noriega, P., Sabater-Mir, J., Perelló, A.: Value alignment: a formal approach. arXiv preprint arXiv:2110.09240 (2021)
2. Fisac, J.F., et al.: Pragmatic-pedagogic value alignment. In: Robotics Research: The 18th International Symposium ISRR, pp. 49–57. Springer (2020)
3. Ji, J., et al.: Beavertails: towards improved safety alignment of LLM via a human-preference dataset. In: Oh, A., Naumann, T., Globerson, A., Saenko, K., Hardt, M., Levine, S. (eds.) Advances in Neural Information Processing Systems 36: Annual Conference on Neural Information Processing Systems 2023, NeurIPS 2023, New Orleans, 10–16 December 2023 (2023). http://papers.nips.cc/paper_files/paper/2023/hash/4dbb61cb68671edc4ca3712d70083b9f-Abstract-Datasets_and_Benchmarks.html
4. Graham, J., et al.: Moral foundations theory: the pragmatic validity of moral pluralism. In: Advances in Experimental Social Psychology, pp. 55–130 (2013)
5. Schwartz, S.H., et al.: Extending the cross-cultural validity of the theory of basic human values with a different method of measurement. J. Cross-cult. Psychol. **32**, 519–542 (2001). Sage, Thousand Oaks
6. Giménez, A.C., Tamajón, L.G.: Analysis of the third-order structuring of Shalom Schwartz's theory of basic human values. Heliyon **5**, e01797 (2019). Elsevier
7. Curry, O.S.: Morality as cooperation: a problem-centred approach. In: The Evolution of Morality, pp. 27–51 (2016)
8. Curry, O.S., Alfano, M., Brandt, M.J., Pelican, C.: Moral molecules: morality as a combinatorial system. Rev. Philos. Psychol. **13**, 1039–1058 (2022)
9. DeBellis M.: The Ethics Ontology: A Universal Moral Grammar. Academia. https://www.academia.edu/15327812
10. Holgado-Sánchez, A., Billhardt, H., Ossowski, S., Fernández, A.: An ontology for value awareness engineering. In: ICAART, vol. 3, pp. 1421–1428 (2024)
11. Giorgis, S.D., Gangemi, A., Damiano, R.: Basic human values and moral foundations theory in valuenet ontology. In: Corcho, Ó., Hollink, L., Kutz, O., Troquard, N., Ekaputra, F.J. (eds.) EKAW 2022. LNCS, , vol. 13514, pp. 3–18. Springer, Cham (2022). https://doi.org/10.1007/978-3-031-17105-5_1
12. Fillmore, C.J.: Frame semantics. In: Linguistics in the Morning Calm, pp. 111–138. Hanshin, Seoul (1982)
13. Minsky, M.: A framework for representing knowledge (1974)
14. Mirzakhmedova, N., et al.: The touch\'e23-valueeval dataset for identifying human values behind arguments. arXiv preprint arXiv:2301.13771 (2023)
15. Asprino, L., et al.: Uncovering values: detecting latent moral content from natural language with explainable and non-trained methods. In: Proceedings of Deep Learning Inside Out (DeeLIO 2022): The 3rd Workshop on Knowledge Extraction and Integration for Deep Learning Architectures, pp. 33–41. Association for Computational Linguistics (2022)
16. Bulla, L., Giorgis, S.D., Gangemi, A., Marinucci, L., Mongiovì, M.: Detection of morality in tweets based on the moral foundation theory. In: International Conference on Machine Learning, Optimization, and Data Science, pp. 1–13. Springer (2022)
17. Baker, C.F., Fillmore, C.J., Lowe, J.B.: The Berkeley FrameNet Project, pp. 86–90
18. Miller, G.A.: WordNet: a lexical database for English. Commun. ACM **38**, 39–41 (1995)

19. Schuler, K.K.: VerbNet: A Broad-coverage, Comprehensive Verb Lexicon. University of Pennsylvania (2005)
20. Kingsbury, P., Palmer, M.: From TreeBank to PropBank, pp. 1989–1993
21. Gangemi, A., Alam, M., Asprino, L., Presutti, V., Recupero, D.R.: Framester: a wide coverage linguistic linked data hub. In: European Knowledge Acquisition Workshop, pp. 239–254. Springer (2016)
22. Jiang, A.Q., et al.: Mistral 7b. arXiv preprint arXiv:2310.06825 (2023)
23. Liu, P., Yuan, W., Fu, J., Jiang, Z., Hayashi, H., Neubig, G.: Pre-train, prompt, and predict: a systematic survey of prompting methods in natural language processing. ACM Comput. Surv. **55**, 195:1–195:35 (2023). https://doi.org/10.1145/3560815
24. Javaheripi, M., et al.: Phi-2: the surprising power of small language models. In: Microsoft Research Blog (2023)
25. Ben Allal, L., Lozhkov, A., Penedo, G., Wolf, T., von Werra, L.: Cosmopedia (2024). https://huggingface.co/datasets/HuggingFaceTB/cosmopedia
26. Bird, S.: NLTK: the natural language toolkit. In: Calzolari, N., Cardie, C., Isabelle, P. (eds.) ACL 2006, 21st International Conference on Computational Linguistics and 44th Annual Meeting of the Association for Computational Linguistics, Proceedings of the Conference, Sydney, 17–21 July 2006. The Association for Computer Linguistics (2006). https://doi.org/10.3115/1225403.1225421
27. Rozin, P., Lowery, L., Imada, S., Haidt, J.: The CAD triad hypothesis: a mapping between three moral emotions (contempt, anger, disgust) and three moral codes (community, autonomy, divinity). J. Personal. Soc. Psychol. **76** 574 (1999). American Psychological Association
28. Gangemi, A.: Norms and plans as unification criteria for social collectives. Auton. Agents Multi Agent Syst. **17** , 70–112 (2008). https://doi.org/10.1007/S10458-008-9038-9
29. Lazzari, N., De Giorgis, S., Gangemi, A., Presutti, V.: Sandra–a neuro-symbolic reasoner based on descriptions and situations. arXiv preprint arXiv:2402.00591 (2024)
30. Sainburg, T., McInnes, L., Gentner, T.Q.: Parametric umap embeddings for representation and semisupervised learning. Neural Comput. **33**, 2881–2907 (2021)
31. Reimers, N., Gurevych, I.: Sentence-bert: sentence embeddings using siamese bert-networks. In: Proceedings of the 2019 Conference on Empirical Methods in Natural Language Processing, Association for Computational Linguistics (2019). https://arxiv.org/abs/1908.10084
32. Ke, G., et al.: Lightgbm: a highly efficient gradient boosting decision tree. In: Guyon, I., et al.: (eds.) Advances in Neural Information Processing Systems 30: Annual Conference on Neural Information Processing Systems 2017, 4–9 December 2017, Long Beach, pp. 3146–3154 (2017). https://proceedings.neurips.cc/paper/2017/hash/6449f44a102fde848669bdd9eb6b76fa-Abstract.html
33. Trager, J., et al.: The moral foundations reddit corpus. arXiv preprint arXiv:2208.05545 (2022)
34. Lewis, M., et al.: BART: denoising sequence-to-sequence pre-training for natural language generation, translation, and comprehension. In: Jurafsky, D., Chai, J., Schluter, N., Tetreault, J.R. (eds.) Proceedings of the 58th Annual Meeting of the Association for Computational Linguistics, ACL 2020, Online, 5–10 July 2020, pp. 7871–7880. Association for Computational Linguistics (2020). https://doi.org/10.18653/V1/2020.ACL-MAIN.703

Static and Adaptive Planning with WoT TD by Generating Python Objects as Intermediary Representations Using Large Language Models

Lukas Kinder(✉) and Tobias Käfer

Institute AIFB, Karlsruhe Institute of Technology (KIT), Kaiserstr. 12, 76131 Karlsruhe, Germany

lukas.kinder@kit.edu

Abstract. This paper presents a novel method for plan generation with Large Language Models (LLMs). We propose utilizing Web-of-Thing Thing Descriptions (WoT TD) to inform the LLM about available devices for interaction. We investigate a novel pipeline in which: (1) The WoT TD gets translated into a Python class, (2) The task in natural language gets translated into code that interact with this class, (3) The generated code gets executed to obtain the plan. During execution we synchronize the state of the Python class with the state of the real device to enable dynamic adaptions of the plan. We evaluate our approach featuring 6 different LLMs. We get performance improvements of up to 14%, when comparing our approach against existing LLM-based planning methods. Furthermore, we explore the influence of different aspects of WoT TDs on planning capabilities. This research paves the way towards more potent LLM planning models by introducing Python classes as intermediaries, simplifying the final planning task while leveraging standardized and accessible domain knowledge provided by WoT TDs.

Keywords: Planning · Large Language Models · Semantic Web

1 Introduction

Planning systems require domain descriptions in order to fit plans to the availabilities and constraints of a given environment. For example, a robot interacting with a device needs to know exactly what the device does, in order to find a sequence of actions to fulfill some goal. The required domain knowledge is usually provided by a human expert, for example in the form of PDDL domain descriptions. However, this can be expensive and the expert needs to be consulted every time a new device is added to the system.

To address this issue, we propose a novel approach that uses Web-of-Things Thing Descriptions (WoT TDs) as domain descriptions for planning systems. WoT TDs are a World Wide Web Consortium recommendation since 2020 and

A. Meroño Peñuela et al. (Eds.): ESWC 2024, LNCS 15345, pp. 256–273, 2025.
https://doi.org/10.1007/978-3-031-78955-7_21

provide a human-readable and machine-interoperable interface for devices [16]. By using WoT TDs, new devices could be easily integrated into the planning system since these descriptions are often provided by the device manufacturers. However, WoT TDs lack the detailed and precise information required for formal planning algorithms, as they do not fully describe the workings of a device. In particular, precise information about the requirements and outcomes of actions is missing.

In this work we investigate how the general world knowledge of Large Language Models (LLMs) can be utilized to fill information gaps in WoT TDs. Previous work already demonstrated that LLMs can be used to generate actionable plans by interpreting tasks in natural language and translating them into executable steps [2,12,13,33,35,39].

In our approach we want to task a LLM to generate a plan by dividing the task into multiple elemental actions that can be executed one by one. This is a process similar to coding a program, in which elemental instructions are chained to fulfill an overall goal. The idea is that if solving a task requires a LLM to have the mindset of a programmer, it may be best to also translate it into a programming task [20,33,37,39]. In a first step we let the LLM translates the JSON-LD file of a WoT TD into a Python class that describes the device. The functions of the Python class correspond to the actions that can be performed with the device. During this step the LLM needs to predict the formal requirements and effect of actions. Afterwards, the LLM tries to accomplish a task given in natural language by calling functions of this class. The plan is generated when running all the generated code. The whole pipeline is shown in Fig. 1.

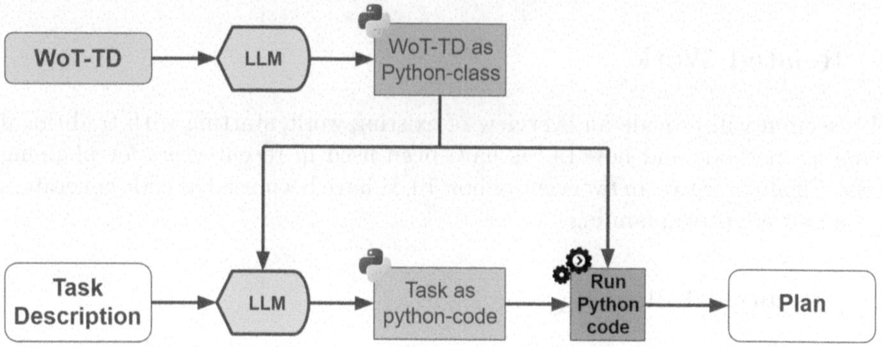

Fig. 1. The pipeline of our approach. First, the (simplified) Web of Things Thing Description gets translated into a Python class. The actions that can be performed with the device become functions of this class. Secondly, the task in natural language gets translated into code that is calling functions of this Python class. Finally, all the generated code gets executed to generate the plan. The color coding in later figures maps them to this pipeline.

We evaluate different approaches using our own benchmark with 123 tasks involving 29 devices, including real-world WoT TDs. For each device we use a simulator to verify that a plan was successful.

Our contributions in this paper are:

- We introduce a novel method that utilises WoT TDs as domain knowledge for LLM planning systems, by writing representations of devices as Python classes.
- We demonstrate that our approach enables adaptive planning, which means that a plan can be adapted to a new situation, if the environment is behaving unexpected [7]. This is done by synchronizing the state of the device with the state of the python class during plan-execution.
- We evaluate our approach against the state of the art models Progprompt [33] and SayCan [2].
- We study how different augmentations of the Web of Things Thing Descriptions influence the performance of our approach.

After elaborating related work in Sect. 2 we will explain our approach in Sect. 3. The comparison of our model with other LLM-based planning methods as well as an ablation study is shown in Sect. 4 and a conclusion can be found in Sect. 5.

This paper is an extension of our previous work "Towards Improving Large Language Models' Planning Capabilities on WoT Thing Descriptions by Generating Python Objects as Intermediary Representations" [17].

All the code, the benchmark and the results of our experiments are available on the projects Git repository[1].

2 Related Work

This section will provide an overview of existing work, starting with traditional planning methods and how LLMs have been used in recent years for planning tasks. Finally, we give an overview of how LLM have been used as code generators and about adaptive planning.

2.1 Traditional Planning

Traditionally, symbolic approaches have been used for robotic planning tasks such as STRIPS or SHOP [8,26,27]. Since its introduction in 1998 the Plan Domain Definition Language (PDDL) and extensions of it have been predominantly been used for planning [1,3,9,10,15]. These approaches usually require a fully observed and unambiguously defined environment. Formal information of the state of the world and the possible actions must be provided. This makes these approaches unsuitable for planning based on WoT TDs as they do not contain information about preconditions and outcomes of actions.

[1] https://gitlab.kit.edu/lukas.kinder/plannning_with_thing_descriptions_akr3.

2.2 LLMs as Planners

LLMs have been a promising approach for robotic planning, if the problem at hand benefits from general world knowledge natural language understanding. The type of useful general information they provide could be for example: "Food can usually be found in the fridge" or "In order to use the device I probably have to turn it on" etc. A challenge with plan generation by the means of a LLM is that even though they are usually able to produce good sounding high-level plans, they struggle to translate the plan into a sequence of executable elemental actions [12,40]. This limitation arises because the data they are trained on may lack the detailed domain-specific knowledge necessary for generating a grounded plan.

In early work, LLMs were tasked with directly producing action sequence as plans that satisfy a task description in natural language. Grounding the model to the domain-specific actions can be done for example by pre-training [14,22]. However, this requires a lot of training data and computational scalability. In the model SayCan, grounding is achieved the LLM scores the likelihood for action being the next step in a plan [2]. This is only feasible, if it is possible to enumerate all possible actions.

One method to mitigate the limitations of LLMs is to refrain from allowing the LLM to generate the plan entirely, instead letting it make calls to external solvers [28,31]. This strategy can be applied in the planning domain, by letting the LLM translate a problem into PDDL and let a symbolic solver determine the correct plan [24]. This however requires precise definition of a formal world-model by the LLM.

2.3 LLMs as Code Generators

With their training data usually containing code data, LLMs can be reasonable code generators [4,6,11]. Therefore it may be beneficial rewrite a problem into a code generation task. Writing code requires to determine small individual steps that together achieve some high level goal. This is the type of thinking that is often required for planning or structured reasoning. Therefore, a LLM may perform better in the familiar framework of a code generation task, if presented with tasks that requires a solution made up by many elemental actions [25].

In the planning domain, this has the advantage that the generated code can often be more easily mapped to the environment. For example by letting a model use template-functions that map to elemental actions [23,33,34,39] or by letting it use predefined class structures that translate well into real-world concepts of interest [37]. The generated code can also be used to solve a variety of reasoning problems. This method extends the traditional Chain of Thought approach [38], because the code can be compiled and executed to calculate an answer [5,20,36].

2.4 Adaptive Planning

Adaptive planning refers to the ability of a planning system to modify its plans in response to changes in the environment or unexpected events. Unlike traditional planning methods that often assume a static and fully observable environment, adaptive planning systems can update their plans based on environmental feedback.

Formal systems for adaptive planning may re-run the entire planning process each time the environment changes. However, to increase efficiency an alternative method is to repair the existing plan whenever changes occur [7,19].

An promising approach to deal with uncertain environments is to use Large Language Models (LLMs). Huang et al. [13] introduced a method where an LLM generates actions while maintaining an "inner monologue". This inner monologue provides the LLM with environmental feedback in natural language relevant for the planning task.

3 Approach

We will describe the task of the model and the challenges with it in Sect. 3.1. Afterwards, Sect. 3.2 explains how the WoT TD is translated into a Python class and Sect. 3.3 explains how the task in natural language gets translated into Python. Finally, we explain in Sect. 3.4 how the entire code is executed in order to generate the plan.

3.1 Task Description

The model has to generate a plan in the form of a sequence of actions that can be performed with a device. The plan should fulfill a task that we give the model in natural language. Since the task description is in natural language, the model needs to interpret what it should do. Examples of task descriptions are "Turn on the lights","Play me a song on the radio with maximum volume" or "Today I have five friends coming over. Make coffee for all of us".

We also give the model a WoT TD, that is has to use to extract domain knowledge about the device. An example of a WoT TD is shown in Fig. 2a. Generally a WoT TD gives information about three interaction affordances: *Properties*, *Actions* and *Events*. A *Property* expresses the state of the device. They can be retrieved and possibly updated. *Actions* can be called in order to invoke an operation of the device. This can for example cause the state of the device to change. *Events* describe a (random) incident with a device that has an impact on it (For example a lamp may overheat). In this paper we will ignore *Events* for our evaluations. The action descriptions in the WoT TD are not detailed enough to explain the entire inner working of the corresponding device. Usually the outcome of an action is not formally given and sometimes an action has requirements that are not indicated. Furthermore, the workings of a device may be influenced by hidden variables not mentioned in the WoT TD.

3.2 Translating the Thing Description Into a Python Class

Translating the WoT TD into Python code is done using a LLM. We instructed the LLM to translated the WoT TD into a Python class as follows:

```
{ "title": "Coffee Machine",
  "properties": {
    "water": {
      "description": "
   Illustrates water level of
   the machine.",
      "type": "boolean"
    },
    "storage": {
      "description": "
   Indicates the remaining
   coffee ground storage.",
      "type": "boolean"
    },
    "on": {
      "description": "Displays
     the current power state of
     the machine.",
      "type": "boolean"
    }
  },
  "actions": {
    "toggle": {
      "description": "Toggles
   on property of the device."
    },
    "refill": {
      "description": "Refills
   the water tank of the
   machine."
    },
    "empty": {
      "description": "Empties
   coffee ground container."
    },
    "make coffee": {
      "description": "Creates
   a medium cup of coffee."
}}}
```

(a) A WoT TD of a coffee machine.

```
class CoffeeMachine:
    def __init__(self):
        self.water = True #
   Illustrates water level of
   the machine.
        self.storage = True #
   Indicates the remaining
   coffee ground storage.
        self.on = False #
   Displays the current power
   state of the machine.

    def toggle(self):
        # Toggles on property
   of the device.
        self.on = not self.on

    def refill(self):
        # Refills the water
   tank of the machine.
        self.water = True

    def empty(self):
        # Empties coffee
   ground container.
        self.storage = True

    def make_coffee(self):
        # Creates a medium cup
    of coffee.

        if not self.on:
            self.toggle()

        if not self.water:
            self.refill()

        if not self.storage:
            self.empty()
```

(b) The corresponding Python class.

Fig. 2. An example of how a WoT TD can be translated into a Python class. Of special interest is the function `make_coffee()`. It is written such that requirements to make a coffee are automatically fulfilled if necessary.

- The class has a variable for each WoT TD *Property*.
- The class has a function for each WoT TD *Action*.

- Descriptions within the WoT TD are preserved in the Python class as comments.
- If an action has prerequisites, the corresponding function should call other functions of the class, such that these prerequisites are fulfilled.

An example of how to write the WoT TD of a coffee machine into a Python class is shown in Fig. 2. Further examples for different devices are shown in the Appendix in Fig. 3 and Fig. 4.

Checking the prerequisites and fulfilling them within the functions, allows to write the subsequent plan in a shorter and less detailed manner. Some actions require a sub-plan to be able to be performed. While creating the overall plan it is not necessary to write out these types of sub-plans anymore. For example, making a coffee requires the sub-plan to turn the machine on, and if necessary refill water and empty the storage. Generating the Python class also necessitates that the LLM decides how actions change the state of the device and what the input of actions are.

The prompt that we give the LLM also includes information about the initial state of the device. In addition to that, the LLM is given examples of how to translate WoT TD into Python classes in its prompt (Few-shot learning). All prompts can be seen in our Git repository.

3.3 Translating the Natural Language Task Into Python Code

After the WoT TD is translated into a Python class, this class is used as a prompt. In addition, the LLM receives the task description in natural language that it has to translate into Python code. This is done using few-shot learning. In the prompt it is also sated that loops or utility functions can be used.

For example, the task"Make 5 cups of coffe" using the Python class in Fig. 2b would correspond to:

```
coffeeMachine = CoffeeMachine()
for i in range(5):
    coffeeMachine.make_coffee()
```

Note that making a coffee may require a sub-plan to turn the device on, refill or empty the machine. This does not need to be included because it is handled withing the function of the class. The model also does not repeat the command `make_coffee()` but can use a loop instead. This is useful because LLMs are notoriously bad in counting tasks [29].

3.4 Running the Code

In a final step all the generated code is executed. The plan is obtained by tracking the timing of function entries and exits within the Python class. The functions of the Python class correspond to the action of the device. Therefore, whenever a function was executed during runtime, we append the corresponding action to the plan.

3.5 Adaptive Planning

As an extension of this approach we also synchronized the state of the Python class with the state of the real device. This can be done by copying the state of the properties of the device to the state of the corresponding variables within the Python class. For example, the coffee machine may run out of water, which is not modeled in the Python class as written in Fig. 2b. However, whenever the water-property of the real device becomes False during plan execution, we also set the water-variable of the Python class to False. We perform this synchronization step every time an action was called during plan execution.

The idea is that the requirement-structures within the functions of the Python class enable to repair the plan correctly. This allows for adaptive planning in which the plan may be adapted during execution, whenever the state of the real device diverges from the state of the Python class. Note that this does not require an additional call to the LLM but the hope is that the generated code is robust enough to deal with unexpected behaviour of the real device automatically. An example of this is shown in Fig. 5 in the Appendix.

4 Experiment

The benchmark we created contains 123 planning tasks. It involves 29 devices that have between 2 and 9 tasks each. Of the WoT TDs 24 of them were written by us and 5 of them are real-world descriptions from companies that provide them for their devices. For each device, we used a device-simulator to verify the success of the plan. These simulators followed the structure of the WoT TDs but could have hidden variables or interactions. For example, the coffee-machine-simulator runs out of water after every 10 cups of coffee (This is not mentioned in the WoT TD in Fig. 2a). The number of elemental steps to fulfill a task ranges between 1 and 173 steps, which is considerably longer than in existing robotic planning benchmarks [21,32].

The LLMs for our experiments were selected such that they had a range of different amount of parameters. We were also interested if models that are already pretrained on code generation would perform better. Therefore we used GPT-3.5, GPT-4, Llama2-7b[2], Llama2-70b[3], CodeLlama2-7b[4] and CodeLlama2-70b[5]. CodeLlama-7b and CodeLlama-70b are version of Llama-7b and Llama2-70b that were further fine tuned on code corpora [30]. In our experiments, we used 4-bit quantized versions of the models.

We will discuss an experiment in which we compare our approach with state of the art models in Sect. 4.1. An experiment in which we investigate which aspect of the Wo TD are most important for plan generation is shown in Sect. 4.2.

[2] https://huggingface.co/TheBloke/Llama-2-7B-Chat-GPTQ.
[3] https://huggingface.co/TheBloke/Llama-2-70B-Chat-GPTQ.
[4] https://huggingface.co/TheBloke/CodeLlama-7B-Instruct-GPTQ.
[5] https://huggingface.co/TheBloke/CodeLlama-70B-Instruct-GPTQ.

4.1 Experiment 1: Comparing Our Approach with Existing Work

For comparison we used the models SayCan [2] and Progprompt [33]. The model SayCan is simply generating the plan in the format:

```
1. action1, 2. action2, ... n. done.
```

The model Propgprompt is generating a plan via code generation: After the actions are provided as an Python import-statement, the LLM is asked to generate code that fulfills a task.

The implementation in the original papers are not suitable for our benchmark, as they did not use WoT TD. Therefore we had to adapt their work as follows:

- The prompt is restructured to include a system message and a user-assistant dialogue for the few-shot examples.
- The WoT TD is provided in the prompt.
- The system message of the prompt explicitly warns the LLM that some action have requirements.
- For SayCan, the model is simply generating the action sequence instead of using the model as a heuristic.
- For Progprompt the actions of the Wot TD are given as an import statement.

In the results below we write SayCan* and Progprompt* to indicate the difference between the original work and our adaptations.

The original work for Progprompt did not utilize loops to repeat an action sequence multiple times. However, this ability is very useful for some of the tasks in our benchmark. Therefore we tested out two versions: For Progprompt* it is stated in its system-message that the LLM should not write loops and for Progprompt* + Loops the LLM is instructed to use loops and examples with loops are in the prompt.

The results for different models with different LLMs is shown in Table 1. Success was measured using the state of the device-simulator after the plan was executed. Overall our method performed best except for when using GPT-4. Synchronizing the state of the Python class with the state of the device increased the performance of our method, except for CodeLlama2-7b and Llama2-7b.

Table 1. Results for the 123 planning tasks for different models with different LLMs.

	SayCan*	Progprompt*	Progprompt* + Loops	Our - No Synchronization	Our - With Synchronization
GPT-4	0.772	0.821	**0.852**	0.813	0.837
GPT-3.5	0.585	0.577	0.683	0.732	**0.772**
Llama2_70b	0.317	0.504	0.488	0.618	**0.650**
CodeLlama2_70b	0.301	0.317	0.325	**0.333**	**0.333**
Llama2_7b	0.276	0.309	0.341	**0.366**	**0.366**
CodeLlama2_7b	0.285	0.447	0.463	0.585	**0.602**

Overall, the GPT-3.5 and GPT-4 models performed considerably better on the benchmark than the Llama models. Our approach results in a considerable improvements for most of the LLMs. This could indicate that representing the device as a Python class in an intermediate step, causes the LLMs to be better in writing plans for it. An obvious reason SayCan under-performed could be that this method does not enable the use of loops. The bad performance of SayCan may also showcase that code-generation models are in general better planners.

Interestingly, there is no clear trend that the models fine-tuned with code-generation perform better. This could be because the programming that needs to be done is not very complicated. There are no advanced mathematical operations, highly nested loops, recursion or knowledge about specialized libraries required. Rewriting a WoT TD into Python code may be a different type of task the CodeLlama-version were trained with, preventing them to generalize well for this new task.

Based on our inspection, most planning mistakes originate from the class generation task and not from translating the task description into code. For example, the models may miss requirements of actions or misinterpret how a variable is used.

4.2 Experiment 2: Exploring WoT TD Performance Through Ablation Analysis

In addition, we also performed an ablation study to investigate which aspects of the WoT-TD are most important for the LLMs abilities to generate a plan. For this purpose we augmented the WoT TD and measured performance under the following conditions:

- **Only Task**: This is a baseline in which we already provide a (correctly implemented) Python class to the LLM and only the task needs to translated into Python code.
- **Unaltered**: The normal WoT TDs are used.
- **No Descriptions**: All descriptions within the WoT TDs are removed.
- **Generic Action names**: The names of the actions within the WoT TDs are replaced with the generic names: `action1, action2` etc.
- **No Descriptions and Generic Action Names**: There are no descriptions and the actions names are generic. Note that under this condition there is no indication of what an action is actually doing.
- **RDF**: The WoT TD are serialised into RDF data in Turtle syntax.

All results with augmented WoT TD are shown in Table 2.

The general trend seems to be that the models perform well as long as there is either a description or the actions have non-generic names. Providing the correct class implementation gives a performance boost for all models. This indicates that even though the LLMs are able to extract a lot of relevant knowledge from the WoT TDs, having a human expert give the correct model is still a superior approach. Providing the WoT TD in Turtle does not change the performance much compared to the standard json format.

Table 2. The results of our approach with different augmentations of the WoT TDs. The condition *Only Tasks* serves as a baseline in which a correct WoT TD to Python class translation was provided and only the code for the task needs to be written. SUCCESS indicates the number of times running the code resulted in a successful plan, verified by the device-simulators. FAILURE indicates the number of times the plans were not successful, ERROR is the number of times the plan could not be executed and TIMEOUT is the number of times running the code caused an infinite loop.

		Success	Failure	Error	Timeout
GPT-4	Only Task	0.967	0.024	0.008	0.0
	Unaltered	0.837	0.106	0.033	0.024
	No Descriptions	0.87	0.057	0.049	0.024
	Generic Action Names	0.87	0.065	0.049	0.016
	No Descriptions and Generic Action Names	0.130	0.780	0.089	0.0
	RDF	0.902	0.024	0.057	0.016
GPT-3.5	Only Task	0.927	0.049	0.016	0.008
	Unaltered	0.772	0.138	0.041	0.049
	No Descriptions	0.659	0.236	0.049	0.057
	Generic Action Names	0.675	0.211	0.033	0.081
	No Descriptions andGeneric Action Names	0.106	0.837	0.049	0.008
	RDF	0.789	0.122	0.081	0.008
Llama_70b	Only Task	0.683	0.236	0.057	0.024
	Unaltered	0.650	0.236	0.106	0.008
	No Descriptions	0.528	0.309	0.138	0.024
	Generic Action Names	0.561	0.309	0.106	0.024
	No Descriptions andGeneric Action Names	0.187	0.659	0.098	0.057
	RDF	0.561	0.195	0.203	0.041
CodeLlama_70b	Only Task	0.593	0.285	0.089	0.033
	Unaltered	0.333	0.415	0.244	0.008
	No Descriptions	0.325	0.407	0.268	0.0
	Generic Action Names	0.301	0.496	0.187	0.016
	No Descriptions andGeneric Action Names	0.195	0.374	0.423	0.008
	RDF	0.317	0.407	0.268	0.008
Llama_7b	Only Task	0.593	0.276	0.106	0.024
	Unaltered	0.366	0.374	0.244	0.016
	No Descriptions	0.374	0.39	0.211	0.024
	Generic Action Names	0.276	0.52	0.195	0.008
	No Descriptions andGeneric Action Names	0.195	0.496	0.301	0.008
	RDF	0.366	0.301	0.325	0.008
CodeLlama_7b	Only Task	0.74	0.211	0.041	0.008
	Unaltered	0.602	0.230	0.171	0.024
	No Descriptions	0.537	0.341	0.057	0.065
	Generic Action Names	0.512	0.341	0.098	0.049
	No Descriptions andGeneric Action Names	0.187	0.659	0.114	0.041
	RDF	0.61	0.22	0.138	0.033

5 Conclusion

This work presented a novel method of how WoT TD can be utilised as a resource to provide LLMs with domain knowledge for planning, emitting the necessity for a human expert to ground LLMs to the environment.

We show that LLMs are successfully able to use WoT TDs as a source of domain knowledge, as long as the WoT TDs either contain descriptions or actions have meaningful names. Even though the WoT TDs do not give a detailed formal description of the workings of a device, the LLMs are able to fill these information gaps using their general world knowledge.

We show the benefit of our approach in which devices are represented as Python classes as an intermediate step. This separates the task of interpreting the workings of a device and generating the plan. We believe that this makes our method more explainable and it is simpler for humans to intervene (For example by changing the Python class). Turning the plan generation into a code generation problem allows to use loops, preventing the LLMs from having to count and having to produce long repeated sequences that may excess the token-limits of LLMs.

We also show that the performance of our approach can be increased by synchronizing the state of the Python class with the state of the device. This allows for adaptive planning in which the plan changes based on environmental feedback.

Acknowledgments. This work has been supported in part by the German federal ministry of education and research (BMBF) in NeSyPlan (FKZ 01IS23052B). We also thank Jan Henze, Nicholas Popovic, Michael Färber and David Paul Mark for fruitful discussions and for help during preparation of the dataset and LLM set-up.

Appendix

```
{"title": "Bedside Lamp",
 "properties": {
   "on": {
     "type": "boolean",
      "description": "True if
  Light is turned on",},
   "brightness": {
      "type": "integer",
      "description": "
  Brightness level of the
  light in percentage",
      "minimum": 0,
      "maximum": 100,
}},
 "actions": {
   "turn on": {
     "description": "Turns the
    light on",
   },
   "turn off": {
     "description": "Turns the
    light off",
   },
   "increase": {
     "description": "Increases
    light by 10%",
   },
   "decrease": {
     "description": "Decreases
    light by 10%",
}}}
```

(a) A WoT TD of a Bedside Lamp.

```
class BedsideLamp:
  def __init__(self):
    self.on = False # True if
   Light is turned on
    self.brightness = 50 #
   Brightness level of the
   light in percentage

  def turn_on(self):
    # Turns the light on
    self.on = True

  def turn_off(self):
    # Turns the light off
    self.on = False

  def increase(self):
    #Increases light by 10%
    if not self.on:
      self.turn_on()

    if self.brightness <= 90:
      self.brightness += 10

  def decrease(self):
    #Decreases light by 10%
    if not self.on:
      self.turn_on()

    if self.brightness >= 10:
      self.brightness -= 10
```

(b) The corresponding Python class.

Fig. 3. An example of how a the WoT TD of a Bedside Lamp can be translated into a Python class. Tasks in our benchmark that involved the bedsit lamp were for example "Give me a brightness of 30" or "Make it is bright as possible".

```
{"title": "Dishwasher",
 "properties": {
   "running": {
     "type": "boolean",
     "description": "States
    whether the dishwasher is
    currently running and
    washing dishes or not",
   },
   "door": {
     "type": "String",
     "description": "
    Represents if the
    dishwasher is currently
    closed or open",
     "characteristics": ["open
    ", "closed"],
   }
 },
 "actions": {
   "close_door": {
      "description": "Closes
    the door",
   },
   "open_door": {
      "description": "Opens
    the door",
   },
   "stop": {
      "description": "Stops
    the washing process",
   },
   "start": {
     "description": "Starts
    the washing process",
}}}
```

(a) A WoT TD of a Dishwasher.

```
class Dishwasher:
  def __init__(self):
    self.running = False  #
   States whether the
   dishwasher is currently
   running and washing dishes
   or not
    self.door = "closed"  #
   Represents if the
   dishwasher is currently
   closed or open

  def close_door(self):
    # Closes the door
    self.door = "closed"

  def open_door(self):
    # Opens the door

    if self.running:
      self.stop()
    self.door = "open"

  def stop(self):
    # Stops the washing
   process
    self.running = False

  def start(self):
    # Starts the washing
   process

    if self.door == "open":
      self.close()
    self.running = True
```

(b) The corresponding Python class.

Fig. 4. An example of how a the WoT TD of a dishwasher can be translated into a Python class. Tasks in our benchmark that involved the dishwasher were for example "Start the dishwasher" or "Wash the dishes. Open the door afterwards".

```
class CoffeeMachine:
    def __init__(self):
        self.water = True # Illustrates water level of the
   machine.
        self.storage = True # Indicates the remaining coffee
   ground storage.
        self.on = False # Displays the current power state of
    the machine.

    def toggle(self):
        # Toggles on property of the device.
        self.on = not self.on

        execute_action("toggle")
        synchronize_state(self)

    def refill(self):
        # Refills the water tank of the machine.
        self.water = True

        execute_action("refill")
        synchronize_state(self)

    def empty(self):
        # Empties coffee ground container.
        self.storage = True

        execute_action("empty")
        synchronize_state(self)

    def make_coffee(self):
        # Creates a medium cup of coffee.

        if not self.on:
            self.toggle()

        if not self.water:
            self.refill()

        if not self.storage:
            self.empty()

        execute_action("make coffee")
        synchronize_state(self)
```

Fig. 5. The Python class as generated by the large language model and additionally adding the functionality to interact with the real device. When calling `execute_action()` an action is performed with the real coffee machine (in practice that can be done using the WoT Scripting API [18]). And while calling `synchronize_state()` the values of the variables are set to the values of the properties of the real coffee machine. These two steps are added at the end of every function.

References

1. Aeronautiques, C., et al.: Pddl| the planning domain definition language. Tech. Rep, Technical Report (1998)
2. Ahn, M., et al.: Do as i can, not as i say: grounding language in robotic affordances. arXiv preprint arXiv:2204.01691 (2022)
3. Baier, J.A., Bacchus, F., McIlraith, S.A.: A heuristic search approach to planning with temporally extended preferences. Artif. Intell. **173**(5–6), 593–618 (2009)
4. Bubeck, S., et al.: Sparks of artificial general intelligence: early experiments with gpt-4. arXiv preprint arXiv:2303.12712 (2023)
5. Chen, W., Ma, X., Wang, X., Cohen, W.W.: Program of thoughts prompting: disentangling computation from reasoning for numerical reasoning tasks. arXiv preprint arXiv:2211.12588 (2022)
6. Denny, P., Kumar, V., Giacaman, N.: Conversing with copilot: exploring prompt engineering for solving cs1 problems using natural language. In: Proceedings of the 54th ACM Technical Symposium on Computer Science Education, vol. 1, pp. 1136–1142 (2023)
7. Ferguson, D., Stentz, A.: Anytime, dynamic planning in high-dimensional search spaces. In: Proceedings 2007 IEEE International Conference on Robotics and Automation, pp. 1310–1315. IEEE (2007)
8. Fikes, R.E., Nilsson, N.J.: Strips: A new approach to the application of theorem proving to problem solving. Artif. Intell. **2**(3–4), 189–208 (1971)
9. Fox, M., Long, D.: Pddl2. 1: an extension to pddl for expressing temporal planning domains. J. Artif. Intell. Res. **20**, 61–124 (2003)
10. Garrett, C.R., Lozano-Pérez, T., Kaelbling, L.P.: Pddlstream: integrating symbolic planners and blackbox samplers via optimistic adaptive planning. In: Proceedings of the International Conference on Automated Planning and Scheduling, vol. 30, pp. 440–448 (2020)
11. Hou, X., et al.: Large language models for software engineering: a systematic literature review. arXiv preprint arXiv:2308.10620 (2023)
12. Huang, W., Abbeel, P., Pathak, D., Mordatch, I.: Language models as zero-shot planners: extracting actionable knowledge for embodied agents. In: International Conference on Machine Learning, pp. 9118–9147. PMLR (2022)
13. Huang, W., et al.: Inner monologue: embodied reasoning through planning with language models. arXiv preprint arXiv:2207.05608 (2022)
14. Jansen, P.A.: Visually-grounded planning without vision: language models infer detailed plans from high-level instructions. arXiv preprint arXiv:2009.14259 (2020)
15. Jiang, Y.Q., Zhang, S.Q., Khandelwal, P., Stone, P.: Task planning in robotics: an empirical comparison of pddl-and asp-based systems. Front. Inf. Technol. Electron. Eng. **20**, 363–373 (2019)
16. Kaebisch, S., Kamiya, T., McCool, M., Charpenay, V., Korkan, E., Kovatsch, M.: Web of things (wot) thing description 1.1. W3C recommendation, W3C (2020). https://www.w3.org/TR/wot-thing-description11/
17. Kinder, L., Käfer, T.: Towards improving large language models' planning capabilities on wot thing descriptions by generating python objects as intermediary representations. In: First International Workshop on Actionable Knowledge Representation and Reasoning for Robots (2024)
18. Kis, Z., Peintner, D., Aguzzi, C., Hund, J., Nimura, K.: Web of Things (WOT) scripting API. W3C Recommendation W3C (2023). https://www.w3.org/TR/wot-scripting-api/

19. Koenig, S., Likhachev, M.: Improved fast replanning for robot navigation in unknown terrain. In: Proceedings 2002 IEEE International Conference on Robotics and Automation (Cat. No. 02CH37292), vol. 1, pp. 968–975. IEEE (2002)
20. Li, C., et al.: Chain of code: reasoning with a language model-augmented code emulator. arXiv preprint arXiv:2312.04474 (2023)
21. Li, C., et al.: Behavior-1k: a benchmark for embodied AI with 1,000 everyday activities and realistic simulation. In: Conference on Robot Learning, pp. 80–93. PMLR (2023)
22. Li, S., et al.: Pre-trained language models for interactive decision-making. Adv. Neural. Inf. Process. Syst. **35**, 31199–31212 (2022)
23. Liang, J., et al.: Code as policies: language model programs for embodied control. In: 2023 IEEE International Conference on Robotics and Automation (ICRA), pp. 9493–9500. IEEE (2023)
24. Liu, B., et al.: Llm+ p: empowering large language models with optimal planning proficiency. arXiv preprint arXiv:2304.11477 (2023)
25. Madaan, A., Zhou, S., Alon, U., Yang, Y., Neubig, G.: Language models of code are few-shot commonsense learners. arXiv preprint arXiv:2210.07128 (2022)
26. Nau, D., Cao, Y., Lotem, A., Munoz-Avila, H.: Shop: simple hierarchical ordered planner. In: Proceedings of the 16th International Joint Conference on Artificial intelligence, vol. 2. pp. 968–973 (1999)
27. Nilsson, N.J., et al.: Shakey the robot. Technical Note 323, SRI A.I. Center (1984)
28. Pan, L., Albalak, A., Wang, X., Wang, W.Y.: Logic-LM: empowering large language models with symbolic solvers for faithful logical reasoning. arXiv preprint arXiv:2305.12295 (2023)
29. Parcalabescu, L., Gatt, A., Frank, A., Calixto, I.: Seeing past words: testing the cross-modal capabilities of pretrained v&l models on counting tasks. arXiv preprint arXiv:2012.12352 (2020)
30. Roziere, B., et al.: Code llama: open foundation models for code. arXiv preprint arXiv:2308.12950 (2023)
31. Schick, T., et al.: Toolformer: language models can teach themselves to use tools. Adv. Neural Inf. Process. Syst. **36** (2024)
32. Shridhar, M., et al.: Alfred: a benchmark for interpreting grounded instructions for everyday tasks. In: Proceedings of the IEEE/CVF Conference on Computer Vision and Pattern Recognition, pp. 10740–10749 (2020)
33. Singh, I., et al.: Progprompt: generating situated robot task plans using large language models. In: 2023 IEEE International Conference on Robotics and Automation (ICRA), pp. 11523–11530. IEEE (2023)
34. Skreta, M., Zhou, Z., Yuan, J.L., Darvish, K., Aspuru-Guzik, A., Garg, A.: Replan: robotic replanning with perception and language models. arXiv preprint arXiv:2401.04157 (2024)
35. Song, C.H., Wu, J., Washington, C., Sadler, B.M., Chao, W.L., Su, Y.: Llm-planner: few-shot grounded planning for embodied agents with large language models. In: Proceedings of the IEEE/CVF International Conference on Computer Vision, pp. 2998–3009 (2023)
36. Wang, X., et al.: Executable code actions elicit better LLM agents. arXiv preprint arXiv:2402.01030 (2024)
37. Wang, X., Li, S., Ji, H.: Code4struct: code generation for few-shot event structure prediction. arXiv preprint arXiv:2210.12810 (2022)
38. Wei, J., et al.: Chain-of-thought prompting elicits reasoning in large language models. Adv. Neural. Inf. Process. Syst. **35**, 24824–24837 (2022)

39. Zeng, A., et al.: Socratic models: composing zero-shot multimodal reasoning with language. arXiv preprint arXiv:2204.00598 (2022)
40. Zhang, H., et al.: Building cooperative embodied agents modularly with large language models. arXiv preprint arXiv:2307.02485 (2023)

Author Index

A. Meroño Peñuela et al. (Eds.): ESWC 2024, LNCS 15345, pp. 275–278, 2025.
https://doi.org/10.1007/978-3-031-78955-7

The manufacturer's authorised representative in the EU is Springer Nature Customer Service Centre GmbH, Europaplatz 3, 69115 Heidelberg, Germany. If you have any concerns regarding our products, please contact ProductSafety@springernature.com

Printed and bound by CPI Group (UK) Ltd, Croydon, CR0 4YY
01/10/2026
02225908-0008